Files and Databases:
An Introduction

Files and Databases:
An Introduction

Peter D. Smith   **G. Michael Barnes**
CALIFORNIA STATE UNIVERSITY, NORTHRIDGE

 Addison-Wesley Publishing Company

READING, MASSACHUSETTS   MENLO PARK, CALIFORNIA
DON MILLS, ONTARIO   WOKINGHAM, ENGLAND   AMSTERDAM
SYDNEY   SINGAPORE   TOKYO   MADRID   BOGOTÁ
SANTIAGO   SAN JUAN

This book is in the Addison-Wesley Series in Computer Science
Michael A. Harrison/Consulting Editor

James T. DeWolf/Sponsoring Editor
Bette J. Aaronson/Production Supervisor
Carol Spencer, Spencer Graphics & Editorial Services/Production Editor
Patti Williams/Text Designer
Hugh Crawford/Manufacturing Supervisor
Bob McCormack and Jean Depoian/Cover Designers

Library of Congress Cataloging-in-Publication Data

Smith, Peter D. (Peter Desmond), 1950–
    Files and databases.

    Includes index.
    1. File organization (Computer science)   2. Data
base management.   I. Barnes, G. Michael.   II. Title.
QA76.9.F5S63   1987CP   001.64′2   85-7356
ISBN 0-201-10746-5

ABCDEFGHIJ-HA-89876

To Kathleen, Evan, and Benjamin
from Peter

To Kristin and Carl
from Mike

Preface

Information is a valuable resource both to people and to corporations. Computer software provides an efficient means of processing information, and database systems are becoming increasingly common means by which to store and retrieve information. The purpose of this text is to give an introduction to file and database systems. We hope to show not only what file and database systems are and what they can do but also how they carry out their functions.

A Bridge between Data Structure and Database Design

We believe that knowledge of both file and database systems is important for two complementary reasons. First, the organization of data in files is the foundation of database systems, and thus an appreciation of file organization techniques gives a better insight into the operation of database management systems (DBMS's). Second, file processing systems have disadvantages that spurred the invention of DBMS's, and therefore studying DBMS principles helps illuminate the limitations of files. Material on files is often overlooked both in introductory data structure texts (which concentrate on main memory structures) and in database texts (which tend to overlook implementation details). Although COBOL texts discuss file operations, they suffer from the problem that COBOL hides implementation details. Furthermore, the nature of the language often makes algorithms obscure. This text is intended to bridge the gap between a first course in data structures and a course in database design.

There is a trend in computer science for topics that once were the province of researchers to be introduced gradually into graduate and then into undergraduate curricula. Such is the case with database theory and practice. Organizations such as IEEE and ACM occasionally make recommendations about the syllabus of various degree programs. The ACM Curriculum Committee on Computer Science has presented recommendations for both undergraduate[1] and graduate[2] degree programs. Our text covers material in both CS.5 (Introduction to File Processing) and CS.11 (Database Management Systems Design) of the undergraduate recommendations. In addition, the ACM Curriculum Committee on Information Systems has made recommendations for both graduate and undergraduate degree programs in information sciences.[3] In terms of these recommendations, this text contains material for IS2 (Program, Data, and File Structures) and IS4 (Database Management Systems).

We assume a certain amount of knowledge on the part of readers and expect familiarity with basic data structures such as records, lists, and trees. We have tried to make the text as independent as possible from particular high-level languages. We use a pseudocode notation for algorithms. However, because the pseudocode is block structured, it will be helpful if readers have had prior experience with a block-structured language. (Note that block structure is indicated by level of indentation. For large blocks or loops we have indicated the range by brackets.) We have also tried to make the book system-free. In our classes we supplement it with material describing specific systems.

One Book for a Variety of Courses

In the first chapter we distinguish between a database and a set of files. We also discuss the evolution of database systems. After this chapter we follow a bottom-up approach, from secondary storage devices to file organizations to database systems. Our text is suitable for different courses. The following figure illustrates recommended paths through the chapters.

---

1. R. H. Austing, B. H. Barnes, D. T. Bonnette, G. L. Engel, and G. Stokes (eds.), "Curriculum '78: recommendations for the undergraduate program in computer science," *Communications of the ACM*, vol. 22, no. 3, pp. 147–166, March 1979.

2. K. I. Magel, R. H. Austing, A. Berztiss, G. L. Engel, J. W. Hamblen, A. A. J. Hoffmann, and R. Mathis (eds.), "Recommendations for Master's level programs in Computer Science," *Communications of the ACM*, vol. 24, no. 3, pp. 115–123, March 1981.

3. J. F. Nunamaker, Jr., J. D. Couger, and G. B. Davis (eds.), "Information systems curriculum recommendations for the 80s: undergraduate and graduate programs," *Communications of the ACM*, vol. 25, no. 11, pp. 781–805, November 1982.

Files course   * —— 1–2 $\big\langle$ $\begin{matrix} 3\text{–}4 \longrightarrow 5\text{–}7 \\ 5\text{–}7 \longrightarrow 3\text{–}4 \end{matrix}$ $\big\rangle$ 8–10 $\diagdown\underline{11\text{–}12}\diagup$ *

Database course   * —— 1–2 $\diagdown\underline{5\text{–}7}\diagup$ 8–14 —— *

Files and
database course   * —— 1–2 $\big\langle$ $\begin{matrix} 3\text{–}4 \longrightarrow 5\text{–}7 \\ 5\text{–}7 \longrightarrow 3\text{–}4 \end{matrix}$ $\big\rangle$ 8–12 $\diagdown\underline{13\text{–}14}\diagup$ *

However, we recommend strongly that in order to get a full perspective, a files course should use portions of the database material in Chapters 11 and 12 and that a database course should use portions of the files material in Chapters 5, 6, and 7.

In Chapter 2 we examine secondary storage devices and some aspects of their interface with users of a computer system. Chapters 3 and 4 concern sequential file processing and sorting techniques. In Chapters 5, 6, and 7 we consider different organizations for direct-access files. In Chapter 8 we present techniques in choosing the appropriate file organization for a particular application. Chapter 9 describes a record design process for integrated file and database systems. Chapter 10 introduces generalized database concepts. Chapters 11 and 12 describe the hierarchical, network, and relational database models. In Chapters 13 and 14 we briefly introduce more advanced topics. Chapter 13 considers concurrency, data integrity, and data security, and Chapter 14 reviews future database technology. Each chapter is pedagogically sound, with chapter summaries and exercises. In addition, an Instructor's Manual accompanies the text.

Acknowledgments

We developed this book from class notes for a sophomore-level class in files and databases. We would like to thank our students for many useful comments on various early drafts. The book has also benefited from numerous suggestions from our colleagues, particularly Amir Asgari. We benefited considerably from the comments of reviewers and would like to express our appreciation to Anthony I. Hinxman, Wang Laboratories; King Lee, California State University, Bakersfield; Izzeldin M. Osman, California State University, Hayward; Charles Shubra, Indiana University of Pennsylvania; Elizabeth Unger, Kansas State University; and Neil W. Webre, California State Polytechnic University at San Luis Obispo. (Naturally, any errors that remain are our own responsibility.) We would like to express our thanks to Jim DeWolf for his confidence in this project and gratitude to Carol Spencer for her guidance during the production process. We are grateful for the loving encouragement provided by our wives Kathleen Smith and Kristin Bruno and by Evan Panas and Carl Barnes.

Northridge, California   P. D. S.
                                                            G. M. B.

Contents

3 *Serial and Sequential Files 55*

7 Multikey Processing 185

8 Integrated File Addressing Techniques 211

9 Normalization 229

10 Database Management Systems 265

11 The Hierarchical and Network Data Models 281

12 The Relational Data Model 305

13 Issues in Database Implementation 327

14 Advanced Database Topics 343

1

Introduction

1.1 Categorizes data processing systems.

1.2 Presents an overview of file systems.

1.3 Presents an overview of a database system.

1.4 Describes a simple data processing application that will be used in later chapters.

Our major objective in this book is to present concepts about file and database processing. In doing so we will cover two broad areas. The first is the application of data structure techniques to secondary memory. The second is the evaluation of alternate solutions to the problem of mapping user views of data onto physical storage. We will examine this problem both in the file environment (the file addressing problem) and the database environment (database models). We will discuss at length a variety of techniques used to store and retrieve information maintained in secondary memory.

Files are used pervasively in both computer system programming and application programming. In computer system programming, files are often required by translators, text editors, and operating systems. For example, file creation, deletion, and maintenance are major tasks for operating systems. Application programs use files to store the source program, the executable program, and data that the program may require. The reader has probably had experience with file processing in introductory computing courses. Databases, on the other hand, are used primarily by application programs to maintain large amounts of information. For example, businesses use databases for personnel records, inventory, accounting, and planning applications.

This chapter sets up a framework that later chapters will fill in; we introduce many terms and concepts that will become clearer as later chapters are read. First, we establish some fundamental ideas

1

about the roles of file and database systems and categorize data processing software according to its use of secondary storage. In addition, we describe the central issues to be discussed concerning file processing and the database processing environments and we distinguish between a collection of files and a database. Finally, we present a data processing example that will be used in later chapters to illustrate file and database techniques.

1.1 Categories of Data Processing Software

In this section we categorize data processing software according to the ways in which the software accesses data on secondary storage devices.

Computer hardware is often classified as belonging to a particular **generation.** For example, the IBM 370 is regarded as a third-generation machine. Although the boundaries for later generations are fuzzy, the beginning of each early generation is associated with a particular hardware development—the invention of the transistor is one example. Software developments are not so easily classified. However, in tracing the origins of database management systems, we find it convenient to suggest a number of **categories** of data-handling techniques. In our scheme we categorize software broadly according to its independence from details of physical data storage. Primitive software has embedded in it much device-specific information. More sophisticated software, on the other hand, allows the user to write programs that manipulate abstract data objects. The mapping of the abstract objects onto actual storage devices is carried out in a manner transparent to the user. As the level of sophistication increases, there is a migration of functions from application programs into system software. There is some correlation between time and software category in that early programs tended to be more device-dependent than current ones. However, because the correlation is not as strong as with hardware, we prefer the term "category" to "generation."

In our categorization we distinguish between the **logical organization** and the **physical organization** of data. The logical organization is the user's view of data. It is concerned with data elements and their relationships. The physical organization is the way in which data is stored in storage devices.

Category 1: No Data Independence

In category 1 software there is no data independence. A category 1 program typically accesses data by specifying absolute store addresses. If the referenced data changes location, then the program has

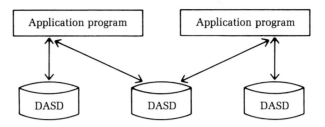

FIGURE 1.1 A logical and physical data dependent configuration

to be modified. Examples of category 1 programs are found at low levels in operating systems. For example, information about free space in a file system may be held in a particular block on disc. For reasons of efficiency, the address of the block may be embedded in programs using it (such as a utility to check file system integrity) rather than being computed or looked up at run time. Category 1 programs are characterized by their intimate involvement with details of secondary storage, typically **direct-access storage devices** (DASD). Figure 1.1 illustrates this direct connection.

Typical operation. A typical operation for a category 1 program is to initiate the transfer of a particular sector of a particular disc into main memory.

Category 2: Physical Data Independence

In category 2 software there is physical data independence but no logical independence. Data processing programs in category 2 typically run under an operating system. The operating system is interposed between application programs and storage devices (see Fig. 1.2).

The operating system now takes care of low-level input/output functions performed by a category 1 program. These include buffering data and responding to device interrupts. Typically, areas of storage can be referred to by name. The operating system maps the name onto an address. For example, users can establish named files of data; **directory** files hold file names and corresponding addresses. If the address of a file changes for any reason, for instance, if the file is recovered from tape after a disc failure, the directory entry will change but accessing programs need not be modified.

However, to operate successfully on a file, a category 2 program must know how the data in the file is organized. For example, it must know about record lengths and the order of fields. Thus, although the program need not be aware of physical organization, it must know

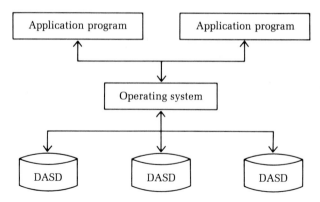

FIGURE I.2 A physical data independent configuration

about the logical organization. This knowledge is typically compiled as part of the program.

Typical operation. A typical operation for a category 2 program is to request the operating system to read record number r from file f. Using directories, the operating system can compute the address of the storage area holding the required information.

Category 3: Partial Logical Data Independence

In category 3 software there is physical independence and partial logical independence. A category 3 program can operate on a variety of files without being modified. Consider a sort utility. To be useful such a utility must be able to operate on data in a number of different formats. When processing a particular file, part of the input to this category 3 program is information about the file format. The distinction between categories 2 and 3 is whether the information required to access a particular file is given at compile time or at run time.

Typical operation. A typical operation for a category 3 program is to request the reading of the next record from a file. Using available information about the format of the file, a request for the appropriate bytes is made to the operating system.

Category 4: Logical and Physical Data Independence

In category 4 software there is both physical independence and logical independence. In a category 4 data processing system, data is stored together with a description of its format. The data definition (the names of elements and their relationships to other elements) is

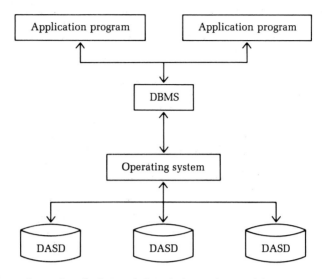

FIGURE 1.3 A logical and physical data independent configuration

no longer part of application programs. Data is fully integrated into databases, and the data definition is available to users of the database. A **database** is a fully integrated collection of files brought together to serve multiple applications. While the database is typically managed by a **database administrator,** ownership of the data is often communal. Data is accessed via a **database management system** (DBMS), which allows the same data to be viewed in a number of different ways. We discuss databases further in Section 1.3. Figure 1.3 illustrates the use of a DBMS.

Typical operation. A typical operation for a category 4 program is to request the reading of the next record of a particular type. The DBMS identifies the logical components making up the record and requests the operating system to retrieve the appropriate information from disc. The record is assembled and returned to the application program.

Whereas category 3 software provides physical independence, a DBMS provides logical independence. High-level languages are extended/augmented to interface with the DBMS. Application programs are independent of logical details as well as physical details. Record format independence is achieved. If a field is added to or removed from a record type, programs not using the field need not be modified.

Note, however, that in some database management systems the application program rather than the DBMS still has to be concerned with the data access paths. Other software has higher-level access methods in addition to those provided by the operating system. In category 4 software the details of retrieving a record from a file given its key have moved from the application program to the DBMS. High-level, nonprogramming, query language interfaces are provided for casual users. Users of query languages are not typically required to have knowledge of access paths.

Category 5: Geographical Data Independence

Currently, category 4 systems are common; however, we can imagine further developments. Often the price paid for generalization and independence is a reduction in efficiency. It is likely that there will be increased hardware support for DBMS functions, for example, processors and storage devices designed to optimize database processing. We consider some aspects of this in Chapter 14.

In a category 5 system there is geographic independence. A database may be distributed over a number of locations instead of being stored at a single site (see Fig. 1.4).

Typical operation. A typical operation for a category 5 program is the same as that for a category 4 program. However, the DBMS, having determined which records have to be retrieved from which files, also has to determine the location of the files and issue the appropriate requests.

Consider an organization such as a bank that maintains many customer account records. An account record is probably accessed most often from one particular location, namely, the customer's branch of the bank. With the introduction of automatic tellers, however, it is desirable to be able to access the record from any of a number of widely spaced locations. In order to minimize communication costs, the bank may create a **distributed database.** Each branch would store the records of its account holders. The branch computers would be linked in a network, and the database software would now be responsible for locating and making contact with the site holding the desired information.

As local area networks proliferate, it is sometimes difficult to determine whether a particular configuration is a distributed database. Ceri and Pelagatti [1] suggest that for a network to be considered a distributed database, each node in the network must be capable of autonomous operations and must also participate in at least one global operation. In the case of a bank, the transfer of funds between accounts at different nodes is such a global operation.

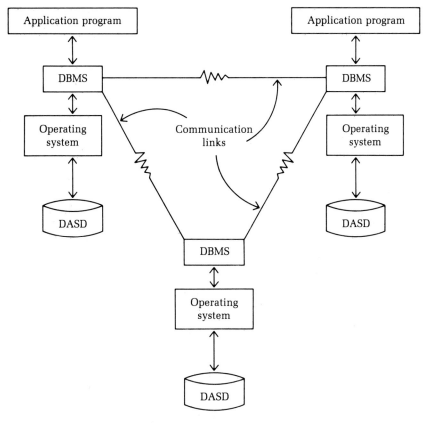

FIGURE 1.4 Category 5 configuration

Distributed databases are an active research area (see, for example, Onuegbe, Rahimi, and Hevner [2] and Epstein and Stonebraker [3]). We consider them further in Chapter 14. For a more detailed treatment of the evolution of databases in general and of particular systems, see Fry and Sibley [4].

Table 1.1 summarizes some of the properties of the five categories of data processing software. In the next two sections we look at properties of file and database systems in more detail.

1.2 File Overview and Terminology

A **file** is typically a collection of records of the same type. This definition includes files of text, which can be regarded as files of one-

TABLE 1.1 Properties of the five categories of data processing software

	Category				
	1	2	3	4	5
Physical independence	No	Yes	Yes	Yes	Yes
Logical independence	No	No	No	Yes	Yes
Geographical independence	No	No	No	No	Yes

byte records. Although files can exist in both primary and secondary memory, they are almost always held in secondary memory, and here we assume that this is the case. Each record in a file consists of a set of fields or data items. As an example, a file of records containing information on the personal computers produced by the XYZ Corporation might contain the two record instances depicted in Table 1.2.

Data files have two salient characteristics. First, they are often voluminous; the capacity of a data file can easily exceed the capacity of primary memory. Consequently, only portions of large files can be held in main memory at one time. Second, data files typically have long lifetimes. A data file often exists before and after the execution of an application program that accesses it.

TABLE 1.2 Example records

Field Name	Record 1	Record 2
Model number	XYZ100	XYZ200
CPU	8086 6MHZ	68010 10MHZ
RAM	272KB	1MB
ROM	384KB	32KB
Discs	1	2
Disc capacity	0 to 128KB	320KB, 20MB
Disc type	RAM	3.5″ floppy, 5.25″ hard
I/O	RS232, parallel	2 RS232, parallel
Display	LCD 16 × 80	Monochromatic 25 × 80
Operating system	MS DOS 2.1	CPM68 or UNIX
Computer type	Lap, 10 lbs	Desktop
Price	$2,500	$6,500

Three issues within the file processing environment are important: file access techniques, the interdependence of application programs and data files, and data redundancy across data files. We briefly present these issues here, and we examine them in detail in Chapters 3 through 9.

File Access Techniques

Given that a file of records exists, what tasks must be accomplished to access a particular record? Who or what is responsible for each of these tasks? Furthermore, how can new records be created and inserted into the file? Numerous file accessing techniques can solve this problem. In Chapter 5 we discuss solutions that are computationally based. Hashing is the major computational technique In Chapters 6 and 7 we discuss the use of additional data structures as techniques for file access. Typically, in all but the simplest file organization, some information about the required record has to be known before it can be accessed. That information (usually a field value) is used to facilitate and verify the file access process.

File and Program Interdependence

A second problem with file processing is the lack of logical and physical data independence between the file and the application program. Logical data dependence means that an application program must know the logical structure of records in a file (their format) and how they are organized within the file in order to access and modify them. For example, if program A creates a file of employee records, the author of an enquiry program B operating on the file must know what record format was used by program A and how the records were placed within the file. Physical data dependence implies that the application program needs to know where a file is located and how the file is mapped onto secondary storage. Over time, these dependencies can cause problems with file maintenance as application programs and computer hardware change. Logical and physical dependence implies that changes to the file, operating system, or hardware may necessitate changes to the application programs.

Data Redundancy

A third problem that plagues file processing is maintaining data consistency with redundant instances of the same data. With many files and with many application programs processing the same files, it is easy for data to become duplicated and for multiple copies of a data item to have inconsistent values. This occurs when different application programs share part of the data stored in a file. To optimize the application programs, the original file may be copied or divided into many files with redundant copies of the same data. Later an application program may update one instance of a data value without updating the redundant copies. After this happens it is difficult to determine which of the data values is valid. Thus there is usually a trade-off between optimizing application processing and maintaining file consistency. Because files exist to store valid information, data consistency should have the highest priority.

Chapters 2 through 9 are concerned with these three file processing problems. These chapters also serve as an introduction to the chapters on database processing. Database technology evolved to solve these and other problems inherent in file processing.

1.3 Database Overview and Terminology

A database differs from a collection of files in three important ways: perspectives on data, data insulation, and data redundancy.

1. A DBMS, by performing a mapping function between application programs and the **logical database,** allows the same data to be viewed in a number of different ways. This mapping is done by the **functional databases.** Functional databases translate the logical representation of the database into representations (perspectives or views) that are useful to different application programs.

2. A second mapping performed by a DBMS serves to insulate application programs from details of physical storage and to some extent provides physical data independence. If the physical layout of data changes for any reason, the application programs need not change; only the mapping changes.

3. As discussed in Section 1.2, data redundancy is not only a waste of space but also gives rise to the possibility of inconsistency. By means of a DBMS many applications can see the data in an optimized structure (their functional database) and yet access the same actual data values (the logical database). However, it may not be possible to eliminate redundancy entirely.

Figure 1.5 shows the stages by which a DBMS maps record requests from an application program onto storage devices. Each of the functional database descriptions, the logical database description, and the physical database description describes a mapping used by the DBMS.

Functional Database Description

The functional database description contains the application program's logical view of data. As illustrated in Fig. 1.5, a particular

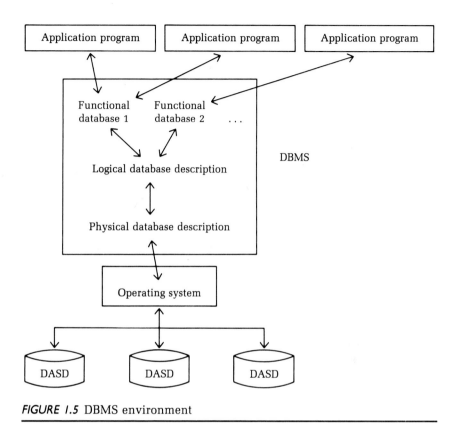

FIGURE 1.5 DBMS environment

functional database may be shared by more than one program. Functional databases are usually established for users by the database administrator.

Consider, as an example, a college data processing system. Three application programs might have differing views as to what constitutes a "professor" record.

Payroll department. The payroll department is interested only in producing paychecks and making appropriate deductions. The payroll program professor record has the fields shown in Fig. 1.6.

Library. The campus library has another view of a professor. The library management is concerned with book circulation. Professors must occasionally be reminded to return books, and the library program generates form letters for this purpose. A professor record in this program has the fields shown in Fig. 1.7.

name	salary	deductions	ss#	home address

FIGURE 1.6 Professor record: payroll program view

Counseling center. The counseling center on campus has an interactive program that enables the staff to put students in touch with useful faculty. This program has a third view of a professor record, that shown in Fig. 1.8.

Thus, three different applications have three different views of what a professor is.

Logical Database Description

Whereas the functional database description describes the logical viewpoint of a particular application program, the **logical database description** describes the logical properties of the entire database. This is the view of the database administrator. Continuing with our example of the professor, the logical database description might include the record types shown in Fig. 1.9.

Physical Database Description

The way in which data is physically placed on storage devices is described in the **physical database description.** For example, the file of PROFREC1 records might be stored sequentially by social security number with an index on the name field. The file of PROFREC2 records might be stored hashed on social security number.

FIGURE 1.7 Professor record: library program view

name	office number	books on loan

FIGURE 1.8 Professor record: counseling center program view

name	office #	home phone	home address	skills

ss#	name	date of birth	home address	home phone

PROFREC1

ss#	dept	salary	deductions	rank	office #	skills	books on loan

PROFREC2

FIGURE 1.9 Logical view of a professor

Distributed systems. In a distributed system the three-level description (functional, logical, and physical) must be extended. For example, there could be four levels:

1. functional database description
2. overall logical description of complete database
3. logical description of the data at a particular node in the network
4. physical description of the database at a particular node

We have presented some issues and features of a DBMS. In Chapters 3 through 8 we will consider a number of different file organizations. In Chapters 11 and 12 we will consider three database models. We will use examples drawn from a common domain in order to highlight differences between file processing and database processing systems. A description of our example domain follows.

1.4 Example Data Processing Application

The example data processing application we present here will be used in later chapters to illustrate file and database techniques. Here we describe the data processing requirements, the resulting processes, and the data that has to be maintained.

SECS Example

The context for the example is a School of Engineering and Computer Science (SECS) in a college. The school administrators process various pieces of information in connection with classes, students, and professors. In particular, at the beginning of each semester, students register for classes. Many courses have prerequisites: for example, a student may not be allowed to enroll in course B unless course A has been completed. A registration program must check prerequisites as well as time clashes, available classroom seating, and so on.

Requirements

The system must allow students to register for classes and must keep records of grades and basic information about faculty and students. Class rosters must be available as required.

Processes

Registration. An interactive registration program is required. Students should be able to register for courses for which they have passed the prerequisite courses. The program should check that the prerequisite has been satisfied and that a student is not registered in two classes meeting at the same time. In addition, a student should not be registered in more than one section of the same course.[1] Some classes (sections of a course) may be restricted to students in a certain major or to those who have completed a certain number of course units. The registration program should help students find classes by listing those for a particular course or those at a particular time.

Roster listing. At any time during or after registration, it should be possible to get a list of the students enrolled in a particular class. This class roster is to be alphabetically ordered by last name.

Grade recording. At the end of a semester a professor should be able to enter student grades in a simple manner. For example, the system could read a class roster, prompt with a student name, and have the professor respond with an appropriate grade.

Data

Students. For each student the system is to hold the student's identification number (which is unique) and the student's name (which may not be unique). Additional information held for each student

---

1. We assume that a course may be offered at different times during the week. For example, an introductory programming course may be offered at 9 A.M. on Mondays and Wednesdays and again at 2 P.M. on Tuesdays and Thursdays. A student should enroll for either the Tuesday/Thursday section or the Monday/Wednesday section of the course.

should include current major, grade point average (GPA),[2] and number of course units completed. Also held for each student is the name of the most advanced prerequisite course completed.

Professors. For each professor the system holds the professor's name and the office number. Each professor has only one office, which may be shared. Professors act as academic advisers to students; each student is assigned to a particular professor, who may be adviser to a number of students. The assignment of students to advisers is to be recorded.

Courses. Each course in the school is assigned a unique name. The data held for a course includes this name and the name of the most restrictive prerequisite course.[3] For example, if course C requires students to have taken course B, and course B requires students to have taken course A, then B rather than A is the most restrictive prerequisite for C.

Grades. It is required that the system keep a record of the grades awarded to students. Because course names may change over time, it will be necessary to record the semester in which the grade is awarded.

Class schedule. It is necessary that information about the scheduling of classes be held. (A student should not be allowed to register for two classes that overlap.) More than one section of a course may be offered. The sections may be at different times and may be taught by different professors. Information held about a course section would therefore include a unique section number, the course name, the start and finish times, the name of the professor teaching it, and the name of the place where the class meets. A professor may teach many courses.

Summary

In this chapter we have seen how data processing systems can be categorized according to how independent an application program is

---

2. Typically a letter grade (A, B, C, D, F) awarded has a numeric value (A = 4, B = 3, C = 2, D = 1, F = 0). The grade for a course is weighted by the number of units for that course (an N-unit class is one which meets N hours a week): GPA = Σ (grade $\times$ units) $/\Sigma$ units. For example, a student awarded a C in a two-unit class and an A in a three-unit class has a GPA for the semester of $(2 \times 2 + 4 \times 3)/5 = 3.2$.

3. We assume (simplistically) that the prerequisite structure is such that there is exactly one such prerequisite course for a particular course. In practice there are likely to be multiple independent prerequisites.

of the logical and physical arrangement of data on which it operates. At one extreme a program has embedded within it actual storage addresses. At the other extreme, a database management system and operating system map the program's view of data onto storage devices. If there are changes in the way data is stored in the latter case, then only the mappings rather than the application programs change. In the case of a distributed system, the program need not even know the location of the site holding the data.

A file is a collection of records typically held in secondary storage. Issues associated with file processing include the mechanisms by which records can be retrieved, the extent to which accessing programs can be data independent, and data redundancy.

Some of the problems with file systems provided the impetus for the development of database management systems. We looked in a little more detail at the way in which a database management system maps user views of data onto physical storage. In our example database the mapping is a three-stage process. The application program perspective of the database (a functional database description) is mapped to the logical database description. The logical database is the description of all the database's record types and their interrelationships. The logical database is mapped onto a physical database description that specifies how data is to be accessed from secondary storage. It is at this stage that file accessing techniques are employed. The physical database description is mapped onto the physical storage devices.

Exercises

1. Classify the data processing programs on a computer system to which you have access. Try to find examples of programs in categories 2, 3, and 4.

2. In the text we described five categories of software. What might be the properties of a category 6 system?

2

Secondary Storage Devices and I/O Control

2.1 Discusses the hierarchy of storage devices and the trade-off between access time and cost.

2.2 Describes devices based on serial tapes.

2.3 Looks at devices that use spinning magnetic tracks.

2.4 Considers some secondary storage devices that, though not common at present, may become important in the future.

2.5 Presents some functions of the operating system concerned with secondary storage devices.

2.6 Looks at the interface that might be provided between users of high-level languages and the file system.

2.7 Presents techniques for data compression.

In this chapter we examine secondary storage devices and consider the interfaces between these devices and programming languages that enable file processing. More specifically, we consider two interfaces—programming languages and operating systems—as depicted in Table 2.1. A programming language enables users' concepts of data storage and retrieval to be expressed in terms of records and files: this is the **logical representation.** An operating system maps records and files onto actual storage devices: this is the **physical representation.** Our discussion begins with secondary storage devices and concludes with the language interface.

Because new storage devices are constantly being developed and existing types improved, figures regarding cost, speed, and capacity can become out-of-date rapidly. Therefore we are reluctant to quantify some of our observations. The reader is advised to consult current

TABLE 2.1 Interfaces

Store	Representation	Interface
User's mind	Conceptual	Programming language
Program	Logical	Operating system
Secondary storage	Physical	

issues of computer periodicals (e.g., *BYTE*, *Datamation*, *Computerworld*) for current figures. Similarly, there is a great diversity of operating systems, and our discussion here is not based on any particular system.

2.1 The Storage Hierarchy

A great number of storage devices are normally found on a computer system, ranging from registers in the CPU to read-only memory (ROM) and random-access memory (RAM) to tapes and discs. In general there is a trade-off between average access time to a storage location in a memory device and the cost of a byte of storage in that device. Fast memories, those with short access times, tend to be expensive. Figure 2.1 plots this relation and indicates where various common storage devices might be placed on the graph. Note that the graph is intended to show relative positions only.

FIGURE 2.1 Memory devices: time/speed trade-off

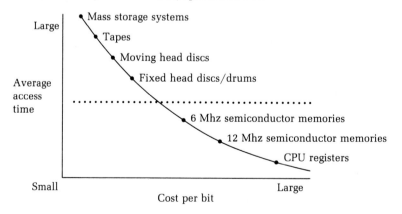

TABLE 2.2 Typical storage device characteristics

Device	Capacity (megabytes)	Cost per Byte (cents)	Average Access Time
Reel-to reel tape	30	.001	300 seconds
Cassette tape	.7	.001	300 seconds
Moving head hard disc (fixed)	465	.004	28 milliseconds
Moving head hard disc (exchangeable)	160	.001	28 milliseconds
Floppy disc	.4	.001	275 milliseconds

Storage devices are often classified as either **primary memory** (sometimes called **internal memory**) or **secondary memory** (sometimes called **external memory**). In Fig. 2.1, devices below the dotted line would be considered primary storage. Central processing units (CPUs) typically require executable instructions to be in primary memory. However, primary storage devices tend to be expensive and are therefore not an economical way of storing large amounts of data over a long period of time. This is why most computer systems provide more capacious and cost effective secondary storage. Table 2.2 gives typical performance figures for some secondary storage devices.

Note that the costs in Table 2.2 do not reflect the spread shown in Fig. 2.1. This is because, in Table 2.2, we have taken into account the cost of device controllers and the fact that total costs will usually be spread over many exchangeable storage media. For example, when calculating storage costs for tapes we have assumed in each case that the cost of the tape drive is spread over a library of 50 tapes. When considering costs for exchangeable hard discs we have assumed a library of 20 discs, and in the case of floppy discs we have assumed a library of 200 discs. With these library sizes and our example prices the cost of storing a byte on each of the exchangeable media is roughly equal.[1]

---

1. We used the following prices in our calculations:
2400′ reel-to-reel tape, $15. Tape drive, $9,000; controller, $3,500.
270′ cassette, $5. Cassette recorder, $80.
160MB exchangeable disc, $500.
465MB disc drive, $19,000, 4-drive controller, $5,000.
Exchangeable disc and controller, $15,000.
5.25″ double-sided, double-density soft-sectored floppy disc, $1.50.
Floppy disc drive and controller, $200.

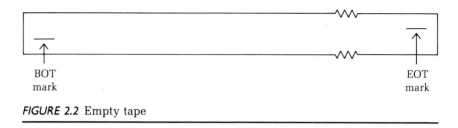

FIGURE 2.2 Empty tape

Typical primary memory has an access time of less than a microsecond. Note from Table 2.2 that even the fastest secondary storage device listed has an access time close to 30,000 times as long. For this reason it is usually important to minimize transfers to and from secondary storage. Hence, likely accessing requirements must be taken into account when mapping files onto secondary storage.

In the next two sections we consider some of the properties of the most common secondary storage devices, those based on tapes and spinning tracks. More esoteric devices are considered in Section 2.4.

2.2 Tape-Based Devices

Many of the properties exhibited by an audio or video tape recorder are found in its computer system counterpart.

1. A drive or deck enables data to be written to or read from removable tapes.
2. Tapes are typically reel-to-reel or cassette.
3. Tapes are serial media; accessing data at the end involves scanning all the intermediate data.

The third property above is the biggest disadvantage of tapes as secondary storage. Access times can be very long if data is required in an order other than that in which it is stored on the tape or if little of the data read is actually used. Advantages of tapes are that they are comparatively cheap, portable, and robust. For example, they are convenient for archiving and distributing data.

Data Tape

A typical tape is a strip of Mylar about half an inch wide coated with a magnetizable material such as chromic oxide. Common reel-to-reel tape lengths are 300 feet, 1200 feet, and 2400 feet. Figure 2.2

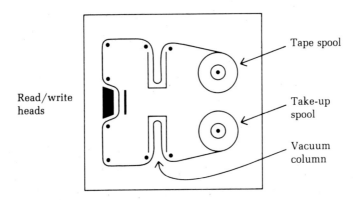

FIGURE 2.3 Tape drive

shows an empty tape. The BOT (beginning-of-tape) and EOT (end-of-tape) marks are aluminum strips that are detectable by the tape drive. When rewinding a tape, for example, the BOT mark, which is about 25 feet from the physical beginning of the tape, enables the drive to stop the tape before it unreels.

Tape Drive

Figure 2.3 depicts a typical tape drive. A tape drive usually operates in one of two modes: **start/stop mode** or **streaming mode.** In start/stop mode the tape drive stops the tape after reading or writing a block of data. Some drives are bidirectional and can read and write data in either direction. A drive reads and writes only when moving the tape at full read/write speed and needs a small but finite time to accelerate to and slow down from this speed. A servo mechanism is used to minimize the possibility of stretching the tape during starts and stops, when the force of acceleration and deceleration can be as high as 25g. (Vacuum columns serve this purpose in the drive of Fig. 2.3.)

A **write permit ring** can be inserted into a slot in the back of a tape reel. When the tape is mounted on the drive, the ring closes a microswitch in the writing circuit. Removing this ring from a tape thus makes it read-only.

Read/Write Operations

Most tape drives write a byte of data across the tape; thus the tape contains a number of parallel **tracks** of information (see Fig. 2.5).

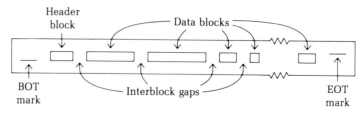

FIGURE 2.4 Tape configuration

Recording density varies among tapes, and better-quality tapes and drives are required for higher densities. The measure of recording density is **bpi** (bits per inch per track). A tape on which data has been recorded at N bpi has N bits stored in a one-inch section of a track. Because bytes are written across the tape (see Fig. 2.5), a tape written at N bpi holds N bytes in a one-inch section. Many reel-to-reel tapes are certified as being reliable up to 6250 bpi. Data is commonly recorded at densities of 800 and 1600 bpi.

The way in which a bit is encoded varies: **NRZI encoding** represents a "1" bit by a change in magnetic polarity and a "0" bit by no change. **Phase encoding** uses three levels of magnetization for "0," "1," and blank. Phase encoding is more resistant to errors caused by dust particles. Because a tape drive is not usually a sealed unit, dust may enter, and particles may be generated due to the contact between the tape and the drive. The magnetic spots that record bits are packed very densely and are vulnerable to dust particles. Dust particles and tape stretching are ways in which data written to a tape may become unreadable, as are magnetic fields that alter the alignment of the magnetized spots.

Data is written to the tape in **blocks** of bytes. A single transfer operation typically moves a block of data between a tape and main memory. Data is written only when the tape is moving at full write speed. In start/stop mode the tape stops after writing a block. The tape drive does not stop the tape instantly, however, and it also requires a small amount of time to accelerate to writing speed. Hence, blocks of data are separated by **interblock gaps**, as shown in Fig. 2.4.

To minimize the tape wasted in interblock gaps, each block on the tape normally contains many logical records. (A logical record is the unit of transfer perceived by the user program.) The number of logical records in a block is the **blocking factor**. For example, if the user program writes 80-byte records but the software packs these into 8000-byte tape blocks, the blocking factor is 100. As the blocking factor

TABLE 2.3 Tape label (header block) format

Bytes	
1–3	Label identifier
4	Label number
5–10	Volume identifier
11	Accessibility
12–37	Reserved
38–51	Owner identifier
52–79	Reserved
80	Label standard version

increases, the number of blocks on a tape, and hence the number of gaps, decreases. Packing and unpacking fixed-length records is relatively simple for a program to do, because only the record length must be known. If the logical records are of variable length, then other information is necessary. For example, there could be a reserved end-of-record character. Alternatively, pointers of various kinds inside the block could identify the points at which records begin.

The first block on the tape, the **header block,** acts as a tape label and typically contains information such as a tape serial number (TSN) and retention date. The TSN is a number allocated to the tape that is unique within a particular institution. It enables the operating system to verify that the correct tape has been loaded. Installations often maintain a pool of tapes from which users may borrow. The retention date is the date on which the tape is due back in the pool. Other information in a header block might include the reel number of a tape if it is part of a multireel data set. Table 2.3 shows the format of an ANSI standard volume label written by the RSTS/E operating system.

Apart from the data bytes, each block usually contains data-checking information. For example, each byte could be supplemented by a parity bit. Thus, if bytes are eight bits long, nine bits are written across the tape. Nine-track tape drives are common. The ninth bit is calculated from the eight data bits in a simple way. This byte-by-byte parity is called **vertical parity.** For instance, the ninth bit could be chosen to be 1 if there are an odd number of 1's in the data bits and 0 if there are an even number of 1's, thus

$$1\ 0\ 1\ 1\ 1\ 0\ 1\ 0\ ①$$

Parity bit

$$0\ 1\ 0\ 0\ 1\ 1\ 0\ 1\ ⓪$$

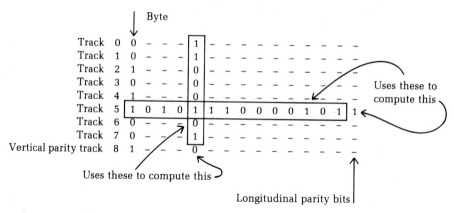

FIGURE 2.5 Tape data block

Parity is often specified as being even (as in this case) or odd. In addition to the vertical parity bits computed across the tape, a **longitudinal parity** bit can be calculated for each track of a block across all the bytes in a block. In this case an extra bit would be written at the end of a track in a block so that the total number of 1's in the track is even (or odd if odd parity is used). These nine longitudinal parity bits are written at the end of the block. Figure 2.5 depicts a block and the parity bits. Values for certain bits have been shown to illustrate parity bit computation (even parity assumed). In practice, additional information is often written. For example, there might be leading and trailing patterns of bytes to enable the reading mechanism to detect the beginning and end of a block. In addition, tapes often contain additional longitudinal error checking information.

For reasons of reliability, tracks are usually written in an order different from that depicted in Fig. 2.5. The part of the byte most likely to change on successive recordings is written on the most reliable part of the tape. The least significant bits are therefore written in the center of the tape. If a single bit of a block becomes corrupted, the combination of longitudinal and vertical parity checks enables the error to be located and corrected. It is also possible to devise schemes that cope with multiple-bit errors.[2] This is left as an exercise for the reader (see Exercise 7).

---

2. See, for example, Hamming [5].

In the following example we show how the capacity of a tape can be estimated.

Example 1. A certain operating system writes user files from discs onto magnetic tapes. The tape drives operate in start/stop mode. The size of files in the **filestore** (collection of user files maintained by the operating system) is measured in 512-byte disc sectors (more on sectors in Section 2.3). How many such sectors can we write on a 2400-foot tape?

To answer this question we need to know (a) how many disc sectors are written onto each tape block, (b) the size of the gap between tape blocks, and (c) the recording density. Let us assume that 20 disc sectors are written onto each tape block (i.e., the blocking factor is 20), that the interblock gap is 0.5 inches, and that the recording density is 1600 bpi. The number of disc sectors on the tape can now be calculated as follows:

Block length = blocking factor × disc sector
                size/recording density
            = 20 × 512/1600 inches
            = 10,240/1600 inches
            = 6.4 inches

Block + gap = 6.9 inches

Tape length = 2400 feet × 12 inches
            = 28,800 inches

Number of tape blocks = tape length/(block + gap)
                      = 28,800/6.9
                      = 4173

Number of disc sectors = number of tape blocks ×
                         blocking factor
                       = 4173 × 20
                       = 83,460

We can also estimate the time required to write a certain amount of data onto a tape. Consider the following example.

Example 2. Suppose that the files of users of the operating system occupy 150,000 disc sectors. As part of system integrity measures, files that have been modified recently are backed up onto tape at the end of a day. On an average day, 20% of the disc sectors are written onto tape. How long will this daily backup take?

To answer this question we need to know (a) the speed at which the tape moves when it is reading and writing and (b) the start/stop times. Assume that the read/write speed is 50 inches per second and that it takes the drive 0.02 seconds to bring the tape up to speed from rest or to decelerate to a stop. We can then estimate the total time needed as follows:

> Block length = 6.4 inches (from Example 1)
> Time to write a block = block length/writing speed
> = 6.4/50 seconds
> = .128 seconds
> Time to write a block plus start and
> stop time (0.02 seconds for each) = .168 seconds
> Number of blocks to back up = 0.2 × 150,000 disc sectors
> = 30,000 disc sectors
> = 30,000/20 tape blocks
> = 1500 tape blocks
> Total time needed for backup = number of tape blocks ×
> time to write one block
> = 1500 × .168 seconds
> = 252 seconds

Note that for the purposes of this simple example we have assumed that data can be transmitted from the CPU as fast as the tape drive needs it.

In summary, tapes are relatively cheap, robust, and compact. They are good for off-line archival storage. However, the time required to access an arbitrary piece of data can be long. They are therefore best suited for data that is processed serially where a large proportion of the data scanned is used and where processing is not time critical.

2.3 Spinning Tracks

The main disadvantage of serial, tape-based devices is that not all data on the tape is equally accessible. There is a large difference between the times required to access the data nearest and the data furthest from the current position on the tape. Efficient access is possible only if the data is processed in the order in which it appears on the tape. This problem has been solved in a variety of devices by rotating a magnetizable surface at high speed past a read/write head. As with a tape system, a track is the projection of a given head position on the recording surface, but a disc contains circular rather than linear tracks. In the worst case, data is less than a single revolution of the track away.

Devices based on the spinning track principle can be classified in many ways. For example, all of the following questions might be asked in an attempt to classify a particular device.

- Is the recording medium detachable from the drive?
- Is there one read/write head per track, or does a moving head serve multiple tracks?
- Are the tracks written on a spinning disc or on a cylindrical drum?
- If a disc is used, is there one platter or several on a common spindle?
- If a single platter is used, is it a hard or floppy disc?
- Do the tracks rotate continuously or only when a read/write operation is performed?
- Do the read/write heads make contact with the track?

A common arrangement is to have a single read/write head per recording surface.[3] The head serves all the tracks on that surface and moves to a particular track when required. This is called a **moving head** system. Discs and drums with a head for each track (i.e., **fixed-head** systems) are becoming rare. The positions that a read/write head can take define a number of concentric tracks on which data can be recorded (see Fig. 2.6a).

A disc pack with more than one recording surface has **cylinders** of tracks. A cylinder is a set of tracks with the same radius. For example, cylinder 200 comprises track number 200 on each of the recording surfaces. A disc drive with one read/write head per surface moves all the heads together. On a normal drive only one of the heads can read or write at one time. If the heads are positioned at a particular track, then all the data in that cylinder is accessible with no further head movement (see Fig. 2.6b). Electronic switching is then used to select the active head. This switching is much faster than the mechanical movement of the read/write head and, for many purposes, can be considered instantaneous.

Data Recording

A hard disc is a rigid metal disc, typically aluminum, coated with a magnetizable material, for example, a mixture of chromic oxide and ferrous oxide. A floppy disc is contained in a plastic envelope with a window through which the read/write head accesses the recording surface. In each case bits are written serially along tracks. Checking information, similar to that found in tape systems, is usually stored together with the data. Check data often takes the form of **check bytes,**

---

3. See Hofri [6] for the properties of discs with two independent read/write heads.

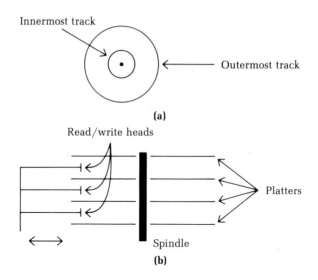

FIGURE 2.6 Disc and drive

that is, bytes that are derived from the data and stored with it. (The section "Low-Level Operating System Functions" later in this chapter examines check bytes more fully.)

A disc must contain **formatting information** so that the recording locations on the disc can be identified. For this reason new discs typically have to be formatted before use. A formatting program writes various pieces of information on each track of a disc; thus the capacity of a formatted disc is likely to be less than that of an unformatted one. **Synchronization bits** are written to enable the servo mechanisms of the drive to detect and correct for fluctuations in the rotational speed of a disc during reading and writing. At the start of each track there might be **track identification bits** and **status bits.** This information allows the hardware to verify a movement of the read/write heads to a particular track.

A track is usually subdivided into a number of **sectors** (see Fig. 2.7). On a **hard-sectored disc** the position of the sectors is defined by holes in the disc. The holes are detectable by the drive. A **soft-sectored disc** has sector defining information written onto it by the formatting program. This information may be as simple as bit patterns indicating intersector gaps. Soft sectoring is more flexible because it may allow users to determine the number of sectors per track.

We saw that many user records can be stored in one tape block. Similarly, and also for reasons of efficiency, many logical records can

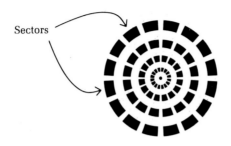

Sectors

FIGURE 2.7 Disc sectors

be stored in one disc sector. For example, six 80-byte records could be packed into a 512-byte sector, or a logical record could span sectors. However, on multiuser systems a central disc, more so than a tape, tends to be a shared resource. Thus a particular user is not likely to have a great deal of control over the size of the physical records.

Some disc drives operate at variable speeds: the rotation rate depends on which track is being accessed. This is done to increase the storage capacity of the disc. Consider a disc processed using a conventional drive; all sectors have the same angular size (see Fig. 2.7). However, those on outer tracks are longer than those on inner tracks because outer tracks have a greater circumference. Because the amount of data recorded in a sector is the same all over the disc, recording density is less on the outer tracks than it is on the inner tracks. With a variable-speed drive some attempt is made to make sectors in all parts of the disc the same length. The drive will slow down as the read/write head moves outward so the rate at which data passes the head is constant.

Read/Write Operations

On most floppy disc systems the drive rotates only when required. Read/write heads make contact with the recording surface. In most hard disc systems the disc rotates continuously. This continuous rotation creates a fast-moving layer of air just above the disc surface. An airfoil moving in this air is kept at a constant distance from the surface. The read/write head is attached to the airfoil. In such systems tolerances are small: even microscopic particles can cause read/write errors or head crashes, which occur when the head makes contact with the disc.

A read/write operation may transfer one or many sectors of information. Given the arrangement of recording surfaces and read/

write heads, the time required for a particular operation, for example, to access, read, and transmit a sector of data, involves five components.[4] These are the times needed:

1. to select the appropriate surface
2. to move the read/write head to the appropriate track (seek delay)
3. for the required sector to rotate around to the location of the read/write head (rotational delay or **latency**)
4. to read the bytes from the disc surface
5. to transmit the bytes to the CPU

The user has no control over the first, fourth, and fifth components. The first is a purely electronic operation, and the time required is negligible. The fourth is dependent primarily on the amount of data read. The fifth depends on the busyness of the channel to the CPU; data may have to be buffered before being sent. We consider the second and third components in more detail.

Head movement. Typically the time required to move the read/write heads is a function of the number of tracks over which the heads must move. The function is not linear. For example, if K milliseconds (ms) are required to move one track, moving N tracks normally takes less than $(N \times K)$ ms. Typical figures are 7 ms for a single track movement, 28 ms for an average track movement, and 50 ms for the worst case (innermost track to outermost track or vice versa).

Rotational delay. On average the user must wait for a disc to make half a revolution for the required data to appear at the read/write position. A typical rotational speed for a constantly rotating disc is 3600 rpm. This yields an average latency of 8.3 ms for all tracks. With a variable speed drive the average latency varies according to the track being accessed. The user has some control over delays due to head movement and rotation, which we look at further in the section entitled "Data Placement" later in this chapter.

In Example 2 we estimated the time required to write parts of a filestore onto tape. We now consider how long it might take to read the same information from discs.

Example 3. In addition to the information given in Example 2, we will make the following five assumptions:

---

4. If the disc is not constantly rotating, time is also needed to bring it up to speed, similar to the time needed to bring a tape up to speed.

1. Data is read one sector at a time, and the time taken to read the sector as it passes under the read/write head is negligible.

2. The data to be read is on a single drive, and the 30,000 sectors are distributed evenly over 500 cylinders; that is, there will be 60 sectors to be read on each cylinder.

3. The disc pack has four recording surfaces and the 60 sectors to be read from a cylinder are distributed equally over those surfaces; that is, each track will have 15 sectors to be read.

4. Head movement time is 7 ms for a single track, and average latency is 8.3 ms. Surface switching times are negligible.

5. The order in which the data within a track is processed is important, so for each sector read, we may have to wait for the sector to rotate to the reading position.

Based on the information given, we can calculate the average total time required to read the information as follows:

$$
\begin{aligned}
\text{Track read time} &= \text{number of sectors to be read} \\
&\qquad \text{in track} \times \text{latency} \\
&= 15 \times 8.3 \text{ ms} \\
&= .125 \text{ seconds}
\end{aligned}
$$

$$
\begin{aligned}
\text{Cylinder read time} &= \text{tracks per cylinder} \times \text{track reads} \\
&= 4 \text{ track reads} \\
&= 4 \times .125 \text{ seconds} \\
&= .5 \text{ seconds}
\end{aligned}
$$

$$
\begin{aligned}
\text{Total read time} &= 500 \text{ cylinder reads} + 499 \text{ cylinder switches} \\
&= 500 \times .5 + 499 \times .007 \text{ seconds} \\
&= 250 + 3.493 \\
&= 253.493 \text{ seconds}
\end{aligned}
$$

Data Placement

How can data be placed on a disc to minimize access times? If the data is to be processed in a predictable order, it is possible to take steps to minimize head movement and rotational delays.

To minimize head movement it is better to treat a disc as a sequence of cylinders rather than a sequence of surfaces. When processing a disc cylinder by cylinder, there is a head movement only after all data in one cylinder has been processed. Thus there is minimal head movement. On the other hand, when processing surface by surface, there is a head movement after each track is processed. If a disc has N recording surfaces, then the number of head movements when processing surface by surface is N times the number when processing cylinder by cylinder.

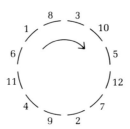

FIGURE 2.8 Hopscotching

Next, consider a number of data items that are to be placed on a particular track and processed in a known sequence. To minimize rotational delay, the items could be located in such a way that a sector containing the item is just coming under the read/write head at the time when it is required. It is likely that data so placed will not appear in consecutive physical sectors but will rather appear in a **hopscotch** pattern (see Fig. 2.8). Here we assume that in the time it takes to process a sector, four others (or, in general, $N \times 12 + 4$ sectors) rotate past the read/write head. Note, however, that this technique assumes that processing time is predictable. It is not likely to be applicable in a multiprocessing system.

Winchester Technology

In the mid-1970s IBM developed Winchester disc packs. Such packs have the read/write heads and the disc platters in a sealed unit. Because the possibility of dust contamination was virtually eliminated, design tolerances could be tighter. Reliability is higher, and the heads can float closer to the disc surfaces, thus allowing greater recording density. Tracks can be packed more than 1000 per inch with bit densities in excess of 12,000 per inch. In contrast, conventional discs have approximately 400 tracks per inch and bit densities of 4000 per inch. Mini-Winchester drives have also been developed, with common disc diameters of 3.5, 5.25, and 8 inches. These drives are small enough to fit into microcomputers. To minimize the effects of data loss, many manufacturers of Winchester drives provide a back-up device. A typical example is a streaming tape cartridge that can be used to load or back up the sealed disc [7].

To summarize, in comparison with tapes, discs provide fast direct access to data. For example, programs that must be loaded quickly into main memory are better stored on disc than on tape. Once the disc address of the program is determined, it can be retrieved in a fraction of a second. If a data record must be updated quickly, as in a seat reservation system, it is impractical to have it stored on tape. (Consider again the average access times given in Table 2.2.) Discs and tapes are the predominant secondary storage media. However, there are alternative devices. We look at four in the next section.

2.4 Esoteric Storage Devices

There have been changes in the types of secondary storage devices used in computer systems. Magnetic tapes were used with some of the earliest computers. Drums were originally the most common direct-access secondary storage device. While tapes are still omnipresent, drums have tended to give way to discs. Discs are now found on all but the smallest computer systems. Other media common at one time, such as punched cards and punched paper tape, have largely been superseded by magnetic devices. In this section we consider some storage devices that, although not commonplace now, may become important in the future. These devices are bubble memories, mass storage systems, content addressable filestores, and optical discs.

Bubble Memories

A bubble memory stores data in the form of magnetic regions or domains that are rotated in a plane of material by a rotating magnetic field. Bubble detection and generation mechanisms are the equivalent of read/write heads. In contrast to discs, there are no mechanical moving parts. Currently bubble memories do not seem to have fulfilled their early promise as rivals to discs [8]. Disc technology has continued to improve, which has kept bubble memories from being widely adopted. Compared with discs, capacities are small and transfer rates low. However, they do have some advantages, including greater reliability, lower access times, smaller size, lower weight, and lower power consumption. They may be a better choice than discs in extreme environments, for example in some military applications or portable personal computers.

Mass Storage Devices

Certain applications have requirements for very large amounts of on-line data. The data might be stored in various ways depending on response time requirements. If short access times are necessary, then one solution is a forest of disc drives. For example, Gifford and Spector [9] describe an airline reservation system with 144 drives.

If comparatively long access times can be tolerated, a mass storage system might be a feasible alternative. Kaisler [10] presents an interesting viewpoint on a number of mass storage devices and applications. Examples of mass storage systems are the IBM 3850 Mass Storage System [11] and the M860 produced by Masstor Systems [12, 13].

The IBM 3850 consists of tape cartridges and hard discs. If a copy of required data is not currently on a disc, the contents of the appropriate cartridge are read onto a disc. This might take as little as ten seconds. From there data is sent to the CPU. If there is no spare disc space, then an algorithm, which takes recent disc usage into account, determines which disc data to overwrite. The capacity of the IBM 3850 storage system can be as high as 472 gigabytes (472 $\times$ 10^9 bytes).

The Masstor M860 is also an on-line cartridge store, but it does not include discs. A maximum M860 configuration can hold 440 gigabytes in 2528 cartridges. The average time to extract a cartridge from the storage area is 2.8 seconds, and in a further 4.6 seconds the cartridge can be loaded and threaded on the data recording device. The average search time is 2.5 seconds. The CPU views the M860 as a tape subsystem. Data can be read in a serial manner or transferred to discs.

Content Addressable Filestores

Data is retrieved from a conventional disc drive by giving the drive the address of the required data. The contents of the appropriate sector(s) are returned. The ICL Content Addressable Filestore (CAFS) [14] is connected to a disc controller and accepts logical requests for data. The disc controller has hardware that can perform key matches. The controller can be loaded with constants for describing record fields and values and with a microprogram to determine if a particular record satisfies a request. The manufacturers claim a search rate of close to a megabyte per second, and use of CAFS has produced significant increases in productivity in a variety of applications [15]. See Addis [16, p. 133] for details of an application and an overview of the CAFS mechanism.

In a conventional data storage system the process of finding a record given a key involves mapping the key onto an address in some way. Much material in the following chapters is concerned with ways of organizing data for efficient retrievals and with the mapping process. Note how CAFS removes the need for this and that the key itself is sufficient for retrievals.

Optical Discs

Magnetic discs hold information in the form of erasable magnetized spots. A typical optical disc holds information in the form of pits or bubbles made by a laser. The laser might write from above and make "pits" [17] or from below and make bubbles [18, fig. 2]. An advantage of the latter is that there is less chance of errors caused by dust. Currently, optical discs are nonerasable, that is, they are write-once read-many-times devices.[5] Reading is also accomplished with a laser and a mechanism that detects the differences in the amounts of reflected light from a pit/bubble and from the normal surface. Resolution can be extremely high, resulting in large storage capacities. For example, the 14-inch high precision platter produced by Storage Technologies holds four gigabytes [19].

The current write-once nature of an optical disc is not a drawback for many applications. For example, in a typical document retrieval system a document is not altered after it has been stored. There are many volumes of legal precedents that could be stored in this way. There are also applications in which it might be an advantage to have data in an unalterable form. For example, accounting information required by auditors could be stored on a write-once disc. Log files from a computer system could also be held in this form. The physical nature of the storage method makes it possible to reproduce optical discs en masse. One can imagine reference material such as encyclopedic data being made available in this way.

One requirement of success for a new type of storage device might be that it can be made to look like an existing device. If, for example, optical discs can be addressed as if they were magnetic discs, they should become very common. Vitter [20] describes some techniques that are effective for applications that are not update-intensive.

2.5 Operating System Interface

In this section we consider some of the operations that might be involved in the transfer of data to and from secondary storage devices. An **operating system** is a program that, in general, is responsible for managing the resources of a computer system for its multiple users. One of the functions of the operating system is to provide a controlled interface between users and secondary storage devices. (Imagine what would happen if every user were free to access the secondary storage in his or her own way.) Figure 2.9 depicts this role.

An alternative view of the role of the operating system is to see it as mapping user views of the storage devices onto the real devices. Typically user views are determined by the programming language

---

5. Erasable optical discs have recently been announced.

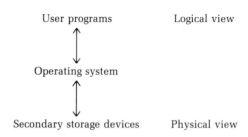

FIGURE 2.9 Operating system role

used. We can thus distinguish between the logical view of the storage and the physical view. The logical view is how the user perceives it, and the physical view is how it really is. For example, a user might view a set of data as a series of 80-byte records, whereas the data is actually stored packed in 512-byte sectors of a disc. When a user requests a logical record, the operating system reads the appropriate sector(s) and extracts the requested bytes. In discussing functions of the operating system in this section, we arbitrarily divide them into low and high level.

Low-Level Operating System Functions

The low-level functions of the operating system are concerned with reliable and efficient transfer of blocks of bytes between main and secondary storage. It is increasingly common for processing in an operating system to be distributed rather than centralized. Thus low-level input/output processing is frequently delegated to **device controllers** or **peripheral processors** having a certain amount of local memory. Functions that can be delegated include error detection and correction, transfer scheduling, data caching, and encryption and compression.

Error detection/correction. We have noted that the electromechanical nature of some secondary storage devices may cause corruption of data. That is, a bit pattern read back from a storage location may not match what was originally written there. There must be some redundancy in the stored data if errors are to be detectable. That is, not all possible bit patterns should be valid. An error detection system might use check bytes.

Writing. The value of the check bytes for a certain set of data is some function of that data. For example, it might be a weighted sum of the data bytes. When data is written, the controller computes check

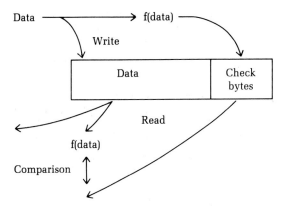

FIGURE 2.10 Data checking

bytes from the data written and writes the check bytes out also, as shown in Fig. 2.10.

Reading. When data is read back, the same computation is performed on the bit pattern read. That is, the controller computes what the check byte values should be, based on the data it read. It then compares the check bytes read from the storage medium with the computed values. A mismatch indicates that data or check bytes have been corrupted. (Note that while a mismatch indicates corruption, a match does not necessarily mean that the data is correct.)

What can be done if an error is detected? In some schemes there may be sufficient information in the bytes read to allow errors to be corrected. (Recall the discussion of tape block errors.) Failing that, the transfer could be repeated a number of times to see if the fault clears. In the case of a disc, the controller could keep a list of addresses of sectors found to be unreliable. Part of the disc could be set aside to hold this information. Taking this idea further, the disc might also have a number of spare sectors invisible to the user. The controller could map addresses of faulty sectors onto addresses of spare sectors in a manner transparent to the rest of the system.

Transfer scheduling. When we looked at disc read/write operations, we saw that head movement time is a significant factor. An intelligent device controller could schedule a series of disc transfers to minimize time lost due to head seeks. For instance, rather than dealing with requests in the order in which they arrive, average time to service a request might be reduced if an "elevator" algorithm were used. In this algorithm priority is given to requests that reference

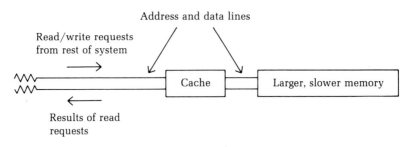

FIGURE 2.11 Cache memory

tracks in whatever direction the read/write head is currently moving. Within this group the closest request wins. A little like an elevator going up and down a building, the read/write heads sweep over the disc.

Data caching. A cache is a comparatively small high-speed memory placed in front of a comparatively large low-speed memory, as shown in Fig. 2.11. When a request is received for a memory access, the memory-accessing mechanism first checks to see if the request can be satisfied from the cache. The slower memory is accessed only if the request cannot be satisfied. If the slower memory must be accessed, a copy of the memory section containing the target location is typically brought into the cache. Note how the disc units of the IBM 3850 Mass Storage System, described earlier, act as a cache to the tape cartridges.

If the cache is already full when a section must be brought in, then various algorithms can be used to select a section to overwrite. For example, the Least Frequently Used (LFU) algorithm chooses the section that has been accessed least often. On the other hand, the Least Recently Used (LRU) algorithm selects the cache section that has been unaccessed for the longest time. (The IBM 3850 uses an LRU algorithm.) The intention of both algorithms is to identify the section least likely to be needed in the future.

When write operations take place there is the problem of keeping the cache and the slower memory consistent. If a **write-through policy** is adopted, changes made to any cache section are immediately made to the corresponding section of the slower memory. Another possibility is to change only the cache section and mark it "dirty." If the replacement algorithm selects a dirty section then it must be written back to the slower memory before being overwritten.

The net effect of the modified read/write operations is that over a period of time the cache will tend to contain copies of frequently accessed areas of the slower memory. This results in a lower average memory access time than if there were no cache present.

A frequent application of the caching technique is to hold commonly accessed sections of main memory (see, for example, Smith [21]). In this case the cache will be constructed of some technology significantly faster than the main memory. Further down the memory hierarchy we can imagine the slower memory being a collection of magnetic tapes and the faster memory being one or more disc drives (as in the IBM 3850). Somewhere in between these applications we can conceive of the slower device being a disc and the faster one being a semiconductor memory. In this case the memory might be in a device controller. Copies of the most frequently accessed disc sectors, for example, those containing disc indexes or directories, would migrate toward the cache.

Caching of main memory achieves its result because of the "property of locality" [22] exhibited by most programs. That is, they tend to access main memory nonuniformly—all parts of the data are not used with the same frequency. In addition, these clusters of data tend to be in use over a period of time. Thus there is likely to be a high **hit ratio.** The hit ratio is the percentage of requests that can be satisfied without accessing the slower memory. It is likely that similar behavior, though perhaps not quite as marked, can be found at other levels in the memory hierarchy.

The operation of the disc cache could be the responsibility of the disc controller and be completely transparent to the rest of the system. The cache would operate at the physical rather than logical level. That is, the controller would not know anything about the significance of data held in any particular disc sector. If the disc is removable, then, depending on the writing policy, the cache may have to be flushed when the disc is removed.

It is worth noting that the operating system usually performs a type of caching when interfacing user programs to files on storage devices. Suppose that a user's file of 80-byte records is stored on a disc with 512-byte sectors. A request from the program for a particular record typically results in the whole of the appropriate sector being read into main memory. A subsequent request for a record in the same sector can be satisfied without accessing the disc (provided that the main memory region has not been overwritten in the meantime).

Encryption and compression. Encryption and data compression/expansion are operations that can also be performed in a transparent way by a peripheral controller. We discuss data compression further in Section 2.7.

An operating system can implement a number of security measures designed to control access to files stored on secondary storage devices. However, these may be rendered useless if the physical medium (disc or tape) is stolen. By storing data in encrypted form the system can make the theft of a storage device less profitable.

Many encryption systems operate by transforming a stream of characters (the **plain text**) into a second stream of characters (the **encrypted text**) using some **key.** It is feasible for the computation involved to be performed by a device controller. Thus the plain text data is never stored on a storage medium. It might be simplest for the controller to take a very low-level view of the storage device, for example, to view a disc as an array of sectors. The key used when storing data on a particular sector might be based on the address of that sector.

High-Level Operating System Functions

We classify as high-level those operating system functions that make access to secondary storage convenient for users. An operating system usually enables users to create and manipulate named files of data. That is, a filestore is mapped onto the storage devices so that sections can be referred to by name. Functions we consider here are filestore structure, security, integrity, and space allocation.

Filestore structure. Information about a user's files is typically held in a directory file. (There can also be directories for complete disc volumes and also directories of users.) The information held in a directory about a file typically includes its name, size, storage address, and date of last modification. In a simple system each user has a single directory containing information about his or her files. It is becoming increasingly common, however, for systems to allow users to create their own subdirectories. This allows related files to be grouped together. Any directory entry can be an ordinary file or another directory. Thus there can be a hierarchical structure of files. Examples of operating systems that support hierarchical filestores are Unix and MS-DOS.

Security. In a multiuser system a user should be able to control access to his or her files. A common security mechanism is to enable the owner of a file to grant and deny various **permissions** to various categories of user. Only the owner of a file should be able to change its permissions. Typical permissions allow a user to delete, read from, write to, append to, and execute a file. Categories of user include the file owner, the users of the system in general, and groups of users specified in various ways. A **permission vector,** a simple data structure recording the access controls on a file, is typically part of the directory entry for that file.

Integrity. Despite error detection and correction methods, files stored on secondary storage devices may become irreparably corrupted due to hardware and software errors. How can this inconvenience be minimized? Programs that update files can do so by creating an updated copy of the file without destroying the old one. Thus a previous version of data may be available if the current one is destroyed. A sound strategy is to make copies of files and store the copies off-line. This responsibility should be undertaken for all users by the operating system. In a **full backup** the complete filestore is copied, but in an **incremental backup** copying is limited to files that have been modified since some reference date. The date-of-last-modification field in a directory entry indicates whether or not a file should be copied. Although there are various backup strategies, the following is one possibility.

- On the first day of each month, copy the complete filestore onto tape.
- Every weekend, make copies of those files that have been modified since the most recent monthly backup.
- Each night, make copies of files that have changed since the immediately preceding weekly backup.

Under this scheme, a file that has become corrupted should normally be able to be restored to its state on the previous night.

Space allocation. Secondary storage space is one of the resources of a computer system that the operating system manages. There are a variety of ways in which the system might keep track of the free space on a storage device such as a disc. An elegant method uses a **bit map** or **bit vector.** The bit map for a disc is stored on the disc. Each bit corresponds to a sector and indicates if the sector is free or has been allocated to a file. (See Chapter 7 for a similar application of bit vectors.) The bit map occupies very little space. The disc on which we store the text of this book contains 171,198 sectors, and a bit map for the complete disc would occupy only 42 sectors.

Systems vary in how they allocate space for a particular file. Some require that a file occupy contiguous sectors; the directory entry for the file identifies the beginning and the length of the file. Alternatively, the sectors of a file could be scattered over a disc. In this case the directory could contain a list of pointers to all sectors, or the sectors could be linked and the directory entry point to the first.

How might available space be shared equitably between users? Three possible strategies are fixed quotas, no quotas, and daily income.

TABLE 2.4 Example of block-day space allocation

Day	Income	In Use	Balance
1	40	5	35
2	40	20	55
3	40	50	45
4	40	32	53
5	40	80	13
6	40	60	−7

Fixed quotas. In the first strategy each user is given a fixed quota of space. The operating system checks when the user logs in and logs out that this quota has not been exceeded. A user exceeding his or her quota is required to delete files before proceeding.

No quotas. In the second strategy there are no quotas at all. However, when the on-line storage is nearly used up, the operating system starts to archive files that have not been used for a period of time. In practice, this might take the form of deleting files that have been inactive for a long period. Naturally, the system ensures that there is already a backup copy of a file deleted in this way.

Daily income. Barron [23, p. 128] describes the allocation method of the Cambridge University operating system. It works in much the same way as a current banking account. The unit of currency is the block-day (a block is the unit of file size). Each user has a certain daily income of block-day that is added to his or her current balance at the beginning of the day. At the end of the day the number of blocks currently used is subtracted from the balance. See, for example, Table 2.4. The system may impose limits on the size of positive balances (for instance, ten times income). Penalties may be imposed when a balance becomes negative. For example, the user may not be able to access files except to delete them.

In summary, the operating system provides a disciplined interface between user programs and secondary storage devices. A responsible operating system implements measures to ensure the integrity and security of stored data. Normally, users need to be able to access records in a file from within a program. We look at the programming language interface next.

2.6 Programming Language Interface

Most high-level languages provide a set of routines through which users can access data stored in files. What primitive file operations should a user of a high-level language be able to perform? Here we consider operations in three areas: file opening/closing, data transfer, and file manipulation.

File Opening/Closing

Typically when a file is connected to a high-level language program, it is associated with a **file variable** of some form. A call to a file opening routine establishes a link between a file variable and a file. The link between the file variable and the file is dynamic rather than static. Thus, use of the file variable as an intermediary between a file and other variables in the program allows file-independent routines to be written. A call to a file closing routine breaks the link. In certain cases, when a file is closed, records may have to be flushed from a main memory buffer to the file. Conceptually, the file variable is a structure that may include a **file pointer** that references the currently accessible file record. Additionally, it may include a buffer for transfers to and from the file.

A file can usually be opened in a number of modes. Examples of modes are append, read-only, write-only, and read-and-write. File opening routines should return appropriate error indicators, for example, if a file opened for reading does not exist. When a file is closed, special action may be necessary in order to make the contents permanent. Table 2.5 contains examples of direct-access file opening and closing routines from common high-level languages. It is assumed in each example that the file variables have already been declared. Even for a particular language, input/output may be specific to the operating system. For this reason we have included the name of the operating systems here. Examples of direct-access file commands have been given, since they are more complex than serial-access file commands.

Data Transfer

A link between a file variable and a file having been established, certain primitive operations are usually provided for transferring data between the file and variables in the program. Usually one record is transferred at a time. There are many variations in the routines provided in high-level languages. Some routines do more conversion than others between the external and internal data representations. Some do more than others in formatting input/output.

The routines that can be applied to a particular file are likely to depend on the mode in which it was opened. We will consider different file types in subsequent chapters, but note here that there are likely to be **serial files,** which can only be read in a serial manner,

TABLE 2.5 File opening and closing in high-level languages

Language	Operating System	Command
File opening		
C	UNIX	filevariable = open(filename, mode)*
COBOL	CP/M	Environment division
		SELECT logicalfilename ASSIGN TO "externalfilename" ORGANIZATION IS INDEXED ACCESS MODE IS SEQUENTIAL RECORD KEY IS keyname
		Procedure division
		OPEN I-O logicalfilename
FORTRAN77	NOS	OPEN(unit#, FILE = 'filename', ACCESS = DIRECT, RECL = recordlength)
Pascal	RSTS/E	RESET(filevariable, 'filename/seek')
File closing		
C	UNIX	CLOSE(filevariable)
COBOL	CP/M	CLOSE logicalfilename
FORTRAN77	NOS	CLOSE(unit#, STATUS = 'DELETE')
Pascal	RSTS/E	CLOSE(filevariable)

*C is a functional language. Thus, most commands return values that can be assigned to variables (for example, the assignment to *filevariable*) or checked for error conditions (see how *flag* and *byte.check* are used in Table 2.7).

and **direct-access files,** where any record in the file is equally accessible. Clearly there are close correspondences here with the serial and direct-access storage devices discussed earlier.

When a serial file is opened for reading, the file pointer is positioned at the beginning of the file. Data is read from the file starting at the pointer position. The pointer advances past the data as it is read. It is possible to detect whether the pointer has reached the end of the file. Table 2.6 presents example serial-file data transfer statements from various languages.

If a direct-access file is being processed the file pointer has to be positioned (either implicitly or explicitly) at the appropriate point in the file before a record transfer can take place. Table 2.7 shows direct-access file data transfer commands.

TABLE 2.6 Serial file data transfer examples

Language	Operating System	Command
C	UNIX	byte.check = READ(filevariable, buffer, byte.count) WRITE(filevariable, buffer, byte.count)
COBOL	CP/M	READ logicalfilename AT END PERFORM routine DISPLAY logicalfilename UPON device WRITE recordname TO device
FORTRAN77	NOS	READ(unit#, format) variable list WRITE(unit#, format) variable list
Pascal	RSTS/E	Text files
		READ(filevariable, variable list) WRITE(filevariable, variable list)
		Record files
		To read GET(filevariable)
		To write filevariable^ := record; PUT(filevariable)

Depending on the file organization, higher-level functions may be available. For example, it may be possible to get a record with a particular primary key or to get the record with the key next in sequence to the current one.

File Manipulation

In some combinations of operating system and programming language it may be possible to issue, in the programming language, commands that manipulate files as single entities. For instance, it may be possible to delete a file, to rename a file, or to change the protection codes of a file from within a program. Such facilities are sometimes provided via a general mechanism that allows users to issue operating system commands from within high-level language programs.

2.7 Data Compression

The cost per byte of secondary storage is declining and is likely to continue to do so. However, it may still be worth considering ways of compressing data without loss of information. Suppose we are able

TABLE 2.7 Direct file data transfer examples

Language	Operating System	Command
C	UNIX	To read flag = LSEEK(filevariable, byte.offset, base) byte.check = READ(filevariable, buffer, byte.count)
		To write flag = LSEEK(filevariable, byte.offset, base) WRITE(filevariable, buffer, byte.count)
COBOL	CP/M	To read MOVE keyvalue TO keyname READ logicalfilename INVALID KEY PERFORM routine
		To write WRITE recordname INVALID KEY PERFORM routine

FORTRAN77*		READ(unit#, format, REC = recordnumber)
		   variable list
		WRITE(unit#, format, REC = recordnumber)
		   variable list

Pascal	RSTS/E	To read SEEK(filevariable, recordnumber)
		To write SEEK(filevariable, recordnumber); filevariable^ := record; PUT(filevariable)

*The example here is in standard FORTRAN77. However, many implementations of the language, including the NOS version used in Tables 2.5 and 2.6, do not adhere to this standard.

to compress, for example, a 100K byte file into 40K bytes. (Of course, we must be able to expand it back again when required.) Such a facility may allow us to hold more data on-line, to reduce the time needed to transmit the data, to postpone purchase of additional disc drives, to reduce the number of tapes needed to back up a filestore, and so on. However, compression and expansion involve computation, so there is a trade-off between the time this takes and the space saved. Utility programs could be made available to enable users to compress and expand files; this may be particularly useful if their storage quotas are fixed. Alternatively, as with many of the storage operations discussed in previous sections, some of the compression (and expansion) techniques could be performed by a device controller in a manner

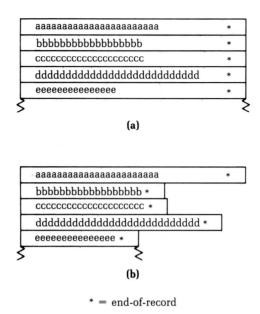

(a)

(b)

* = end-of-record

FIGURE 2.12 Data compression: trailing blank elimination

transparent to the rest of the system. In this case, however, it is important to use a technique with low overhead. In addition, because of the likely variety of file types, it would be desirable to have a method that adjusts dynamically to the data being read. We now look at some compression techniques.

Elimination of Trailing Blanks

Consider a file of fixed-length records containing, for example, personnel data. There are likely to be many records that do not fill the space allowed. A simple compression technique is to suppress a sequence of spaces at the end of a record. The corresponding expansion is simple if the record length is known. The first record in the file might be left uncompressed to give this information. Figure 2.12(a) shows the beginning of an uncompressed file and Fig. 2.12(b) the compressed version.

Run Length Encoding

We can generalize the previous technique and replace a sequence of N occurrences of some character K by three bytes:

<escape code>< N >< K >

The "escape code" indicates that the following byte is to be interpreted as a count rather than as a character code. The third byte is the character being repeated. Space is saved if N is larger than 3. The first example below shows a (contrived) source file and the second example the compressed version.

1. "Wheeeeeee. . . . ." cried the skier.

2. "Wh~7e~9." cried the skier. (~ = escape code)

This technique is likely to produce larger savings when applied to data files than when applied to text files, which do not usually have strings of identical characters. The technique may not be applicable at all to executable files because there may not be a spare bit pattern to act as an escape code.

Record Differences

Kang *et al.* [24] describe a data compression technique in which the records in a file are regarded as the nodes in a complete undirected graph. The distance between any pair of records is a function of the differences between the values in corresponding fields and the lengths of the fields. Using these distances, a minimum spanning tree[6] is computed. In the compressed version of the file a record is represented by (1) a pointer to the record that is its parent in the spanning tree and (2) the values of the fields that are not the same as those in the parent. The distance measure ensures that a record and its parent are similar.

Special Fields

Certain fields such as names and dates can be subjected to special treatment. These kinds of fields may form a significant part of a file of correspondence. Martin [25, ch. 32] outlines some techniques. Names, for example, have a skewed distribution: certain names are more common than others. A table of common names could be established and occurrence of those names replaced by a single byte pointer to the table entry preceded by an escape character.

Rubin [26] shows how this technique can be generalized. Bit patterns not being used to represent individual characters or strings can

---

6. A spanning tree of a graph is a tree that reaches every node of the graph. The minimal spanning tree is the spanning tree with the smallest total path length.

be used to represent commonly occurring strings of characters. The same technique could then be applied to the resulting file, to the result of compressing that file, and so on.

Variable-Length Codes

Significant savings are possible by adopting variable- rather than fixed-length character codes. Short codes would be allocated to the more frequent characters. Huffman [27] outlines a technique for producing an optimum set of variable-length codes. For best results the compression should be a two-pass process. In the first pass the frequencies of the characters in the file are determined. In the second pass the file is encoded using an optimum coding scheme based on the frequencies. Pechura [28] gives details of an implementation of a two-pass algorithm. A disadvantage of this approach, however, is that the coding scheme is likely to be file-specific. Thus a translation table of some form would have to be stored as part of the compressed file. Another disadvantage is that its two-pass nature means that the file contents could not be compressed on the fly, for example, as they are being received from the CPU.

Cormack [29] has devised and implemented what might be classified as a one-and-a-half-pass technique. Rather than using a single frequency distribution of characters (and corresponding set of codes) for compressing an entire record, his scheme uses different code tables for compressing different types of field. The tables are based on large samples of data. The compression algorithm uses the type of the current character to determine the table to use when compressing the next one. Suppose, for example, we have an alphabetic field followed by a numeric one. The alphabetic field would be compressed using a set of codes based on the frequency of alphabetic characters only. On detecting the transition to numeric character the algorithm would switch to a table of codes for numeric characters. The result is that this compression method can save more space than the normal Huffman technique.

A technique requiring only one pass over the data is possible. Good results can be obtained if the coding scheme changes dynamically.[7] Initial codes are assigned as if each character were equally frequent. As it is received, each character is encoded using the current scheme, and the frequency table is then modified to take into account the occurrence of the character. A change to the coding scheme may result. This approach is unlikely to compress the data in a file as

---

7. See, for example, Gallagher [30].

much as the two-pass optimum scheme above. However, there is now no need to store a code as part of the compressed file.

Welch [31] surveys data compression techniques and presents adaptive compression and expansion algorithms. His compression technique maps variable-length character strings onto fixed-length codes. The algorithm has been implemented in hardware, and quoted performance figures are 1.5 memory cycles for each input character and 1.5 cycles per output code. The algorithm exploits a number of types of redundancy found in computer files.

Addressing Problems

Application of a compression technique to a set of data is likely to change its size. In addition, compression is likely to be nonuniform. This may lead to problems in addressing the data. Consider a direct file in which records originally the same size are compressed to varying degrees. How can we tell where the Nth record is located without performing a serial scan or setting up pointers? Other problems may arise depending on where in the computer system the compression takes place. For example, consider the case where compression of data is performed by a disc controller and disc space is allocated by the operating system. The operating system handles the data in its uncompressed form and bases space allocation on that. Welch concludes that disc compression is best handled by the CPU. Tape data, however, is not so problematical except for some cases where drives are bidirectional; in this case compression may be oriented to a single direction.

Summary

We have briefly surveyed some secondary storage devices, operating system functions, and language interfaces to files.

We observed that there is a hierarchy of storage devices with a general trade-off between access time and cost per byte. The access times of secondary storage devices are orders of magnitude longer than those of main memory (primary storage). Tape-based devices are suitable for serial processing but too slow for direct access. Devices based on spinning magnetic tracks are currently the most common direct-access secondary storage. Because of long access times care must be taken when placing data in secondary storage.

We noted that an operating system is a program responsible for the management of the resources of a computer system. One of its tasks is the provision of a reliable, disciplined, usable interface between user programs and secondary storage devices. At a low level it handles the transfers of blocks of bytes between primary and secondary storage devices. At a higher level it allows users to manipulate named files of data. The operating system manages free space and implements security and integrity measures.

High-level languages provide mechanisms for attaching files to programs. Typically, routines are available for transferring records to and from files. We discussed data transfer for serial- and direct-access files. In some cases it may be possible to manipulate files as single entities.

There are a variety of techniques for compressing data. While they lead to a reduction in storage requirements, this saving must be weighed against the computation involved in compression and expansion.

Exercises

1. A given disc has 512 bytes in each sector, 11 surfaces on which to record information, 200 tracks per surface, and 20 sectors on each track.

   a) What is the total capacity of the disc (in megabytes)?
   b) How many 120-byte logical records can be stored on 10 cylinders of this disc if we assume that no logical record is split across a sector boundary?

2. A certain computer system has disc drives and a single tape drive. The specifications of a disc pack are as follows:

   512 bytes per sector   25 sectors per track
   800 tracks per surface   20 surfaces per pack

   Assume that the contents of the two packs are written onto tape with a blocking factor of 25, that is, there are 25 sectors per tape block. Recording density is 1600 bpi and interblock gaps are 0.5 inches long.

   a) How many 2400-foot tapes will be needed?
   b) What percentage of the last (unfilled) tape will be used?

3. The recordable part of a certain magnetic tape is 2400 feet long. Recording is at a density of 1600 bpi, read/write speed is 50 inches per second, interblock gaps are 0.5 inches long, and both start and stop times are 0.01 seconds.

   a) If the size of a logical record is 200 bytes, how many records need to be written per tape block in order to have N% tape utilization (i.e., N% of the tape is occupied by data as opposed to interblock gaps)?

b) How long will it take to write A blocks where each block is B bytes long?

4. Design a set of routines that simulates a disc and the operating system interface. Constants represent physical characteristics (for example, tracks per surface, and number of disc units). Your routines should at the lowest level simulate read/write requests for complete physical records. Next, they should enable a user to create files and take care of the mapping problems. Finally, users should be able to define logical record types and issue requests in terms of logical record numbers. Your routines should handle mapping from internal system buffers.

5. Write a program that tabulates the capacity of a 2400-foot tape in megabytes. Assume 0.5-inch interblock gaps. Use densities of 800 bpi and 1600 bpi and block sizes ranging from 512 bytes to 10,240 bytes in steps of 512 bytes.

6. Assume a disc has the following characteristics:

512 bytes per sector   25 sectors per track
800 tracks per surface   20 surfaces per pack

If average latency is 8.3 ms, single track seek time is 7 ms, and maximum track seek time is 50 ms, compute the amount of time required to read the complete disc (a) cylinder by cylinder, and (b) surface by surface.

7. Vertical and longitudinal parity checks on a tape block allow single-bit errors to be located. Devise a scheme that enables two-bit errors in a block to be located. (Hint: consider multiple parity bits.)

8. Associated with a 500-sector disc is a 20-sector cache. Assume that 25 ms is required to load a sector from disc to cache, 0.5 ms is required to fetch data from cache to main memory, and 1 ms is required to determine if a copy of a sector is in the cache. Write a program to tabulate the average time required to perform a sector read for each hit ratio from 49% to 99% in steps of 2%.

9. The management of your local computer center has been considering the following two strategies as alternatives to the daily/ weekly/monthly backup described in the text.

Strategy 1: A daily backup now backs up only those files changed that day. A weekly backup copies only those files changed during the current week. The monthly backup, as before, copies everything.

Strategy 2: To avoid losing as much as a complete day's changes to a file, files modified during the previous hour are copied every hour. Each run of the backup program has an associated (increasing) generation number. The number of the generation (if any) on which a particular file has been copied is part of its directory entry. Every three months all files are backed up.

Evaluate these two strategies and the one in the text. Give consideration in your answer to the following:

- restoration of a single file accidentally erased from disc
- recovery of the complete filestore after a disc crash
- vulnerability of backup copies (given that tape writing and storage are not 100% reliable)

10. Assume that under operating system 1 (OS-1) files must occupy contiguous sectors but that under operating system 2 (OS-2) they need not.

   a) Under which system do you think it would be easier to implement direct-access files? Give reasons for your choice.

   b) Under which system do you think it would be easier to implement extensible files? Give reasons for your choice.

11. Devise three ways in which OS-2 of Exercise 10 might identify the sectors belonging to a particular file.

12. What disc maintenance utility are users of the OS-1 system of Exercise 10 likely to need? What limitations may OS-1 have with respect to concurrent file creation?

13. Compare the three suggested schemes for allocating file space to users. What are the advantages and disadvantages of each? Consider the points of view of a user and the computer system manager.

3

Serial and Sequential Files

3.1 Presents a program design methodology that can be applied to many problems involving serial file processing.

3.2 Examines an update algorithm for a sequential file of records.

3.3 Looks at the general problem of merging N sequential files.

In this chapter and in Chapters 4 through 7 we will discuss a variety of file organizations, that is, a variety of ways in which data can be arranged in a file. With each file organization we will consider access techniques, or ways in which the data structure is manipulated. Choice of organization for a particular application will depend on the processing requirements of that application. In this chapter we are concerned with serial and sequential files. In Chapter 5 we will examine files organized using hashing. In Chapters 6 and 7 we will look at indexed files.

We define a serial file as one in which records are accessible only in linear order. That is, if we wish to access the Ith record in a serial file it is first necessary to process the preceding $I - 1$ records. Note that this property is shared with serial storage media, such as the tapes discussed in Chapter 2. Most programming language environments support serial files; some, for example standard Pascal [32], support no other file type. To update a serial file it is normally necessary to read from the old file and write to a new file, making appropriate changes during the copying process. In some ways the serial file represents the null file organization—there is no assumption made about the position of any record in the file.

A **sequential file** has the property that records can be accessed in order of some key. In practice this will usually be in **primary key** order. The primary key of a record is a field or combination of fields that uniquely identifies that record. For example, in a file of telephone customers, the combination of name and phone number is probably unique. In a file of employee records, both social security number and employee identification number are candidate primary keys. The primary key would be selected from the set of **candidate keys** according to processing requirements. The sequential property could be achieved by the physical positioning of records in the file, by explicit pointers, or by a combination of both. Again, the file must usually be copied to update the file and preserve the sequence of the records.

In many applications using serial files, the records in a file are arranged in key order. Thus the file is both serial and sequential. However, we think it is worthwhile to make the distinction between the two terms. In this and the following chapter we examine file operations that require only the serial or sequential properties. In later chapters we will look at techniques that require direct access to records.

3.1 Serial Files—Program Design Methodology

Because of the limited way in which a serial file can be accessed, its structure can be described simply. Jackson [33] devised a design methodology that is useful in problems involving serial files (but not limited to such problems). The methodology exploits the simple structure of serial files. We describe the design method here as an introduction to serial files and because it is a useful design tool.

The essence of Jackson's design method is that the control structure of a program is derived from the structure of all the files on which the program operates. Having derived the program control structure, the primitive operations required in processing the files are assigned to appropriate points in the structure. A skeleton program can be produced from this augmented control structure. The relationship between control and data structures may be familiar to you from consideration of simple data structures. For example, consider the relationship between iteration and an array. Note how nested iteration is an appropriate way of processing a multidimensional array. Similarly, recursion is a natural way of processing data structures such as linked lists and trees.

Notation

Jackson presents notation for describing a linear data stream in terms of structures that are related to the three structured programming constructs: sequence, selection, and iteration. In addition, composition may be used to build structures of unlimited size.

Sequence. Figure 3.1(a) shows how sequential data can be represented. The figure indicates that an X consists of an A followed by a B followed by a C. For example, a listing produced by a compiler

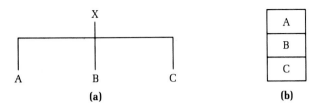

(a) (b)

FIGURE 3.1 Notation for sequence

might consist of a header followed by a list of the program lines followed by a summary report. Figure 3.1(b) shows the corresponding control flow: A is executed first, then B is executed, then C is executed.[1]

Selection. Figure 3.2(a) uses notation showing that an X consists of either an A or a B or a C. Compare this with Fig. 3.1(a) and note the presence of the ° symbols indicating that a choice has to be made. For example, a summary report from a compiler may consist of one of two options: either a "Compiled OK" message or information about errors found in the program. Figure 3.2(b) represents the corresponding control flow. Either A, B, or C is executed, depending on the value of X.

Iteration. Figure 3.3(a) shows notation used to represent the fact that an X consists of zero or more occurrences of an A. For example, a program listing consists of zero or more listings of individual program lines. Figure 3.3(b) shows a representation of a corresponding

FIGURE 3.2 Notation for choice

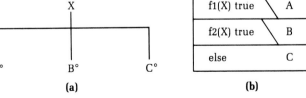

(a) (b)

1. Our notation for control flow is loosely based on Nassi-Shneiderman diagrams.

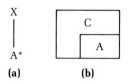

FIGURE 3.3 Notation for iteration

iterative control structure. It indicates that A is executed as long as C is true. That is, A is executed zero or more times.

In practice, a program listing consists of one or more lines rather than zero or more lines. This fact is taken into account in the structure diagram shown in Fig. 3.4. This diagram brings together all the components of the compiler output we have been using as examples.

Design Method Overview

Jackson's methodology involves devising structure diagrams for both program input and program output. After the data structure of the input and output has been described, a control flow structure for the program is derived. The program structure is such that there are correspondences between all data structure elements and elements

FIGURE 3.4 Example structure diagram

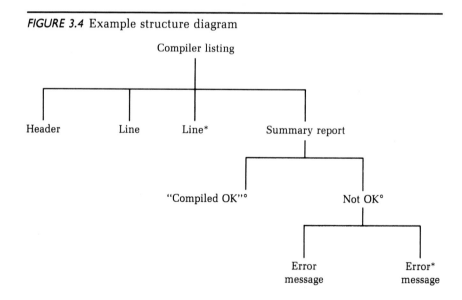

```
<count>
<name>
<info 1>
<info 2>
       .
       .
       .
<name>
<info 1>
       .
       .
       .
ZZZZ
```

FIGURE 3.5 Structure of student record file

of the control structure. Finally, the primitive operations required in processing the data are identified and assigned to appropriate points in the control structure. We now present a simple example of program development using Jackson's methodology. For more details of the design method and further examples, see Jackson's text [33]. Also, Molluzzo [34] develops programs for two problems using Jackson's methodology and compares them with traditional solutions.

Design Example

The problem we consider is one of processing a file of information about students. The file contains information about the performances of each of a number of students in various examinations and homework assignments. Figure 3.5 is a diagrammatic representation of the contents of the file.

The first item in the file is a count of the number of records that follow, including the sentinel record ZZZZ. This count is a file integrity check. In the file, a student's name is followed by zero or more records containing information about that student. We will assume that each such record contains either a homework or an examination score and that the two types of scores will be processed differently when computing an overall total. Figure 3.6 shows a structure diagram for the input file using Jackson's notation.

A program is required that will summarize information in the input file. The output file is to consist of one line for each student containing the student's name, the number of scores computed, and a weighted total. Figure 3.7 shows how the output file can be described using Jackson's notation.

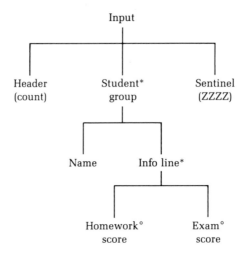

FIGURE 3.6 Structure diagram—student input file

We can now derive a control structure based on these input and output data structures. The aim is to arrive at a control structure such that all data structure elements have a correspondence with a control structure element. Jackson suggests beginning with the data structures and identifying correspondences. Our example has two data structures with the correspondences shown in Fig. 3.8. We process one input file to give one output file; within that, one student group yields

FIGURE 3.7 Structure diagram—report output file

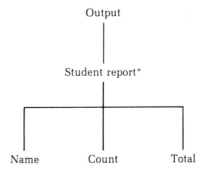

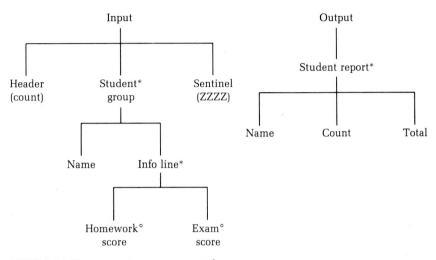

FIGURE 3.8 Data structure correspondences

one student record. The header and sentinel are consumed during processing but generate no part of the output structure. Thus we arrive at the top-level program structure shown in Fig. 3.9.

The next level down on the input structure contains an iteration (info line). However, there is no corresponding iteration on the output structure. Count and total are derived from a set of info lines. The next level in the program structure should therefore be a sequence in which input is processed and output produced. Figure 3.10 shows a possible complete program structure.

In Jackson's method, the next step after the design of the program control structure is the identification of primitive processing operations. These primitive operations are then attached to appropriate

FIGURE 3.9 Top two levels of program structure

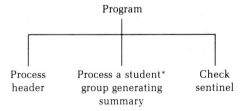

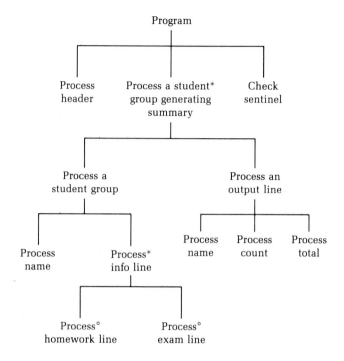

FIGURE 3.10 Control structure—report generation program

points in the program structure diagram. The primitive operations for our example are:

1. Open files
2. Close files
3. Initialize total-records-read
4. Read record from input and add 1 to total-records-read
5. Initialize count-for-student
6. Add 1 to count-for-student
7. Write count-for-student
8. Initialize total
9. Add exam score to total
10. Add homework score to total
11. Write total
12. Read total-records-expected

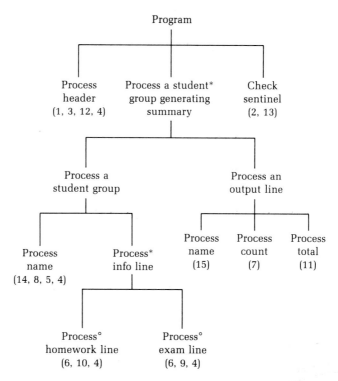

FIGURE 3.11 Structure of Fig. 3.10 with primitive operations assigned

13. Process total-records-expected and total-records-read

14. Save student name

15. Write student name

Figure 3.11 shows the program structure diagram of Fig. 3.10 with the primitive operations assigned. (The numbers in parentheses are from the list above.)

In allocating the primitive operations to tree leaves we have jumped ahead a little. Jackson recommends a read-ahead strategy when reading from the file. That is, a file that has been opened for reading should be read immediately. After the current record from the file has been completely processed, another record is read. In this way, on entry to a record processing routine there will always be a record available. This has been taken into account in Fig. 3.11 and is the reason why operation 4 appears at more than one point in the tree.

```
open files (*1*)
read total-records-expected (*12*)
initialize total-records-read (*3*)
read record and add 1 to total-records-read (*4*)

while not rec = ZZZZ
        save name (*14*)
        count-for-student ← 0 (*5*)
        read record and add 1 to total-records-read (*4*)
        initialize total (*8*)

        while exam or homework record
                add 1 to count-for-student (*6*)
                if exam
                    then add exam score to total (*9*)
                    else add homework score to total (*10*)
                read record and add 1 to total-records-read (*4*)

        write name (*15*)
        write count-for-student (*7*)
        write total (*11*)

    if total-records-read ≠ total-records-expected (*13*)
        then display error message

close files (*2*)
```

FIGURE 3.12 Pseudocode solution

The next step in the development of a final program might be a pseudocode version derived from the augmented program structure tree. In Fig. 3.12 we present pseudocode for the program we are developing. Identifying numbers of the primitive operations are added as commentary. After the pseudocode program has been written, it is usually quite easy to produce a program in a particular programming language.

Structure Clashes

Structure clashes arise when the input and output structures conflict. In such cases it is not possible to find a program structure that will match both. One example of a structure clash is found in data analysis in cases where the boundaries of the units being analyzed do not match the boundaries of the input units. Jackson considers telegram analysis. Suppose that telegrams (with appropriate delimiters) have been packed into 80-character records and that a program that produces a summary of each telegram is required. There is no

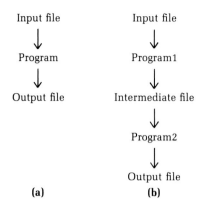

FIGURE 3.13 A resolution of structure clashes

correspondence between the iteration in the input (80-character records) and the iteration in the output (telegram summaries). There is no common unit of iteration for the control structure.

Conceptually, a solution to this problem is to use intermediate files. That is, if the solution depicted in Fig. 3.13(a) is not possible, then the one in Fig. 3.13(b) may be. In the case of the telegram problem, the intermediate file could be a file of one-byte records. In practice, the functions of the two programs of Fig. 3.13(b) can be combined through use of a technique called **program inversion.** In this technique a program that reads records from a file or writes records to a file is transformed into a subroutine that processes a single record. Thus, for example, Program1 could be inverted in this way and made into a subroutine of Program2, so that there is a single program again. For further details of structure clash resolution, see Jackson's text and Stubbs [35, 36].

Our look at Jackson's design method has necessarily been brief and somewhat superficial. In his text, Jackson works through 16 examples presenting subtleties of his method that we cannot include here. One problem for which Jackson develops a solution is that of collating two or more input files. We consider two examples of this type of problem in the next two sections. First, we consider how a sequential file of records might be updated. Second, we see how any number of sequential files might be merged.

3.2 Master File Update

A common data processing problem is to update a file of records (the **master file**) with a set of **transactions.** A transaction might be (1) an

Key	Name	Major	Address
21023	Jones, L.	Math	123 Short Street
24019	Webster, P.	CS	9092 Hillview, #21
24909	Able, C.	Phys	8291 Tampa
27301	Carter, F.	Math	12321 Mountain, #100
29976	Reed, A.	CS	457 Willow
35879	Freeman, J.	Biol	12003 Mountain, #47
36212	Dyson, R.	Phys	1893 Prairie, #22
37450	McNeil, K.	Psch	2098 Short Street
37900	Jones, A.	CS	1773 Willow

(a)

Delete 35879
Change major of 24019 to Math
Insert new record 37450   White, W.   Psch   17 Short Street
Change address of 29974 to 18938 Mountain
Insert new record 24750   Green, J.   Chem   12003 Mountain, #12

(b)

FIGURE 3.14 Master file and set of transactions

insertion of a new record, (2) a deletion of an existing record, or (3) a modification of an existing record. For example, a college might update its roster of students from time to time. Records corresponding to students no longer enrolled will be deleted, records for new students will be added, and changes of major, name, address, and so on, for continuing students will be recorded. Figure 3.14(a) shows an example master file and Fig. 3.14(b) a set of transactions. (Note that some of the transactions are erroneous—more on this later.)

In certain applications it is important for changes to a file to be made in real time, because programs that access the file may be running continuously. The most up-to-date values should be available to such programs. A ticket reservation system is an example of such an application. In other situations it may be acceptable to have a longer delay between the receipt of a new value and the changing of a record because the data file is accessed infrequently. The college student roster might be an example of such an application. Files must be kept on-line in real-time updating. In addition, the files must be organized so that an arbitrary record can be located quickly. (We will consider such organizations in Chapters 5 and 6.) Where a delay is acceptable, a possible strategy is to batch together a number of changes and periodically run an update program. It is this **batch updating** process that we consider here. In some applications the data may be brought on-line only for updating and occasional processing

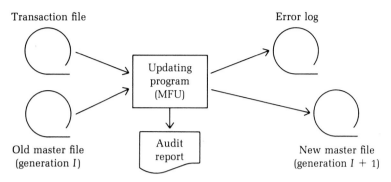

FIGURE 3.15 Master file update

Batch Update

We will update the example master file shown in Fig. 3.14 by means of a program that reads it and a file of transactions and produces a third file: an updated master file (see Fig. 3.15). An error log will contain reports of erroneous transactions, and an audit report will keep a record of the entire run of the program. The update program produces, in effect, a new **generation** of the master file without destroying the current one. If the new generation is corrupted, it can be reconstituted from an earlier generation and the appropriate transaction file(s) (see Fig. 3.16). The number of noncurrent master files (and corresponding transaction files) kept by an organization would be determined by the storage costs and the costs that would be incurred should the master file become irrevocably corrupted.

The master and transaction files must be ordered if the updating process is to be efficient. Therefore we use sequential files. The files

FIGURE 3.16 Generations of master file

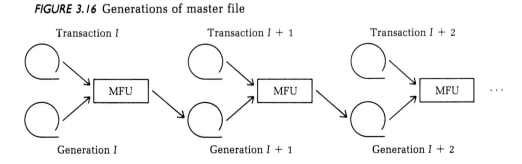

Key	Type	Parameters
24019	M	3 Math
24750	I	Green, J. Chem 12003 Mountain, #12
29974	M	4 18938 Mountain
35879	D	
37450	I	White, W. Psch 17 Short Street

FIGURE 3.17 Transactions file

must be sequenced in the same way so that the transactions appear in the same order as the records to which they apply. In what follows we will assume, without loss of generality, that records in a sequential file are in ascending order of some unique key. Figure 3.17 shows the transaction file for the transactions of Fig. 3.14(b).

The uniqueness property of the key in the master file ensures that a transaction will be unambiguous. In the transaction records the character following the key indicates which of the three transaction types it is—a modification (M), an insertion (I), or a deletion (D). In the case of a modification, the next value is the number of the field to be changed (counting the key as field 1). This is followed by the new value for the field.

Transactions are often generated in an order bearing no relation to the key values. For example, checks are unlikely to be presented at a bank in order of their account numbers. In such cases it is necessary to sort the transaction file. In Chapter 4 we will discuss techniques for sorting arbitrarily large files of records.

Since both the master file and the transaction file are sequenced by key, an update algorithm could consider each key value in turn and take appropriate action depending on whether there are transaction records and/or a master file record with the key. However, rather than iterate through all possible keys, for reasons of efficiency we just consider in turn each key value represented either in the transaction or the old master file. With one exception, which we consider on page 71, the set of transactions for one key value does not affect the set of transactions for any other key value.

The update algorithm should be robust. Errors should be reported if an attempt is made to delete or modify a record that does not exist. Attempts to modify the contents of nonexistent fields should also be detected. Because no two records in the master file can have the same key, insertions have to be checked to make sure that they do not result in key duplication. The error log that might be produced during the updating of the file of Fig. 3.14(a) with the transactions of Fig. 3.17 is as follows:

Key   Error message

29974: Modification error—nonexistent record
37450: Insert error—record already exists

Rather than clutter the updating program with a great deal of data validating, a more elegant solution is to develop a second program that performs checks on the transaction file prior to the update. Although this second program could not detect all the errors outlined above, it would catch enough to make it worthwhile, and the updating program would be simpler. For example, it would be easy to verify that the transaction file is correctly sequenced and that all transactions codes are valid. Exercise 2 at the end of the chapter concerns such a program.

The master file update algorithm in Fig. 3.18 is based on one presented by Dwyer [37].[2] The algorithm assumes that the records are in ascending key sequence and that each file is terminated by a sentinel record having a key higher than any valid key.

The algorithm considers, in ascending order, each key value represented either in the transaction file or in the old master file. In each iteration of the main loop, the variable *currentkey* takes the value of the next represented key. If there is a record in the old master file with that key, then the flag *allocated* is set true and the record is moved to the buffer *master*. Any transactions with the same key as the current key are then applied to the buffer in the following manner.

Insertion. The parameters of the insertion transaction are used to create a new record in the buffer. The *allocated* flag is set to true. If it was already true, an error should be reported because an attempt has been made to insert a record with the same key as an existing one.

Deletion. The *allocated* flag is set to false. If it was already false, an error should be reported because an attempt has been made to delete a nonexistent record. Setting *allocated* to false ensures that contents of the buffer are not written to the new master file.

Modification. If *allocated* is false, an error should be reported because a modification has been attempted on a nonexistent record. Otherwise, the appropriate changes are made to the contents of the buffer according to the parameters of the transaction. No change is made to *allocated*.

---

2. Dwyer gives a COBOL procedure division that we have translated freely into our pseudocode.

```
(* In the algorithm
     currentkey : the current key value being considered
     allocated    : a flag indicating the status of the current key
     trans-record: holds a transaction record
     old-record   : holds a record from the old master file
     master       : buffer for next record to be output to the new master file
*)

open transaction, old-master and new-master files

get trans-record from transaction file
get old-record from old-master file

currentkey ← smaller (key(old-record), key(trans-record))

while currentkey ≠ sentinel
    │   (* determine initial status of this key *)
    │   allocated ← (currentkey = key(old-record))
    │
    │   if allocated
    │      then master ← old-record
    │            get old-record from old-master
    │
    │   while key(trans-record) = currentkey
    │      │   (* process one transaction *)
    │      │   apply trans-record to master
    │      └── get trans-record from transaction file
    │
    │   (* check final status of key *)
    │   if allocated
    │      then write master to new-master file
    └── currentkey ← smaller (key(old-record), key(trans-record))

write sentinel to new-master file
close transaction, old-master and new-master files
```

FIGURE 3.18 Pseudocode master file update

After all transactions with the value of the current key have been processed, the value of *allocated* is checked. If it is true, the buffer contents are written out to the new master file. After all valid keys have been processed, a sentinel is written to terminate the new master file. Figure 3.19 shows the file of Fig. 3.14(a) after the valid transactions of Fig. 3.17 have been applied.

Problem Transactions

In practice, certain types of transactions cause problems and cannot reasonably be detected by a transaction verification program. While the fundamental algorithm of Fig. 3.18 is sound, difficulties arise in

Key	Name	Major	Address
21023	Jones, L.	Math	123 Short Street
24019	Webster, P.	Math	9092 Hillview, #21
24750	Green, J.	Chem	12003 Mountain, #12
24909	Able, C.	Phys	8291 Tampa
27301	Carter, F.	Math	12321 Mountain, #100
29976	Reed, A.	CS	457 Willow
36212	Dyson, R.	Phys	1893 Prairie, #22
37450	McNeil, K.	Psch	2098 Short Street
37900	Jones, A.	CS	1773 Willow

FIGURE 3.19 Updated master file

the application of transactions to the current master. Inglis [38] considers the problem of a sequence of records in the transaction file consisting of an insertion followed by some modifications for a particular key value. If the insertion is rejected because the key is already allocated, the status of the modification transactions is ambiguous. Are they to be considered changes to the old record or to the record that the user intended to insert? Inglis offers a solution involving the suspension of the master file record, and he presents a decision table that shows how this new category affects the procedure of applying a transaction to a master record. A solution suggested by Dwyer [39] simply requires the update program to report the ambiguity. The update is then rerun with a corrected transaction file.

Changes to key field. Earlier we assumed that one transaction group does not affect any other. An exception to this occurs when a transaction changes the value of the field on which the file is sequenced. Some update programs do not permit this type of change. However, for completeness, we present two ways in which changes to the sequencing field could be implemented.

Solution 1. One solution to this problem is to deal with changes to the key-sequence field before the main update program is run. Each modification record that changes the key field is turned into a pair of amendments: the first deletes the existing record and the second inserts a new one. The difficulty with this solution is that the nonkey fields of the record, which have to be part of the insertion transaction, may not be known without reference to the master file.

Solution 2. A second solution is to use two passes for the update rather than one. During the first pass the old record is deleted and an appropriate insertion transaction is generated and written to a

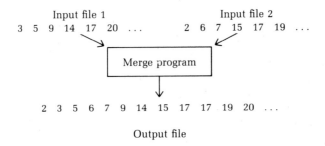

Input file 1   Input file 2

3   5   9   14   17   20   ...   2   6   7   15   17   19   ...

Merge program

2   3   5   6   7   9   14   15   17   17   19   20   ...

Output file

FIGURE 3.20 File merging

scratch file (a temporary working file). The information required to generate the insertion transaction is available in the old master file. The master file produced by the first pass could be considered generation I.5. Following the first pass, the scratch file is sorted. The second pass uses the sorted scratch file and generation I.5. It inserts the new records and produces generation $I + 1$. The two-pass process can be improved by observing that certain insertions can be dealt with during the first pass. If the new key is greater than the key of the last record output to generation I.5, then the new record can be put on one side and inserted into generation I.5 at the appropriate point. A scratch file may be necessary in which to hold such records until they are written.

3.3 Sequential File Merging

In this section we look at the problem of merging N sequential files. Figure 3.20 illustrates what we mean by merging. In this example we are merging two files of integers (i.e., performing a two-way merge) by producing an output file that contains, in order, all the integers in the input files. In a special sense the master file update program performs a two-way merge. It too is an algorithm that compares keys on records from each input file. The processes performed are different, however. N-way merging has a number of applications. For example, several transaction files might be merged into one prior to a master file update. In Chapter 4 we will see how N-way merging is used in file sorting algorithms.

We assume that records in a sequential file are available, via an accessing mechanism, in the order of some predetermined key. This ordering can be achieved by having the position of the next record in sequence determined implicitly or explicitly by the current record.

In an implicit system, records are physically adjacent in some address space. The position of the next record can thus be derived from the position of the current one. An explicit system stores the address of the next record in the current one. We assume in what follows that a get-next-record operation is generally available and that this operation causes the record with the next highest primary key to become available.

The algorithm for merging N sequential files into one is relatively straightforward; the only part needing particular care is processing the end-of-file conditions. You are probably familiar with the basic algorithm, having seen, in a data structures course, algorithms for merging two ordered lists to form a third list. The main point to note about the file version is that it is necessary to hold in main memory only one record from each of the files being merged. Thus files of unlimited length can be merged. The amount of main memory available limits only the **merge order,** that is, the number of files that can be merged simultaneously.

Basic Algorithm

In each iteration of the algorithm the main memory record with the lowest key is written to the output file and replaced by the next record from the appropriate input file. If there are no more records on a particular file, then the element of memory holding records from that file is set to $+\infty$, that is, a value larger than any legal key. This effectively causes the element to be ignored in comparisons. The algorithm terminates when the search for the smallest element returns $+\infty$. This indicates that all data has been read. A pseudocode algorithm for merging together N sequential files is shown in Fig. 3.21.

There may be applications in which there is no $+\infty$ key. Consider, for example, vehicle records in a state in which any combination of letters and digits is a valid license number. The primary key is license number, but there is no key that is not valid. This is not a problem, assuming that the end of the file is detectable. The solution is to keep a count of the number of input files that have been completely read and terminate the algorithm when this count reaches N. A set of flags could be used to indicate which main memory records should be ignored when scanning for the lowest key value.

Efficiency Considerations

If N is large, it may be useful to consider efficient ways of finding the record with the smallest key. A linear search of *Buffer* is not very efficient. At most one element of *Buffer* will be different from the previous iteration; thus much of the work done will have to be repeated. If we impose a binary tree on top of *Buffer*, so that the elements of *Buffer* are the leaves of the tree, the number of comparisons

```
(* In the algorithm
    N     : the number of input files
    Buffer: an array of records, 1 record for each input file
    s     : index to Buffer and input files
    stop  : a flag indicating if merging stops
*)

open N input files and 1 output file

(* initialize records *)

loop from i = 1 to N
    if file i is empty
        then Buffer[i] ← +∞
        else read first record from file i into Buffer[i]

(* merge *)

stop ← false
repeat
        find smallest element of Buffer (assume Buffer[s])
        if Buffer[s] = +∞
            then stop ← true
            else output Buffer[s]
                if end-of-file(file s)
                    then Buffer[s] ← +∞
                    else read next record from file s into Buffer[s]
      until stop

close files
```

FIGURE 3.21 Pseudocode N-way file merge

can be reduced. We can find the smallest element in approximately $\log_2 N$ comparisons rather than $N - 1$ comparisons.

At first it might appear that a candidate structure is a tournament tree such as that shown in Fig. 3.22. Here N is 11. Each internal node holds the "winner," that is, the smaller of its two descendants. The root node therefore holds the smallest key, which is the one we need.

After using the record with the smallest key, we need to replace it and update the tree so that the new smallest key emerges. The replacement for 4 in our example will have to be compared with 11, 9, 24, and 34. Unfortunately, these records are not situated very conveniently in the tree. One solution is to adopt the suggestion of Knuth [40, 5.4.1] and hold "losers" rather than winners in the internal nodes. This makes sense because 11, 9, 24, and 34 are the losers in contests with 4. Figure 3.23 shows the tree that would result if we had the same contents of *Buffer* as in Fig. 3.22 but stored losers rather than winners.

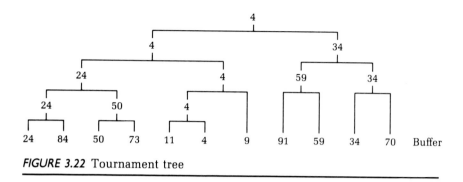

FIGURE 3.22 Tournament tree

In a knock-out tournament every person apart from the overall winner loses exactly once. The tree of Fig. 3.23 shows the point at which each key loses. There are $N - 1$ internal nodes, and the value in each leaf, apart from the smallest (the winner), appears once in an internal node. Note that the records with which we compare the successor of 4 now lie on the path from 4 to the root and that this is true for every leaf node.

After an element of *Buffer* has been replaced, we need to update the tree and find the index of the new smallest element of *Buffer*. This process is relatively straightforward. Assume that each internal tree node has two components:

loser : index of appropriate element in *Buffer*
parent : pointer to parent node (null in the case of the root)

Figure 3.24 is a pseudocode algorithm indicating how the tree is updated assuming that we have just replaced *Buffer*[s]. It should be clear that this fragment can be incorporated into the algorithm of Fig.

FIGURE 3.23 Tree of losers

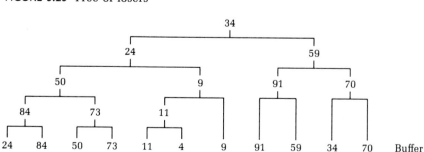

```
(* In the algorithm
    T        : a pointer to an internal node in the tree of losers
    topoftree : a flag indicating if updating has reached the root
*)

T ← parent of Buffer[s]
topoftree ← false

repeat if key(Buffer(loser(T))) < key(Buffer[s])
          then interchange loser(T) and s
       if T = root
          then topoftree ← true
          else T ← parent of node pointed to by T
       until topoftree
```

FIGURE 3.24 Pseudocode tree update

3.21 just after *Buffer*[s] is replaced. The value of the variable s produced by the algorithm of Fig. 3.24 is the index of the new smallest element in *Buffer*. Thus s is correct for the next iteration of the algorithm of Fig. 3.21. The initialization section of Fig. 3.21 has to be augmented. That is, after the contents of *Buffer* are read from the files to be merged, the loser tree must be constructed. The details of this part of the algorithm are left as an exercise for the reader (see Exercise 6). Figure 3.25 shows the revised *N*-way merging algorithm.

The binary tree occupies main memory space and thus reduces the amount available for *Buffer*. However, in practice, rather than buffer space, the limiting factor on the order of the merge is usually an operating system limit on the number of files that can be open simultaneously.

Summary

In this chapter we have looked at serial and sequential files. We classified as serial any file that can be accessed only in a linear manner. This can be contrasted with direct files, which we will discuss in Chapter 5. Files of text, for example, those containing the chapters of this book, are typical serial files. We classified as sequential a file on which some accessing method operates that can return records in some predetermined sequence. Typically this will be primary key order. The sequential property makes many operations easier to perform. We presented Jackson's design methodology, and looked at batch master file update and *N*-way merging.

```
(* In the algorithm
    N          : the number of input files
    Buffer     : an array of records, 1 record for each input file
    s          : index to Buffer and input files
    stop       : a flag indicating if merging is complete
    T          : a pointer to an internal node in the tree of losers
    topoftree : a flag indicating if updating has reached the root
*)

open N input files and 1 output file

(* initialize records *)

loop from i = 1 to N
    if file i is empty
        then Buffer[i] ← +∞
        else read first record from file i into Buffer[i]

s ← index of smallest element of Buffer
build initial tree of losers

(* merge *)

stop ← false
repeat
        if Buffer[s] = +∞
            then stop ← true
            else output Buffer[s]
                if end-of-file(file s)
                    then Buffer[s] ← +∞
                    else read next record from file s into Buffer[s]
                (* update tree *)
                T ← parent of Buffer[s]
                topoftree ← false
                repeat if key(Buffer(loser(T))) < key(Buffer[s])
                            then interchange loser(T) and s
                        if T = root
                            then topoftree ← true
                            else T ← parent of node pointed to by T
                        until topoftree
        until stop

close files
```

FIGURE 3.25 Pseudocode N-way file merge (revised)

You are probably familiar with the relationship between the structure of data and the structure of programs operating on that data. In this chapter we examined a technique suitable for designing programs that operate on serial files. The input and output files are represented by tree structures, and a corresponding program structure is derived. The primitive processing operations required are associated with leaves of the tree. A skeleton program can be generated from this structure. Special action is needed, however, if the input and output files have conflicting structures.

The updating of a master file of records in a batch rather than in an on-line environment can be considered a merging operation. Typically a file of transactions is used. The two files are sequenced in the same way. The update operation produces a new generation of the master file without destroying the old one. We presented an algorithm based on the notion of considering key values in turn.

An advantage of sequential files is that the contents of two or more of them can then be merged in a simple way. We presented an algorithm for merging N files sequenced in the same way. In addition, we considered a technique for making selection of the next output record more efficient. Efficiency of this subalgorithm is important when many files are being merged simultaneously.

Exercises

1. A line printer file at a certain computer installation consists of a header page followed by a listing of the file contents. The format of the header page depends on whether the file is generated by the ABC or by the XYZ operating system. In the case of an ABC file the header is a simple banner. In the case of the XYZ system the header consists of a user name followed by zero or more lines of routing information. The file contents appear on one or more pages after the header page. (Empty files are detected and discarded at an earlier stage of processing.) Both the ABC and XYZ systems start each content page with the name of the file and the current date. The ABC system, in addition, puts the page number at the foot of each content page. Draw a Jackson diagram that represents the structure of line printer files at this installation.

2. Devise a record format for a transaction record and then write and test a program that checks a transaction file. Your program could generate both error messages and warnings. For example, an error message would be output if records are found out of sequence. A warning would be generated if there is both a modification and a deletion transaction for a particular key.

3. Write a program that can generate an arbitrarily large sequential file. One way of doing this is to use a random number generator and tables of possible field values (see [41]). Extend your program so that it can also generate transaction files.

4. Implement and test a master file update program that warns of ambiguous transactions. Your program need not deal with transactions that change the key on which records are sequenced (they could be flagged as errors).

5. Extend your answer to Exercise 4 so that changes to a key can be performed.

6. Implement the algorithm of Fig. 3.25. Test it by performing two-way, three-way, and four-way merging. Ensure that your program works correctly when some (or all) of the input files are empty.

7. Write a program that detects differences between two serial files. Output should be a set of transformations, in some suitable form, that will change one file to the other. How will your solution depend on the amount of main memory available? Try to find the smallest sufficient set of changes.

8. Various reports that could be useful to authors can be generated on a piece of text, for example, average sentence length, readability indexes, and detection of wordy phrases. An example system is the Writer's Workbench [42, 43]. Devise and implement a small system of your own.

9. Write a program that updates a file of bank account records. The master file, sequenced by account number, contains the account number and present balance. A transaction record contains an account number and amount (which may be negative) to be added to the current balance. In addition to the normal error reporting, your program should reject transactions that overdraw an account.

10. A certain computer system keeps a file of the times at which people log on and log off. In the case of a log-on, the user, terminal, and time are recorded. In the case of a log-off, only the terminal and time are recorded. A record is written to a serial file in each case. The beginning of a typical log file is as follows:

cc-jpj	tty09	May 14 09:21
pds	tty12	May 14 09:30
	tty09	May 14 09:35
322-mxm	tty04	May 14 09:40

```
322-jrt        tty00    May 14 09:42
               tty04    May 14 09:50
                 .
                 .
                 .
```

The management requires a program that will read the serial file and output a summary of system usage. The program should show the user, the terminal, log-on and log-off times, and connect time for each connection to the system. In the event that the user is still logged on, this should be indicated. Output from the program when given the file above might be as follows:

```
cc-jpj         tty09    May 14 09:21 – 09:35   (00:14)
pds            tty12    May 14 09:30 – still logged on
322-mxm        tty04    May 14 09:40 – 09:50   (00:10)
322-jrt        tty00    May 14 09:42 – still logged on
```

Draw Jackson diagrams for the input file and output file. Is there a clash between the two structures? If not, devise a program structure. If there is a clash, devise a solution to the problem.

11. Write and test a program based on your answer to Exercise 10.

12. Design and implement a simple mailing list program. A user of your program should be able to add to, delete from, and modify entries in a file of names, addresses, and other information (such as hobbies, birthday, and sex). A user should be able to print out subsets of entries specified in a variety of ways. Examples of subsets are females born in July, and Californians interested in bird watching.

4

External Sorting

4.1 Presents an overview of the most common external sorting strategy, in which sorted sequences of records are produced and then merged.

4.2 Examines techniques for producing the initial sorted sequences.

4.3 Considers some ways in which the sequences can be distributed and merged into a sorted file.

In Chapter 3 we discussed sequential files and looked at a batch master file update. A sequential file may have to be produced from an unsequenced collection of records, and a set of amendments usually must be sorted before a batch update. While batch updating is likely to become less important with the growth of on-line record processing systems (where amendments are processed immediately rather than being batched), database bulk loading or reorganizing often requires presorting of records. This is done so that the program runs at a reasonable speed and produces a well-organized database. In this chapter we consider the problem of sorting a large file of records.

The factor that makes file sorting a different problem from sorting an array is that typically there will be more records to be sorted than can be held simultaneously in the main memory space of a program. We will therefore consider **external sorting** algorithms, where the majority of data is, at any time, outside main memory. In contrast, internal sorting algorithms keep all the data in main memory throughout the sorting process. Hardware sorting devices have been proposed,[1] but we will limit our discussion to algorithms for conventional machines.

---

1. See, for example, Miranker, Tang, and Wong [44].

4.1 Overview of External Sorting

In this section we consider the problem of sorting a file of records. There are many orderings of a file of records corresponding to the different ways of comparing two records. For example, comparison may be based on a hierarchy of fields: records may be sorted by field 1 within field 2 within field 3 and so on. Without loss of generality we will assume in what follows that records are to be sorted into ascending order by some unique key.

Criteria for evaluating external sorting algorithms are different from those for internal sorts. The efficiency of an algorithm for sorting an array in main memory is often expressed in terms of the number of times a comparison has to be made between a pair of array elements. However, the time required to execute an external sort is normally dominated by input/output time. It follows that we should aim to minimize transfers to and from main memory rather than comparisons between the keys of records.

We have a choice between sorting a file *in situ* (in its original position) and using a method that requires additional storage space. One advantage of *in situ* sorting is that it allows us to sort larger files with a given total storage capacity. A disadvantage is that system crashes during a sort may leave the file in a strange state. (This can be circumvented by making an off-line copy before sorting.)

If we choose to sort a file *in situ*, then we may naturally turn to internal sorting algorithms and treat our file as an array of blocks. Clearly this requires a direct-access file. Quicksort [45] is one of the better internal sorting algorithms. Six and Wegner [46] describe EX-QUISIT, an algorithm based on Quicksort, which sorts a direct access file *in situ*. It requires that there be room in main memory for two file blocks. However, for good performance, the choice of pivot element is critical. EXQUISIT (and Quicksort) can perform very poorly if the initial ordering of records to be sorted is unfavorable.

In this chapter we present algorithms that, while unspectacular, are safe. Their performance is guaranteed, independent of the ordering of the initial file. The algorithms we consider are classified as **sort-merge.** They sort a file by the divide-and-conquer technique in that small sections of the file are sorted and then the sorted sections are merged together. Thus we have a two-stage process:

1. *Sort stage.* Records are read from the input (unsorted) file and sorted **partitions** (sometimes termed **runs** or **strings**) of records are written to output files. Records within a partition are in the correct order relative to each other.

2. *Merge stage.* Partitions generated in the sort stage are merged,

109	49	34	68	45	2	60	38	28	47	16	19	34	55
98	78	76	40	35	86	10	27	61	92	99	72	11	2
29	16	80	73	18	12	89	50	46	36	67	93	22	14
83	44	52	59	10	38	76	16	24	85				

FIGURE 4.1 Example input file

producing longer and longer partitions. Merging stops when there is only one partition: the required sorted file.

The sort-merge approach works because the sort stage can be adapted to available main memory. Furthermore, the merge stage needs only space in memory for one record from each of the partitions being merged. Each of the two stages benefits from an increase in available main memory. The more memory there is, the longer the initial partitions are likely to be. There are therefore likely to be fewer partitions generated from a given input file, and thus the merging stage requires fewer iterations. In addition, an increase in the number of partitions that can be merged at one time increases the merge order and also leads to a shorter merge phase. Note that with the sort-merge method a file can be sorted even if main memory can hold only two records. This is the extreme case. The capacity is large enough to produce partitions two records in length and to perform a two-way merge. Of course, in this case sorting would take a long time!

It is worth observing that the sort-merge algorithms require only serial files. External sorting can therefore be implemented using programming languages that support only serial files. (On early computers, which had tape drives but no discs, much use was made of algorithms of this type.)

4.2 Generating Sorted Partitions

Although there are many ways of producing partitions from an unsorted file, we consider only the following three methods in this section:

1. internal sorting
2. replacement selection
3. natural selection

To compare the three algorithms, we show how each would process the input file shown in Fig. 4.1. Only the keys of the records are shown; the first record has key 109, the second 49, and so on. We will

34	45	49	68	109
2	28	38	47	60
16	19	34	55	98
35	40	76	78	86
10	27	61	92	99
2	11	16	29	72
12	18	73	80	89
36	46	50	67	93
14	22	44	52	83
10	16	38	59	76
24	85			

FIGURE 4.2 Partitions from internal sorting

assume in our discussion of the algorithms that main memory can hold M records. Keep in mind that our objective is to produce sorted partitions that are as long as possible.

Internal Sorting

The simplest strategy of all is to read M records at a time from the unsorted file, to sort them using an internal sorting method, and then to output them. Note that all partitions produced in this way, except perhaps for the last, will contain exactly M records. Figure 4.2 shows the partitions produced from the input file of Fig. 4.1 using a memory size (M) of five.

Replacement Selection

Internal sorting does not take advantage of any partial ordering that may exist in the input file. The replacement selection algorithm, on the other hand, does exploit such ordering. Consider the following strategy for producing sorted partitions.

1. Read in M records from the unsorted file.

2. Output the record with the smallest key.

3. Replace it by the next record on the input file. If the new record cannot be part of the current partition (that is, if its key is smaller than that of the last record output), mark it "frozen." (Frozen records are ignored when searching for the record with the smallest key.) If there are any unfrozen records, return to step 2.

4. Start a new partition. That is, unfreeze the frozen records and go to step 2.

A pseudocode algorithm for replacement selection is given in Fig. 4.3. Two flags are associated with each record. One indicates whether or not the record has been written to the output. The other indicates whether or not the record is frozen, that is, whether or not it is usable in the production of the current partition. Although it is possible to combine these two flags into a single indicator, we leave them separated for clarity. The inner loop in the pseudocode outputs records to the current partition. Each cycle of the outer loop produces one partition.

It should become clear that the replacement selection algorithm can take advantage of partial ordering of the records in the input file. The closer the input file is to the desired final order, the more often the replacement record can be used in the current partition. Hence partitions will tend to be longer than those generated using internal sorting. It can be shown that the expected partition length when using replacement selection is $2 \times M$ records.[2]

Figure 4.4 shows the partitions output from the replacement selection algorithm when the input is the file listed in Fig. 4.1. Again it is assumed that main memory can hold five records and, in this case, the necessary flags.

Natural Selection

One of the disadvantages of the replacement selection algorithm is that toward the end of producing a partition most of the main memory space is occupied by frozen records. These records cannot contribute to the current partition. The natural selection method devised by Frazer and Wong [48] avoids this by having a "reservoir" on secondary storage into which frozen records are placed. The production of a partition now terminates when this reservoir overflows or the input file is exhausted. Figure 4.5 gives a pseudocode algorithm for the production of partitions using natural selection. Recall that we are assuming that main memory can hold M records; we assume that the reservoir can hold M' records. Frazer and Wong observed that when the reservoir and main memory have the same capacity and both can hold more than about 30 records, the expected partition length is about $M \times e$ (i.e., $M \times 2.718 \ldots$) (hence the choice of name for the algorithm). Figure 4.6 shows the partitions generated by the natural selection algorithm given the input file of Fig. 4.1. For this example it is assumed that both main memory and the external reservoir can hold five records.

---

2. See, for example, Knuth [40, 5.4.1] and Bradley [47, 5.3.1].

```
(* In the algorithm
    M       : the number of records in the buffer
    Buffer  : the buffer—an array of records
    written : an array of flags indicating if corresponding buffer records have been written
    frozen  : an array of flags indicating if corresponding buffer records are frozen
    last-key: holds the value of the key of the last record output
*)

(* set flags and read initial buffer *)
loop from i = 1 to M
    written[i] ← true

i ← 0
repeat i ← i + 1
    │   read Buffer[i] from input
    │   written[i] ← false
    └── until end-of-file(input) or i = M

(* generate sorted partitions *)
while not end-of-file (input)

    │   │   (* generate one sorted partition *)
    │   │   (* initialize frozen flags *)
    │   │   loop from i = 1 to M
    │   │       if not written[i]
    │   │           then frozen[i] ← false
    │   │
    │   │   while any unfrozen records remain
    │   │       │   (* write one record to sorted partition *)
    │   │       │   find smallest unfrozen record (assume Buffer[s])
    │   │       │   append Buffer[s] to sorted partition
    │   │       │   last-key ← key(Buffer[s])
    │   │       │   written[s] ← true. frozen[s] ← true
    │   │       │   if not end-of-file (input)
    │   │       │       then read new Buffer[s] from input
    │   │       │           written[s] ← false
    │   │       │           if key(Buffer[s]) ≥ last-key
    │   └── └──             then frozen[s] ← false

(* write out remaining records in buffer *)
output unwritten records in ascending key order
```

FIGURE 4.3 Replacement selection algorithm

Comparison of Partition-Forming Algorithms

In general we want partition-forming algorithms to generate long partitions so that the amount of merging required will be small. However, there may be other factors to consider when choosing an algorithm.

An advantage of using internal sorting to produce the initial par-

```
34  45  49  60  68  109
 2  16  19  28  34   38  47  55  76  78  86  98
10  27  35  40  61   72  92  99
 2  11  16  18  29   50  73  80  89  93
12  14  22  36  44   46  52  59  67  76  83  85
10  16  24  38
```

FIGURE 4.4 Partitions from replacement selection

titions is that the partitions produced are all the same length, except possibly for the last. This can simplify merging; the merging algorithm may be easier to develop if the size of each partition is predictable.

Replacement selection, on average, produces longer partitions than internal sorting. Although variability of partition length may complicate merging, it is simple to detect boundaries between partitions written to the same file.

Natural selection tends to produce longer partitions than either internal sorting or replacement selection. However, there are input/output transfers to and from the reservoir during initial partition formation. Neither of the other two methods incurs this cost. Our aim is to minimize total sorting time, which in practice means minimizing the total number of input/output transfers. However, the reduction in merging brought about by having longer initial partitions may more than offset the number of reservoir transfers.

To summarize, the closer the initial file is to the desired final order, the larger the differences in partition lengths are likely to be among the three algorithms (see Exercises 3 and 4). The longer partitions may, however, require a more complex merge stage.

4.3 Distribution and Merging

Suppose that the sort stage produces R partitions. The optimal way of merging them is to have each partition in a separate file and then to perform a single R-way merge. However, in practice there will be operational restrictions. The most likely of these is on the number of files that a program can have open at any time. Therefore merging typically requires a series of **phases.** During each phase records are read from one set of files and merged partitions are written to a second set of files. There are many merging strategies, each having requirements regarding the distribution of the initial partitions. In the following we will assume that at any time we can have at most F files

```
(* In the algorithm
      M, M'            : the number of records in the buffer, external reservoir
      Buffer           : the buffer—an array of records
      written          : array of flags—have buffer records been written?
      frozen           : a similar array indicating if records are frozen
      reservoir-count : count of records currently in the reservoir
      no-space         : flag set when reservoir overflows
      done             : flag set when replacement of a record is complete
      last-key         : holds the value of the key of the last record output
*)

(* set flags and read initial buffer *)
loop from i = 1 to M
        written[i] ← true
i ← 0
repeat i ← i + 1
    │   read Buffer[i] from input
    │   written[i] ← false
    └── until end-of-file(input) or i = M

(* read from file and output partitions *)
repeat (* output one partition *)
    │       reservoir-count ← 0
    │       no-space ← false
    │       repeat (* output one record *)
    │       │       output smallest unwritten record (assume Buffer[s])
    │       │       last-key ← key(Buffer[s])
    │       │       written[s] ← true
    │       │       if not end-of-file (input)
    │       │           then done ← false
    │       │               repeat if key(next record in input file) ≥ last-key
    │       │               │       then read next input record into Buffer[s]
    │       │               │           written[s] ← false
    │       │               │           done ← true
    │       │               │       else if reservoir-count < M'
    │       │               │               then read next input record into reservoir
    │       │               │                   add 1 to reservoir-count
    │       │               │               else no-space ← true
    │       │               └── until done or no-space
    │       └── until end-of-file(input) or no-space
    │       output unwritten buffer records in ascending key order, set
    │           corresponding elements of written to true
    │
    │       (* set up buffer for next partition *)
    │       if reservoir-count > 0
    │           then move min(reservoir-count,M) records from reservoir
    │               to buffer, set corresponding elements of written
    │               to false, and decrease reservoir-count
    │       if buffer not full and not end-of-file(input)
    │           then fill buffer as much as possible from input
    │               setting corresponding elements of written to false
    └── until no unwritten records in buffer
```

FIGURE 4.5 Natural selection algorithm

```
34   45   47   49   60   68   109
 2   16   19   28   34   38   40   55   61   76   78   86   92   98   99
10   11   16   27   29   35   50   67   72   73   80   89   93
 2   12   14   18   22   36   44   46   52   59   76   83   85
10   16   24   38
```

FIGURE 4.6 Partitions from natural selection

open for reading or writing. The larger the value of F, the faster merging is likely to proceed. A limit on the value of F is most likely to arise from an operating system restriction. For example, the system under which this book was prepared prohibits users from having more than 16 files open at a time.

We will consider three distribution and merging strategies:

1. balanced N-way merging
2. optimal merging
3. polyphase merging

A measure of the efficiency of the merging stage of an external sorting algorithm is the number of **passes** over the data required to merge the partitions together. The number of passes is defined as follows:

$$\text{Passes} = \frac{\text{total number of record reads}}{\text{total number of records in the sorted file}}$$

That is, the number of passes is the average number of times a record is read during the merging. For every read there is a corresponding write, so the number of passes is a measure of the total input/output required.

Balanced N-way Merge

In the balanced N-way merge the available files are divided as equally as possible into two sets. The initial partitions are distributed as evenly as possible on the files in one set. During each phase of the merge, records on the input files are read and merged partitions are distributed cyclically onto the output files. At the end of a phase what was the input set becomes the output set and vice versa. The method is balanced in the sense that each of the files in the input set contains approximately the same number of records. Figure 4.7 contains a pseudocode algorithm for the balanced N-way merge. The variable input-set-first is used to remember which of the two sets of files (the files numbered 1 through N or those numbered N + 1 through F) is

```
(* In the algorithm
    N                : size of one set of files (F − N is the size of the other)
    input-set-first : used to differentiate between the input
                       and output sets during the current phase
    outsetsize      : size of the output set
    base            : the number, in the range 1 through F, of the first output file
    outfilenum      : the number of the current output file
    partitioncount: count of partitions written during this phase
*)

N ← F div 2      (* N is roughly half F *)
input-set-first ← false

repeat (* set up files *)

        change value of input-set-first
        if input-set-first
          then open files 1 through N for reading
               open files N + 1 through F for writing
               outsetsize ← F − N
               base ← N + 1
          else open files 1 through N for writing
               open files N + 1 through F for reading
               outsetsize ← N
               base ← 1

        (* perform a phase *)

        outfilenum ← 0
        partitioncount ← 0

        repeat merge partition from each input file onto file numbered (base + outfilenum)
               increment partitioncount by 1
               outfilenum ← (outfilenum + 1) mod outsetsize
             └─ until end-of-file on all input files

        rewind input files and output files

      └─ until partitioncount = 1

if input-set-first
  then sorted file is N + 1
  else sorted file is 1
```

FIGURE 4.7 Balanced N-way merge algorithm

currently the input. The value of *input-set-first* is established at the
start of each phase. During a phase, records are read from the input
files and merged partitions are written to the output files. Partitions
are written cyclically to the output files in order to distribute them
as evenly as possible. If exactly one partition is written out during a
particular phase, then merging is over. The value of *input-set-first*
implicitly identifies the file containing the final sorted records.

TABLE 4.1 Balanced N-way merging

	File 1	File 2	File 3	File 4
Initially	10×1	10×1		
After phase 1			5×2	5×2
After phase 2	3×4	2×4		
After phase 3			1×8,1×4	1×8
After phase 4	1×16	1×4		
After phase 5			1×20	

Consider 20 initial partitions and 4 files. We will use $i \times j$ to represent i partitions each containing j records. Table 4.1 shows how merging proceeds when using the balanced N-way algorithm with F equal to 4.

Recall from our earlier discussion that, in practice, initial partitions will be long and will vary in length. However, so that we can compare the three merge algorithms in a simple way, we assume that each initial partition contains exactly one record. Initially the 20 partitions are distributed evenly on files 1 and 2; thus each of these two files is shown as 10×1.

In the first phase, files 1 and 2 are the input files and files 3 and 4 are the output files. In phase 1, partitions of length 1 are read and, since we are performing two-way merging, partitions containing two records are produced. There are ten partitions produced, which are distributed over files 3 and 4. In phase 2, files 3 and 4 become the input files and files 1 and 2 become the output files. Partitions containing four records are produced, which are the result of merging partitions containing two records. Five partitions are produced in phase 2 and distributed over the two output files. The algorithm proceeds in this way until one phase, in this example phase 5, produces exactly one partition.

Note that the balanced N-way merge algorithm, although simple, is far from the best. We are performing only $(F/2)$-way merging instead of $(F-1)$-way merging, which is the best we could do (there must always be at least one output file). In addition, depending on the number of initial partitions and the value of F, during certain phases partitions are liable to be copied from one file to another without being merged with anything. In our example, a partition of length 4 is copied from file 1 to file 3 during phase 3. During phase 4 the same partition is copied from file 3 to file 2.

TABLE 4.2 Optimal merging

Phase	Input 1	Input 2	Input 3	Out	Reads
1	1:1	2:1	3:1	21:3	3
2	4:1	5:1	6:1	22:3	3
3	7:1	8:1	9:1	23:3	3
4	10:1	11:1	12:1	24:3	3
5	13:1	14:1	15:1	25:3	3
6	16:1	17:1	18:1	26:3	3
7	19:1	20:1	21:3	27:5	5
8	22:3	23:3	24:3	28:9	9
9	25:3	26:3	27:5	29:11	11
10	28:9	29:11		30:20	20
				Total	63

The number of passes that the balanced N-way merge algorithm requires is always the same as the number of phases. This is because all the records are read in each phase. For our 20-partition example, therefore, there are five passes. We will see that this simple relationship between phases and passes does not hold for the other two algorithms.

Optimal Merge

The optimal merge algorithm was described by Lewis and Smith [49]. Initial partitions are written to separate files, and a record is kept of the length of each partition. Thus we have a set of files, each containing one partition. As with the other algorithms we examine, merging proceeds in a number of phases. During each phase the $F-1$ shortest partitions are read and merged, and the merged partition is written to an output file. The input files are then removed from the set of files, and the output file is added to the set. The process of merging is repeated until the set contains only one file. Table 4.2 shows how this algorithm operates on the 20 partitions of the earlier example; again we assume that each initial partition contains exactly one record and that $F = 4$. We use x:y to represent file number x containing a partition of y records. For example, file 21, containing 3 records, is created in phase 1. In phase 7 file 21 is merged with files 19 and 20 to create file 27, containing 5 records. The number of passes required is 63/20, or 3.15.

The algorithm is not truly optimal because the input files in a phase may be very different in length. The effective merge order is reduced when input from some of the files has been exhausted.

TABLE 4.3 Polyphase merging

	File 1	File 2	File 3	File 4	Reads
Initially	13×1	11×1	7×1		
After phase 1	6×1	4×1		7×3	21
After phase 2	2×1		4×5	3×3	20
After phase 3		2×9	2×5	1×3	18
After phase 4	1×17	1×9	1×5		17
After phase 5				1×31	31
				Total	107

Polyphase Merge

The polyphase merge algorithm has neither of the disadvantages of the balanced N-way merge and does not require the record keeping of the optimal merge. However, it does require a more complex initial distribution of partitions. We will consider two algorithms—one for a special case and one for a general polyphase merge.

Table 4.3 shows how the merging of 31 partitions with $F = 4$ would proceed. (The number of partitions and their initial distribution are carefully chosen.) We assume again that each initial partition contains exactly one record. We use the notation introduced earlier for the balanced N-way example, that is, $i \times j$ represents i partitions each containing j records.

In phase 1 we are producing partitions containing three records because we are merging partitions of length 1 from each of three files. We can produce only seven partitions before we reach the end of file 3. This leaves six partitions unread on file 1 and four partitions unread on file 2. In phase 2 we produce partitions of length 5 because we are merging partitions of lengths 1, 1, and 3. We can produce only four such partitions before we reach the end of file 2. Merging proceeds in this way until phase 5 produces the sorted file. The number of passes required is 107/31, or about 3.45.

The general algorithm will be able to merge an arbitrary number of partitions. However, it will be convenient to consider first an algorithm that requires that the total number of partitions be one of a special set of numbers.

Special case. The problem with the polyphase merge is knowing how the initial partitions are to be distributed so that the algorithm can merge them optimally. To determine the initial distribution we work back from the final one. Consider the case where $F = 4$; that is, in any phase there are three input files. We are concerned with

TABLE 4.4 Derivation of initial distributions

Produced by Phase				Total Partitions
Last	1	0	0	1
Last − 1	1	1	1	3
Last − 2	2	2	1	5
Last − 3	4	3	2	9
Last − 4	7	6	4	17
	13	11	7	31

the number of partitions on each of these input files. The final distribution is one partition on one file. Before the final phase we must therefore have one partition on each of the input files. We denote this as

$$1 \quad 1 \quad 1$$

Three-way merging will then produce the final partition. Before the next to the last phase we must have

$$2 \quad 2 \quad 1$$

so that when we merge we produce one partition (before reaching the end of the shortest file). This, together with the two files with one partition remaining on them, gives us the 1 1 1 distribution. In general, if at any phase we want to produce

$$a \quad b \quad c \quad \text{partitions,}$$

then the phase before must leave us with

$$a + b \quad a + c \quad a \quad \text{partitions}$$

so that when we merge we produce

$$a = \text{minimum } (a, a + b, a + c) \text{ partitions,}$$

leaving b partitions on one file and c partitions on another. Table 4.4 shows how this works when $F = 4$. Working back from the desired final configuration, we arrive at the distribution of

$$13 \quad 11 \quad 7$$

used in the example of Table 4.3.

You may observe that this merging method, when $F = 4$, will work optimally if the total number of initial partitions is in the series

   1   3   5   9   17   31   ...

These numbers are in fact part of a generalized Fibonacci series. The appropriate series when $F = 4$ is the series of order 3, which is

   1   1   1   3   5   9   17   31   57   ...

Each of the first three terms is 1. Each succeeding term is the sum of the three that precede it. In general, the series $T_1, T_2, T_3, \ldots$ is defined

$$T_i = 1 \qquad\qquad i < F$$

$$T_i = \sum_{k=i-F+1}^{i-1} T_k \qquad i \geq F$$

Special case algorithm. We know in this special case that the total number of initial partitions is a member of the appropriate Fibonacci series. We have seen how each term in the series is associated with a particular distribution of partitions. We have also seen how a distribution is derived from the distribution for the preceding term in the series. This suggests the following algorithm for distributing a number of partitions onto files. Again we illustrate using $F = 4$.

   We regard

   1   0   0

as our first target distribution and write the first partition onto one of the three files. If a second partition is generated, then we know this target is no good and switch to the next target (see Table 4.4), that is

   1   1   1

The second and third partitions are written to the two remaining input files. If a fourth partition is generated, then this target is also no good and we replace it by

   2   2   1

The fourth and fifth partitions are written to files that are short of their target number of partitions. We know in this special case algorithm that when the partitions are all distributed some target distribution will have been matched exactly. Therefore it does not matter to which of those files short of its quota we write a partition. Distribution of partitions proceeds in this way until there are no more.

   Next, we consider a more general algorithm where it is no longer critical that the total number of partitions to be merged be a member of the appropriate Fibonacci series.

General algorithm. We have seen how distribution and merging works optimally if the number of partitions is a member of an appropriate Fibonacci series. If the total is not guaranteed to be a member of the series, a solution is to introduce **dummy partitions.** Dummy partitions do not occupy file space; in fact, they exist only as numbers in a table. We introduce sufficient dummy partitions to make the total number of partitions a term in the series.

The use of dummy partitions has consequences for the section of the sorting algorithm that merges partitions. It must be able to distinguish between dummy partitions and real ones. How are dummy partitions regarded in relation to the files containing real partitions? Note that during merging, the partitions toward the beginning of a file are read more often than those toward the end (consider the example of Table 4.3). It makes sense, therefore, to treat the dummy partitions as if they appeared at the beginning rather than at the end of a file. In this way real input/output is minimized. For the same reason, it is desirable to spread the dummy partitions as evenly as possible over the files.

Figure 4.8 shows a general implementation of the polyphase algorithm.[3] Variable *LEVEL* and tables *A* and *D* are used in the following way. During the distribution phase, the variable *LEVEL* records how many targets have been reached. When merging, *LEVEL* is decreased after each phase; when it reaches zero we have finished. Table *A* at any time holds a target distribution of partitions. Each target is a row similar to those in Table 4.4. Table *D* holds the number of dummy partitions required to bring the number of actual partitions on each file up to the appropriate quota in the target. Thus, as we put real partitions on the file, the elements of *D* are decreased. If table D contains all zeros, we have reached the current target. If, at this point, we have not yet come to the end of the input file, then the target is replaced as in the earlier special case algorithm. The elements of D are modified accordingly. Note that the real partitions are distributed across the files in such a way as to even out the number of dummy partitions.

In order to take dummy partitions into account, the merging process operates as follows for each merged partition produced.

```
if D[k] > 0 for all k                    1 ≤ k ≤ (F − 1)
   then increase D[F] by 1
        decrease D[k] by 1               1 ≤ k ≤ (F − 1)
   else merge 1 partition from each FILE[k] where D[k] = 0
        decrease D[k] by 1                where D[k] > 0
```

---

3. This algorithm is based on one presented by Knuth [40, 5.4.2] and is a generalization of that presented by Gilstad [50].

(* In the algorithm
    A   : a table holding the current target distribution
    D   : a table holding the number of dummies assumed on each file
    LEVEL: holds the number of merge phases needed
    FILE : an array of file variables/channels
    Pntr : indicates where the next initial partition should be written
*)

(* initialization *)
set A[1] ... A[F − 1] and D[1] ... D[F − 1] to 1
set A[F] and D[F] to 0
set Pntr to 1
set LEVEL to 0
open file i for writing on FILE[i] $1 \le i \le F - 1$

(* generation and distribution of initial partitions on files 1 through F − 1 *)
generate a partition and write to FILE[Pntr]
decrease D[Pntr] by 1
while not end-of-file(input)
      if D[Pntr] < D[Pntr + 1]
        then Pntr ← Pntr + 1
        else if D[Pntr] = 0
            then (* revise target *)
                add 1 to LEVEL
                a ← A[1]
                loop from k = 1 to F − 1
                    D[k] ← a + A[k + 1] − A[k]
                    A[k] ← a + A[k + 1]
            Pntr ← 1
      generate partition and write to FILE[Pntr]
      decrease D[Pntr] by 1

close files on FILE[1] ... FILE[F − 1]
loop from i = 1 to F − 1
    open file i on FILE[i] for reading
open file F on FILE[F] for writing

(* merge section *)
while LEVEL > 0
    (* perform a merge phase *)
    repeat Merge partitions from files on FILE[1] ... FILE[F − 1] onto the file on FILE[F]
      until end-of-file (FILE[F − 1])
    decrease LEVEL by 1
    rewind and close files on FILE[F] and FILE[F − 1]
    open file on FILE[F] for reading
    open file on FILE[F − 1] for writing
    (* reallocate files to channels, make corresponding changes to D *)
    FILE[1], FILE[2], ... , FILE[F] ← FILE[F], FILE[1], ... , FILE[F − 1]
    D[1], D[2], ... , D[F] ← D[F], D[1], ... , D[F − 1]

FIGURE 4.8 Polyphase sort-merge algorithm

9	7	4		Actual partitions
4	4	3	0	+ D (number of dummies)
13	11	7		Total

File 1	File 2	File 3	File 4
Ra	Rb	Rc	
Rd	Re	Ri	
Rf	Rh	Rn	
Rg	Rk	Rq	
Rj	Rm		
Rl	Rp		
Ro	Rt		
Rr			
Rs			

FIGURE 4.9 Trace of partition distribution

Figure 4.9 shows the results of the distribution phase of the polyphase algorithm of Fig. 4.8. As with the earlier balanced N-way and optimal examples, we use 20 partitions and $F = 4$. Note that because 20 is not a term in the modified Fibonacci series, 11 dummy partitions are required to bring the total to 31, the next term in the series. The real partitions, in the order in which they are generated, are denoted Ra, Rb, . . . , Rt. Figure 4.9 also shows the final contents of table D, which holds the distribution of dummy partitions.

Table 4.5 traces the merging stage of the polyphase algorithm. Dummy partitions are shown (as D) in the positions that the merging algorithm assumes they occupy. When real partitions are merged, we concatenate the partition identifiers. Thus, for example, Rabi represents the merge of Ra, Rb, and Ri and is itself merged later. A total of 31 partitions are merged: 20 real partitions and 11 dummies. The number of passes required is

$$\frac{\text{Total reads}}{20} = \frac{10 + 9 + 12 + 11 + 20}{20} = \frac{62}{20} = 3.1$$

Note that only real reads are counted.

Comparison of Distribution and Merging Strategies

Balanced N-way merging is simple to implement but not very efficient. The algorithm designated as optimal is not the best in all cases, as we have demonstrated with our example, and has record-keeping overhead. The overhead with the polyphase algorithm is

TABLE 4.5 Trace of partition merging

	File 1	File 2	File 3	File 4
Initially	D	D	D	
	D	D	D	
	D	D	D	
	D	D	Rc	
	Ra	Rb	Ri	
	Rd	Re	Rn	
	Rf	Rh	Rq	
	Rg	Rk		
	Rj	Rm		
	Rl	Rp		
	Ro	Rt		
	Rr			
	Rs			
After phase 1	Rg	Rk		D
(10 reads)	Rj	Rm		D
	Rl	Rp		D
	Ro	Rt		Rc
	Rr			Rabi
	Rs			Rden
				Rfhq
After phase 2	Rr		Rgk	Rabi
(9 reads)	Rs		Rjm	Rden
			Rlp	Rfhq
			Rotc	
After phase 3		Rrgkabi	Rlp	Rfhq
(12 reads)		Rsjmden	Rotc	
After phase 4	Rrgkabilpfhq	Rsjmden	Rotc	
(11 reads)				
After phase 5				Ra . . . t
(20 reads)				

proportional to the order of the merge rather than the number of partitions. See Knuth [40] for a more detailed analysis and description of sorting algorithms.

Summary

We have considered the problem of sorting a large file of records. The algorithms we examined can be termed external sorting algorithms in that most of the data at any time is held outside main memory. We looked at algorithms that sort in a divide-and-conquer manner. In the first stage of the sort operation, comparatively small sections of the unsorted file are sorted. In the second stage, the sorted partitions are merged in a number of phases into a sorted file.

Sorted partitions can be generated from an unsorted file in many ways. We examined three: internal sorting, replacement selection, and natural selection. The methods differ in the extent to which they are able to take advantage of any partial ordering in the unsorted file and produce longer partitions. Longer partitions will require fewer partitions and less subsequent merging. However, extra storage, internal or external, is needed by the better algorithms.

Similarly, sorted partitions can be distributed and then merged in many ways. To minimize total sorting time we try to minimize the number of input/output transfers. Balanced N-way merging was the first algorithm considered. It is simple but comparatively slow: only half the available files are used for input during merging. Optimal merging allocates one partition to each of a number of files and then produces the sorted file by merging the smallest partitions into a new partition at each phase. Polyphase merging was the final algorithm considered. It merges faster than the other two but requires a relatively complex distribution based on the properties of Fibonacci series.

Exercises

1. Why are algorithms such as Shellsort, bubblesort, and heap sort not very suitable for external sorting?

2. Assume that each book published has a unique number (the ISBN) that is printed in each copy of the book. Assume that whenever a copy of a book is sold its ISBN is appended to a serial file called BOOKSOLD. Outline an algorithm by which a list of the top ten best-selling books could be obtained from BOOKSOLD. Each entry in the list should consist of an ISBN and the number of copies sold. The list entries should be ordered by copies sold. (The system on which your solution is to run has very limited main memory and disc space but a large number of tape drives.)

3. Implement the three algorithms for creating initial partitions. Use a random number generator to create a large unsorted file. Tab-

ulate the average length of partition generated for each algorithm for a variety of main memory capacities.

4. Modify the file creation mechanism of Exercise 3 so that one aspect of the "sortedness" of the input file can be varied in a simple way. For example, arrange that with probability P, a record is in the desired final relationship with its predecessor in the file. Keeping the main memory capacity constant, tabulate the average partition lengths of the three algorithms for various values of P.

5. During natural selection, reservoir overflow causes the contents of main memory to be output, which terminates the current partition. What would be the consequences of switching to a replacement selection algorithm at this point, that is, outputting the smallest main memory element, replacing it by the next input, possibly freezing it, and so on? Consider the current partition and future partitions.

6. A certain external sorting program forms initial partitions using internal sorting and merges the partitions using balanced N-way merging.

   a) Assuming that the input file contains X records, how many read operations are required in stage 1 (partition formation)?
   b) Assuming that main memory can hold exactly M records, give an expression for P, the number of initial partitions generated.
   c) Assuming that F files are used in the balanced merging (F is even), give an expression for T, the number of phases required to merge P partitions.
   d) Assuming that the system takes 0.01 seconds to perform a read or a write operation and that processing time can be ignored, how long will it take to sort a file of 51,200 records if $M = 50$ and $F = 8$?

7. You have been put in charge of the records office of a large college. Each student record contains demographic data and a list of classes in which the student is currently enrolled. Transactions on the serial student record file are applied in batches as described in Chapter 3 (see pp. 67–70). The transactions must be sorted before being applied (using the method of Exercise 6). You have to decide how big the batches should be. What factors would you take into account?

8. Consider the following partition generating and merging strategy. M records are read from the unsorted file, sorted, and written to a file. The next M records are read, sorted, and merged with the

first partition to form a partition of $2 \times M$ records. Similarly the next M records are read, sorted, and merged to form a partition of $3 \times M$ records. We proceed in this way until the partition consists of the entire file to be sorted. Compare this strategy with balanced N-way merging. What is the total number of reads required by each method to sort a file of X records?

9. Tabulate the number of passes and phases required by an optimal merge algorithm for a variety of values of F and the number of initial partitions.

10. Tabulate the number of passes and phases required by Knuth's polyphase merge algorithm for a variety of values of F and the number of initial partitions.

11. A certain sort program uses a total of five files in the distribution and merging parts of a sort-merge algorithm. It uses Knuth's algorithm. From a particular unsorted file, 49 partitions are generated.

   a) Will any dummy partitions be required? If so, how many?
   b) What is the final target distribution used in the distribution section of the algorithm?
   c) How many phases are required to merge the partitions together?
   d) How many passes are needed to merge the partitions? (Assume that all initial partitions are the same length.)

12. Knuth's algorithm goes to some trouble to distribute the number of dummy runs evenly over the files. Is it worth it? Modify your program of Exercise 10 so that partitions are written to the first file until its quota is reached, then to the second file, and so on. What differences do you observe in the output?

13. Tabulate, using simulation or otherwise, the maximum space needed for files during the course of merging partitions using Knuth's polyphase algorithm. Assume that the space occupied by a file is not reusable until all the records in the file have been read. Express your answers as multiples of the size of the initial unsorted file. Try values of F (number of files) from 4 through 10 and 100, 150, 200, ..., 1000 initial partitions.

14. A simple spelling checker might work as follows. The file of text to be checked is read and a scratch file is created containing the words of the file, one to a line. The scratch file is then sorted. The sorted file is run against an alphabetically ordered dictionary file. Words not found in the dictionary are written to a log of possible spelling errors. Implement a spelling checker of this form. How will your sort and comparison programs deal with upper-

and lowercase letters? Extend your checker so that it records the position in the source file of each suspected error.

Suggestions for Further Reading

H. Lorin, *Sorting and Sort Systems* (Reading, Mass.: Addison-Wesley, 1975). An informal introduction to various aspects of sorting. Part 2 of the text covers external sorting.

5

Direct Files

5.1 Discusses the pointer concept and its extension to files.

5.2 Covers the basic addressing problem and considers techniques involved in organizing a direct file using hashing.

5.3 Describes a technique that uses a main memory table so that retrievals from a direct file can be made in one access.

5.4 Examines techniques for organizing a direct file in cases where the number of records in the file at any time is highly variable.

5.5 Describes a novel use of hashing in the creation of a robust filestore.

In this chapter we examine direct files. A direct file, or direct-access file, is a file in which any record can be accessed without reference to other records. In serial files, on the other hand, a record is available only when the preceding records have already been processed. It may be useful to think of a direct file as being similar to an array of records, whereas serial files have properties in common with singly linked lists.

In addition, direct files may be stored in a different way from the way serial files are stored. In the case of direct files it is normally necessary to be able to compute (or otherwise determine) quickly the address of the storage location holding a particular record. For efficiency of access, direct files are normally stored on direct-access devices, for example, discs, rather than on serial devices, such as tapes.

Some of the techniques with which you are probably familiar in the context of arrays can be applied to direct files. For example, a record can be located in an ordered file using a logarithmic search. However, due to the comparatively long access times of secondary storage devices (see Chapter 2) and the fact that the file may contain a very large number of records, some caution is needed.

5.1 Addressing and Pointers

Addressing

Consider the problem of obtaining the address of the secondary storage element containing the Ith logical record in a file. In the case of a disc file, the address of an element might consist of unit, cylinder, track, and sector numbers. A number of steps are typically involved in translating a user program's request for record I into the address of the physical record containing it. The first step might be to identify the starting position of the Ith record relative to the beginning of the file. This is typically a simple computation:

$$\text{Starting position} = (I - 1) \times \text{record length}$$

Later steps might express this position in terms of physical records and then, using the file's directory entry, as an actual disc address.

Variable- versus fixed-length records. We implicitly assumed in the discussion above that all records in the file were the same length. In practice, programming languages that allow users to create direct files usually do require that all records in the file be of the same type. However, what if we have data that is logically variable in length, that is, variable-length records? One solution is to pad out the records to some maximum length. Another is to factor out the variable-length part. Consider the following example.

A tax authority keeps records on local residents. Included in a record are the license numbers of all vehicles owned. The records are thus logically of variable lengths; not everyone owns the same number of vehicles. It is possible to assume a fixed maximum number of vehicles per person, but this has two consequences. First, much space may be wasted because the majority of people probably have far fewer than the maximum number of vehicles. Second, we can never be sure that the "maximum" will not be exceeded. Possible factoring solutions include the two shown in Figs. 5.1 and 5.2.

In Fig. 5.1 the fixed-length part of a resident's data is kept in file A, and the variable-length part (list of vehicles) is held as a series of (fixed-length) records in file B. The link between the two files is made implicitly by the social security number field, which we assume uniquely identifies a resident.

Figure 5.2 shows another technique for handling variable-length information. This method might be appropriate if there is no unique key for linking files or if the space that the key occupies is considered too great for the key to appear in both files. Each record in file A contains a count of the number of vehicles owned by a particular

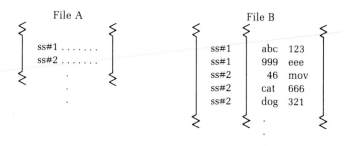

FIGURE 5.1 Record factoring

resident and a pointer to file B. The pointer points to the first vehicle owned by the resident. What is a disadvantage of this second technique? Consider what happens if cars are bought and sold.

Pointers

Given that records in a file are directly addressable, users may wish to address them directly or from other records in a file. The latter case gives rise to **linked storage.** (We assume that you are already familiar with the power and usefulness of linked structures.)

We start with the concept of a pointer to a record. A pointer, in general, is data from which the address of the object being pointed to can be determined. The concept extends easily from main memory to secondary storage. We discuss five possible pointer implementations in order of the time required to translate the pointer into an address. The fastest method is presented first and the slowest last.

FIGURE 5.2 Record factoring

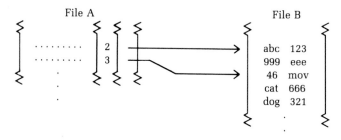

Secondary storage address. In effect, a secondary storage address is an absolute address, and no further address translation is necessary. Thus it is a fast mechanism. However, such addresses are rarely available to high-level language programmers. In addition, this type of pointer is vulnerable in the sense that the position of the file containing the target record may change for a number of reasons. For example, a collection of files may be moved in order to compact free space. In this case pointers consisting of secondary storage addresses would have to be updated.

Record number. A second possibility is to use, as a pointer to a record, its record number in the file. However, the position of the target record within the file may change because of record movements. For example, a file may be compacted following a record deletion. Despite this, record number is a common pointer implementation in many high-level languages.

Offset. If the target record and the record containing the pointer are in the same file, the number of records between them in the file could be used as a pointer. Also, the amount of space needed for a pointer field can be reduced if most pointers are to nearby records. This technique might be used, for example, when implementing a tree as a file of node records. Although this method of calculating an address is a fraction slower than using the record number, updating of some pointers might be avoided in the case where a block of records moves.

Indirect address. If there are many pointers to a particular record, as there might be, for example, in a representation of a graph, it might be appropriate to point to records indirectly. That is, records point to a table that points to records. If the position of the target record changes, only the table entry for that record needs to be modified.

Symbolic. All of the methods that we have discussed thus far are vulnerable to changes in the position of the target record. Methods that are not vulnerable in this way are based on the contents rather than the position of the target record. For example, the primary key of a record can be used as a pointer to it. In a sense, however, this just defers the problem because the pointer mechanism then relies on the existence of a mechanism for translating a primary key into an address (unless the storage device is content-addressable). Thus, while symbolic pointers never need to be changed, translation into an address is probably slow. Note that symbolic pointers were used in Fig. 5.1. The social security number field in file B can be regarded as a pointer to file A.

Pointers are important in many of the techniques examined later in this chapter. The first technique we consider is the use of key-to-address transformations as a solution to the record-addressing problem.

5.2 Hashing

The record-addressing problem is concerned with locating a record in a file given some unique attribute of that record (for instance, the primary key). When the primary key is an integer, the most direct solution is to treat the key as the address to use when storing the record. Given the key of a record to be located, retrieval is then easy. In practice, however, such a simple relationship between primary key and record address is rarely possible; keys are often nonnumeric or are very large integers. For example, at California State University, Northridge, student identification numbers are seven digits long. We could create a file of 10,000,000 empty records and thus have a one-to-one correspondence between record addresses and possible student identification numbers, but this would waste a great deal of storage space. Because of the way that identification numbers on our campus are constructed, no currently valid number is less than 5,800,000 or greater than 8,700,000. In addition, only about 40,000 students are active at any time. It would therefore be more efficient to set up a file with space for 40,000 records.

In general, the **address space,** the set of possible addresses in the file that is constructed, is likely to be very much smaller than the **key space,** the set of legal keys. We therefore arrive at the idea of mapping the key space onto the address space. A convenient mechanism for doing this is a **hash function** whereby

$$\text{address} \leftarrow \text{hash (key)} \qquad \text{address} \subset \text{set of valid addresses}$$

Direct mapping is clearly just a special case of this. The hash function is so named because the key is often hashed, that is, chopped or messed up, to produce the address. A record is stored by transforming the key into an address and storing the record at that address. This process is often referred to as **hashing.** A record is retrieved by a similar process: the address is computed from the key and the record is fetched. Typically this technique is very fast. Whereas the time to search a serial or sequential file tends to rise with the number of records in the file, this is not necessarily the case with a file organized using hashing.

The technique outlined above is, however, a simplification. In practice, one must consider a number of design factors when creating a file using hashing:

1. the number of records that can be held at the same address in the file, that is, the size of a **bucket**

2. the packing density: what should be the ratio of the number of records put in the file to the total capacity of the buckets?

3. the hash function: what transformation should be applied to a key to give an address?

4. the overflow resolution technique: given that buckets are finite in size, what method should be used to deal with bucket overflow?

Bucket Size

A bucket is a region of a file considered to have a single address as far as the hash mechanism is concerned. A bucket may hold more than one record. For example, a file with space for 1000 records could be regarded as consisting of 1000 buckets each of size 1. The size of the address space in this case is 1000. Alternatively, the file could be viewed as having 500 buckets of size 2, or 250 buckets of size 4, and so on. In the case of a bucket size of 5, records 1 through 5 in the file would be in bucket 1 and considered to have address 1, records 6 through 10 would have address 2, and so on. Bucket size is typically related to the physical characteristics of the storage device and is chosen so that all records in a bucket can be fetched in a single access. There is a **collision** during an insertion when two records hash to the same bucket address. Two keys that hash to the same address are sometimes termed **synonyms.** Collisions are not a problem if the bucket is not full, because the records are simply stored in available spaces in the bucket. **Overflow** occurs during insertion when a record is hashed to a bucket that is already full.

As bucket size increases, the probability of overflow decreases but the time taken to search for a record in the bucket may increase. However, the cost of accessing a bucket element once the bucket is in main memory is normally small compared with the time required to fetch a bucket. If bucket search time is critical, there are fast techniques for storing and retrieving records in a bucket. Hashing is one example!

Running example. A university administration wishes to store basic biographical information about students so that it can be retrieved very quickly. Each student record is 80 bytes long. Secondary storage devices on the university computer have physical records that are 512 bytes long, and up to 1024 bytes can be fetched in one read operation. The designers choose a bucket size of 12, which is the largest possible bucket fetchable in a single read. The 64 bytes available after the 12 logical records are stored can be used for pointers, counters, and so on. For example, it would be desirable on fetching a bucket to know quickly how many record places were occupied.

Packing Density

The number of logical accesses required to perform an insertion or retrieval operation tends to rise as the file fills. This is understandable; if more of the slots are occupied it is more likely that the hashing function will generate the address of an occupied slot during insertion or the address of a slot containing an unwanted record during retrieval. On the other hand, it may be economically undesirable to have files containing a lot of empty space. We define the **home buckets** of the file as those with addresses that can be produced by the hash function (there may be other buckets used for overflow only). Now we can define **packing density** as follows:

$$\text{Packing density} = \frac{\text{number of records in file}}{\text{total capacity of home buckets}}$$

As a rule of thumb, it is often found that collisions become unacceptably frequent if the packing density exceeds 70%, although this depends on bucket size. Given the choices for bucket size and packing density, we can estimate the number of records that will overflow the home buckets. What follows is the derivation of a formula that yields the expected percentage of record overflows for a file with a given bucket size and packing density.

Assume that there are N home buckets, that each has a capacity of C records, and that K records are put into the file. The packing density is

$$\frac{K}{C \times N} \quad \text{(which must be} \leq 1\text{)}$$

The probability of a given bucket receiving exactly I of the K records is

$$P(I) = \frac{K!}{I! \times (K - I)!} \times \left(\frac{1}{N}\right)^{I} \times \left(1 - \frac{1}{N}\right)^{K-I} \quad \text{(see footnote 1)}$$

Note that this assumes a uniform distribution of records into buckets,

---

1. If the hash function is uniformly distributed, we can make two assumptions. First, we assume that the probabilities associated with a record being inserted into a home bucket are independent. Second, we assume that the

that is, a perfect hash function. Given function P defined above, the probability of exactly J records overflowing from a given bucket with capacity C is P(C + J). Thus the expected number of overflows from a given bucket is

$$P(C + 1) + 2 \times P(C + 2) + 3 \times P(C + 3)$$
$$+ \ldots + (K - C) \times P(K)$$

$$= \sum_{j=1}^{K-C} j \times P(C + j)$$

The expected number of overflows from all the home buckets is

$$N \times \sum_{j=1}^{K-C} j \times P(C + j)$$

which we can express as a percentage of the records put into the file:

$$100 \times \frac{N}{K} \times \sum_{j=1}^{K-C} j \times P(C + j)$$

Note that any bias in the address transformation function toward particular addresses is likely to increase this percentage. We should regard the figure produced in this way as a minimum percentage. Given the formulas above, we can plot expected overflow against packing density for a particular bucket size. Table 5.1 shows the expected percentage overflow for various combinations of bucket size and packing density.[2]

---

expected probability that a record will be inserted into one of N specific home buckets is $1/N$. Thus, the probability that a specific set of I records will be inserted into a given home bucket (e.g., bucket B) is $(1/N)^I$. As you can see, this is the second term in expected probability expression. The third term is similar. It describes the expected probability that the remaining $(K - I)$ records will be inserted in different home buckets (not B). The term $(1 - 1/N)$ is the probability that a record will not be inserted into a particular home bucket.

So far we have been discussing the probability that I of K records will be inserted into a particular home bucket and that the remaining $(K - I)$ records will not be inserted into that bucket, that is, $(1/N)^I \times (1 - 1/N)^{K-I}$. However, there are a number of ways that K records could be taken I at a time. This is the first term in the above expression: $K!/[I! \times (K - I)!]$. In summary, then, the first term is the number of different ways I records could be inserted into a specific home bucket while the remaining $(K - I)$ records are inserted into other home buckets.

2. In the calculations, the file was assumed to contain 200 buckets.

TABLE 5.1 Expected file overflow

Bucket Size	% Packing Density									
	50	55	60	65	70	75	80	85	90	95
2	10.27	11.90	13.56	15.25	16.94	18.65	20.35	22.04	23.71	25.37
3	5.92	7.29	8.75	10.30	11.92	13.59	15.30	17.05	18.81	20.58
5	2.44	3.36	4.45	5.68	7.07	8.58	10.21	11.93	13.73	15.60
8	0.83	1.33	2.01	2.87	3.94	5.20	6.65	8.26	10.03	11.93
12	0.24	0.47	0.84	1.38	2.13	3.11	4.33	5.79	7.48	9.36
17	0.06	0.15	0.32	0.63	1.12	1.85	2.84	4.12	5.69	7.53
23	0.01	0.04	0.12	0.28	0.58	1.08	1.86	2.96	4.40	6.18
30	<0.01	0.01	0.04	0.11	0.29	0.63	1.22	2.14	3.45	5.16

Running example. The designers of the student record retrieval system aim to have about 30% of the file empty. Given the current and projected student population, the administration determines that the system should be capable of holding up to 60,000 student records at any time. The file will therefore contain 7143 home buckets (60,000/ 12 × 10/7 rounded up). Given a packing density of 70% in conjunction with a bucket size of 12, the formula developed above indicates that we can expect at least 2.13% of the records put in the file to overflow home buckets (see Table 5.1). Provision must therefore be made for at least 1278 overflow records.

Transformation Function

The third design factor we consider is the function that transforms a key into a bucket address. When hashing to secondary rather than primary storage, the time taken to compute the hash function is normally insignificant compared with bucket access time. It may therefore be worth having a relatively complex transformation in order to minimize secondary storage accesses. It is desirable that the mapping be uniform, that is, that there be no bias toward any particular addresses. If there is such bias, then records hashing to the favored addresses are likely to overflow home buckets and take longer to store and retrieve. It may be easier in many cases to reduce the transformation to bit operations. Martin [25] suggests a three-step key-to-address transformation:

Key

1. Transformation of the key, which may not be numeric, into an integer A. This transformation should not involve any loss of

↓
↓
A

      information: that is, if necessary, the key could be recreated
      from A.

2. Transformation of A into an intermediate integer B. The range
   of B is the same order of magnitude as the target address space.
   (For example, if the address range is 0–999, B might be a ten-
   bit integer.) A is transformed into B in such a way that the
   expected set of A values produces no bias toward particular
   values of B.

↓
B

3. Transformation of B into an address. This can be accomplished
   by multiplying by an appropriate scaling factor (for example,
   999/1023 for our example above).

↓
Address

Step 2 is normally the crucial one. Methods based on division, that
is,

$$B \leftarrow A \bmod T$$

often give good results. Ghosh and Lum [51] showed that if goodness
is measured in terms of overflows, division is better than the randomization method, which is theoretically perfect. The randomization
method would hash a key to a particular bucket out of N buckets
with probability $1/N$. More important, it would hash two consecutive
keys to the same bucket with probability $(1/N)^2$. Why might division
be better? In practice, the set of keys to be hashed may contain clusters
of adjacent values. Typically, step 1 of the three-part operation will
produce clusters of consecutive integers. (This is the case, for example, if the key is considered a base K integer where K is the size
of the alphabet from which its characters are drawn.) The division
method spreads out the clusters because it ensures that two consecutive values for A produce different values of B. Consider the example
of Table 5.2, which shows some keys and typical results for steps 1
and 2.[3] The set of original keys contains two subsets of clustered
records. Step 1 produces the set of A values containing two subsets
of consecutive integers. However, we can see from the third column
how the division method ensures that the integers in a cluster produce
different B values.

---

3. The A values are the keys considered as a base 38 number. Space $= 0$,
Hyphen $= 1$, A–Z $= 2$–27, 0–9 $= 28$–37. A B value is the corresponding A
value mod 3001.

TABLE 5.2 Typical A and B values

Keys	A Values	B Values
ASM0343L	290219317455	1919
ASM0343M	290219317456	1920
ASM0343N	290219317457	1921
T121-B	1726095549	1376
T121-C	1726095550	1377
T121-D	1726095551	1378
T121-E	1726095552	1379

Some values of the divisor T are better than others. Buchholz [52] suggested that T be the largest prime number less than the number of buckets. Lum, Yuen, and Dodd [53] tested a number of key-to-address transformation methods and found division to work well. They advise that although T need not be a prime number it should not have a prime factor less than 20.

Trial and error may be a reasonable way of deriving a hash function. A representative sample of key values can be run through the function and the results considered for unacceptable bias (see Exercise 10).

Note that if we hash records into a file we typically lose the capability to process them in sequential order. However, certain techniques will preserve the order of the records (see the note on order-preserving hashing on page 135).

Running example. Student identification numbers are seven digits long and are of the form YYSDDDD, where YY is the year of application (last two digits), S is the semester of application (2 = spring, 3 = summer, 4 or 5 = fall), and DDDD is an integer consecutively allocated from 0000 up within a semester. (Because more than 10,000 applications are received during the fall, the number allocated after YY49999 is YY50000.) In the light of the discussion above, the designers decide to use a division operation on the student identification number to produce an address. Because 7143 (the number of buckets computed on page 113) has a small factor (3), they increase the size of the address space to 7151, which is the next highest prime number. The remainder when dividing the five digits SDDDD by 7151 should give an acceptable hash value.

Overflow Strategy

Overflow occurs when a record hashes to a full bucket. When this happens, the problem is (1) to find space for the record and (2) to arrange matters so that the record can be found when searched for. We will look at two broad categories of solutions, open addressing and chaining. These solutions can be categorized respectively as a computational and as a data structure approach. In the first, addresses of buckets to search are calculated dynamically. In the second, chains of overflow records are rooted in the home buckets.

Open addressing. The first solution requires a mechanism that, from the key of the record, generates a list of bucket addresses. That is,

$$A_i = f(i, key) \qquad i = 0, 1, 2, \ldots$$

If, when storing the record, bucket A_i is full, bucket A_{i+1} is examined. When retrieving a record, buckets are examined until one is found that either contains the required record or has an empty space. An empty space indicates that the record being searched for is not in the file. This method of resolving overflow was proposed by Peterson [54], who termed it **open addressing.** A good function f should ensure that each integer 0 through $N - 1$ (N is the number of home buckets) appears in the generated list of bucket addresses.

A simple class of functions is represented by

$$A_i = (i \times step + hash(key)) \bmod N$$

If the value of $step$ is chosen to have no factors in common with N, then the first N elements of the list will be all the possible bucket numbers.[4] This method of computing addresses is called **linear probe.** When using linear probe it is a good idea to remember the value of hash(key). If this address appears later in the list, we can stop the generation of addresses because from then on we will merely be repeating earlier ones.

Linear probe suffers from two forms of **clustering.** That is, there are two ways in which records tend to bunch together in particular buckets instead of being spread evenly throughout the file. Clustering is undesirable because it increases the average number of accesses required for storage and retrieval. The two forms of clustering are primary and secondary clustering, and there are ways of minimizing them.

Primary clustering. Primary clustering occurs because buckets probed when processing a record hashing to the first bucket in a

---

4. If N and $step$ do have factors in common, then the number of different addresses in the list is N divided by the highest common factor of N and $step$.

TABLE 5.3 Linear probe sequence

Key	Hash	Probe Sequence						
1234	25	25	28	0	3	6	9	...
245	28	28	0	3	6	9	12	...
1054	0	0	3	6	9	12	15	...
100	7	7	10	13	16	19	22	...
1591	10	10	13	16	19	22	25	...
323	13	13	16	19	22	25	28	...

sequence are also used by records hashing to the second and subsequent buckets in that sequence. For example, if the number of home buckets (N) is 31, a simple mechanism for generating a sequence of overflow addresses is

$$A_i = (i \times 3 + \text{hash(key)}) \bmod 31$$

Table 5.3 shows the addresses of buckets probed for a number of different keys. Overflow from bucket 25 to bucket 28, for instance, increases the probability that bucket 28 will overflow. Overflow from both buckets will compete for space in bucket 0, and so on.

A solution to the primary clustering problem is to use a nonlinear function for generating the sequence of probe addresses. If, for example, we use

$$A_i = (i \times 3 + i^2 \times 5 + \text{hash(key)}) \bmod 31,$$

we get the probe sequences of Table 5.4. Note how buckets having the same probe sequence in Table 5.3 (for example, 7, 10, and 13) now have different sequences. Also, note that the method described above for deciding when to stop address generation does not work for nonlinear functions. This is because even if the same address appears

TABLE 5.4 Nonlinear probe sequence

Key	Hash	Probe Sequence						
1234	25	25	2	20	17	24	6	...
245	28	28	5	23	20	27	13	...
1054	0	0	8	26	23	30	16	...
100	7	7	15	2	30	6	23	...
1591	10	10	18	5	2	9	26	...
323	13	13	21	8	5	12	29	...

TABLE 5.5 Double hashing

Key	Hash	Hash2	Probe Sequence							
1234	25	11	25	5	16	27	7	18	29	...
366	25	12	25	6	18	30	11	23	4	...
831	25	27	25	21	17	13	9	5	1	...
100	7	4	7	11	15	19	23	27	0	...
224	7	8	7	15	25	0	8	16	24	...
4471	7	29	7	5	3	1	30	28	26	...

more than once in the list of addresses, its successors on each occasion are likely to be different.

Secondary clustering. Use of nonlinear rather than linear probe does not eliminate secondary clustering. Secondary clustering occurs because, using simple open addressing as described above, all records with the same original home bucket follow the same sequence of overflow buckets. Defects in the design of the original hash function are likely to be perpetuated. Suppose that the hash function of the examples of Tables 5.3 and 5.4 were poorly designed and that far too many records hashed to bucket 25. From Table 5.4 we can see that if the nonlinear probe were being used we would expect buckets 2, 20, 17, 24, and so on, to become full quickly.

A solution to the secondary clustering problem is to use **double hashing.** In this method the probe sequence is produced in the following way:

$$A_0 = \text{hash(key)}$$
$$A_i = (A_{i-1} + \text{hash2(key)}) \bmod N \quad i > 0$$

Recall that N is the number of home buckets. Hash2 should produce an integer that is relatively prime to N, that is, has no factors in common with N. In this way the probe sequence will include all bucket numbers from 0 through $N - 1$. The two hash functions should be independent: the probability that hash(key1) will equal hash(key2) and hash2(key1) will equal hash2(key2) if key1 is not the same as key2 should be approximately $(1/N)^2$. Note that if N is prime, hash2 could return any positive integer less than N and each bucket would be probed. (See Knuth [40, 6.4] for suggestions on the design of hash2.) Table 5.5 illustrates double hashing. It shows, for a small number of keys, the two hash values and part of the sequence of buckets probed.

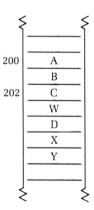

FIGURE 5.3 Example file fragment

Again we are assuming 31 home buckets. The two functions used in the example of Table 5.5 are:

hash(key) = key mod 31

hash2(key) = 1 + (truncate(key/31) mod 29)

Deletions. You may have realized that deletions from a file may be a problem in the case where overflows are handled by open addressing. A search may stop prematurely because an empty record space is found in a bucket. This suggests that the record being searched for is not in the file. Consider, for example, the file of Fig. 5.3.

Assume that records A, B, C, and D hash to 200 and that records W, X, and Y hash to 202. If the records are inserted into the file in the order A, B, C, W, D, X, Y and overflow is resolved using linear probe with step size 1, then the records will be placed as shown. What happens if record W is to be deleted and we simply remove it from the file? Can we still find D, X, and Y successfully? Consider two possible solutions to the problem: (1) marking deleted records (logical deletion) and (2) rehashing.

The first solution, called logical deletion, is to mark the record "deleted" in some way rather than removing it. For example, we would set the primary key to some "impossible" value, such as −1 for keys that are normally only positive integers. Locations that contain "deleted" records are treated as empty by the insertion algorithm so they can be reused. However, they are not considered empty by the retrieval algorithm. The difficulty with this solution is that once a record slot becomes nonempty, it never becomes empty again. The only possible transitions are

empty $\rightarrow$ used
deleted $\rightarrow$ used
used $\rightarrow$ deleted

Unsuccessful searches terminate only when an empty record slot is found; therefore they take longer and longer as empty space becomes scarcer and scarcer. To maintain the performance of the file it may be necessary, from time to time, to replace the hash file by a new one that contains only empty and used record slots. This could be done easily by first setting up an empty file of the appropriate size and then scanning the current file. Nonempty records that are not marked deleted are hashed into the new file.

Another solution to the deletion problem is to remove the record from the file in the usual way, that is, to make the slot empty, but then **rehash** certain of the remaining records in the file. Rehashing a record involves deleting it and then inserting it. A copy of the record is made, its slot is marked empty, and the copy is reinserted into the file as if it were a new record. The problem here is knowing which records to rehash. In a simple case, where overflow is resolved using linear probe and a step size of 1, the only records that need to be rehashed are those positioned between the deleted record and the next free space. These are the only records that could have overflowed from the deleted space. Consider Fig. 5.4. Figure 5.4(a) shows the file of Fig. 5.3 after record W has been removed. Figure 5.4(b) shows the effect of rehashing records Y, X, and D. With more complex open addressing schemes, however, it may not be as easy to identify the records to rehash. In addition, rehashing may be comparatively time-consuming.

Chaining. A second solution to the problem of overflows is called chaining (sometimes referred to as **closed addressing**), in which lists of records that have overflowed are rooted in appropriate home buckets. The overflow records are put in any convenient place, perhaps in a separate overflow area or in an arbitrary bucket that is not full. In contrast to open addressing, the location used does not typically depend on the contents of the record. We consider three variations on the basic idea outlined above: (1) separate lists, (2) coalescing lists, and (3) directory methods.

Separate lists. In the separate lists method we link together records overflowing from the same home bucket. The list is rooted in that bucket. Only the records on the list need be examined when searching, and because any one might be the one looked for, comparisons

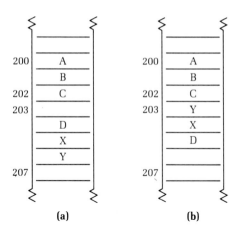

FIGURE 5.4 Rehashing

are minimized. Deletions are straightforward. If we delete a record from a home bucket, we can replace it by one on the overflow list. If we delete a record on a list, it is removed from the list in the conventional way.

Coalescing lists. The separate lists method requires a comparatively large amount of space for pointers. A second possibility is to store records in spare space in home buckets. Each bucket has a single pointer pointing to the next bucket to try when searching. Pointers are established as records overflow. This method reduces pointer overhead, but many more records may have to be examined when searching.

Directory methods. Typically, in methods involving directories, room is allocated in a home bucket beyond that needed to store records. The extra space is used to hold pointers to records overflowing from the bucket and their keys. As long as all overflows can be pointed to in this way, this method is fast. If the space allocated to the directory of pointers is used up, then the pointers may have to identify lists of records rather than individual records.

Comparison of open addressing and linked storage. Knuth [40, 6.4] compared retrievals done from files organized using open addressing (linear probe) with retrievals from files where overflow was handled by separate lists. Open addressing performed well unless the file was almost full. Chaining methods performed well but required extra space for pointers.

TABLE 5.6 Example address and signature sequences

Key	Buckets					Signatures				
WHITE	85	87	89	91	93 ...	00101	01001	10100	10111 ...
BLUE	85	86	87	88	89 ...	00110	00011	00110	10000 ...
LILAC	85	90	95	0	5 ...	01000	10100	11000	10100 ...
RED	85	92	99	6	13 ...	00010	11000	11110	10010 ...
GREEN	85	86	87	88	89 ...	00011	00100	10001	00111 ...

Running example. The university administrators want fast retrieval even in the worst case. The file designers decide to have overflow handled by separate chains. They decide on a separate overflow area on each disc cylinder for the buckets on that cylinder. A separate set of cylinders is provided in case any of the primary overflow areas becomes full.

In the next two sections we look at how disc accesses can be saved by the use of data structures in main memory. In Section 5.3 we consider table-assisted hashing, which enables retrievals from a file to be fast even though insertions may be slow. In Section 5.4 we examine three extensible file organizations where both retrievals and insertions may be fast.

5.3 Table-Assisted Hashing

Larson and Kajla [55] describe a file organization based on hashing that guarantees retrievals in one access to secondary storage. This is accomplished by means of a table in main memory that has one entry for each bucket in the hash file.[5] Although insertions may take a long time, retrievals are very fast.

The technique requires mechanisms that will generate a sequence of bucket addresses and a parallel sequence of k-bit **signatures** from a record key. (Compare this with Larson's dynamic hashing technique described later in this chapter.) Table 5.6 shows example sequences with k = 5.

Consider the following as an informal introduction to the insertion process. Suppose our file has a bucket size of 3 and we insert the

---

5. The table entries would be saved on disc when the hash file is closed and read into main memory when the hash file is opened.

records in the order shown in Table 5.6. The home bucket of each is 85, so after three insertions bucket 85 will be full and will contain WHITE, BLUE, and LILAC. (No signatures are stored in the buckets.) What happens when we want to insert RED? If more records hash to a bucket than that bucket can contain, the records are sorted according to the appropriate signature for each record. The result for bucket 85 is as follows:

RED   (signature 00010 = 2)
WHITE   (signature 00101 = 5)
BLUE   (signature 00110 = 6)
LILAC   (signature 01000 = 8)

Now we find a separating signature value such that all records with a lower signature can be placed in the bucket. The value we select is the smallest signature in the set of records that overflow the bucket. In our example this value is 8. This separating value is put into the table entry for the bucket, and thus table entry 85 in our case now contains 8. Records with smaller signatures are put in the bucket. Bucket 85 now contains RED, WHITE, and BLUE. Record LILAC is now the insertion problem; it will be put in bucket 90.

Retrievals

Retrieval of records is very efficient with table-assisted hashing. From the key to be searched we generate:

$Bucket_1$, $Bucket_2$, $Bucket_3$, $Bucket_4$, ...

$Signature_1$, $Signature_2$, $Signature_3$, $Signature_4$, ...

We want the smallest i such that:

$Signature_i$ < Table[$Bucket_i$]

This is the number of the only bucket in the file where the record might be stored.

Insertions

The insertion algorithm operates similarly to retrievals in that it begins by searching for the record to be stored. This will bring us either to a full or a nonfull bucket. If the bucket is not full, then the record is inserted and we have finished. If the bucket is full, then its records are sorted as described earlier. It is likely that most of these records will be reinserted into the bucket, but it is not impossible that all records will overflow. Consider the case where all the signature values are the same. Typically, overflow records will be added to a list of records to be reinserted into the file.

When a sort and distribution is performed on a bucket, the table entry for the bucket decreases. Consider, for example, the insertion of the record GREEN into our example file. The search for GREEN would bring us to bucket 85; its signature for that bucket is 3, which is less than the table entry. The current bucket contents and the new record would be as follows:

RED   (signature 00010 = 2)
GREEN   (signature 00011 = 3)
WHITE   (signature 00101 = 5)
BLUE   (signature 00110 = 6)

BLUE is added to the reinsert list, and the table entry for bucket 85 is changed to 6. It follows from this discussion that the initial value for table entries should be $+\infty$ or, in practice, k 1's. This bit pattern should therefore not be a valid signature. It is clear that an insertion or reinsertion may cause one or more records to be added to the reinsert list, and thus it may take a long time for all records to be reinserted into the file.

Deletions

Larson and Kajla make no reference to the deletion of records. However, it is not a difficult problem, and we leave it as an exercise for the reader (see Exercise 9).

Table-assisted hashing is good for applications where retrievals are more frequent than insertions. Larson and Kajla present results from the use of table-assisted hashing to organize a file of user-identifiers. The file is accessed frequently by an operating system to validate log-ins. The contents of the file, however, change comparatively rarely.

In the next section we consider extensible files. Here, too, main memory structures of various forms help reduce disc accesses.

5.4 Extensible Files

Up to this point we have considered hashing as operating on fixed-length files. In our design process we chose a bucket size and a packing density. In conjunction with an expected number of records, this fixed the number of buckets allocated to the file. We assumed implicitly that the number of records in the file at any time would not vary a great deal. In many applications, however, the number of records in the file is likely to grow and shrink by large amounts. If K is the number of records stored in the file at any time, and K ranges between Kmin and Kmax, cases where the value of Kmax divided by Kmin

(which we will call SPAN) is large may cause problems. If we have
a fixed file size, then when K is close to $Kmin$, space may be unacceptably underutilized. When K is close to $Kmax$, the packing density
is high and storage and retrieval times may be long. Rehashing is one
solution. When the number of records in the file differs significantly
from the original estimate, a new file of a more appropriate size can
be created and the records hashed into it using a suitably modified
hash function. In practice, however, this is likely to be very time-
consuming. In addition, the file is likely to be unavailable while rehashing is performed, which may be unacceptable in many
applications.

A number of hashing techniques have been developed for organizing files with high SPAN values. We will consider three of them.
Each technique assumes that physical blocks can be allocated to a
file and deallocated as required. This is reasonable: an operating system does this as files are created and deleted. We classify the techniques described in this section as implementations of **extensible files,**
in contrast with conventional hashing, which uses fixed-length files.
Each technique implements solutions to the following problems:

1. splitting a bucket when it becomes full
2. dispersing records between old and new buckets
3. minimizing bucket accesses during retrieval
4. deleting records from the file

The techniques we consider are virtual hashing, described by
Litwin [56], Larson's dynamic hashing [57], and the extendible hashing scheme devised by Fagin et al [58]. (Note that we use the term
"extensible" to describe a class of techniques, while Fagin et al. use
the term "extendible" for their particular organization.) In each of
these file organizations the number of buckets in the file grows and
shrinks relatively smoothly with the number of records stored. There
are no overflow buckets, and deletions are quite simple. Retrievals,
successful or not, typically require only one or two accesses to secondary storage. In what follows we assume that buckets are of fixed
size and that each has a capacity of C records.

Virtual Hashing

Virtual hashing is characterized by the use of multiple related
hash functions rather than a single function. Division is the basis of
hashing. The initial file contains N buckets, and initially, the function
used when hashing into any of the buckets is

address = key mod N

A novel feature of the method is the action taken when a bucket

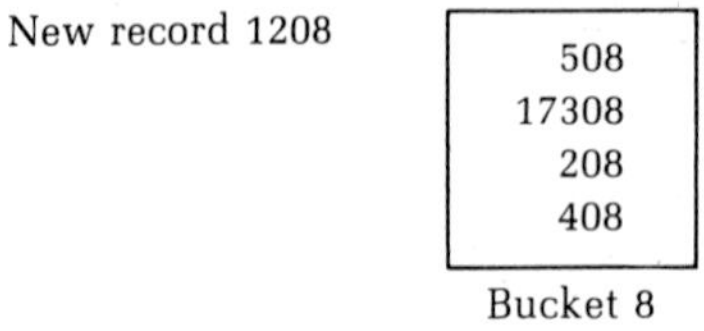

New record 1208

```
        508
       17308
        208
        408
```
Bucket 8

FIGURE 5.5 Bucket overflow

overflows. The $C + 1$ records (current bucket contents plus potential insert) are rehashed using a function related to but different from the one producing the collisions. For example, assume that $N = 100$ and $C = 4$. Figure 5.5 represents an overflow condition: bucket 8 is full and a record with key 1208 is to be inserted into the file.

The current hash function for the bucket is the original one:

address = key mod 100.

The five records will be rehashed using function:

address = key mod (2N)   (i.e., address = key mod 200)

Bucket 108 will therefore be required and is allocated to the file. After rehashing, which we can regard as a splitting of bucket 8, we get the configuration of Fig. 5.6.

Suppose that record 1608 is now inserted into bucket 8 and then record 5808 comes along. We need to split bucket 8 a second time, and on this occasion we use

address = key mod (4N)   (i.e., address = key mod 400)

Bucket 208 is allocated to the file. Figure 5.7 shows the contents of the three buckets after the second split.

In general, if we are splitting a bucket that has been involved as the destination of S previous splits, we use the function

FIGURE 5.6 Buckets after rehashing

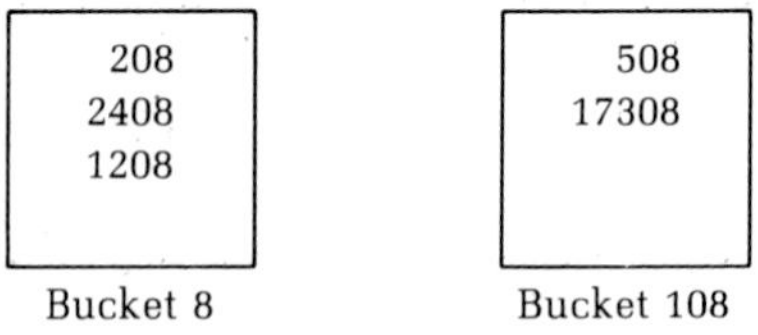

```
        208
       2408
       1208
```
Bucket 8

```
        508
       17308
```
Bucket 108

2408	508	208
1208	17308	5808
1608		

Bucket 8   Bucket 108   Bucket 208

FIGURE 5.7 Buckets after second split

$$\text{address} = \text{key mod } (2^{S+1} \times N)$$

Litwin [56, p. 518] gives a formal definition of the splitting process, which in effect is

Let h_j denote the function: key mod $(2^j \times N)$ $j = 0, 1, 2, \ldots$

Let $C_{m,j}$ denote the set of keys which h_j maps onto m
    $m < 2^j \times N$

To split $C_{m,j}$ we use h_{j+1} restricted to $C_{m,j}$

A split will generally send records to two buckets: the one being split and a newly allocated one that will therefore be initially empty.

Given a history of splits, how do we know which bucket should be regarded as the prime bucket for a record with a particular key? For example, in the file above, how are we to search for a record with key 208? Which hash function do we apply to the key? Litwin shows how the splitting history can be represented as a graph and, more usefully, as a bit string. He presents an algorithm that computes the primary address of an arbitrary key.

Litwin's suggested virtual hashing scheme (VH1) splits buckets as outlined above only if the overall load factor of the file, or the number of records in file divided by the capacity of allocated buckets, exceeds some threshold. Until that level is reached, overflow is handled by separate chaining.

A disadvantage of virtual hashing is that it appears to waste space because when a new bucket is allocated buckets with addresses between it and the previous end of file may also be allocated. This may be the case if insertions are clustered. However, in practice, the total amount of space used is likely to depend on the way in which bucket addressing is implemented. We can imagine the buckets being mapped onto a contiguous area of storage.

Dynamic Hashing

Initially, a file organized using Larson's dynamic hashing consists of N buckets, where N is the range of the hash function. Each bucket

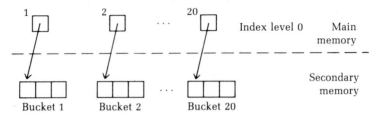

FIGURE 5.8 Initial dynamic hash file

is pointed to by a cell in main memory, and bucket address is therefore not as important as in Litwin's technique. Figure 5.8 depicts an initial file configuration when N = 20 and C = 3. Note that the part of the structure above the line is in main memory and the part below is on disc. We term the main memory structure the **index.** (We consider indexes in general in Chapter 6.) The initial index has just one level, which we denote level 0.

A hash function (H_0) transforms a key into an address of a level 0 index element (1 through N). The appropriate bucket is accessed by following the pointer. If a record is to be inserted into a bucket that is already full, then a new bucket is allocated to the file. In contrast to Litwin's virtual hashing, the address of the new bucket is not important. The C + 1 records are distributed between the old and new bucket. What was one pointer to the old bucket turns into an internal node of a binary tree with two children pointing to the old and new buckets. Figure 5.9 depicts the file of Fig. 5.8 after bucket 2 has split.

As records continue to be inserted into the file and splitting continues to occur, the index tends toward a forest of N binary trees. The

FIGURE 5.9 File of Fig. 5.8 after bucket split

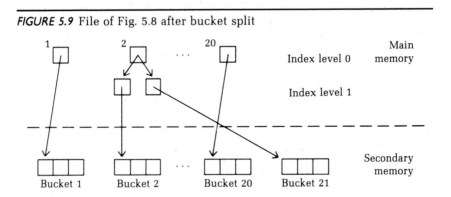

TABLE 5.7 Typical values for H_0 and B

Key	$H_0(key)$	$B(key)$
157	2	10100 ...
95	1	00011 ...
88	1	01100 ...
205	2	10010 ...
13	1	10111 ...
125	1	10001 ...
6	1	01000 ...
301	1	00110 ...

roots of the trees are at level 0. The internal and external nodes can be represented very simply. The conventions proposed by Larson are as follows:

Internal node (0, parent pointer, left child pointer, right child pointer)

External node (1, parent pointer, count, bucket pointer)

Two questions come to mind. First, when dispersing records between two buckets, how do we decide which goes where? Second, hash function H_0 brings us to the appropriate binary tree in the index. How do we decide which of the buckets pointed to by the leaves of that tree is the one to fetch?

These questions are related. When deciding whether to put a record in the old or the new bucket, we must do so in a way that does not depend on the other records in the bucket. Otherwise, conditions might be different when we search for the record later. Larson's solution is to have a second function B that, given a key, returns an arbitrarily long binary string, that is, a sequence in which each element is either 1 or 0. Table 5.7 shows typical keys, values of arbitrary H_0, and the beginning of the strings generated by some arbitrary B.

If the bucket being split is pointed to from a node at level I in the tree, then we use the value of the $(I + 1)$st digit of $B(key)$ to determine if a record goes in the left (old) or right (new) bucket. For example, we could adopt the convention that 0 signifies left and 1 signifies right. Consider the records of Table 5.7. If we assume a bucket size of three then the first five records can be inserted without difficulty. Figure 5.10 depicts the file at this point.

If we insert a record with key 125, then the first bucket splits. We allocate a new bucket to the file. The full bucket is pointed to by a leaf at level 0, so we use the first digit in the $B(key)$ strings. Records

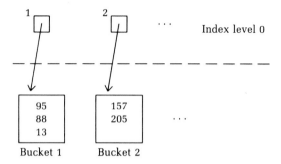

Index level 0

95
88
13

157
205

· · ·

Bucket 1   Bucket 2

FIGURE 5.10 Dynamic hash file after five insertions

with keys 95 and 88 go in the left bucket, and records with keys 13 and 125 go in the right bucket. Figure 5.11 depicts the file after the split. We have labeled the branches of the tree for convenience. Note that a result of the splitting strategy used is that all records in a bucket pointed to by a leaf node at index level J have the same first J bits of $B(key)$.

In the search for a record, $H_0(key)$ identifies the appropriate tree and $B(key)$ is used to traverse it to a leaf. The combination of the two functions uniquely identifies a leaf in the forest of trees and hence a bucket in the file. As with Litwin's method, the bucket identified in this way is the only one we need to examine. If the record is not in there, it is not in the file at all.

FIGURE 5.11 File of Fig. 5.10 after split

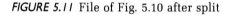

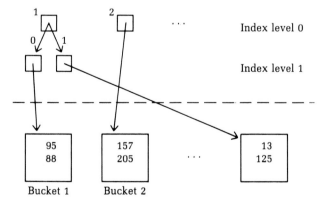

Index level 0

Index level 1

95
88

157
205

· · ·

13
125

Bucket 1   Bucket 2

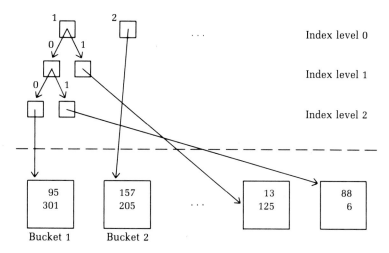

FIGURE 5.12 File of Fig. 5.11 after split

A search is the first step in the insert procedure. For example, consider the insertion of the next record from Table 5.7, that is, the one with key 6. $H_0(6)$ brings us to tree 1, and we use $B(6)$ to traverse to a leaf. In this case we need only one digit. The record is inserted in the last space in bucket 1. Suppose we now insert a record with key 301. Application of functions H_0 and B again bring us to bucket 1. The bucket is full, so it splits. It is pointed to by a leaf at index level 1, so this time we use the second digit of the binary strings to disperse the records. Figure 5.12 shows the result.

There are various ways of constructing function B. One possibility is to use the key of the record (or in general some function H_1 of the key) as the seed for a pseudo–random number generator. Each pseudo–random integer generated is then transformed into a binary digit. It is desirable that the transformation produce 0 and 1 with equal probability. One possible transformation is to use the parity of the binary representation of the integer. Figure 5.13 depicts this implementation of function B.

In Fig 5.13, b_i represents a binary digit generated. We have shown the general form of a class of pseudo–random number generators. In practice B would probably be written as a function that, given a key K and an index I, returns the Ith binary digit in the sequence generated from K.

It is worth noting that if function B is implemented in the manner described, a problem occurs if all records to be dispersed have the

Key

↓

$X_0, X_1, X_2, X_3 \ldots$

↓ ↓ ↓ ↓

$b_0, b_1, b_2, b_3 \ldots$

$X_0 = H_1(\text{key})$ $X_{i+1} = (X_i \times a + b) \bmod c$ $b_i = \text{parity}(X_i)$

FIGURE 5.13 Possible implementation of function B

same value of X_0. The result will be that the binary strings of the records will be identical and hence the records can never be split into two sets. The system could monitor the variety of X_0 values in a bucket, but human intervention may be necessary.

Larson analyzes expected storage utilization and shows it to be approximately 69% all the time. However, additional space beyond that required for the buckets would normally be required to store the index when the file is not in use. Frost [59] presents algorithms for writing the index out to a file and for recreating it from the file.

There may be a hidden overhead in dynamic hashing. Because of the discontiguous way in which the index evolves, nodes on a path from root to leaf may be widely separated in main memory. In a virtual memory system, several page faults may be incurred during a tree traversal. Dealing with a page fault may require a disc access. In addition, if the file is large, the index may be too big to fit in main memory and at least the lower levels may have to be kept on secondary storage. Thus access times are further increased.

Variations on dynamic hashing have been described by Scholl [60]. In one variation, overflow buckets are introduced and bucket splitting deferred. In this way storage utilization can be improved at a cost of longer average access times.

Extendible Hashing

The extendible hashing organization of Fagin *et al.* [58] is similar to Larson's dynamic hashing in that a two-level organization is used. Extendible hashing uses a **directory** and a set of "leaves." Each leaf consists of a bucket of records and an integer header. The directory consists of a similar header (d) and 2^d pointers (not necessarily distinct) to leaves. Figure 5.14 shows a typical configuration.

While Larson's method uses, in effect, two hash functions and Litwin's uses a large set of related functions, extendible hashing uses

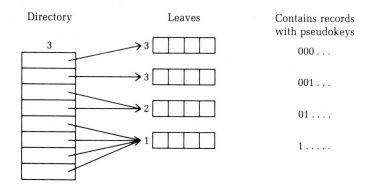

FIGURE 5.14 Typical extendible hash file

a single hash function. The function operates on the key of a record and produces a fixed-length bit string denoted the **pseudokey.** The header of a particular leaf indicates the number of prefix bits that the pseudokeys of the bucket records have in common. To find a record, the first d bits of its pseudokey are used as an index into the directory. This yields a pointer to the appropriate leaf to search. For example, suppose that we are searching the file of Fig. 5.14 for a record with key X and that the pseudokey derived from X is 1010000100010. We use the first three bits of the pseudokey to form an index (5) into the directory. Entry 5 points to the fourth leaf, so this is where we search for the record with key X. Extendible hashing improves on dynamic hashing in that only one page fault is risked in the directory/index search.

If we wish the system to grow completely naturally, we could allocate a single leaf initially. The directory will have a single entry pointing to the leaf. The initial value of the directory header and the leaf header will be zero. However, we would usually choose to have an initial file containing N buckets. The value of d will be $\lfloor \log_2 (N - 1) \rfloor + 1$ and the directory will have 2^d entries.

To store a record, the first d bits of its pseudokey are used to access the directory and the record is placed in the leaf pointed to. If the leaf is full, a new one is allocated. (As with dynamic hashing, the address of the new leaf is unimportant.) Assume that the header for the old (full) leaf is T. The $C + 1$ records are dispersed between the new and old leaf according to bit $T + 1$ of their pseudokeys. The headers for the new and old leaves are both given the value $T + 1$. Other adjustments depend on the relationship between the new header value ($T + 1$) and the directory header (d). Two cases must be considered: when $d \geq T + 1$ and when $d < T + 1$.

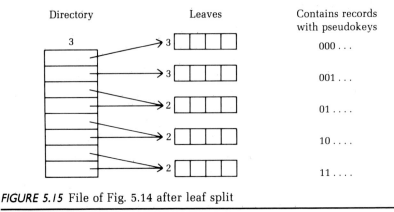

FIGURE 5.15 File of Fig. 5.14 after leaf split

Case 1: d ≥ T + 1. In this case the group of pointers pointing to the old leaf are split in two. Half will point to the new leaf and half to the old leaf, depending on the dispersal of records. For example, suppose that the fourth leaf in the file of Fig. 5.14 splits. Figure 5.15 shows how the file might change. Note that the four pointers originally pointing to the fourth leaf have been divided into two groups that point to the old and new leaf.

Case 2: d < T + 1. In this case the size of the directory must be doubled so that it can differentiate between the old and new leaves. The value of d therefore increases by 1. Leaves not involved in the split will find themselves pointed to by twice as many pointers as before. Figure 5.16 shows what happens to the configuration of Fig. 5.15 after the first leaf splits. The directory rewrite is a simple operation that can be performed with a linear scan.

Deletions

Deletions from extensible files do not present the problems noted earlier with open addressing in normal hashing. A record can be removed from a bucket and the remaining records shuffled up. What if we delete the last record in a bucket? Consider the three extensible file techniques discussed.

With Litwin's virtual hashing, an empty bucket can be deallocated from the file and appropriate adjustments made to the data structure that records splits. We assume that a bucket can be deallocated from a file without affecting higher-numbered buckets.

In the dynamic hashing organization we need to consider whether the bucket from which a deletion has been made has a **buddy bucket.**

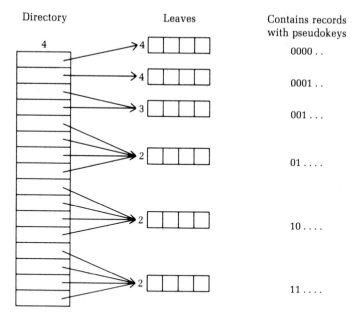

FIGURE 5.16 File of Fig. 5.15 after leaf split

Bucket A is buddy to bucket B if the two buckets are pointed to by external nodes with the same parent. If the total number of records in two buddies will fit into a single bucket, then the two records can be put in one of the two buckets. The empty bucket is then deallocated and the index tree adjusted.

The buddy bucket concept appears in the extendible file organization too. Buddy buckets have the same header value (T), and the pseudokeys of the records they contain have $T - 1$ prefix bits in common. For example, the first two buckets in Fig. 5.16 are buddies. If space permits, they can be combined after a deletion. The new header value will be $T - 1$. If all leaf headers are now less than the directory header, the directory can be halved in size and pointers adjusted.

Order-Preserving Hashing

In the section on the transformation function earlier in this chapter we mentioned the possibility of hashing preserving the sequence of records. Here we consider this idea very briefly. There would appear to be two difficulties in order-preserving hashing. First, we would seem to need a hash function such that

$$A < B < C \Rightarrow hash(A) < hash(B) < hash(C)$$

Second, such a "linear" transformation would appear to have the disadvantage of preserving any clustering in the keys to be hashed. Both of these problems can be solved. For example, we do not have a hash function at all if we use the key directly. Clustering need not be a problem if the hash file is made up of a dynamically changing index (a forest of binary trees) and a collection of buckets. Consider how this might operate. A certain number of the first bits of a key are used to select a tree in the index. The remaining bits are used to traverse the tree to a root. Records in a bucket have keys with the same prefix bits and would be kept in order. Insertion and retrieval proceeds in a way similar to Larson's dynamic hashing. Processing records in sequence is accomplished by taking each tree in turn, performing an appropriate traversal, and fetching the buckets pointed to by the leaves. Tamminen [61] has investigated the performance of an order-preserving hash file. There are other, perhaps better, ways of providing both sequential and fast access to a record. We consider some of them in Chapter 6.

In the final section of this chapter we examine a practical application of some of the techniques described earlier. We will see how hashing has been used in the implementation of a reliable filestore.

5.5 Filestore Reliability through Hashing

We discussed filestore organization briefly in Chapter 2. Conventionally, a disc contains directories and ordinary files. Directories contain names and addresses of ordinary files. A problem with this arrangement is that if a directory file becomes corrupted, ordinary files may become inaccessible even though they are perfectly sound. This is particularly likely to happen on a floppy disc–based system, where read/write heads make contact with the recording surface. The directory is likely to be the most frequently accessed part of the disc and hence the most likely to fail.

A novel alternative to the usual arrangement of directories and files has been proposed by McGregor and Malone [62]. Accessing block number I of a file F using a conventional directory system might involve:

1. looking in the directory to find the entry for F and the disc address of the beginning of the file

2. computing the address of the Ith block (this is reasonably straightforward if the file occupies a contiguous area on the disc)

In contrast, McGregor and Malone's organization views a disc as a series of **logical tracks,** each of which contains a fixed number of sectors. One sector on each track, the "key sector," is reserved for system use. A file is considered to consist of a number of blocks grouped into logical tracks. To access block *I* of a file their system:

1. computes the number of the logical track within the file that contains the *I*th block. For example, suppose we wish to retrieve block 57 (of file TESTDATA) and that there are 22 user-accessible blocks in a track. Block 57 is located in the third track of the file.

2. concatenates the file name with the logical track number to form a key. The key in our example is TESTDATA3.

3. looks up the key in a small table of (key, address) pairs. If present, the address is read from the table. (The table stores the addresses of recently accessed tracks.)

4. hashes the key if it is not in the table and, in a conventional way, searches for the track that has the key stored in its key sector. A simple linear probe is used to resolve collisions. (In practice, the entries in the table of step 3 are reserved for recently accessed tracks that are not at the address generated by hashing the key.)

Reserved keys are used to identify free tracks and tracks found to contain sectors causing read/write errors. Stored keys are transparent to the user.

Within the limitations of the size of the key sector a hierarchical filestore could be simulated. In a hierarchical file system, users may create subdirectories to an arbitrary depth. There is usually some mechanism for changing the current or "working" directory. Suppose, for example, that a user has subdirectories DATA and PROGRAMS and in each subdirectory there are files called PROG1 and PROG2. If the current directory is DATA, then a reference to "PROG1" is taken to be a reference to the file in that subdirectory. There is usually a notation for giving "absolute" file references that are independent of the current directory. For example, /DATA/PROG1 would always identify the PROG1 file in DATA. This notation can be simulated in the hash-organized file by allowing a character such as a solidus ("/") to appear in file names. Thus X would represent a normal file X, /Y/X could represent file X in subdirectory Y, /Z/Y/X could represent a file two levels down the tree, and so on.

In conventional file systems, protection codes for a file are normally held in its directory entry. The hashing-based alternative allows different parts of a file to have different protection. Another advantage over conventional systems is that sparse files can be stored in a space-efficient manner. Consider, for example, the requirements of Litwin's virtual hashing.

McGregor and Malone found the first solution to the deletion problem outlined in the open-addressing part of Section 5.2, logical deletion, to be unsatisfactory. To maintain overall performance, rehashing is used. Tracks between the deleted one and the next free one are rehashed. Consider Fig. 5.4 and imagine that the record slots are the logical tracks of the disc. If we delete the file track that was at disc track 203, then the disc is as shown in Fig. 5.4(a). Tracks in locations 204, 205, and 206 are rehashed. In some cases, as shown in Fig. 5.4(b), file tracks may be repositioned on the disc as a result. The hashing-based file system described here has been implemented with good reliability on both floppy discs and large multiplatter discs.

Summary

In this chapter we have discussed direct files, that is, files where a mechanism is available that makes all records accessible at all times. We have seen how the main memory pointer concept can be extended to direct files, and we considered a variety of ways in which a pointer could be implemented. The techniques vary in the amount of translation required to produce a secondary storage address from a pointer and in their vulnerability to changes in the position of the target record.

Fast storage and retrieval of records can result if there is a connection between the key of a record and the address where the record is stored. Typically the address space and key space vary widely in size, so we arrive at the idea of hashing—the mapping of a key onto an address. Various design decisions are required when organizing a file using hashing. For example:

1. What transformation will be used? We saw that methods based on division give good results.

2. How many records will be stored at the same address? That is, what size should the bucket be? We saw the trade-off between bucket search time and probability of bucket overflow.

3. How should the capacity of the file relate to the number of records anticipated? We saw how high storage density increases the probability of bucket overflow.

4. What action should be taken if a particular bucket is full and another record has to be stored there? We considered a variety of computation-oriented and data structure-oriented techniques.

Main memory data structures can be used to reduce the number of disc accesses required in searching and update operations. We saw how tables and trees could be used.

Conventional hashing is good when the number of records stored in a file at any time is close to some predicted number. However, if there is a wide range in the number of records stored, then other techniques are more appropriate. In general, the size of the address space has to vary to maintain a reasonably constant storage density. We examined three techniques: virtual hashing, dynamic hashing, and extendible files. Each allows the number of buckets in a file to vary. They differ in the mechanisms by which the buckets are accessed.

Finally, we saw how hashing has been used to implement a reliable filestore. Reliability is achieved through being able to access blocks of a file directly rather than having to go via a potentially unreliable directory. Use of hashing enables the direct access to be performed in reasonable time.

Hashing in its simplest form can be viewed as a computational technique (as opposed to a data structure technique) for organizing data in direct files. In the next chapter we look at ways of achieving fast access using data structures.

Exercises

1. In a hash-organized file, what are the consequences of having more than one record with the same key? Consider a sequence of insertions and (logical) deletions of a set of records with identical keys. What behavior is exhibited?

2. A possible measure of the sortedness of a file of N records is the number of pairs of records that are out of order expressed as a fraction of the total number of pairs $N!/[2 \times (N - 2)!]$. For benchmarking sorting algorithms, it would be convenient to be able to generate a file with an arbitrary degree of sortedness by this measure. Outline how this could be done.

3. In order to avoid excessive probing, 70% is often regarded as an upper limit on the fullness of a hash file. Investigate what happens to probe lengths as a file fills as follows. Establish a file of 1000 empty records. Fill X% of the records. Insert 50 further records and record the average number of record reads required during an insertion. Plot this number against X. Try values of X from 50 to 96 in steps of 2.

4. In Section 5.2 we suggested a method for hashing student identification numbers. Consider each of the following functions and indicate why it might be inferior to the method chosen.

   a) Add up the last four digits and multiply the result by 99/36.

b) Use the first two digits.

c) Concatenate the third and last digits.

5. Larson's dynamic hashing technique uses binary trees in the index. What would be the consequences of using eight-way trees instead? In your answer make reference to the hash functions, the bucket splitting process, and expected storage utilization.

6. Larson's function B (see Section 5.4) produces a bit string from a key. It can be implemented using pseudo–random numbers. Why would it probably be a mistake to use function H_0 as the means of deriving the seed (X_0) from the key?

7. The highway patrol in a certain state wish to establish a file of vehicle records accessible by license number. Help them by designing a suitable hash function. Assume that there will be 200,000 buckets in the file. License numbers have the following characteristics:

a) Numbers have at least one and no more than seven alphanumeric characters. Most are six or seven characters long.

b) Many plates are of the form llldddd or dlllddd, where d represents a digit and l a letter.

8. How could bit lists be used to improve the efficiency of overflow resolution methods in conventional hashing? (Hint: Consider how input/output transfers might be reduced.)

9. How are records deleted from a file organized using table-assisted hashing? When a record is deleted, is more than one bucket affected? If so, how? What changes, if any, are made to the table?

10. Choose a set of keys, for instance, names of people in your address book or names of radio stations.

a) Design hash functions that map the keys onto the integers 1 through 50.

b) Devise a method of measuring the goodness of a hash function. Use it to evaluate your answers to a).

11. Implement dynamic hashing. Devise a way of storing the tree structure on a file so that it can be preserved when the file is closed. Try trees of various orders, that is, binary trees, three-way trees, four-way trees, and so on. Devise benchmark operations to access and update your file organizations. Plot performance measurements against tree order.

12. Implement extendible hashing. Generate a random initial file and measure the average performance of the system over a large set

of random retrievals, insertions, and deletions. Compute the theoretical expected values. How do they compare?

13. Create a file of the career records of major league baseball players. For example, a record could contain name, games played, lifetime batting average, and number of home runs. Construct the file so that records can be accessed very quickly by name of player. Write two associated programs

    a) to find and retrieve an arbitrary record given a player's name
    b) to update information from game records

14. One advantage of a conventional filestore organization is that it is easy to get a list of names of files currently on disc. Before reading McGregor and Malone's paper, devise a way in which users might be able to get such a listing quickly from a hash-organized disc.

15. What properties does a true hierarchical filestore have that are not present in McGregor and Malone's system? How would you extend their technique to give a user the illusion of a true hierarchical filestore?

6

Indexed Files: Primary Key Indexing of Sequential Files

6.1 Looks at the properties of static indexes—those having a fixed structure.

6.2 Examines the properties of dynamic indexes—indexes where the structure may vary as the indexed file changes.

6.3 Compares the properties of static and dynamic indexes.

Hashing, which we described in Chapter 5, is a computational technique for organizing files. Records in hashed files can be stored and retrieved quickly. The technique is computational in the sense that the address of a required record is, to a large extent, computed from data values in that record. One of the disadvantages of a hash file is that records are difficult to process in key order, which might be important if we want to access all records with keys in a certain range. **Indexing** is a data structure-based technique for accessing records in a file. It is a data structure technique in the sense that a search of a data structure yields the required address. In this technique a main file of records is supplemented by one or more indexes. Indexes may be part of the main file or be separate files, and may be created and destroyed as required without affecting the main file. When changes are made to the main file, appropriate update operations must be carried out on any indexes to that file.

Index files can be compared with the index or table of contents of a book. Consider the index of a book. It consists of a number of entries, each of which is a pair:

topic, page number(s)

Book indexes are usually arranged alphabetically, which makes it easy to find a particular topic and hence the pages on which it is mentioned. An index file is like a book index. Index files typically contain records of the following form:

key value, pointer(s) to main file

The pointers reference records in the main file that have the particular key value. In this chapter we discuss primary key indexing, in which an index entry identifies a unique record in the main file. In Chapter 7 we will look at secondary indexing, in which many records may have a particular value of a secondary key. The space requirements of an index depend to a large extent on the nature of the file being indexed and on the type of index. For example, there is an upper bound on the size of a primary key index to a fixed-length file.

In this chapter we discuss using data structure techniques rather than computational techniques to solve the file accessing problem. We consider the efficiency of the data structures and the operations required to maintain optimum efficiency. It is important to remember that when we discuss "records" in an index, for example, in a node of a search tree, we mean records of the form shown above rather than records of the main file.

Although indexes to sequential files are common, nonsequential files can also be indexed. A sequential file is typically in sequence only with respect to one key. For example, a file of insurance records ordered by policy number would be nonsequential with respect to a second key such as name of policyholder. Hash files, such as those examined in Chapter 5, are unlikely to be in order by any key at all.

Without data structures, processing records with respect to a key other than the one by which the file is sequenced is likely to be inefficient. Consider the file of insurance records. To find a record when given the name of the policyholder, we would probably have to perform a linear search through the file. If we needed a list of policyholders according to date of birth, we would probably have to perform a sort operation.

Except in certain reference books, topics in the body of a book do not normally appear in alphabetical order. Books can therefore be regarded as nonsequential from the point of view of topic. (They are usually sequential from the point of view of chapter and section number.) Indexes help to locate topics. In the remainder of this chapter we consider index organization in the context of indexed sequential files.

A sequential file, you will recall, is one in which records can be accessed in sequential order, which is usually primary key order. An indexed sequential file is a sequential file supplemented by an index structure. The purpose of the index is to speed up access to a particular record. Normally the index is effective only when the file being indexed is stored on a direct-access device. Unindexed sequential files, on the other hand, could reasonably be stored on serial devices.

There are alternatives to indexing as a technique for achieving fast access to sequential files, but they tend to be comparatively slow or restrictive. A binary search is one possibility, but it requires that for a given I it must be possible to compute the address of the Ith record in the file. If sequencing is implemented by pointers rather than physical adjacency, this may not be feasible. Even if it is possible to compute the address, performance of a binary search algorithm is not impressive. Suppose that there are M logical records in a file and that they are packed N to a physical record. The average number of physical accesses required to find a record using a binary search is about $(\log_2\lceil M/N\rceil) - 1$. We will not give further consideration to other methods of access because indexing is more useful.

The way we organize an index file will depend on the operations we wish to perform via the key field. Possible operations include retrieval of individual records and processing of all records in key order. If the index is used only to locate a record with a particular value of a key, then hashing may be a suitable way of organizing it. However, if the index is the means of accomplishing both sequential processing and fast individual record access, then a tree structure is a better choice. This is because sequential processing is accomplished by simple tree traversal and the nature of the tree also allows a particular record to be located quickly. The indexes we examine in this chapter are based on trees.

Because the main file is sequenced, it may not be necessary for the index to have an entry for each record. Figure 6.1 shows a sequential file with a two-level index. Level 1 of the index holds an entry for each three-record section of the main file. In a similar way, level 2 indexes level 1. It may be sufficient for an index to a sequential file simply to identify the part of the main file containing the desired record. The final part of a search operation can then be a simple linear or binary search of the identified section. Typically this will be a search, in main memory, of a physical record retrieved from the file. Consider the book analogy. The table of contents acts as an index in our sense of the term. The file (book) is in sequence by the key being indexed (chapter and section numbers). Section numbers in the body of the text may be long (for example, *p.q.r.s.t*). In the table of contents, however, entries may be limited to *p.q.r*, leaving the reader to interpolate to find more precise subheadings. Thus, while there is still a search space, it has been reduced through use of the index.

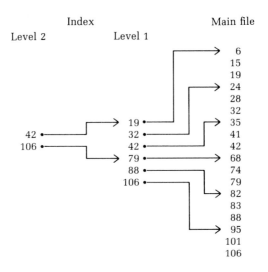

FIGURE 6.1 File with two-level index

Indexed sequential organization is straightforward apart from the problem of inserting new records into the file. The problems are to preserve the sequence of the records and to update the index appropriately. Two broad classes of solutions to these problems are static index techniques and dynamic index techniques.

Although the contents of a **static index** may change as we perform insertions and deletions on the main file, the structure of the index does not change. Typically the insertion algorithm uses overflow areas. This method, however, tends to lead to gradual loss of efficiency for search and update operations, and periodic maintenance is required to restore performance. Typically this involves running a stand-alone program that writes a new version of the main file eliminating overflow lists. The index is rebuilt during the rewriting. The IBM ISAM system [63; 25, ch. 20] uses static index structures.

A **dynamic index** adapts as records are inserted into and deleted from the main file. In some sense, maintenance of efficiency is an integral part of the insert and delete algorithms. There is no need to run a separate maintenance program periodically. Dynamic indexing methods are characterized by the splitting and joining of nodes in the index tree. The IBM VSAM system [64; 25, ch. 20] uses dynamic indexing.

Both static and dynamic indexes are useful depending on the type of application. We will compare their efficiency in carrying out the following file operations:

1. searching for a record with a given key
2. inserting a new record
3. deleting a record with a given key

6.1 Static Indexes

One approach to organizing a tree in a static index structure is to keep its structure fixed and to deal with insertions by means of overflow lists at the leaves. As you will see, it will be useful to include information about overflows in the index.

Organization of the Index

A static index can be regarded as a series of tables of fixed size. The lowest-level table indexes the main file itself, the next highest level indexes the lowest level, and so on. Figure 6.1 showed a small example file with two levels of indexing. A level 1 index entry holds the highest key value in a three-record section of the main file together with a pointer to the section. A typical entry is

42 , <pointer to section with 42 as its highest key>

The choice of three for the size of the main file section is arbitrary here. In practice it is likely to be related to the size of physical and logical records (recall the distinction made in Chapter 1). For example, if the storage device can transfer up to 1024 bytes in one access and logical records are 80 bytes long, each main file section will probably contain 12 records. Thus a complete section can be read in one disc access. The index holds the highest key in each physical record. In a level 2 index entry we hold, together with an appropriate pointer, the highest key value in each three-record section of the level 1 index. Again, the choice of three here for the section size is arbitrary. Given particular file characteristics and properties of the storage media, it is possible to calculate the number of index levels and the total space they occupy (see Exercise 1).

Why do we index a section by its highest rather than its lowest key? To answer this question, let us follow the retrieval of the record with key 28 from Fig. 6.1. We begin at the top of the tree with the level 2 index. We select the smallest index entry with key greater than or equal to the target key. In this case we select 42. The associated pointer points to the level 1 section that contains the following entries:

19 →
32 →
42 →

Using the same selection criteria, we follow the pointer associated with entry 32 in the level 1 index. The pointer gives us the address of the section in the main file containing

    24
    28
    32

When we search this, we find the record with key 28. If we had been looking for a record with key 29 instead, the search would fail when key 32 was encountered.

By holding the highest rather than the lowest key in the index, we avoid an extra comparison at each index level during a search operation. This is because the pointer to the lowest value and the key of the largest value together define a search subspace. For example, the pointer associated with entry 32 in the level 1 index points to the section starting with 24. Any record with a key in the range of 24 through 32 will be in that section. If we hold the lowest key, we would have to look at the next index entry to establish the upper bound on the subspace. You can see that this is true by drawing the structure of Fig. 6.1 and replacing the high key values with the appropriate low key values. Retrace the search for record with key 28 and see how the number of key-key comparisons differs.

Insertions

Next, let us examine the way in which the file and indexes change when insertions are made into the main file. We will insert records with keys 7, 33, and 18. These insertions will cause overflow conditions that must be resolved.

Insert 7. When we insert a record with key 7, the index structure leads us to the first section of three records in the main file. This is where the record with key 7 would be if it were in the file. To preserve the record sequence, the new record must be inserted after the one with key 6. Therefore the record with key 19 is moved out of the main file section and into an overflow area. Figure 6.2 shows the new configuration.

We assume that there is space at the end of each section of records in the main file for a pointer to a list of records that have been moved out of the section. (In our example above, user records occupy 960 out of 1024 bytes, leaving ample room for such a pointer.) Observe that sequential processing of the file is slowed by the need to make an access to the overflow area between records with keys 15 and 24. However, access to an arbitrary record need not be slowed if we modify the level 1 index. Suppose that in addition to holding the

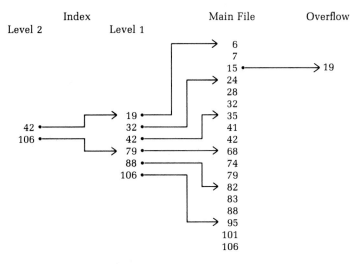

FIGURE 6.2 File with overflow

highest key in either the main file section or its overflow list, it also holds the highest key in the main file section alone. With this information we can tell whether to look for a particular record in the main file or in the overflow area. In the case of our example the level 1 index entry for the first main file section is now

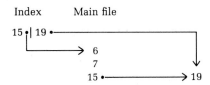

The entry indicates that 15 is the highest key in the section and that 19 is the highest key when the overflow list is taken into account. To go directly from the level 1 index to the appropriate overflow list we will need a pointer from the level 1 index entry to the list. However, in subsequent diagrams we will show the key values in the level 1 index entries but omit pointers to overflow lists to prevent the diagrams from becoming cluttered.

Insert 33. Key 33 lies between the key ranges of the records stored in the second and third three-record sections of the main file. Examination of the level 1 index indicates that if the record with key 33 were already in the file it would be in the third section; its key is greater than the largest key recorded for the second section. Hence

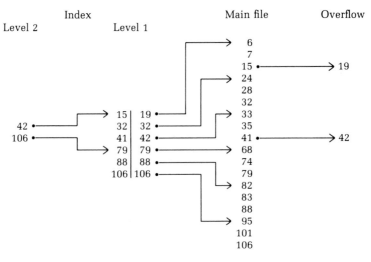

FIGURE 6.3 File with overflow

the new record is inserted into the third section; Fig. 6.3 shows the new configuration. Although the two overflow lists are separate in the diagrams, there is no reason why they should not be stored interleaved in the same file (see the discussion on physical organization of overflow area below).

Insert 18. Key 18 is lower than the highest key associated with the first file section (19) but higher than the last key in the main file section (15). The new record is therefore put directly into the overflow list. Figure 6.4 shows the new configuration. Although sequential accessing of the file may not be slowed further as a result of this insertion, a retrieval of record with key 19 is likely to take longer than before.

Physical Organization of Overflow Area

Above, we discussed in abstract terms how insertions into the main file might be handled. How might an overflow scheme be implemented? One possibility is to write the initial sequential file cylinder by cylinder on a disc, leaving a number of tracks free on each cylinder. Records overflowing from sectors in a cylinder would be placed in the spare tracks in the same cylinder, that is, in a cylinder overflow area. In this way no disc head movement would be required when following a pointer from the main file. If overflows are confined to such areas, sequential processing is reasonably fast. However, what happens if there are enough insertions in one part of the file to

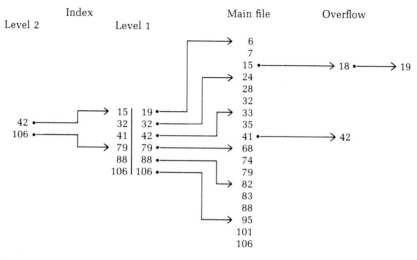

FIGURE 6.4 Overflow chain

exhaust a particular cylinder overflow area? Such clustered insertions—insertions with a small range of key values compared with the
key range of the file as a whole—are a problem for indexed sequential
file organizations. In a static organization, such as that described above,
they will result in long overflow lists. One solution is to provide a
number of spare cylinders that can be used by overflows from any
cylinder. However, if these have to be used, both sequential and direct
processing of the file begin to require time-consuming disc head
movements. Performance degrades rapidly.

A weakness of the static organization is its potential degradation
of performance as insertions are made. In a typical application we
would expect that there would be more retrievals than insertions or
deletions, so it is important that they be as efficient as possible. In a
static organization maintenance programs may have to be run periodically to restore performance levels. During these runs the file is
likely to be inaccessible. In contrast, dynamic indexes, which we discuss next, may gradually change shape in order to preserve efficiency.
Compared with static indexes, more work may be done when a record
is inserted or deleted, but there is no need for separate periodic
maintenance.

6.2 Dynamic Indexes

Many dynamic indexes are implemented as trees. In this chapter we
consider four common tree structures and compare them in terms of:

1. depth (minimum for given number of records)
2. ease of maintenance
3. maximum order

The four tree types are binary, AVL, multiway, and B-trees. We assume that you are familiar with the basic concepts of a tree data structure and terms such as "root" and "node." We adhere to the convention of depicting a tree with the root uppermost and regard the root as the top of the tree.

Binary Trees

Binary trees suffer from two disadvantages compared with other trees: long retrieval times and the effort needed to maintain efficient access. Binary trees have a branching factor of two, that is, each node has at most two immediate descendants (children). Consequently, the minimum height of a tree containing N records is $\lfloor \log_2 N \rfloor + 1$. For example, a tree of 100 records has at least seven levels. If a tree is held on secondary storage, then there tends to be a proportional relationship between the number of node reads and the number of physical seeks. It is therefore desirable to have short trees to minimize the number of physical accesses. Because of the small branching factor, binary trees tend to be tall. For best performance the tree should be balanced in the sense that the sum of the lengths of the paths from the root to the nodes is minimized. After an insertion or a deletion the tree may have to be rebalanced. The operations required to balance an arbitrary tree are relatively complex.[1]

AVL Trees

AVL trees, devised by Adel'son-Vel'skii and Landis [66], are restricted-growth binary trees. They were invented as a solution to the balancing problem encountered with normal binary trees. An AVL tree is not necessarily perfectly balanced. In a perfectly balanced binary tree the number of nodes in the two subtrees of an arbitrary node differ by at most 1. In an AVL tree the heights of the two subtrees differ by at most 1. The balancing operations are simpler than those for ordinary binary trees, but AVL trees still have comparatively long search times. Bounds have been established for the height of an AVL tree containing N records as follows:

---

1. See, for example, Martin and Ness [65].

$$\log_2 (N + 1) \leq \text{height} \leq 1.4404 \log_2 (N + 2) - 0.328$$

Considering again a tree with 100 records, we have

$$6.658211 \leq \text{height} \leq 9.282961$$

The search problem persists because we still have tall trees.

Multiway Trees

Multiway trees are a generalization of binary trees. Instead of containing a record and two pointers, as in a binary tree, a node contains R records and $R + 1$ pointers. This alleviates the long retrieval times found with binary trees. The increase in the branching factor typically makes the tree shorter than the corresponding binary tree for the same number of records. However, complex balancing operations may be required as records are inserted and deleted.

B-trees

B-trees were devised by Bayer and McCreight [67]. They have neither the retrieval nor the maintenance problems of binary trees because they are multiway trees with efficient self-balancing operations. We will therefore consider them in some detail.

B-trees are balanced multiway trees. A node of the tree may contain several records and pointers to "children." We use the term "child" to refer to the immediate descendant of a node; hence "siblings" refers to nodes with the same parent. The operations of retrieval, insertion, and deletion are guaranteed efficient even in the worst case.

B-tree definition. We follow Knuth [40, 6.2.4] rather than Bayer and McCreight and define a B-tree of order M to be a tree with the following properties:

1. No node has more than M children.
2. Every node, except for the root and the terminal nodes, has at least $\lceil M/2 \rceil$ children.
3. The root, unless the tree only has one node, has at least two children.
4. All terminal nodes appear on the same level, that is, are the same distance from the root.
5. A nonterminal node with K children contains $K - 1$ records. A terminal node contains at least $\lceil M/2 \rceil - 1$ records and at most $M - 1$ records.

Recall that we are considering index structures: a record in the tree will therefore consist of a key and a pointer to the main file. We can

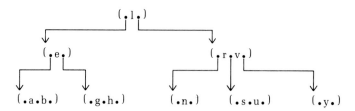

FIGURE 6.5 Example B-tree

speak of a B-tree of order 8 ($M = 8$), a B-tree of order 197 ($M = 197$), and so on. The integer M imposes bounds on the "bushiness" of the tree. While the root and terminal nodes are special cases, normal nodes have between $\lceil M/2 \rceil$ and M children and $\lceil M/2 \rceil - 1$ and $M - 1$ records. For example, a normal node in a tree of order 11 has at least 6 and not more than 11 children. The lower bound on node size ensures that the tree does not get too tall and thin, since this results in slow searches. The upper bound on node size ensures that searches of an individual node will be fast. When implementing the tree, for example, as a file of records, the upper bound allows us to define an appropriate record type. The lower bound ensures that each node is at least half full and therefore that file space is used efficiently.

The definition above only determines the structure of a B-tree; to be useful there must be some ordering of the records in the tree. In what follows we will make the following assumptions:

1. Within a node of $K - 1$ records, records are numbered $R_1, R_2, R_3,$ ..., R_{K-1} and pointers to children are numbered $P_0, P_1, P_2, \ldots,$ P_{K-1}. Thus a typical node may be depicted as follows:

P_0	R_1	P_1	$\ldots$	R_{K-1}	P_{K-1}

2. Records in the subtree rooted in P_0 have keys less than the key of record R_1. Records in the subtree rooted in P_{K-1} have keys greater than the key of record R_{K-1}. Records in the subtree rooted in P_i ($0 < i < K - 1$) have keys greater than the key of record R_i and less than the key of record R_{i+1}.

Figure 6.5 shows an example B-tree. In this and subsequent examples we will assume that the keys of the records in the tree are single characters. Only the keys will be shown, but remember that in fact there are also pointers to a main file.

It is not always possible to determine the order of a tree by looking at it. The tree of Fig. 6.5 must be at least order 3 because some nonroot nodes have three children. At the same time it must be less than order 5 because some nodes have only two children. It is therefore a tree of order 3 or order 4.

We present algorithms and performance figures for each of the search, insert, and delete operations. Note that in the insert and delete operations the balance of the B-tree is maintained.

B-tree terminology. We will term **adjacent siblings** two nodes that have the same parent and are pointed to by adjacent pointers in the parent. Thus in the tree of Fig. 6.5 (.n.) and (.s.u.) are adjacent siblings, whereas (.n.) and (.y.) are not adjacent siblings. Adjacent siblings are pointed to by P_{i-1} and P_i (for some i). We will term record R_i the **separating record** for the two siblings. Thus in the tree of Fig. 6.5 adjacent siblings (.s.u.) and (.y.) are separated by record with key v.

Searching B-trees. When searching for a record with a given key we start by examining the root node. We search the node for the required record. If the record is not found, comparisons with the keys in the node will identify the pointer to the subtree that may contain the record. If the selected pointer is null, then we are at the lowest level in the tree and the record we are searching for is not present in the tree. If the pointer is not null, then we read the node pointed to, that is, the root node of the subtree, and repeat the operation. Figure 6.6 contains a pseudocode algorithm for the search.

Performance of the B-tree search algorithm. Assume the B-tree is of order M and that it contains N records. Consider the null pointers in the terminal nodes. (In the literature [67, 40] these pointers are often regarded as pointers to leaves.) An in-order traversal of a B-tree will alternate between null pointers and records and will start and finish with a null pointer. There are therefore N + 1 null pointers in a tree containing N records. From the definition of the tree, all the null pointers are at the same level; assume this is level h where the root is considered to be level 1. Thus in Fig. 6.5, null pointers are at level 3. The worst case when searching the tree will require h node reads: one at each level 1 through h. We can derive an expression for h in terms of N and M as follows:

At level 2 the minimum number of nodes is 2.

At level 3 the minimum number of nodes is $2 \times \lceil M/2 \rceil$.

$$\vdots$$

At level h + 1 the minimum number of nodes is $2 \times \lceil M/2 \rceil^{h-1}$.

(The null pointers in the terminal nodes might be regarded as pointers to nodes at a nonexistent level h + 1.)

(* In the algorithm
    Found: a flag to indicate if the record has been found
    K   : key of record being searched for
    P   : holds a pointer to a node
    N   : record count
*)

Found ← false
read root

repeat
        N ← number of records in current node
        case
            K = key of record
                in current node: found ← true
            $K < key(R_1)$: $P ← P_0$

            $K > key(R_N)$: $P ← P_N$

            otherwise   : $P ← P_i - 1$ (for some i where $R_i - 1 < K < R_i$)
        endcase
        if P not null
            then read node pointed to by P
until Found or P is null

FIGURE 6.6 B-tree search algorithm

We know there are $N + 1$ null pointers, and therefore

$$N + 1 \geq 2 \times \lceil M/2 \rceil^{h-1}$$

which yields

$$h \leq 1 + \log_{\lceil M/2 \rceil} [(N + 1)/2]$$

This gives us an upper bound on the height of a B-tree of order M containing N records and hence an upper bound on the number of node reads during a retrieval. The minimum number of node reads is clearly one. This is the case where the record being searched for is found in the root.

    Tree-balancing operations are required in two cases when performing insertions or deletions on a B-tree. In the insertion operation a node can overflow because the definition of the tree imposes an upper bound on node size. We can resolve overflow by redistributing records in existing nodes or by splitting the overlarge node. When deleting, on the other hand, we may have node underflow because a node may become smaller than the lower bound on node size. Underflow can be resolved either by redistribution or by **concatenation** of two nodes.

Before
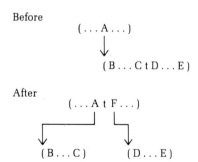

FIGURE 6.7 B-tree node split

B-tree insertion. New records are always inserted into a terminal node. In our diagrammatic representation of a tree, every null pointer represents an insertion point where a new record might go. In Fig. 6.5, for example, records with keys greater than l but less than r would be inserted in the node containing n: to the left of n if less than n and to the right if greater than n. To determine the appropriate insertion point for a particular new record, the insertion algorithm starts by searching for the new record as if it were already in the tree. The search algorithm will bring us to the appropriate point in a terminal node.

As stated earlier, a problem with inserting records is that nodes can overflow because there is an upper bound to the size of a node. What if the node into which we have inserted a record now exceeds the maximum size? This situation can be resolved using **redistribution** or **splitting.** We talk about the possibility of redistributing records during insertions in the section on B*-trees later in this chapter. Here we consider how a node might be split. On overflow, the node is split into three parts. The middle record is passed upward and inserted into the parent, leaving two children behind where there was one before. Suppose that the order of the B-tree is M. The largest number of records allowable in a node is therefore $M - 1$. Splitting an overfull node with M records can be depicted as follows:

Figure 6.7 shows how a pointer to one of the two children is inserted into the parent in addition to a record. As usual, lowercase letters here represent records. Uppercase letters represent pointers. F is a pointer to a newly allocated node.

Splitting may propagate up the tree because the parent into which we inserted a record may have been at its maximum size. Therefore it will also split. If it becomes necessary for the root of the tree to split, then a new root is created that has just two children. This is a valid node because of the third property of a B-tree listed on page 153. If the root splits, then the tree grows by a level. This is the only way that a B-tree grows a level. We can regard the terminal nodes as being the fixed level of a tree that grows up or down only at the top (root). Note that no explicit balancing operations are required in the insertion algorithm.

Figure 6.8 contains a pseudocode algorithm for the insertion of a new record. The insertion algorithm assumes the existence of a stack and a temporary node, called TOOBIG, in main memory. This node has room for one more record and one more pointer than the maximum node allowed in the B-tree. It is used as temporary working space when a node splits.

The insertion algorithm starts by searching for the record to be inserted. This is done in order to bring us to the appropriate terminal node in the tree. During the search, whenever we move from a parent node to one of its children, we push the address of the parent node onto the stack. Later, this will enable us to move from a node to its parent by unstacking an address. The stack mechanism is adequate because the only nodes we are interested in are the direct ancestors of the terminal node where we start insertions. Use of the stack means there is no need for any node to contain a pointer to its parent.

An insertion of a record into the current node can have two possible results. The insertion may occur without any maintenance operations being required, or it may cause overflow.

Case 1: nonoverflow insertion. The current node is not full. In this case we insert the record. We also insert an appropriate pointer so that the number of pointers in the node is still one greater than the number of records. The algorithm terminates.

Case 2: overflow insertion. The current node is full. In this case we copy it into the overlarge node TOOBIG, which has room for one more record and one more pointer than the maximum allowed in a tree node. We then put the records and pointers in TOOBIG back in the tree to effect the splitting operation. The center record is identified; if M is even an arbitrary choice is made between the two central records. Records and pointers to the left of the center record are put back in the current node, the remainder of which is cleared. Records and pointers to the right of the center record are put in a new node.[2]

---

2. We assume that there is a mechanism for allocating new nodes to the tree. A file of node records is a reasonable implementation of the B-tree. We could

```
(* In the algorithm
    In-rec   : the record to be inserted into the tree
    Finished: a flag to indicate if insertion has finished
    Found    : a flag to indicate if record has been found in tree
    P        : holds a pointer to a node
    TOOBIG: an oversize node
    N        : record count
*)

(* Search tree for In-rec forming stack of node addresses. *)
Found ← false
read root
repeat
            N ← number of records in current node
            case
                key(In-rec) = key of record
                            in current node: found ← true
                key(In-rec) < key(R₁)          : P ← P₀

                key(In-rec) > key(Rₙ)          : P ← Pₙ

                otherwise                       : P ← Pᵢ ₋ ₁ (for some i where
                                                            key(Rᵢ ₋ ₁) < key(In-rec) < key(Rᵢ))

            endcase
            if P not null
                then push onto stack address of current node
                        read node pointed to by P
    until Found or P is null
if Found
    then report record with key = key(In-rec) already in tree
    else (* insert In-rec into tree *)
        P ← nil
        Finished ← false
        repeat if current node is not full
                    then put In-rec and P in current node
                        Finished ← true
                    else copy current node to TOOBIG
                        insert In-rec and P into TOOBIG
                        In-rec ← center record of TOOBIG
                        current node ← 1st half of TOOBIG
                        get space for new node, assign address to P
                        new node ← 2nd half of TOOBIG
                        if stack not empty
                            then pop top of stack
                                    read node pointed to
                            else (* tree grows *)
                                get space for new node
                                new node ← pointer to old root, In-rec and P
                                Finished ← true
                until Finished
```

FIGURE 6.8 B-tree insertion algorithm

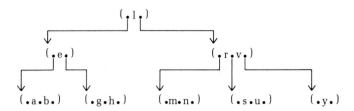

FIGURE 6.9 B-tree of Fig. 6.5 after inserting m

The center record and a pointer to the newly allocated node now have to be inserted into the parent of the current node. The algorithm therefore iterates until at some level no further splitting is needed. If the root has to split, the new root will contain, in addition to the record and pointer passed up from below, a pointer to the old root.

Consider the tree of Fig. 6.5 and the successive insertion of records with keys m, j, p, and d. We will assume the tree to be of order 3. It follows that the largest node can hold two records and three pointers and that the smallest node can hold one record and two pointers. TOOBIG can hold three records and four pointers.

Insert m. This is a simple insertion. The key is greater than l but less than r, so the record goes into the node with n. Because there is enough room in this node for a new record, the insertion algorithm finishes. Figure 6.9 shows the new tree.

Insert j. The record with key j should go in the node currently containing g and h. However, this node is at its maximum size, so records g, h, and j are put into the TOOBIG node. The middle record (h) is then inserted into the parent node. The remaining records form two children where there was one child before. Figure 6.10(a) shows the intermediate step and Fig. 6.10(b) the final result of inserting a record with key j into the tree of Fig. 6.9.

Insert p. When we insert a record with key p into the final tree of Fig. 6.10, we find that the splitting operation occurs at two levels.

keep a list of the records not currently used in the tree. When a new node is required by the insertion algorithm one could be taken from the list. (We will see on page 166 that the deletion algorithm sometimes discards nodes from the tree. They would be added to the free node list.) Only if the list were empty would the insertion algorithm need to invoke mechanisms to extend the file.

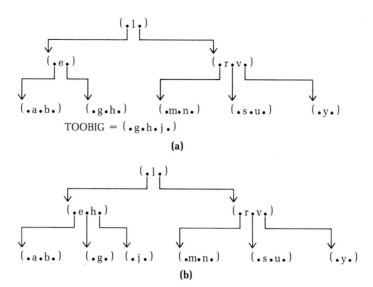

FIGURE 6.10 B-tree of Fig. 6.9 after inserting j

Initially the record is put in TOOBIG with records m and n (see Fig. 6.11a). When this splits, record n is passed up to be inserted into the parent. However, the parent is already full, so TOOBIG holds the parent and record n (see Fig. 6.11b). When TOOBIG is split, record r is passed up to the root. The final tree is shown in Fig. 6.11(c).

Insert d. The insertion of the final record into our tree causes splitting to occur all the way up to the root and the tree to grow one level. Initially record d goes into TOOBIG together with records a and b (see Fig. 6.12a). When TOOBIG splits, record b is passed up to the parent. However, because the parent is already full, its contents are copied with record b into TOOBIG (see Fig. 6.12b). When TOOBIG splits again, record e is passed up to the root. Because the root is already full, TOOBIG is set up again containing the old root and record e (see Fig. 6.12c). When TOOBIG splits for the final time, a new root is created and the tree grows by a level. Figure 6.12(d) shows the final tree.

Performance of the insertion algorithm. The best case for the insertion algorithm is when there is room for the new record in the initial node. In this case we have to read h nodes (where h is the height of the tree) and write one node. The worst case is illustrated by our last example. If the tree is split all the way up to the root, then h + 1 new nodes are created (where h is the height of the tree before

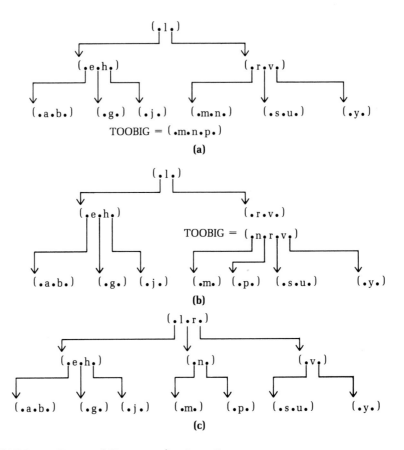

FIGURE 6.11 B-tree of Fig. 6.10 after inserting p

insertion). That is, we must read h nodes and write $2h + 1$ nodes. Knuth [40] reports that the average number of nodes split during an insertion is $1/(\lceil M/2\rceil - 1)$, where M is the order of the tree. Thus, as M increases, the average number of node splits decreases. For example, if M is 10, the expected number of splits per insertion is 0.25. This drops to 0.02 when M is 101. The minimum and maximum number of node reads are both h. This is because insertion is always initially into a terminal node. The minimum number of node writes is one when, as in the case of our first example, the record can be inserted in a lowest-level node. The maximum number of node writes is $2h + 1$, which occurs when the root splits and the tree grows a level.

   An alternative to splitting as a means of resolving an overlarge node is to redistribute records in a local area of the tree. If an adjacent

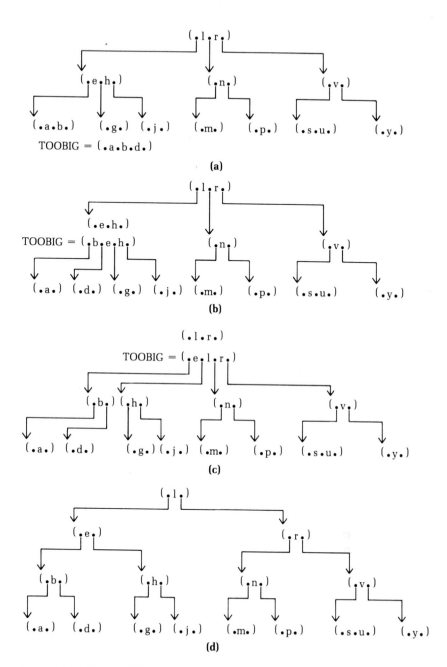

FIGURE 6.12 B-tree of Fig. 6.11 after inserting *d*

sibling of the overlarge node has spare room, records can be moved from one node to the other. Naturally, the ordering of records in the tree must be preserved. We have not, however, included redistribution in the insertion algorithm. This is left as an exercise for the reader (see Exercise 11). Redistribution will, however, be discussed in the context of deletions from a B-tree.

B-tree deletions. As in the insert operation, we always start the delete operation at the lowest level of the tree. If the record we need to delete is not in a terminal node, then we replace it by a copy of its successor, that is, the record with the next highest key. The successor will be at the lowest level (see, for example, the tree of Fig. 6.5). We then delete the successor record. (Note that using the predecessor rather than the successor would work just as well.) A problem with deletions is that after a record has been removed from a node we may have **underflow;** the node may be smaller than the minimum size. This situation can be resolved by means of redistribution or concatenation.

Redistribution is possible when an adjacent sibling of the node with underflow has records to spare; that is, it contains more than the minimum number of records. Redistribution involves moving records among the adjacent siblings and the parent; thus the structure of the tree is not changed. Concatenation, which is performed when redistribution is not possible, involves the merging of nodes and is the complement of the splitting process we saw with insertions. If concatenation is performed, the structure of the tree changes. Changes may propagate all the way to the root. In extreme cases the root node is removed and the tree shrinks by one level. Figure 6.13 contains a pseudocode algorithm for the deletion of a record from a B-tree.

The deletion algorithm starts by searching for the record to be deleted. As with the insertion algorithm, node addresses are put on a stack during the search to make it simple to move from a node to its parent later. If the record is not in a terminal node, then we cannot delete it directly. Instead, we move to its successor (stacking addresses again) and replace the record to be deleted by a copy of its successor. Because of the structure of a B-tree, the successor of any record not at the lowest level will be in a terminal node. The redundant lowest-level record is then deleted. Thus in all cases deletion involves removing a record from a terminal node. The successor of record R_i is the first record in the subtree pointed to by P_i. It can be located by moving down the P_0 pointers in that subtree until the lowest level is reached.

In addition to removing the record from the current node, we also remove one of the adjacent pointers. In this way the number of records

(* In the algorithm
   Finished   : a flag that indicates if deletion has finished
   TWOBNODE : an oversize node that is about 50% larger than a normal node
   A-sibling   : an adjacent sibling node
   Out-rec   : the record to be deleted from the tree
*)

search tree for Out-rec forming stack of node addresses
(see Fig. 6.8 for details)

if Out-rec is not in terminal node
   then search for successor record of Out-rec at terminal level (stacking node addresses)
      copy successor over Out-rec
      terminal node successor now becomes the Out-rec

(* remove record and adjust tree *)

Finished ← false
repeat
      remove Out-rec (record R_i) and pointer P_i
      if current node is root or is not too small
        then Finished ← true
        else if redistribution possible (* an A-sibling > minimum *)
           then (* redistribute *)
              copy "best" A-sibling, intermediate parent record, and
                current (too-small) node into TWOBNODE
              copy records and pointers from TWOBNODE to "best"
                A-sibling, parent, and current node so A-sibling and
                current node are roughly equal size
              Finished ← true
          else (* concatenate with appropriate A-sibling *)
              choose best A-sibling to concatenate with
              put in the leftmost of the current node and A-sibling the
                contents of both nodes and the intermediate record
                from the parent
              discard rightmost of the two nodes
              intermediate record in parent now becomes Out-rec
    until Finished

if no records in root
   then (* tree shrinks *)
      new root is the node pointed to by the current root
      discard old root

FIGURE 6.13 B-tree deletion algorithm

in the node will still be one less than the number of pointers. We choose, arbitrarily, to delete the pointer following the deleted record. If the new node size is not below the minimum, the algorithm terminates.

We can deal with underflow either by redistribution or by concatenation. Usually a too-small node can be resolved by redistributing records in a local area of the tree. Redistribution is possible if either adjacent sibling contains more than the minimum number of records. Redistribution involves moving records from the selected adjacent sibling through the parent to the too-small node. We assume in the algorithm the existence of a temporary main memory variable TWOBNODE. This has to be big enough to hold the contents of the too-small node, one of its adjacent siblings, and a record from the parent. If M, the order of the tree, is odd, then the capacity of TWOB-NODE must be

$1.5M - 1.5$ records $(1.5M - 0.5$ pointers$)$.

If M is even, then the capacity must be

$1.5M - 2$ records $(1.5M - 1$ pointers$)$.

Redistribution involves bringing into TWOBNODE the contents of the too-small node, one of its adjacent siblings, and the appropriate separating record from the parent. These records and pointers are then redistributed in a way similar to the splitting of TOOBIG in the insertion algorithm. The central record from TWOBNODE is the one written back to the parent. The left and right halves remaining are written back to the two siblings.

Given a choice of sibling nodes to use, we might reasonably choose to use the one that will cause the new sizes of the two sibling nodes to be closest to 75% full. They would then be as far as possible from the two size bounds. We could thus hope to minimize the possibility, assuming insertions and deletions to be equally likely, of future expensive splitting, concatenation, or redistribution operations. To avoid additional node reads when deciding which sibling to use, parent nodes could hold, together with each pointer to a child, a count of the number of records the child contains. However, while this would speed up the delete operation, maintaining the counts would be a considerable overhead in the insert operation.

Redistribution is not possible if the too-small node does not have an adjacent sibling node that is more than minimally full. In this case we have to use concatenation. We merge the too-small node with one of its adjacent siblings and the appropriate separating record from the parent. The resulting node replaces one of the concatenated nodes that is then discarded.

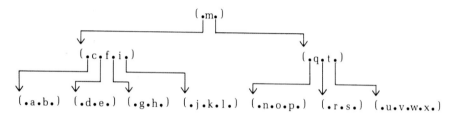

FIGURE 6.14 Example B-tree

If we examine the properties of the B-tree, we see that concatenation is possible only in relatively rare circumstances. If M, the order of the tree, is odd, then concatenation is possible only if an adjacent sibling is minimally full, that is, contains $(M - 1)/2$ records. If the sibling were larger than this, the node would exceed the maximum size after concatenation. If M is even, then concatenation is possible only if a sibling is minimally full or contains one record over the minimum. We are unlikely, therefore, to have a choice between siblings with which to concatenate. However, if there is such a choice, we could again choose the sibling that results in the size of the new node being furthest from the two extremes.

Concatenation of two children removes a record from the parent; the separating record that is used in forming the new node has to be deleted from the parent node. If the parent node becomes too small by this deletion, then the problem of resolving a too-small node has to be solved at the next level up. In the most extreme case, concatenation takes place all the way up the tree. It may be that we remove the only record in the root, leaving just a pointer. In this case we can discard the root; the node pointed to by the pointer becomes the new root. This is the only way in which the height of a B-tree can decrease.

Consider the tree of Fig. 6.14 and the successive deletion of records with keys j, m, r, h, and b. We will assume the tree to be of order 5; it follows that the largest node can hold four records and five pointers and the smallest node two records and three pointers. TWOB-NODE can hold six records and seven pointers.

Delete j. The first deletion is a simple one from the lowest level of the tree. The tree after deletion is shown in Fig. 6.15.

Delete m. In this case the record to be deleted is not at the lowest level in the tree, so we replace it with a copy of its successor (the record with key n) and then delete the lowest-level successor. The resulting tree is shown in Fig. 6.16.

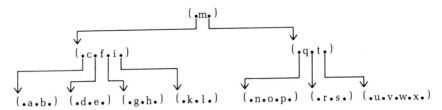

FIGURE 6.15 B-tree of Fig. 6.14 after deleting j

Delete r. Deletion of record r makes the resulting node too small. However, we can resolve the situation without altering the structure of the tree by redistributing records, because one of the adjacent siblings is more than minimally full. Records in the two adjacent siblings, together with the separating record in the parent, are thus brought into TWOBNODE and redistributed. Figure 6.17(a) shows the tree after the initial deletion and also shows the contents of TWOBNODE. Figure 6.17(b) shows the tree after redistribution.

Delete h. When we delete the record with key h, the resulting node is again too small. However, in this case we cannot resolve it using redistribution because neither adjacent sibling has records to spare. We therefore use concatenation. Records and pointers from the too-small node and the separating record from the parent are inserted into an adjacent sibling. The too-small node is then discarded. Figure 6.18(a) shows the tree after the deletion and shows the choice of adjacent sibling. Figure 6.18(b) shows the tree after concatenation.

Delete b. When the record with key b is deleted from the tree of Fig. 6.18(b) we have underflow. This is resolved using concatenation. However, in this case, removing a record from the parent causes it in turn to become too small (see Fig. 6.19a). The too-small node cannot be resolved using redistribution because its only sibling is minimally full. Therefore concatenation takes place at this level, too. The result

FIGURE 6.16 B-tree of Fig. 6.15 after deleting m

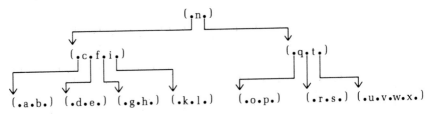

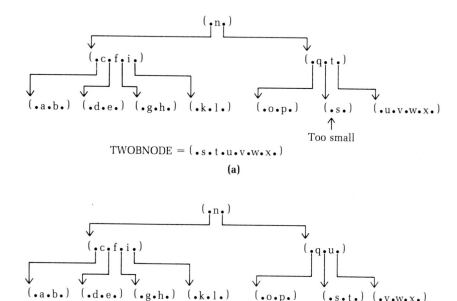

TWOBNODE = (.s.t.u.v.w.x.)

(a)

(b)

FIGURE 6.17 B-tree of Fig. 6.16 after deleting r

is shown in Fig. 6.19(b). Note now, however, that bringing a record down from the root causes the root to contain no records. It can therefore be removed; thus the final tree is as shown in Fig. 6.19(c).

Performance of the deletion algorithm. The best case of the deletion algorithm is illustrated by our first example, that is, when the record to be deleted is at the lowest level. In this case we have to read h nodes (where h is the height of the tree) and write one node (to put back the modified node). The worst case, according to Bayer and McCreight [67], occurs when concatenation occurs at all but the first two nodes in the path from the root to the lowest-level deletion node, the child of the root has underflow, and the root itself is modified. In this case, $2h - 1$ nodes are read and $h + 1$ nodes are written. However, because the majority of records are at the lowest level, Bayer and McCreight report that on average during a delete operation the number of node reads is less than $h + 1 + 1/k$ and the number of node writes is less than $4 + 2/k$, where $k = \lceil M/2 \rceil - 1$.

A number of variations on the B-tree data structure have been devised. Typically, each is designed to overcome some of the deficiencies of the B-tree. In the next two sections we consider two such variations: B*-trees, which arise from a suggestion by Bayer and McCreight [67], and B⁺-trees, which were suggested by Knuth [40].

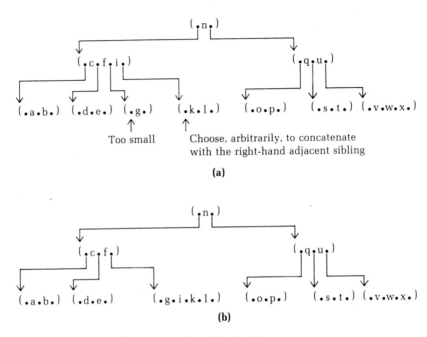

(a)

(b)

FIGURE 6.18 B-tree of Fig. 6.17 after deleting h

B*-trees

Searches. The B*-tree performs searches in the same way as the B-tree, except that there are different bounds on node sizes (see page 173).

Insertions. Bayer and McCreight [67] considered making the insertion operation of a B-tree more efficient by reducing the number of occasions when a node had to be split. If the node into which we need to insert a record is full, we might in certain circumstances be able to solve the overflow problem by local redistribution of records rather than by splitting the nodes. Here we consider three possible techniques for redistributing records: right-only, right-or-left, and right-and-left. The names are derived from the adjacent sibling nodes involved.

Right-only redistribution. The right-only redistribution process is similar to the redistribution in the B-tree deletion algorithm of Fig. 6.13. The proposed algorithm examines the right sibling of the node that is too full (or the left sibling if there is no right one). Redistribution is possible if the sibling node is not full. Thus we must split a node only if the sibling is full. When we do split, we distribute records

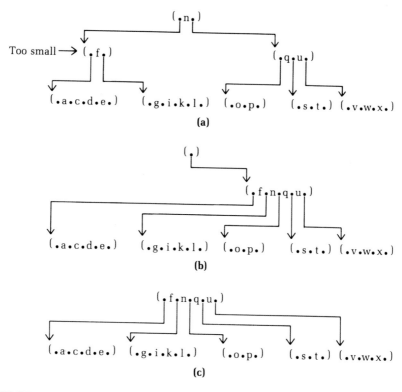

FIGURE 6.19 B-tree of Fig. 6.18 after deleting b

from the two adjacent siblings (one full, one overfull) into three nodes: the two siblings and a new node. One effect of this splitting strategy is that tree nodes will now be at least two-thirds full instead of at least half-full, as in a B-tree.

Right-or-left redistribution. Right-or-left redistribution is similar to right-only redistribution except when the right sibling is full. In this case, the left sibling is checked for possible redistribution. Nodes are split only when both siblings are full. Again, we distribute records from two full nodes into three nodes. Right-or-left distribution post-pones node splitting, so the resulting tree will contain nodes that are, on the average, fuller than with the right-only technique.

Right-and-left redistribution. We could go further than the right-or-left redistribution. At the time a node is split in the right-or-left technique we are likely to have copies of the three nodes and the two parent records in main memory. These are the originally full node,

TABLE 6.1 Redistribution costs

	Required Disc I/O								
	Best Case				Worst Case				
Right-only redistribution	r	r	w	w	r	r	w	w	w
Right-or-left redistribution	r	r	w	w	r	r	r	w	w	w
Right-and-left redistribution	r	r	w	w	r	r	r	w	w	w	w

its right and left siblings, and the separating records in the parent node. At this point we could redistribute three nodes into four. With this algorithm the lower bound on node size would in most cases be raised to three-quarters full. However, not every node has two siblings, so the split routines involving the right or left sibling only would have to be employed occasionally.

We can compare the expected performance characteristics of the three possible redistribution techniques based on the number of reads and writes required on the B*-tree file under the following three assumptions. First, we assume that all nodes required will be available in main memory. Second, we assume that the necessary preconditions for the technique have been satisfied. For example, in the case of the right-and-left technique, we assume that the node has both a right and left sibling. Third, we assume that each technique has a roughly equal probability of propagating splits up the tree. Thus, in this comparison we examine only the local effect of the three redistribution techniques on the sibling nodes. That is, we do not include rewriting the parent node in our metrics, as it is a constant. Table 6.1 presents the number of reads (r) and writes (w) required for the three techniques.

The best case for each technique is when the right sibling is not full. Two nodes are read and then written back. The worst case for the right-or-left technique, for example, is when the right sibling is full and thus the left sibling must be read. The left sibling is full, so we have to split and write three nodes. Recall for comparison that a split-on-overflow strategy results in a "r w w" case with nodes at least half full. What, then, are the advantages of local redistribution? There are two. First, the nodes are used more efficiently with a minimum capacity of $\lfloor (2M - 2)/3 \rfloor$ records in the case of the first two techniques and $\lfloor (3M - 3)/4 \rfloor$ records in the third case. Second, with redistribution, splitting does not propagate up the tree. Note, however, that the range of node size in a B*-tree is smaller than that in a B-tree of the same order. If the tree is volatile, there may consequently be more occasions on which underflow or overflow has to be resolved.

With these redistribution assumptions and the analysis above, the right-only redistribution technique seems preferable. The right-only

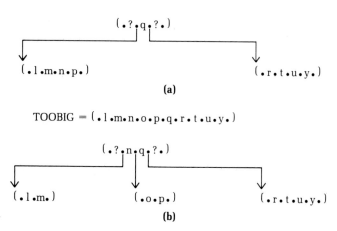

FIGURE 6.20 Node splitting in B*-tree

technique is simple and gives the advantages of redistribution with little I/O overhead. Therefore, our further discussion will assume a right-only redistribution algorithm.

For an example of a case where node-splitting is necessary, assume that we have a B*-tree of order 5, with the three nodes depicted in Fig. 6.20(a). An attempt to insert a record with key o into the B*-tree will result in a merging and splitting sequence that transforms the tree in Fig. 6.20(a) into the tree in Fig. 6.20(b). Records with keys shown as ? are not relevant to the example.

The root node has no siblings. What happens if it needs to split? As before, the central record will become the new root and the remaining parts of the old root will form the first level of the tree. However, to ensure that these children are not smaller than the new minimum size we defined above, the upper bound on the root has to be modified. For a B*-tree of order M the upper bound of the root node will now be $2\lfloor (2M - 2)/3 \rfloor$ records. When the root splits, it will leave two nodes each containing $\lfloor (2M - 2)/3 \rfloor$ records. Thus we now have a tree with two different node capacities (root node and other nodes).

Knuth [40, 6.2.4] termed the tree that results from these modifications a B*-tree. A B*-tree of order M has the following properties:

1. No node apart from the root has more than M children.

2. Every node, except for the root and the terminal nodes, has at least $\lfloor (2M - 2)/3 \rfloor + 1$ children.

3. The root, unless the tree has only one node, has at least two children and at most $2\lfloor (2M - 2)/3 \rfloor + 1$ children.

TABLE 6.2 Maximum and minimum node sizes

		M = 20	M = 21	M = 22
B-tree (order M)				
Minimum records (root)	1	1	1	1
Maximum records (root)	$M - 1$	19	20	21
Minimum records (nonroot)	$\lceil (M - 2)/2 \rceil$	9	10	10
Maximum records (nonroot)	$M - 1$	19	20	21
B*-tree (order M)				
Minimum records (root)	1	1	1	1
Maximum records (root)	$2 \lfloor (2M - 2)/3 \rfloor$	24	26	28
Minimum records (nonroot)	$\lfloor (2M - 2)/3 \rfloor$	12	13	14
Maximum records (nonroot)	$M - 1$	19	20	21

4. All terminal nodes appear on the same level, that is, they are the same distance from the root.

5. A nonterminal node with K children contains $K - 1$ records. A terminal node contains at least $\lfloor (2M - 2)/3 \rfloor$ records and at most $M - 1$ records.

Table 6.2 shows maximum and minimum node sizes for root and nonroot nodes. The figures for a B-tree and a B*-tree are given for trees of order 20, 21, and 22.

Deletions. What do we do if a deletion leaves a node too small? As in the case of a B-tree, we can locally redistribute records if an adjacent sibling has records to spare. If there is no such sibling we must concatenate. Note that the only concatenation normally allowable is of three nodes into two. (The exception is when the only two children of the root are concatenated and the tree shrinks a level.) What happens, however, if we are dealing with a node at one end of a tree level? Such a node has only one adjacent sibling. See, for instance, node X in Fig. 6.21(a) or (b). We know that node W is minimally full; otherwise redistribution would have been possible. However, we cannot necessarily concatenate V, W, and X. If V is not minimally full, the result will be too large to fit into two nodes. One solution is to redistribute a single record so that W is now too small and X is minimally full. Now we have an instance of the more general case. Redistribution can be tried; if it turns out that V is minimally full, then V, X, and W can be concatenated.

Comparison with B-tree. The height (h) of a B*-tree of order M containing N records is given in the following expression:

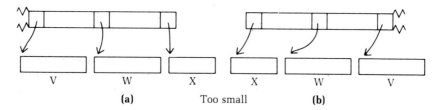

(a)   Too small   (b)

FIGURE 6.21 Node underflow—special case

$$h \leq 1 + \log_{\lceil (2M-1)/3 \rceil} [(N + 1)/2]$$

Searching a B*-tree is faster on average than searching a B-tree for a particular N and M due to the higher average branching factor. However, B-trees are better for applications where insertions or deletions are more common than searches. B*-trees are thus better when searching is the most common tree operation.

B^+-trees

Knuth [40, 6.2.4] proposed a variation on B-trees that for clarity Comer [68] designated the B^+-tree. Records in a B^+-tree are held only in the terminal nodes of the tree. The terminal nodes are linked together to facilitate sequential processing of the records and are termed the **sequence set**. Nonterminal nodes are indexes to lower levels in a way similar to the structure of Fig. 6.1. Nodes in the index levels contain only key values and tree pointers. There is no need for terminal nodes to have tree pointer fields. Thus terminal nodes have a different structure from nonterminal nodes. In fact, there is no reason why the index part of the tree should not be stored on a different device than the terminal nodes.

Figure 6.22 shows a B^+-tree. To make the distinction clear, index records in the tree are shown thus:

[key. .]

and keys are shown as single letters. The records in the tree are those of the B-tree of Fig. 6.5. The records were inserted into the B^+-tree in arbitrary order; thus the index structure shown is one of many possibilities.

Recall that terminal nodes contain records and index level nodes contain only keys. In addition, for efficiency, node capacity is likely to be a function of the physical record size. Therefore it is likely that the order of a B^+-tree index will be different from the capacity of the terminal nodes in its sequence set. Suppose, for example, that physical

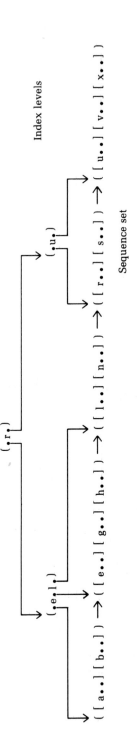

FIGURE 6.22 Example B⁺-tree

records are 512 bytes long, that index records are composed of an 8-byte key and a 4-byte pointer to the file being indexed, and that internal tree pointers occupy 2 bytes. We can pack 42 index records in a 512-byte terminal node and leave 8 bytes for the pointer to the next terminal node. In the index levels we can have 50 eight-byte keys and 51 tree pointers in each 512-byte node and have 10 bytes free in which to store the number of records currently in the node.

The properties of a B^+-tree of order M are as follows:

1. The root node has 0, 2, or $\lceil M/2 \rceil$ through M children.
2. All nodes except the root and terminal nodes have at least $\lceil M/2 \rceil$ children and not more than M children.
3. All terminal nodes appear at the same level; that is, they are the same distance from the root.
4. A nonterminal node with K children contains $K - 1$ keys.
5. Terminal nodes represent the sequence set of the data file and are linked together.

Insertions. If the node splits when we insert a record into a terminal node of a B^+-tree, we put a copy of the key of the central record in TOOBIG into the index. We then divide all the records in TOOBIG between the old node and a new node. Thus the central record will also be in one of the two halves after splitting. If an index node has to split, the algorithm is the same as for a conventional B-tree and the central record is passed up to the parent. Figure 6.23 shows the evolution of a B^+-tree. It is only one of the possible ways in which the tree of Fig. 6.22 might have evolved. For this example we assume that terminal nodes can hold two or three records and index nodes one or two keys. Figure 6.23(a) shows the tree after only three records have been inserted. Insertion of a record with key n causes the terminal node to split in two and the key r to be passed into the index. It is the first key in the index. This is shown in Fig. 6.23(b). Figure 6.23(c) shows the tree after records with keys e and s have been inserted. Insertion of a record with key l causes another terminal node to split and a second key to be inserted into the index. This is shown in Fig. 6.23(d). Finally, insertion of a record with key v causes a terminal node to split, a key to be inserted into the index, and the root of the index to split. Now we have two index levels, as shown in Fig. 6.23(e).

Deletions. When a record is deleted from the B^+-tree and no redistribution or concatenation is needed, no changes need be made to the index. Even if the key of the record to be deleted appears in the index, it can be left as a separator. Figure 6.24 shows the tree of Fig. 6.22 after the deletion of record with key e.

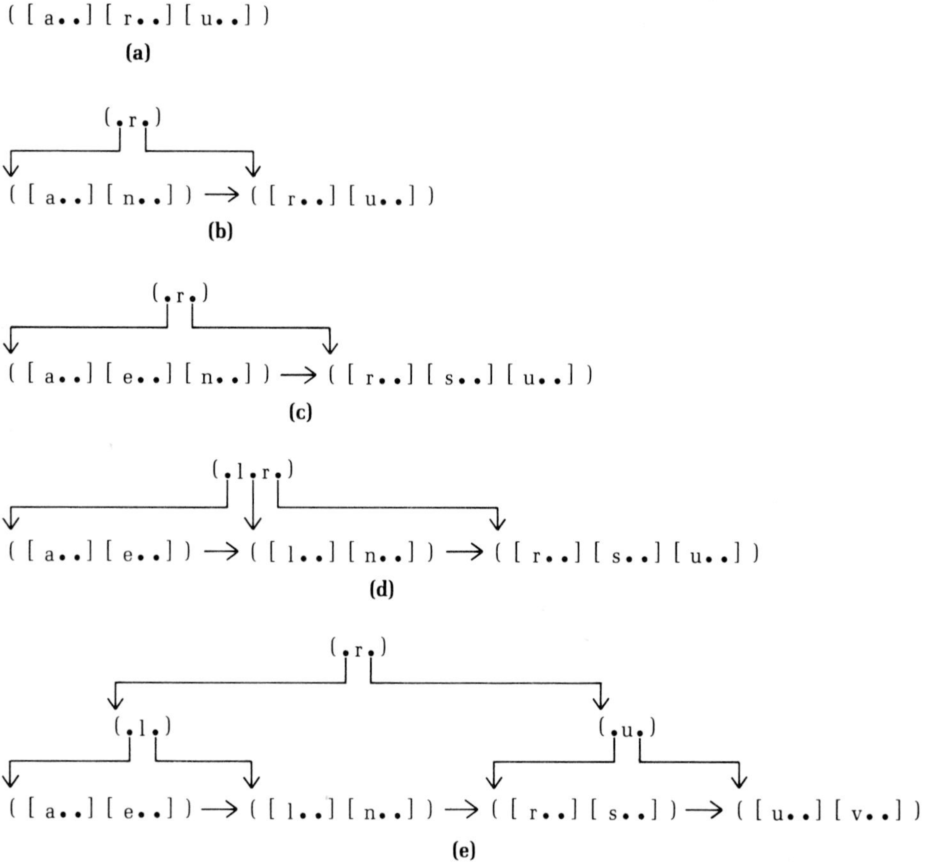

([a . .] [r . .] [u . .])

(a)

(. r .)

([a . .] [n . .]) → ([r . .] [u . .])

(b)

(. r .)

([a . .] [e . .] [n . .]) → ([r . .] [s . .] [u . .])

(c)

(. l . r .)

([a . .] [e . .]) → ([l . .] [n . .]) → ([r . .] [s . .] [u . .])

(d)

(. r .)

(. l .)   (. u .)

([a . .] [e . .]) → ([l . .] [n . .]) → ([r . .] [s . .]) → ([u . .] [v . .])

(e)

FIGURE 6.23 Evolution of B^{+}-tree

Deletions that result in redistribution of records cause changes in the content but not the structure of the index levels. Figure 6.25 shows the tree of Fig. 6.24 after the deletion of record with key s.

Finally, deletions that result in concatenation of terminal nodes also cause deletions from the index levels. Figure 6.26 shows the effect of deleting a record with key g from the tree of Fig. 6.25.

Comparison with B-tree. All searches in a B^{+}-tree have to go down to the terminal nodes. However, because the index levels hold only keys rather than complete index records, searching time is comparable with a B-tree holding the same number of records. Sequential processing in a conventional B-tree is more complex than traversing a linked list (see Exercise 7) and may also require that more than one

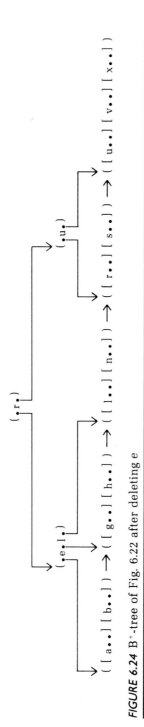

FIGURE 6.24 B⁺-tree of Fig. 6.22 after deleting e

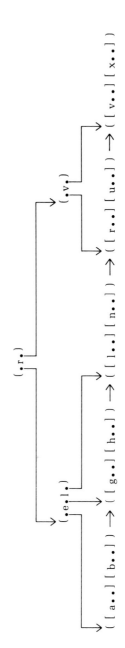

FIGURE 6.25 B⁺-tree of Fig. 6.24 after deleting s

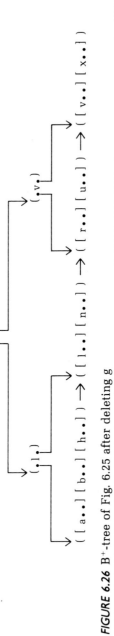

FIGURE 6.26 B⁺-tree of Fig. 6.25 after deleting g

node be held in main memory simultaneously. In a B$^+$-tree, getting the next record in sequence requires at most one node read. B$^+$-trees are therefore good in applications in which both direct and sequential processing are required.

6.3 Comparison of Static and Dynamic Indexes

Held and Stonebraker [69] compared the properties of static index structures typified by ISAM with those of dynamic structures typified by B-trees and VSAM. They suggest that while a dynamic structure is easier to reorganize, there is a price to pay for this and that the costs are threefold.

First, there may be pointers into the B-tree from other files. For example, the B-tree may be the main file with index files pointing into it. Certain operations on a B-tree may require a record to be moved from one node to another (see the insert and delete examples). Such movements are likely to require changes to the pointers to the records that are moved; recall our discussion of pointers in Section 5.1. Thus the insert and delete operations on the B-tree may have hidden overheads.

Second, there may be concurrency problems in multiuser systems. One user may try to access a B-tree while another is updating it. The problem of locking out nodes is not trivial.[3]

Finally, B-trees need explicit pointers in nonleaf nodes because nodes can be split dynamically. A B-tree node can therefore hold fewer records than a node of the same total size that does not require such pointers. The branching factor is therefore smaller and the height of the tree likely to be greater than that of a static structure holding the same number of records. Operations such as search, insert, and delete will therefore tend to take longer than they would for a static index to a file with no overflows.

Summary

In the same way that a book index or table of contents provides a fast way to access parts of a book, indexes provide fast access paths to records in a file. We can create and destroy indexes without affecting the main file, but they may need to change as the indexed file changes. Primary key indexing typically involves identifying the record with

---

3. See, for example, Lehman and Yao [70].

a given primary key. Secondary indexing, similar to a book index, is typically concerned with locating all records having a particular value of a secondary key. We look at secondary indexing in Chapter 7.

We identified two categories of index structure: static and dynamic. A static index keeps the same structure while insertions and deletions are performed on the main file. Although retrievals tend to take longer as overflow lists get longer, performance can be restored by periodic maintenance. A dynamic index, on the other hand, adapts as the main file changes.

Indexes are often tree-structured because search operations are efficient and sequential processing is normally easy. A B-tree is a multiway tree with bounds on the node size. The B-tree organization is particularly suitable because the search, insert, and delete operations are guaranteed efficient even in the worst case. We also compared the B-tree with two variations: B*-trees and B$^+$-trees. Good examples of some of the techniques described in this chapter can be found in a description of the INGRES database system by Stonebraker et al. [71].

Exercises

1. Suppose that you are storing a file of N records on a disc that can transfer up to B bytes in one access. We will term this amount of data one disc block. Each of the N records is L bytes long, of which K bytes is the key.

   a) How many disc blocks does the file occupy, assuming that no record spans two blocks?

   b) How many blocks (on the same disc) would level 1 of a static index occupy? Assume that a pointer occupies two bytes and that an index entry at level 1 contains two keys and two pointers.

   c) How many levels of index will there be in total? Assume that if the level I index occupies only one block, then there are no level J indexes ($J > I$).

   d) What is the total amount of space occupied by the indexes in question c?

2. There may be advantages in storing the indexes to a file and the file itself on separate devices. What are the implications of an increase in the size of the disc block on the device holding the index? Assume:

   main file: 10000 records
   main file block size: 1024 bytes
   record length: 80 bytes

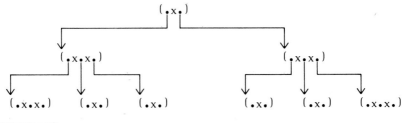

FIGURE 6.27

___

key length: 8 bytes
pointer length: 2 bytes

Using the formulas from Exercise 1, or otherwise, compute the number of index levels and total index space for each index block size from 256 bytes to 3072 bytes (in steps of 256 bytes).

3. Derive expressions for (a) the minimum and (b) the maximum number of records in a B-tree of order M with records at L levels in the tree.

4. A B-tree of order 6 contains 17 records. The keys of the records are

   8, 13, 26, 28, 41, 49, 54, 67, 83, 84, 96, 107, 132, 146, 151, 154, 170

   The tree has three levels (the root and two levels below). Draw the tree. Draw it also as it appears after each operation in the following sequence.

   a) Delete record with key 83.
   b) Delete record with key 67.
   c) Delete record with key 26.

5. Fig. 6.27 is a B-tree of order 3, with x's marking the locations of the records. The tree in fact holds records with the following single-character keys:

   P, Y, A, Q, F, W, J, T, B, L, M, D, U

   a) Draw the tree, showing where each record would appear.
   b) Draw the relevant parts of the tree as they would appear after each step in the following sequence of operations.
      (1) Insert record with key X.
      (2) Delete record with key Q.
      (3) Delete record with key M.
      (4) Insert record with key C.

6. We implicitly assumed in discussing B-trees that a tree does not

contain two or more records with the same key. Will the search, insert, and delete algorithms work if there are duplicate keys? Why or why not?

7. Devise an algorithm for traversing a B-tree. Generalize your solution so that it can output in sequence all records with keys greater than K1 and less than K2, for arbitrary K1 and K2. Implement your solution and ensure that it gives sensible output for any K1 and K2.

8. What are the advantages and disadvantages of storing a file of records as a B-tree in contrast to simply having a B-tree index to the file?

9. Consider a situation where a hash file of records is being generated and a B-tree index to the file is required. The records are generated in ascending key order. The B-tree could be generated in parallel with the hash file, in which case the index entries would be inserted into the tree in ascending order. Alternatively, the tree could be generated after the hash file is complete. In this case a sequential pass through the hash file would generate index entries in random order. What difference, if any, would the choice between these two strategies have on the efficiency of subsequent (a) insertions, (b) deletions, and (c) searches?

10. Consider a file organized using table-assisted hashing and a file organized as a B-tree. Assume that in both files there are no two records with the same key. What are the comparative advantages and disadvantages of the two organizations (a) when inserting records into the file, and (b) when retrieving records from the file?

11. Modify the insertion algorithm of Fig. 6.8 to delay node splitting as described in the section on B*-trees. It should prefer redistribution over splitting and not split if there is an adjacent sibling that is not full.

7

Multikey Processing

7.1 Examines threaded files, which are files in which records with the same value of a particular attribute are linked together.

7.2 Discusses the multilist organization, in which an index identifies sublists of records with common attributes.

7.3 Examines inverted files, which are special cases of the multilist organization. An inverted file is sufficient by itself to answer certain types of queries.

7.4 Presents a simplified view of STAIRS, an information retrieval system based on inverted files.

7.5 Considers possible implementations of the index structures required by the multilist organization.

7.6 Discusses aspects of maintenance for secondary indexes.

7.7 Describes grid files, which are multikey file structures.

In Chapter 6 we were concerned with the retrieval of records by a single key: the primary key. We saw how indexing can be used regardless of whether the main file is sequenced by the key. For primary key indexing, each index entry identifies a unique record in the main file. Many applications, however, require **multikey retrieval**, that is, the retrieval from a file of all records having some combination of attribute values (possibly including the primary key). For example, a realtor might want to retrieve from a file of house records all those for properties with

- a swimming pool or sauna
- two bathrooms
- at least four bedrooms

For scholarship purposes, a college dean might want to generate a list of all students with

- U.S. citizenship

- physics or math major

- GPA of at least 3.3

- student identification number less than 150,000

There are likely to be many records in a file with the same value of a particular secondary attribute. Indexes of various forms are one mechanism for finding them. Typically a secondary index can produce a list of pointers to records having a particular value of a secondary key. With this capability it is easy to satisfy combinational requests, such as the two examples above, by performing set union and intersection operations on the lists.

A secondary index provides a fast way to locate all records with a particular attribute value. However, there is a price to be paid. Indexes take up space, and if the file is changed frequently, much time may be spent updating secondary indexes. The user has to weigh the cost of retrievals with and without a particular index against index maintenance costs. Clearly the relative frequency of retrievals and file modifications will be a factor.

Multikey queries involving ranges of attribute values are awkward to deal with using conventional indexes. They might be better served by the grid file organization. In this chapter we look at both secondary key indexing and grid files.

The example data collection we will use is a file of records containing information about used cars. (This is of particular interest to the authors, neither of whom can afford a new one.) Cars have various nonunique attributes, including manufacturer, model, and color.

7.1 Threaded Files

In a threaded file a pointer field is associated with each indexed secondary key field. The value in the pointer field identifies the next record in the file with the same value of the secondary key. Thus a number of **threads** run through the file. The index for an attribute contains one entry for each value of that attribute found in the file. An entry points to the first record having the attribute value and acts as a header of a linked list. The pointers embedded in the file can be followed to find other records with the same attribute value. In this way we can identify all records with a particular attribute value.

Consider a file in which records have k attributes and suppose that two of these attributes are threaded in the manner described. If the first of the two attributes has N different values and the second

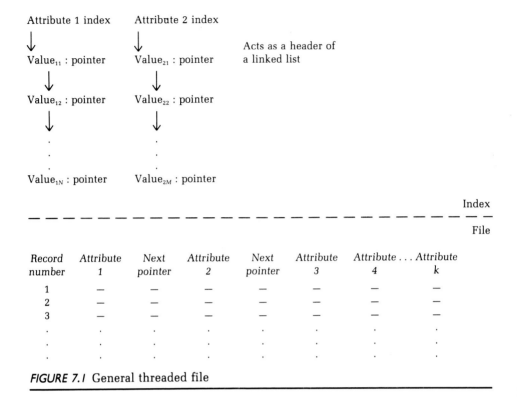

FIGURE 7.1 General threaded file

has M different values, then the general form of the file and indexes would be as shown in Fig. 7.1.

Figure 7.2 shows part of a file of car records with one set of threads (for manufacturer) and part of the corresponding index. To find the cars made by a particular manufacturer, we find the manufacturer in the index and follow the thread through the file. When a record is added to a threaded file, the appropriate threads must be extended. If the new record contains an attribute value not previously represented in the file, then a new entry will be required in the appropriate index.

What if we want to satisfy a query involving two attributes, for example, finding all green Fords? There are at least three options:

1. We could traverse the list of Fords, checking each record to see if it is a green car.

2. We could traverse the list of green cars (using the color index and then a color thread), checking each to see if it is a Ford. Given a choice between this and the previous option, we would want to

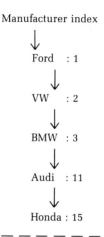

Manufacturer index

Ford   : 1

VW   : 2

BMW : 3

Audi : 11

Honda : 15

Rec. no.	Manuf.	Next Manuf.	Model	Color	License
1	Ford	4	Pinto	White	HORS4ME
2	VW	6	Bug	Red	SKIBNY
3	BMW	9	322i	Black	DADIOU1
4	Ford	5	Mustang	White	VALEGRL
5	Ford	7	Pinto	Blue	RATFACE
6	VW	8	Rabbit	Black	910VCD
7	Ford	10	Pinto	White	PACMAN
8	VW	12	Rabbit	Blue	BYE4NOW
9	BMW	16	320	Red	CMEGO
10	Ford	14	Mustang	Blue	DPGURU
11	Audi	?	5000	White	OU2LNCH
12	VW	13	Jetta	Black	1GWN821
13	VW	?	Bug	Green	BUG4AJS
14	Ford	18	Mustang	Red	1ABA800
15	Honda	?	Civic	Green	COMPSCI
16	BMW	17	320	White	4AUH2OS
17	BMW	?	322i	Blue	GOTTAGO
18	Ford	19	Tempo	Black	L8AGAIN
19	Ford	20	Pinto	Red	LUV2SKI
20	Ford	?	Mustang	Green	MYWHLS
.	.	.	.	.	.
.	.	.	.	.	.
.	.	.	.	.	.

FIGURE 7.2 Threaded file

traverse the shorter list. For this reason it would be desirable for an index entry to include thread length.

3. We could traverse the two threads simultaneously and perform a matching operation. We would maintain a pointer to the next record on each list and advance the smaller of the two pointers. When the pointers coincide we have found a green Ford; we then advance both pointers. For example, suppose records for Fords are at addresses

1, 4, 5, 7, 10, 14, 18, 19, 20, 49, and 53

and that records for green cars are at addresses

13, 15, 20, 25, 31, 39, 40, 46, 47, 48, and 53.

We would initially point to records 1 and 13, getting these values from the manufacturer and color indexes respectively. The Ford pointer would be advanced using the pointers embedded in the file until it exceeds (at 14) the green pointer, which would then be advanced in turn. Proceeding in this way, we find that the pointers coincide at 20 and 53. Note that this merge technique requires that pointers be in numerical order. However, this is not a problem if care is taken when insertions, deletions, or modifications are performed.

The third technique seems to require more record seeks than the first two. However, we can separate the pointer fields from the associated key fields and store them in a separate index file. Because records in this index file are smaller than those in the main file, the packing density is higher. The number of times a logical record is read is higher with the third technique than it is with the first two methods. However, because of the higher packing density, the number of times a physical record has to be read may in fact be lower.

7.2 Multilists

In the multilist organization the threads in the main file have the same structure as in the threaded file organization but the index entries are different. Instead of an index entry pointing simply to the beginning of a thread, it now points to every kth record on the thread (for some value of k). That is, the index entry for a particular attribute value identifies every kth record with that value. (The simple threaded file of Fig. 7.2 could be regarded as a multilist organization with k = ∞.) In effect, we have a number of sublists of length k. There is a pointer in the index to each sublist. An index entry now has two links: one to the entry for the next value of the attribute and a second

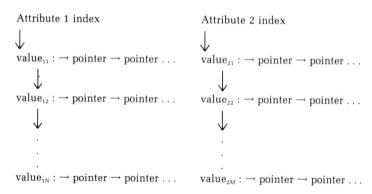

FIGURE 7.3 Multilist index

to a list of pointers to the main file. With this additional information in the index, performance of merge operations can be speeded up. The additional values are used to perform look-ahead checks. Figure 7.3 shows the general form of a multilist index, assuming the same file parameters used for Fig. 7.1.

Figure 7.4 shows the file of Fig. 7.2 with two representative indexes. Here we have used a value of 3 for k. Consider now how the search for green Fords might proceed. The Ford pointer and the green pointer are initialized to 1 and 13 respectively, using the manufacturer and color indexes. Whenever we need to advance a pointer, we have a choice between

1. advancing it to the next element in the current sublist using the pointer embedded in the file, or
2. advancing it to the beginning of the next sublist using the pointer in the index.

We choose the larger of the two values, provided that it does not take us beyond the other pointer. Figure 7.5 is a trace of the values taken by the two pointers when searching for green Fords (recall the assumptions made in Section 7.1 about the positions in the file of records of green cars and Fords). Values marked with an asterisk (*) indicate that the value was taken from the index rather than the file.

7.3 Inverted Files

Our initial threaded file represents one extreme of the multilist organization, with $k = \infty$. The other extreme is when $k = 1$; in this case the index points to every record with a particular attribute value.

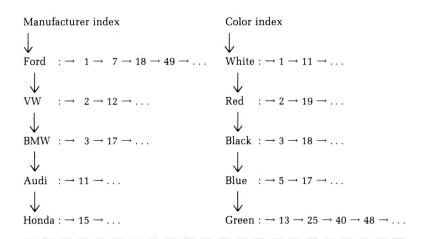

Manufacturer index

Ford : → 1 → 7 → 18 → 49 → ...

VW : → 2 → 12 → ...

BMW : → 3 → 17 → ...

Audi : → 11 → ...

Honda : → 15 → ...

Color index

White : → 1 → 11 → ...

Red : → 2 → 19 → ...

Black : → 3 → 18 → ...

Blue : → 5 → 17 → ...

Green : → 13 → 25 → 40 → 48 → ...

Rec no.	Manuf.	Next Manuf.	Model	Color	Next Color	License
1	Ford	4	Pinto	White	4	HORS4ME
2	VW	6	Bug	Red	9	SKIBNY
3	BMW	9	322i	Black	6	DADIOU1
4	Ford	5	Mustang	White	7	VALEGRL
5	Ford	7	Pinto	Blue	8	RATFACE
6	VW	8	Rabbit	Black	12	910VCD
7	Ford	10	Pinto	White	11	PACMAN
8	VW	12	Rabbit	Blue	10	BYE4NOW
9	BMW	16	320	Red	14	CMEGO
10	Ford	14	Mustang	Blue	17	DPGURU
11	Audi	?	5000	White	16	OU2LNCH
12	VW	13	Jetta	Black	18	1GWN821
13	VW	?	Bug	Green	15	BUG4AJS
14	Ford	18	Mustang	Red	19	1ABA800
15	Honda	?	Civic	Green	20	COMPSCI
16	BMW	17	320	White	?	4AUH20S
17	BMW	?	322i	Blue	?	GOTTAGO
18	Ford	19	Tempo	Black	?	L8AGAIN
19	Ford	20	Pinto	Red	?	LUV2SKI
20	Ford	?	Mustang	Green	?	MYWHLS

FIGURE 7.4 Multilists

Ford pointer	Green pointer	Comments
1	13	
7*		Skip over 4
10		Cannot skip ahead to 18
14		
	15	
18		
	20	
19		
20		Match
49	40*	Optimal pointer advance
	48*	
	53	
53		Match

FIGURE 7.5 Trace of multilist search

If such an index exists for an attribute, then there is no need for a pointer field for that attribute in the main file. We consider a multilist organization with k = 1 to be an **inverted file**.

According to Salton and McGill [72, p. 24], who cite a report from the National Bureau of Standards [73], "virtually all the commercially available [information retrieval] systems are based on inverted file designs." Information retrieval systems in this context tend to be document retrieval systems. In such systems, documents such as journal articles are stored together with keywords or index terms indicative of their content. Users of information retrieval systems typically express requests in the form of Boolean expressions. For example, to find information about the health hazards of visual display terminals, a user might enter:

```
FIND 'HAZARD' AND ('VDU' OR 'VDT' OR 'TERMINAL')
```

This means that the user wants documents that have been indexed by the term "hazard" and also by one of the terms "VDU," "VDT," and "terminal." The user interface is usually more sophisticated, however. For example, the user can find out how many documents are indexed with a particular term and can ask for a list of more precise or more general terms. Users may be able to form sets of documents and include references to them in queries. The MEDLARS system of the National Library of Medicine [74] is an example of an information retrieval system with a very large document collection. In the next section we will examine another system (IBM's STAIRS [75]) in some detail.

We can define the degree of inversion to be the percentage of attributes indexed in this way. If the file is 100% inverted, then every attribute is indexed. Figure 7.6 shows the threadless file and part of the inverted file index for the file of Fig. 7.2.

The main file can be thought of as a function that, when given a record address, returns the attribute values of the record at that address:

File (address) → (attribute, value), (attribute, value), . . .

An example would be

Car file (3) → (Manuf., BMW), (Model, 322i), (Color, Black), . . .

Index files typified by the index structure of Fig. 7.6 represent the inverse function. We can give such indexes an attribute-value pair and have a list of addresses of records with the specified attribute value returned:

File (attribute, value) → address, address, . . .

An example is

Index-to-car file (Manuf., BMW) → 3, 9, 16, 17, . . .

An index file that identifies each record with a particular attribute value is thus termed an inverted file because in some sense it is functionally the inverse of the main file.

In practice it might be advantageous to use something other than the address of a record as a pointer to it (recall some possibilities outlined in Chapter 5, pp. 107–108). There are likely to be many pointers to a particular record and hence many changes required to position-dependent pointers if the main file record moves. The primary key is a position-independent pointer, but accessing is slow because of the need to translate the key to an address at some stage.

If the main file is 100% inverted, it is redundant for certain purposes because the inverted file contains the necessary information. For example, if we want to know only how many green Fords are in the main file, the inverted file can tell us. If, however, we want a list of the license plates of the green Fords, we must access the main file.

7.4 STAIRS: An Application of Inverted Files

IBM's STAIRS (STorage And Information Retrieval System) is a powerful document retrieval system. Users can retrieve documents based on their content. For example, they can retrieve documents containing an arbitrary word, or those satisfying a complex Boolean expression

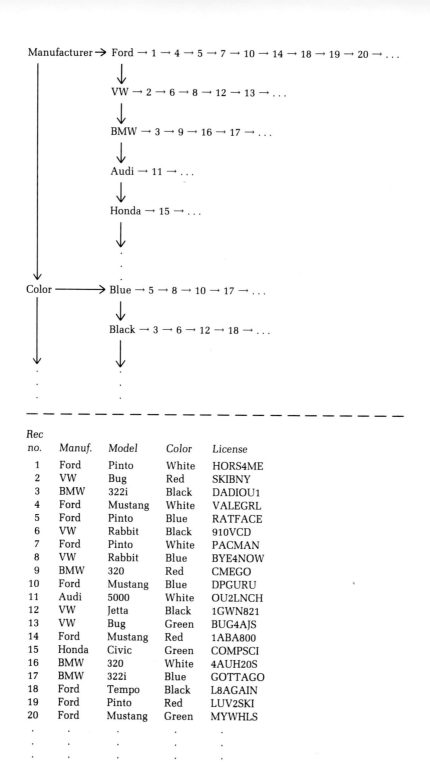

Manufacturer → Ford → 1 → 4 → 5 → 7 → 10 → 14 → 18 → 19 → 20 → ...

VW → 2 → 6 → 8 → 12 → 13 → ...

BMW → 3 → 9 → 16 → 17 → ...

Audi → 11 → ...

Honda → 15 → ...

Color ────→ Blue → 5 → 8 → 10 → 17 → ...

Black → 3 → 6 → 12 → 18 → ...

Rec no.	Manuf.	Model	Color	License
1	Ford	Pinto	White	HORS4ME
2	VW	Bug	Red	SKIBNY
3	BMW	322i	Black	DADIOU1
4	Ford	Mustang	White	VALEGRL
5	Ford	Pinto	Blue	RATFACE
6	VW	Rabbit	Black	910VCD
7	Ford	Pinto	White	PACMAN
8	VW	Rabbit	Blue	BYE4NOW
9	BMW	320	Red	CMEGO
10	Ford	Mustang	Blue	DPGURU
11	Audi	5000	White	OU2LNCH
12	VW	Jetta	Black	1GWN821
13	VW	Bug	Green	BUG4AJS
14	Ford	Mustang	Red	1ABA800
15	Honda	Civic	Green	COMPSCI
16	BMW	320	White	4AUH20S
17	BMW	322i	Blue	GOTTAGO
18	Ford	Tempo	Black	L8AGAIN
19	Ford	Pinto	Red	LUV2SKI
20	Ford	Mustang	Green	MYWHLS

FIGURE 7.6 Inverted file

FIGURE 7.7 STAIRS file hierarchy

of words. In addition, they can retrieve documents where given words appear in the same text unit such as a sentence or paragraph. It is also possible to retrieve those documents containing an arbitrary phrase.

The STAIRS system has this capability because it indexes every word occurrence in the text, in contrast to most document systems, which index a few selected keywords. STAIRS can thus be classified as a full-text document retrieval system.[1] In this section we give a brief description of the file structures that make retrievals efficient and show how queries are answered. The file structures we describe are simplified versions of the actual STAIRS structures.

File Structure

The STAIRS system contains five levels of data structures/files, as depicted in Fig. 7.7. The lowest level in the structure, the documents file (or files), contains the machine-readable documents. The only change from the conventional representation of a document is that each paragraph is tagged with a label such as TITLE, TEXT, ABSTRACT, and so on. In addition, the document contains end-of-sentence codes that the system can recognize.

The next level in the structure, the index, has one entry for each document. The entry contains information such as a pointer to the document, protection codes, and date of entry into the system. The

---

1. Full-text systems do have disadvantages, however. See, for example, Blair and Maron [76].

three file levels above the index refer to a document by a unique document number: the number of its entry in the index.

The occurrence file contains one record for each word occurrence in the document collection. The information recorded for each word occurrence is:

- document number
- paragraph code
- sentence number
- position within sentence

The entries in the occurrence file are ordered so that all records for a particular word are contiguous. Within this grouping, records are sorted in the order of the four fields listed above.

The dictionary, as might be expected, contains an entry for each different word in the document collection (including such common words as "the," "of," and "in"). Summary information, such as the number of times the word occurs and the number of different documents in which it occurs, is stored together with the word.

Large dictionaries in book form usually have a thumb index, which enables the user to find an alphabetical section rapidly. The matrix takes this one step further. It has 26 × 27 entries, each of which identifies the start of a section of the dictionary for words beginning with a particular pair of letters. (The twenty-seventh entry is a space character, thus allowing one-letter words to be indexed.) In fact, the matrix eliminates the need to store the first two letters of words in the dictionary. This key compression saves a certain amount of space.

Figure 7.8 represents a small part of the top three levels of an example file collection. We assume in this example that in the document collection, "macabre" is alphabetically the first word starting with the letters "ma." Also, we assume that the word "mainframe" occurs a total of 109 different times and in 20 different documents.

Answering Queries

Using the STAIRS system, how do we find all documents containing a phrase such as "fast breeder reactor"? We perform a three-way merge on the occurrence lists of the three words. We wish to identify sentences in which all three words occur and the position of "fast" is one before the position of "breeder," which in turn is one before the position of "reactor." Thus we look for three records, one from each list, which have the same document number, paragraph code, and sentence number and which have the required relationships between the position-within-sentence fields.

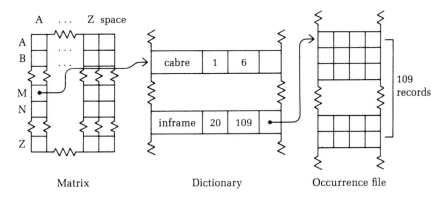

FIGURE 7.8 Top three levels of the STAIRS hierarchy

Given the file structures described above, other types of queries can be processed efficiently. The following are four examples (using our own query language).

1. Users can restrict searches to particular parts of a text, for example,

   FIND 'BREEDER REACTOR' IN TITLE

   The extension to the merging process is straightforward.

2. Users could specify stems as in

   FIND 'HISTORY OF COMPUT*'

   Records from lists for all words beginning "comput" will be considered for the third position.

3. Users could specify words that should not appear in the same sentence. For example, a user could be interested in fatigue in the context of people rather than metals and input something like

   FIND 'FATIGUE' BUT NOT 'METAL' IN SENTENCE

4. In some cases it may not matter in which order words appear. For example, a user may be interested in information retrieval systems and input something like

   FIND 'INFORMATION' | 'RETRIEVAL'

   Now documents containing either the phrase "information retrieval" or the phrase "retrieval of information" will be retrieved.

An advantage of the file hierarchy is that a user of the system can enquire about the vocabulary of the document collection without going beyond the top two levels. By using the matrix and dictionary the user can quickly find out how often a word occurs and in how many documents. The user may then wish to refine the search terms

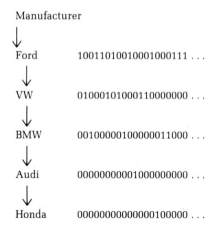

FIGURE 7.9 Bit vector index

to provide more or less output. In response to a query the system can report the number of documents satisfying it, taking into account protection codes, without having to go to the documents themselves.

7.5 Index Implementation

With the multilist and inverted file indexes described in Sections 7.2 and 7.3 there is a problem of maintaining variable-length lists for each attribute value. This is one of the major problems of multilist indexing. In this section we consider two alternatives to simple lists: bit vectors and a general graph structure.

Bit Vectors

A bit vector in the context of indexes is an array of two-valued objects having as many elements as there are records in the main file. Each element indicates whether or not the corresponding main file record has a particular attribute value. Figure 7.9 shows the (partial) bit vectors for the manufacturer attribute of the car file of Fig. 7.2.

Graph Structure

We can save a certain amount of space in a structure such as the index of Fig. 7.6 by combining those list elements that point to the same main file record. Thus each main file record is represented in an inverted directory file by a single node that is on as many lists as there are indexed attributes. (We therefore have a graph structure.)

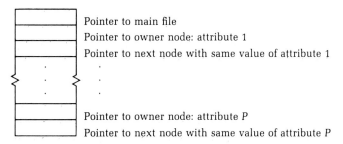

Pointer to main file
Pointer to owner node: attribute 1
Pointer to next node with same value of attribute 1

Pointer to owner node: attribute P
Pointer to next node with same value of attribute P

FIGURE 7.10 General graph node

A node will have, for each indexed attribute, a pointer to the next node representing a main file record with the same value of that attribute. It is convenient if each node also contains a pointer back to the owner of the list, that is, the index entry for the particular attribute value. Figure 7.10 shows what a node might look like. Figure 7.11 shows a small part of the graph structure for our car file. Only nodes for records 1, 4, and 5 are shown.

Consider how the problem of finding green Fords might now be solved. We choose, arbitrarily, one of the two attributes, for example, manufacturer. We follow the manufacturer pointers from the first node pointed to by "Ford." At each node visited we check the owner of the color attribute to see if it is "green."

Depending on the type of retrieval required, combining the various nodes for a main file record into a single node may reduce the number of accesses needed to the index structure. Note that the structure we have described is almost equivalent to the suggestion made at the end of Section 7.1 to put threads in a separate file.

Comparison of Bit Vectors and Graphs

Bit vectors may at first appear to have higher storage costs than graph structures. However, suppose that the main file contains M records, that P different attributes are indexed, and that the attributes have an average of N different values. The storage required for the bit vectors is

$N \times M \times P$ bits

Assuming that we are combining nodes as described above, the storage for the comparable part of the graph structure (M nodes) is

$M \times (2 \times P + 1)$ pointers, which equals $(2 \times M \times P) + M$ pointers

Roughly speaking, if the number of different values of an attribute is

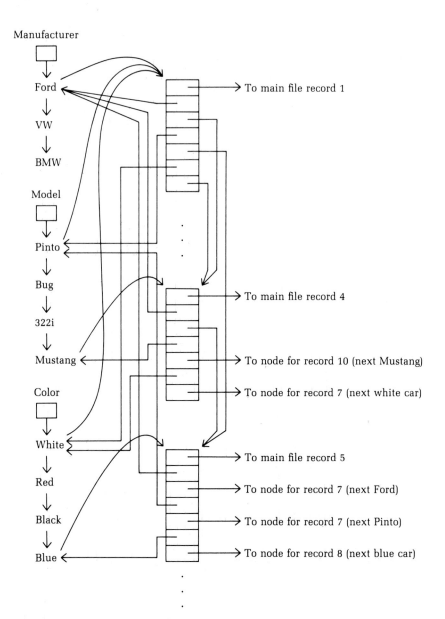

FIGURE 7.11 Partial graph structure

less than the number of bits required to hold two pointers, then a set of bit vectors occupies less space than the comparable graph structure. A hybrid system might be a preferred compromise; bit vectors would be used for attributes with few different values and lists would be used for attributes with many different values.

The biggest advantage of bit vectors is the speed with which simple set operations can be performed on conventional hardware. Most computers have machine-level instructions for performing logical operations on bit patterns. In contrast, list merging is comparatively slow.

7.6 Index Maintenance

Secondary indexes, like primary indexes, must reflect the contents of the main file at all times. Although there is only one primary index, there may be several secondary indexes. Thus maintenance of correct index entries may become a big overhead. In this section we consider how bit lists and graph structures compare in the amount of maintenance required. We also look at some aspects of storing linked structures.

Updating

An inverted file must be updated in three cases: when we insert a new record into the main file, when we delete a record, or when we change the value of a secondary key of an existing record. In the case of an insertion or a deletion, all indexes for the file have to be modified. In the case of a single field modification, one index at most has to be updated.

To delete a record from the main file we could simply mark it deleted. The alternative is to rewrite the file and omit the deleted record. The marking operation is a logical rather than a physical deletion. Logical deletion is simpler. A disadvantage of physical deletion is that records may change position in the file and thus require changes in pointers to them. We must perform the same type of deletion we perform on the main file record on all bit list indexes to the file. However, regardless of the technique used on the main file, either deletion technique is viable for linked-list indexes. If list elements are ordered to facilitate merging, a deletion may require a list traversal and take a considerable amount of time. An advantage of physical deletion is the reduction in list length; this makes subsequent traversals shorter.

For some insertions we may be able to reuse logically "deleted" records in the main file, in which case there is no problem in updating a bit vector. However, depending on the implementation, bit vectors

FIGURE 7.12 List nodes

might be awkward to deal with if the main file increases in length. Every bit vector would have to be lengthened. Adding records to a graph structure is, of course, not a problem. However, if the elements of the list are ordered, lengthy traversals may again be necessary.

If we change the value of an attribute (for example, the color of a used car from green to red), the changes in the bit list are very small. We simply clear a bit in one list (green) and set it in another (red). When we modify an attribute in a graph structure, on the other hand, we must release the node from one inverted attribute list and assign it to another. Observe from Fig. 7.11 that we must usually change three pointers in this operation.

Both the insertion of a new record and a change in an attribute value might introduce an attribute value not previously represented in the file. In the case of a bit vector, we must create a new vector with exactly one bit set. In the case of the graph structure, there will be a new list with exactly one node.

Reliability

Secondary storage tends to be more vulnerable than primary storage to data corruption. Some of the data structures we have described above can be rendered useless if a critical pointer is damaged. We might therefore consider methods of making the structures more robust, that is, less likely to be damaged irreparably. A general technique might be to provide two or more paths to any record. A file maintenance program can check the integrity of access paths. A damaged path can be detected in a number of ways. For example, a record addressed by a pointer may be missing information identifying it as part of the file. If a damaged path is detected, we can possibly use another route and repair it. This recovery principle suggests that a double-linked circular list is preferable to a single-linked list.

In fact, double-linked lists need not cost any more in storage space. Figure 7.12(a) shows a node from a conventional double-linked list; as usual an uppercase letter represents a pointer and a lowercase letter a data item. Figure 7.12(b) shows how the two pointers can be combined into one. *A,B* represents some function of *A* and *B* from which each can be recovered given the other. Exclusive-or is a candidate function. Arriving at this node from A (the address of the node to the left), we can extract from A,B the value of B (the address of the next node to visit). Similarly, we can move from right to left. Thus double linking is achieved using only one pointer field. Another solution to this problem is a coral-linked structure (see Martin [25, ch. 23]). In summary, path duplication leads to a more robust list structure and can be achieved with no additional storage.

Inverted files are a good way of answering multikey queries that are Boolean expressions. However, from the discussion above it is clear that they may not be suitable when the main file is highly volatile. A large overhead may be involved for insertions and deletions. Also, retrievals may be slowed down when an inverted list must be fetched from secondary storage. Grid files have been proposed as an alternative way of answering multikey queries. We consider this organization next.

7.7 Grid Files

Nievergelt, Hinterberger, and Sevcik [77] describe a secondary key accessing technique using grids that performs well on both stable and volatile files. We describe the method briefly here; see the original source for more details.

Design Aims

The design aims of the grid file organization are fourfold:

1. *Point queries.* The processing of a completely specified query should require no more than two disc accesses. A completely specified query (or **point query**) is one in which a single value is specified for each key attribute. An example from the car file is:

   find Manufacturer = VW, Model = Jetta, Color = Black,
   License = 1GWN821

2. *Range queries.* Processing of range queries and partially specified queries should be efficient. Two examples of such queries are:

   find Manufacturer = VW, Model = Bug, D < license < X
   find Manufacturer = Ford, Color = Green

3. *Dynamic adaptation.* The file structure should adapt smoothly to insertions and deletions.

4. *Symmetry.* All key fields, whether primary or secondary, should be treated equally. (Compare this with the inverted file organization, in which record location typically depends on the primary key only.)

Ideal Solution

Assume that records have k keys (in the case of the car file, k = 4). Consider the k-dimensional space defined by the k sets of attribute values. Modifying the bit vector idea of Section 7.4, we can conceive of a k-dimensional bit matrix. Dimension i of this matrix would have as many elements as attribute i has different values. If a particular element of the k-dimensional matrix is set to 1, this indicates that a record exists with the corresponding set of k attribute values. If the bit is 0, then no such record exists. Note that the matrix of bits is therefore a complete representation of the set of records.

This organization satisfies the four design aims above, although we have assumed nothing about how it might be stored. Processing point queries involves examination of a single element. Processing range queries involves processing all elements in a particular j-dimensional matrix j ≤ k). Insertions and deletions are carried out by setting and clearing appropriate single elements of the matrix. All key fields are treated equally.

The k-dimensional matrix, however, is an ideal rather than a practical file organization. In practice the matrix would be far too large to store. If a file has records with 4 keys and each attribute has 100 different values, the matrix will have 100,000,000 elements. The grid file organization that we discuss next is in some ways an approximation of the matrix ideal.

Practical Grid File Implementation

In the grid file organization the size of the matrix is reduced by partitioning sets of attribute values. For example, we could partition the set of colors into four subsets. If we regard attribute values as character strings, we might have

$$Color < F$$
$$F \le Color < K$$
$$K \le Color < Q$$
$$Q \le Color$$

Thus the color lemon, for example, falls into the third partition (K ≤ lemon < Q). The partition points are held in **linear scales.** The set of k linear scales, one for each attribute, defines a **grid** on the k-dimensional attribute space. The space is thus divided into **grid blocks.** The number of grid blocks is much smaller than the number of elements in the matrix. What we have lost, however, is the one-to-one correspondence between elements of the grid/matrix and possible records.

In the grid file organization, records are stored in buckets. Buckets have a fixed size, but there can be arbitrarily many of them in a file (as in the extensible file organizations of Chapter 5). The dynamic assignment of buckets to grid blocks is maintained in the **grid directory.** The grid directory consists of linear scales (described above) and a **grid array,** where each element contains a pointer to a bucket. While each element of the grid array points to exactly one bucket, grid array elements, which form a k-dimensional rectangle, may point to the same bucket. The bucket pointed to by an array element is the only bucket in the file where records with the corresponding attribute values are stored.

We can represent the partitioning of the Color attribute described above by the following linear scale

Color   (F, K, Q)

Suppose that the other three attributes are partitioned similarly and that the linear scales are

Manufacturer (G, R)
Model   (C, H, N, T)
License   (B, M, S)

Consider the record with

Manufacturer = Ford, Model = Pinto, Color = Blue,
   License = BBC1500

The partitions into which the attribute values fall are 1, 4, 1, and 2 respectively. Therefore, the bucket pointed to by

grid-array [1, 4, 1, 2]

is the only place where the record would be stored.

The grid array of pointers is normally so large that it must be held in secondary memory. On the other hand, the linear scales would normally fit into main memory. Next we consider how well the grid file organization achieves the four design aims of point queries, range queries, dynamic adaptation, and symmetry.

Performance of Grid Files

Point queries. In response to a point query, each of the k specified attribute values is first transformed into a grid index using the appropriate linear scale. The element of the grid array selected by the set of k indexes can now be fetched from disc. Nievergelt, Hinterberger, and Sevcik make a number of suggestions for implementing the grid array. The calculations involved in mapping a rectangular k-dimensional array onto linear memory are not complex. The address of a particular element is easy to compute, and the element can be fetched in one access. A second disc access fetches the bucket pointed to from the array element. Thus the first design aim is achieved.

Range queries. The second design aim is to answer range queries efficiently. To satisfy this aim it must be possible to move efficiently along an arbitrary axis of the grid array. That is, given the address of a particular element, it must be easy to compute the address of the next or previous element in any of the k dimensions. For example, to satisfy the range query

Manufacturer = VW, Model = Bug, D < license < X

we need to process records in buckets pointed to by elements in the rectangle

grid-array [3, 1, 1 . . . 4, 2 . . . 4]

A linked list implementation of the matrix would satisfy this requirement. An array implementation enabling direct access of an element given its indexes would also be suitable.

Dynamic adaptation. The third design aim is that the organization should adapt smoothly to insertions and deletions. Let us consider these in turn.

Insertions. If a record must be inserted into a bucket that is already full, then a new bucket is allocated to the file and records are distributed between the two buckets. There are two cases to consider: when the full bucket is pointed to by more than one pointer and when the bucket is pointed to by only one pointer.

If the full bucket is pointed to from more than one element of the grid array, we do not need to make changes to the partitioning. Records are distributed between the two buckets according to current partitioning, and some of the pointers change from the old to new bucket.

Suppose, for example, that the grid element representing records with

      Color < F
G ≤ Manufacturer < R
H ≤ Model < N
      License < B

and the grid element representing records with

      Color < F
G ≤ Manufacturer < R
N ≤ Model < T
      License < B

both point to the same bucket and that this bucket overflows. A new bucket is allocated to the file, and one of the two elements of the grid array is changed to point to it. Records in the overflowing bucket are distributed between the two buckets according to whether the value of the model attribute is less than N.

If only one grid element points to a bucket, then the grid must be refined. One of the subranges represented by the bucket contents must be divided. A new partition point is added to the appropriate linear scale. One bucket is assigned to each half of the original grid element, and the records are distributed according to the new partitioning.

Suppose that after further insertions there is overflow in the bucket pointed to by the element representing records with

$$\text{Color} < F$$
$$G \leq \text{Manufacturer} < R$$
$$N \leq \text{Model} < T$$
$$\text{License} < B$$

Assume further that only one element points to this bucket. We therefore need to split one of the subranges. Choosing, arbitrarily, the Manufacturer dimension, we could insert a partition at M. The corresponding linear scale is now

Manufacturer (G, M, R)

The number of elements in the grid array increases by 33% because the manufacturer dimension now has four rather than three subranges. Most of the new elements will point to an existing bucket. For example, the element representing records with

$$F \leq \text{Color} < K$$
$$G \leq \text{Manufacturer} < M$$
$$\text{Model} < C$$
$$M \leq \text{License} < S$$

will point to the same bucket as the element representing records with

$$F \leq \text{Color} < K$$
$$M \leq \text{Manufacturer} < R$$
$$\text{Model} < C$$
$$M \leq \text{License} < S$$

We need to allocate a new bucket to the file and distribute records from the overflowing one. The two buckets will now be pointed to by the array elements representing

$$
\begin{aligned}
\text{Color} &< \text{F} \\
\text{G} \le \text{Manufacturer} &< \text{M} \\
\text{N} \le \text{Model} &< \text{T} \\
\text{License} &< \text{B}
\end{aligned}
$$

and

$$
\begin{aligned}
\text{Color} &< \text{F} \\
\text{M} \le \text{Manufacturer} &< \text{R} \\
\text{N} \le \text{Model} &< \text{T} \\
\text{License} &< \text{B}
\end{aligned}
$$

Deletions. To maintain reasonable storage utilization, two candidate buckets might be merged if their combined number of records falls below some threshold. The records would be moved into one of the buckets and pointers to the other reassigned to it. The empty bucket would be deallocated from the file. Note that not every pair of buckets can be merged. Only elements that form a k-dimensional rectangle can point to a particular bucket.

Symmetry. The symmetry of the matrix ideal is preserved in the grid organization. There is no performance difference between primary and secondary indexing because all indexed attributes are treated in the same way.

Summary

Multikey indexing involves finding all records with particular combinations of key values. This contrasts with primary key indexing, discussed in Chapter 6, where we were concerned with finding the record with a particular (unique) primary key.

One approach to multikey retrieval is to link together in some way records with the same value for a particular secondary key. The linkage might be embedded in the file of records itself or in an index. If such an index identifies all occurrences of a particular attribute value, it is an inversion of the main file. One disadvantage of inverted files is the maintenance problem, that is, the extent of the updating required when the main file changes. Another disadvantage is the amount of computation involved in answering range queries.

Grid files are an alternative way of satisfying multikey queries. In effect, a representation of the k-dimensional key space is partitioned into grid blocks that contain buckets of records. The grid file organization adapts smoothly to insertions and deletions and allows single record and range queries to be answered efficiently.

Exercises

1. Implement a multilist merging algorithm. For two multilist structures, your algorithm should find the elements common to the two sets of sublists with minimal sublist accesses.

2. Consider the highway patrol of Chapter 5. Rather than having the license plate of a suspect vehicle, they are more likely to have a partial description, such as "blue Ford Mustang, 1978 or 1979 model." Design a suitable file structure that allows the fast retrieval of records for cars matching such partial descriptions.

3. Consider the problem of the highway patrol again. We saw in Chapter 5 how we can quickly retrieve records when given a license plate number. What happens if only partial information is available? Suppose, for example, that a license is identified only as A?B9?63. How could the records of all cars that match be found? Would index files help? If so, how many would you set up? Assume maximum of seven alphanumeric characters in a license. Could queries of the following form be answered?

   "First character 1 or L, then AB23, then either O or Q"

4. A library wishes to record information about books and borrowers in such a way that it is possible to determine very quickly:
   a) those books (if any) currently on loan to a given borrower
   b) whether or not a particular book is on loan and, if so, who the borrower is

   Describe the files you would create to support such a query program. Show how queries of the two types above would be answered using your files.

5. What are the advantages and disadvantages of bit lists compared with list structures in each of the following cases?
   a) the main file is a fixed-length hash file
   b) the main file is an extensible hash file

6. When completing a crossword puzzle, a solver may sometimes have partial information about a word. For example, a seven-letter

word with second letter T, third letter O and sixth letter G might be represented:

– T O – – G –

It would be convenient to have a program that listed those words in a dictionary which match a pattern of this form. Design appropriate files and a program which would find matching words quickly.

7. You have been given a set of machine-readable documents and the task of creating the five levels of STAIRS files. Describe your solution to the problem.

8. Implement and test double linking of lists using the single pointer method of Fig. 7.12.

9. Implement a grid file organization. Establish a set of "benchmark" queries and file modifications. Monitor the performance of the file in carrying out the benchmark operations. Try different bucket sizes.

8

Integrated File Addressing Techniques

8.1 Reviews properties of file organizations.

8.2 Considers factors that influence the selection of a file organization.

8.3 Looks at some of the anomalies that might arise when using an integrated set of files.

8.4 Proposes a solution to the data processing problem of Chapter 1.

8.5 Presents the major advantages and disadvantages of using files.

In this chapter we review the file organizations described in earlier chapters and consider factors that designers might consider when choosing a file organization. In addition, we outline some of the problems that might arise when using an integrated set of files. We return to the data processing problem outlined in Chapter 1 and describe a possible solution using files. Finally, we look at the advantages and disadvantages of files.

8.1 Review of Files

The major problem in organizing files is to arrange the data in a file so that the accessing requirements of application programs can be satisfied efficiently. A set of interfacing routines to each file organization implements various accessing mechanisms. Thus the organization of a file is its structure; the access techniques are the ways in which that structure is manipulated. In Chapters 3, 5, 6, and 7 we presented a number of different file organizations and accessing techniques oriented toward single- and multiple-key processing.

TABLE 8.1 File organizations and accessing requirements

Organization	Single Record by Primary Key	All Records in Primary Key Order
None	Slow	Slow
Sequential	Slow	Fast
Hashed	Fast	Slow
Indexed sequential	Okay	Fast

Single-Key File Processing

In single-key file processing, records are stored and retrieved according to the value of a single key, typically the primary key. Common accessing requirements are for a single record with a particular primary key and the retrieval of all records in primary key order. Table 8.1 shows four file organizations and their suitability for these accessing requirements.[1] The "none" entry corresponds, for example, to a serial nonsequential file or to a direct-access file where records are placed in arbitrary locations. If there is no requirement for fast query processing and a large proportion of the records read in a scan of a file are used, then a sequential organization (considered in Chapter 3) is adequate. Files organized using hashing (examined in Chapter 5) are suitable in cases where independent individual retrievals are performed and fast response is needed. That is, the result of a query is either one record or none and there is no connection between one retrieval and the next. An indexed file organization (see Chapter 6) is also an appropriate organization for this kind of retrieval.

Files organized using hashing are not useful if it is necessary to find all records with a key in a particular range. To satisfy such a request efficiently the system must be able to process records in key sequence. Sequential files are one solution. However, if only a small section of file is to be retrieved, then it is desirable to be able to find the beginning of that section quickly. Indexed sequential files (see Chapter 6) are thus more appropriate.

Multikey File Processing

If records are to be retrievable by more than one key, then the primary key organizations above are not the best solution because

---

1. Informally, our categories of slow, ok, and fast might correspond to times proportional to N, $\log N$, and 1 respectively for each record retrieved from a file of N records.

they are asymmetric in their treatment of record fields. In Chapter 7 we considered multiple-key retrievals. Inverted file organizations are a common method of performing such retrievals. However, they can be time-consuming when updates are performed. Grid files are in some ways a better way of performing multikey retrievals. First, existence queries can be answered in no more than two disc accesses. Second, the index structure adapts smoothly to main file insertions and deletions.

8.2 Choice of File Organization

The problem in selecting a particular file organization is to choose a structure that will satisfy certain requirements. For example, a user may need to retrieve records in sequence and may also need fast access to a particular record. In this case, suitable organizations include hash files in which the key order is preserved, B-trees, and ISAM files.

It is difficult to determine the best file organization and the most efficient access technique for a given situation. A good approach is to simulate the behavior of a number of candidate organizations. Davis and Coumpas [78, 79] describe an interactive dynamic file organization model. A user of their system inputs file characteristics, user requirements, and hardware characteristics. The system can respond with performance and cost figures for a number of different file organizations. Let us examine more closely the input parameters for the simulator.

The simulator requires three sets of input parameters: file characteristics, user requirements, and hardware characteristics. File characteristics are logical properties of the file. They include, for example, the number of records in the file and the average attribute length. User requirements are concerned with the accesses and changes to the file. This includes, for instance, the number of deletions per day and the number of times a month the whole file is read serially. Hardware characteristics are parameters of the available storage devices. These characteristics include block size, tracks per cylinder, and storage cost per megabyte.

The output from the model is a pair of tables, one containing nine performance figures and the other showing costs. In both tables the information is shown at various points in the lifetime of the file. The nine performance figures include the time required to insert a record, the time required to fetch an arbitrary record, and the time required to read the entire file serially. The costs that are reported include both storage and processing costs. Processing costs include the cost of reorganizing the file.

Davis and Coumpas compare six file organizations: indexed sequential, direct, inverted, multi-ring, sequential, and pile. There seems to be no reason why the system could not be extended to model other file organizations. However, in the absence of a modeling program to provide quantitative information, a user might use the following parameters to evaluate candidate organizations: time, file-use ratio, space, and volatility. These parameters overlap to a certain extent with those of Davis and Coumpas.

Time

Consider the programming time required to develop and maintain file processing software. A more complex file organization would require more time to develop file access and maintenance software. In addition, there are "hidden" software development and maintenance times. If a particular organization requires that updates be processed in a particular sequence, then the time required to sort them must be included in its processing cost. Monitoring and evaluating the performance of a file organization also requires some time.

File-Use Ratio

The **file-use ratio** of a file in a particular run of an application program can be defined as the number of records used divided by the number of records in the file. If the ratio is high, indicating that most of the records in the file are used, then a serial file or a sequential file organization is acceptable. If the ratio is low, then a better choice would be an organization in which it is possible to focus quickly on the needed record with minimal accesses of the unneeded records.

Complicating factors arise, however, when using a file-use ratio analysis. Consider an application that, when run, uses 30% of the logical records in a file. If the file is organized as a hash file, then, in principle, only the 30% of records in the file need be accessed. However, in practice, overflow resolution may make the percentage of records accessed higher than 30%. Depending on the blocking factor, the percentage of physical records accessed may be higher still. On the other hand, if the file is organized sequentially, then a large proportion of the records must be read (depending on the position of the last record processed). In addition, there may be processing required (e.g., sorting) so that the accesses are made in sequential order. It is difficult to say that if the file use ratio exceeds X% a serial organization should be used. Obviously, when the file-use ratio is low, say between 5% and 10%, then direct storage is likely to be better. Each application is likely to be unique, however, and a simple simulation will probably give useful indicators on which to base an informed decision.

TABLE 8.2 Space overheads of some file organizations

Organization	Overhead
B-tree	Pointers to nodes. Average node utilization approximately 75%.
Grid file	Linear scales, grid array. Likely to be unused space in buckets.
Dynamic hashing	Index trees, bucket space approximately 69% full.
Table-assisted hashing	Table (main memory), unused bucket space.
Conventional hashing	Unused bucket space, may require pointer space for overflows

Space

When computing space requirements, the designer should take both primary and secondary storage into account. Many file organizations require space in addition to that used by the records themselves. Table 8.2 gives some examples. Hashing, for example, may be ruled out if space on secondary storage is at a premium. In addition, certain organizations we have considered, such as dynamic hashing and grid files, work best if certain tables are in main memory. These organizations may not be feasible on some configurations even if a large amount of disc space is available.

In addition to the space taken up by the file itself, space may be needed during an update operation if the file is not updated *in situ*. Even though such space is likely to be needed only temporarily, it must be available when required.

Volatility

How often is the file changed? If the file changes frequently, an organization with many indexes may require a lot of processing. It is useful to distinguish between two types of changes: (1) those that add records to and delete records from a file and (2) those that modify existing records. Is there real growth in the number of records in the file or growth only if deleted records are not reused? Some organizations such as B-trees adapt as deletions are made. Others, such as ISAM, may not and may require periodic runs of a file-rewriting program to maintain efficiency. How often do fields of records change value? Are some fields more volatile than others? For example, consider seven fields that might be found in a student record.

date of birth, sex, name, major, address, class year, GPA

From left to right they are increasingly likely to change. In some cases

STUDENTS (SID,   SNAME,   MAJOR,   REQ.UNITS)
key is sid

100	A. Brown	Art	60
115	J. Fisher	CS	68
116	K. Wong	Psych	65
118	J. Gomez	CS	68
261	A. Brown	Math	55

FIGURE 8.1 Example student records

it is worth splitting records and establishing two files, one volatile, the other stable.

It is clear that a number of factors have a bearing on the choice of a file organization for a particular record type, given the requirements of application programs. In many applications, individual file design will be preceded by a partitioning of attributes into record types, giving rise to a set of integrated files. By a set of integrated files, we mean files where the value of a field of a record in one file may be dependent on a field value in a second file. An example of integrated files is a pair of files that have common attributes. In the next section we see why some care is needed in partitioning attributes.

8.3 Integrated Files and Update Anomalies

Update anomalies are undesirable side effects that occur when performing insertion, modification, or deletion transactions on an integrated set of files. Update anomalies are to be avoided because they violate the semantics of the information represented by data items within the files. Anomalies can be minimized by partitioning attributes carefully. In this section we give examples of some of the problems that can arise. In Chapter 9 we describe design techniques for minimizing the potential for anomalies in a set of files or a database.

We will use the specification STUDENTS in Fig. 8.1 to illustrate update anomalies in the following discussions. The attributes SID, SNAME, MAJOR, and REQ.UNITS represent respectively a unique student identification number, the student's name, the student's major, and the required units for completing that major.

Modification Anomalies

A **modification anomaly** can occur when there are redundant data values for the same attribute within and across record instances. For example, in STUDENTS a modification of REQ.UNITS for the CS

STOCK (DEALER, TITLE, PUB, COST)
composite key is (dealer, title)

Tams	Pascal	Acme	24.00
Waldens	Cobol	Tops	10.00
Tams	Data S.	Acme	26.00
Union	Files	Tops	9.20
Union	Cobol	Tops	10.50
Waldens	DB Org.	Acme	35.00

FIGURE 8.2 Example book/dealer records

major from 68 to 65 requires changes in values in two records. If MAJOR and REQ.UNITS are attributes in other record types, then other records associating CS with 65 would also have to be updated. If the modification were performed on only one record type, there would be inconsistent data values across the collection of record types. A modification anomaly occurs whenever an attribute's value is changed in a manner that produces inconsistent data values with respect to the underlying semantics of the record specifications.

Deletion Anomalies

What would happen if the record with a SID of 116 were deleted from the STUDENTS file? Information would clearly be lost. Actually, more information may be lost than was intended. In our example the following three facts are lost. The first fact is the intended deletion. The second and third facts are **deletion anomalies**.

1. A record with the value 116 for attribute SID existed.
2. The attribute MAJOR can have the value PSYCH.
3. The REQ.UNITS for PSYCH major is 65.

Insertion Anomalies

Suppose we try to insert partial information into the file, for instance, the fact that MAJOR can be HISTORY and requires 70 units. We could only do this directly if there were a student to insert whose major is history. Temporary solutions such as using arbitrary dummy keys are unsatisfactory because they will later have to be modified and updated when an actual instance (a history major) is inserted. This side effect is an **insertion anomaly**. Consider, as a second example, the records of Fig. 8.2. They contain data about book dealers, titles, publishers, and costs.

STUDENTS.1 (SID,   SNAME,   MAJOR)
key is sid

100	A. Brown	Art
115	J. Fisher	CS
116	K. Wong	Psych
118	J. Gomez	CS
261	A. Brown	Math

MAJORS (MAJOR,   REQ.UNITS)
key is major

Art	60
CS	68
Psych	65
Math	55

FIGURE 8.3 Revised student records

Given file STOCK, one could not answer queries about the costs of a particular book title unless a dealer had that title in stock. (Note the use of a **composite key** in Fig. 8.2. Composite keys are candidate keys that contain more than one attribute. They are needed when there is no single attribute candidate key.)

Modification, deletion, and insertion anomalies can be minimized by design. Try the update modification we attempted on STUDENTS in Fig. 8.1 on the two record specifications of Fig. 8.3. Note that the probability of a modification, deletion, or insertion anomaly has been reduced. This is because the specifications in Fig. 8.3 are less complex: they represent single associations, not multiple associations. As we will see in Chapter 9, file design is a process of decomposing complex record specifications into simple record specifications. A good rule of thumb is one record specification per concept (association among attributes).

We now turn to the data processing problem of Chapter 1 and illustrate how suitable file organizations might be derived. The derivation of record types is informal compared with the methodology we will use in Chapter 9.

8.4 Example File Processing Application

In Section 1.4 we outlined a simple data processing problem in a School of Engineering and Computer Science (SECS). The problem concerned the management of student records and registration. Now we consider how a solution might be implemented using the file techniques we have examined. First, we consider the required operations and determine the data needed to support them. Second, we determine suitable organizations for the files.

Operations and Data

Three principal operations are required:

1. registration of students in course sections (classes)
2. production of class rosters
3. grade recording

Registration of students. Students register individually. Information must be available about courses already passed so that course prerequisites can be checked. One solution is to have a file of student records, each containing basic demographic information about the student and information about courses he or she has passed. However, in the light of the volatility discussion above, it is probably better to split student information into two files. One (the grade record file) will contain information about courses passed. Records in this file change comparatively infrequently. A record will contain information about one grade awarded to one student. We will make the simplifying assumption that although students may retake courses, the file holds only the best grade awarded to a particular student in a particular course. The second file (the student file) will contain basic demographic data and summary information such as the name of the most restrictive prerequisite course passed. In addition, a record in the student file will contain the names of the courses in which the student is currently enrolled. Records in this file will be modified frequently during registration.

The school catalog indicates, for each course, the name of the prerequisite course (if any). This information is required by the registration program and is independent of whether or not the course is actually offered in a particular semester. Therefore we will establish a course file. There will be one record for each course. A course record indicates the restrictions, if any, on enrollment in that course.

The final checks on registration are concerned with individual classes. A particular class is offered at a particular time and place. It is likely to have a limit on enrollment and may have enrollment requirements beyond those for the course in general. We will therefore establish a schedule file, containing one record for each class being offered.

Production of class rosters. During and after registration we need to be able to produce an alphabetically ordered list of the students

TABLE 8.3 Required file accessing

		Program	
File	Registration	Roster Printing	Grade Recording
Grade record	Read only		Read/write
Student	Read/write	Read only	Read/write
Course	Read only		
Schedule	Read/write	Read only	Read only
Professor		Read only	Read only

enrolled in an arbitrary class. Most of this information is available in the student file. In addition, we need information about the professor teaching the class. We will therefore have a professor file. The professor file will have one record for each faculty member and will contain information such as name, department, and office number. It will be convenient to assign a unique identification number to each professor or to use a unique attribute such as social security number.

Grade recording. We envisage grade recording as an interactive operation performed by a professor. In response to a class number the grade recording program outputs the details of the class, for instance, the course of which it is a section, the time at which it meets, and so on. If there is no error in the class number, then the program prompts with a series of student names. The professor enters the appropriate grades, which are recorded in the grade record file. The files established to support registration and roster listing will also support grade recording.

Table 8.3 summarizes the files and accessing programs we have arrived at. It shows the kind of access, if any, that each program makes to each file. Next we consider organization of the records in each of the files.

File Organization

We have decided that the data processing needs of SECS can be served by establishing the five files of records described above. Next we consider ways in which the files should be organized.

Grade record file. A grade record is accessed in two ways. First, the registration program needs to know if student X has passed course Y. Second, the grade recording program needs to add records containing information about grades awarded. Records will be accessed frequently during registration. Many records will be added and a few

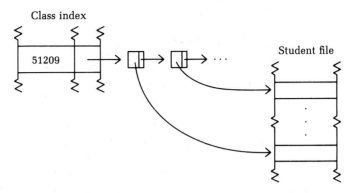

FIGURE 8.4 Class index entry

modified at the end of a semester. Given these requirements, a hash file suggests itself. The key is the pair of attributes (student identification number, course name).

The growth pattern of the file is unusual. At periodic intervals the size of the file is likely to increase by large amounts. Conventional hashing by itself is not adequate, although we could have a maintenance program that would rehash the file to a larger one during an inactive period. However, a better solution is to use an extensible hashing technique with guaranteed fast retrieval, perhaps dynamic hashing.

Student file. The student file is accessed in two ways. First, the registration program requires single student records. Second, the grade recording and roster printing programs require the records of all students in a particular class. Each record will be accessed and modified a few times during registration and a few times at the end of a semester. New records will be added and existing ones deleted two or three times a year.

If we assume that the number of students is large (e.g., tens of thousands), it is inefficient to have the grade recording and roster printing programs perform serial searches to find all students in a particular class. One way of dealing with the requirements of these two programs is to index the student file on class. Each entry in the class index points to a list of pointers to records of students enrolled in the class. This structure and a typical index entry are illustrated in Fig. 8.4. That is, we invert the student file on the class attribute. When a student adds a class, a pointer to the student record is added to the appropriate list. For fast retrieval, entries in the class index are hashed on class number.

We can assume that class sizes are not gigantic, so it is reasonable to sort selected student records into alphabetical order as part of the roster printing operation. This avoids the overhead involved in keeping student records linked in alphabetical order. Similar sorting may also be part of the grade recording program.

For certain purposes, such as registration, it seems sensible to have students identify themselves by a unique key, for example, their identification number, rather than by their name. There is no requirement to print out the entire student file in any particular order, so hashing the student file on identification number is appropriate.

Course file. Only the registration program needs to access the course file. It retrieves a single course record identified by a particular course name. Accesses will be very frequent during registration. However, records will be added to or deleted from the file comparatively rarely during a year. Consideration of these factors suggests a hash file where the hash function converts a course name to an address and is carefully designed to minimize, if not eliminate, overflows.

Schedule file. The schedule file is accessed in a number of ways. All three programs require single class records. We assume that each class, that is, each section of a course, has a unique section number. This number will be the key. In addition, when assisting a student looking for classes, the registration program has to be able to retrieve records of classes in a particular course and/or at a particular time. Class records will be accessed very frequently during registration. If any class has a size limit, then the corresponding record in the schedule file will contain a count of seats remaining. Such records will be updated frequently. Class records may be updated due to changes in teaching assignments. Occasionally, new records may be added to the schedule file. On rarer occasions a record will be deleted.

The majority of accesses to the schedule file will be by class number. Fast response is needed. One possibility is to hash records by this number.

How can we find all classes of a certain course? We cannot assume that class number is a convenient function of course name and class time. Just as we inverted the student file on class number, we invert the schedule file on course name. An entry in the course index identifies the classes in a particular course.

How do we respond to a request for all classes meeting during a certain time? Let us assume that a user specifies a day pattern, a start time, and a finish time. For example, a request for a class that meets on Monday and Wednesday mornings from nine o'clock to noon might be input as

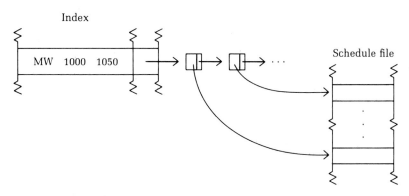

FIGURE 8.5 Schedule file inverted

MW 0900-1200

In response, the user needs a list of classes that meet only on the specified days and that both start and finish in the specified period. Requests of this form are likely to be frequent during registration, so sequential searching of the schedule file, though simple, is not a good solution. The number of different day patterns is likely to be small compared with the number of course sections. Similarly, the number of different times at which classes start and the number of different class lengths are comparatively small.

A possible way of satisfying requests of the form above is to invert the schedule file by a composite key, namely

day pattern, start time, finish time

Each entry in the index points to a list of pointers to appropriate records in the schedule file. Figure 8.5 shows the structure and a typical index entry. The next problem is how to organize the index entries.

If the index entries are ordered by finish time within start time within day pattern, then a user is interested in a contiguous subsection of them. Figure 8.6 illustrates the ordering of the entries and the subsection that would be of interest in the case of the query above. (Entries marked ⇐ satisfy the example constraints.) Users must be able to locate the beginning of the subsection quickly and process the entries in sequence efficiently. A B$^+$-tree is a data structure with appropriate properties. To find the first index record with a key satisfying the user's query we search the B$^+$-tree with an artificial key derived from the query. In the case of the example above we search with

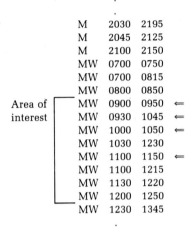

M	2030	2195
M	2045	2125
M	2100	2150
MW	0700	0750
MW	0700	0815
MW	0800	0850
MW	0900	0950	⇐
MW	0930	1045	⇐
MW	1000	1050	⇐
MW	1030	1230
MW	1100	1150	⇐
MW	1100	1215
MW	1130	1220
MW	1200	1250
MW	1230	1345

Area of interest brackets MW 0900–MW 1200.

FIGURE 8.6 Fragment of schedule file index

MW 0900 0000

It is easy to process records in a B$^+$-tree in sequence because they are held in the terminal nodes and the terminal nodes are linked in sequence. We traverse the index records until we detect that no further record can satisfy the user's constraints. In this way we can quickly identify and process the range of entries. This is a possible solution to the problem of finding classes that fit in specific time intervals. There are others (see Exercise 2).

Professor file. The professor file is accessed only by the roster printing program and grade recording programs. Both programs need to retrieve the record with a given unique professor identification number. Accesses will be comparatively rare. Updates will be rare too. Access time does not appear to be critical. We can therefore save space by using a sequential file rather than a hash file.

Table 8.4 summarizes the files and organizations we have devised. Two of the files are indexed; the other three stand alone.

Review of Example

Even though our example is a small one, we have shown how many of the organizations discussed in earlier chapters can be applied. We have inverted files, hash files, and B-trees. Our particular example

TABLE 8.4 Example SECS file organizations

Index(es)	File
	Grade record file (hashed on {student identification number, course})
Index on class number (hashed on class)	Student file (hashed on student identification number) Course file (hashed on course name)
B$^+$-tree index on {day pattern, start time, finish time} Index on course name (hashed on course)	Schedule file (hashed on class number)
	Professor file (sequential on professor identification number)

had no requirements for sequentially processing a file, but it is not difficult to imagine such an application. For example, the alumni association may wish to send mail to all students. The printers of the schedule of classes may wish to process all classes in a particular order. We leave it to the reader to determine the effect of these additional requirements (one example is given in Exercise 4).

8.5 Advantages and Disadvantages of Files

We can regard files as natural extensions of main memory data structures. They have two main advantages: size and permanence. The size of a file in many cases is limited only by the number of discs and tapes available for its storage. Multi-megabyte files are not uncommon. A data structure exists until the space it occupies is needed for some other purpose. Main memory is typically too limited to allow a data structure to exist beyond the run of the program that creates it. It is also too volatile and not an appropriate medium for permanent data. Secondary storage, on the other hand, is much cheaper; files stored in this way can be kept for many years.

Although access times differ, many techniques applicable to main memory data structures extend naturally to files. Practically all programming languages provide an interface of some kind to files. The interface is a close one that allows efficient processing. Thus files are a simple and convenient way of storing data so that it may be accessed over a period of time and by a number of different programs.

Advantages of Using Integrated Files

There are five main advantages to using an integrated file processing environment. First, because file-based programming is relatively straightforward, the data processing staff do not need to use advanced programming techniques. Thus, software personnel may be more readily available and less expensive to hire. Second, there is no added expense in terms of purchasing and maintaining software to handle the file-program interface. Third, it is relatively easy to maintain the integrity of a set of files against system failure. Fourth, because of the relatively simple interface between a program and a file, transfers are relatively efficient. Finally, limited concurrent access makes recovery from crashes relatively simple.

Disadvantages of Using Integrated Files

There are four main disadvantages to using an integrated file processing environment. First, there is a large degree of dependence between programs and data. Programs are not insulated from changes in the logical and physical organization. Second, answering new requests or producing one-of-a-kind reports is difficult when using files. Third, only a limited degree of concurrent data access is usually possible. If a program has a file open for writing, other programs are usually prevented from reading any part of it. Fourth, in an integrated file environment, mechanisms for communicating data modifications across applications tend to be external to rather than part of the file system itself. In a multiuser environment it is difficult to control, document, and disseminate changes to file structures. Data integrity is not maintained by the system but rather is the responsibility of application programs.

Summary

We consider the file organization problem to be one of arranging data in a file appropriately for given retrieval requests. There may be single-key or multikey requests. Examples of single-key requests are

```
GET RECORD WITH PRIMARY KEY = 'X'
GET RECORD WITH NEXT HIGHEST PRIMARY KEY
GET RECORDS WITH 'D' < PRIMARY KEY < 'G'
```

Hash organizations and (indexed) sequential files are appropriate for single-key requests. Typical multikey requests include

```
GET ALL RECORDS WITH ATTRIBUTE A = 'X' AND ATTRIBUTE B = 'Y'
GET ALL RECORDS WITH ATTRIBUTE A = 'X' OR ATTRIBUTE A = 'Y'
```

Indexes are one solution to multikey requests, although grid files are in some ways a better solution.

The choice of an organization for a particular file depends on file characteristics, user requirements, and hardware characteristics. Ideally one would like to be able to simulate a number of different candidate organizations and measure the cost and performance of each. In the absence of such a system, factors such as file volatility, file-use ratio, and available time and space should be taken into account.

We examined some of the problems that might arise when using integrated files. Update anomalies are one potential problem. (In Chapter 9 we will look at techniques for minimizing the potential for anomalies.)

To illustrate some of the points raised in our discussion, we considered a solution to the SECS data processing problem using file techniques. In devising a solution we looked at the information required by each program and suggested a set of files. For each of the files in turn we considered the accessing requirements and file volatility. Taking these into account, we suggested possible organizations.

Files provide useful data structures with properties (size, permanence) beyond those of normal main memory structures. Files can be accessed efficiently. However, the close connection between files and accessing programs can cause serious problems. The lack of an intermediate mapping between logical and physical organization necessitates changes to application programs when a file organization is changed. These issues are addressed by database management systems, as we will see in Chapter 10.

Exercises

1. Suppose that secondary storage were free. Would this change the way in which files are organized?

2. How can the proposed index to the schedule file of the SECS example be improved?

3. Implement and test a simple student registration system along the lines of the design above.

4. The SECS administrators decide they would like to introduce an on-line transcript service, whereby a student could enter his or her identification number and get a chronologically ordered complete list of courses taken and grades awarded. You have been asked to implement this service. What changes, if any, would you make to the file organizations developed in the chapter?

5. Read the papers by Davis and Coumpas [78, 79]. Implement a dynamic file organization model of your own. Test at least one organization that they did not.

6. A large manufacturing company has given you the task of devising an organization for its file of parts records. Each record in the file contains information about a particular part. The fields include number (which is unique), description, price, and quantity on hand (QOH). There are about 10,000 records. The file is accessed in a number of ways:

   a) Twice a year a catalog is produced containing the information in the parts records in ascending order of part number.
   b) Once a day the QOH field of about 100 records is increased to reflect deliveries made from the manufacturing plant.
   c) Several times during an hour the QOH field of a record is decreased as shipments are made out of the warehouse.
   d) Many times an hour customers make telephone enquiries about a part, referring to it either by part number or by description.

   Describe how you would organize the file, including any index files you would create. Give reasons for your choice of organization. State clearly any assumptions you make.

7. Suppose that the company of Exercise 6 makes weekly changes to its catalog; it adds some new parts and deletes some obsolete ones. Would your solution to Exercise 6 be different? Give reasons for your answer.

8. Consider the mailing list exercise of Chapter 3 (Exercise 12). What factors would you take into account when deciding whether to use a serial file, an indexed file, or a hash file as a means of organizing the records?

Suggestions for Further Reading

O. Hanson, *Design of Computer Files* (Rockville, Md.: Computer Science Press, 1982).

9

Normalization

9.1 Presents a taxonomy for describing associations that can exist among entity attributes.

9.2 Explains the process of normalization as a technique for minimizing anomalies and data redundancy.

9.3 Illustrates the record design process with an example set of entity specifications derived from the data processing environment of Section 1.4.

When we use an integrated set of files, as described in Chapter 8, or a database management system (DBMS) as presented in Chapter 10, we must pay close attention to the associations among attribute values. We call a logical collection of attribute values an **entity**. We use this term synonymously with "logical record." An **entity specification** is the declaration, or naming, of an entity's attributes. Because an attribute of one entity specification may also be an attribute of another entity specification, updates to one entity may cause inconsistency among redundant data values in other entities. We described such update anomalies in Chapter 8. Careful entity specification will minimize these update anomalies. Thus we present principles of good entity specification to emphasize its relevance both to integrated file and to database information processing environments.

Normalization is a process used to design an optimum set of entity specifications for all types of record modifications. The goal of normalization is to design entity specifications that facilitate the enforcement of rules about how attributes are associated. Once normalization has been performed, the logical declaration of entities and associations among entities can be developed. In general, the normalization process generates many simple entity specifications from a few semantically complex entity specifications.

Normalization helps reduce file maintenance problems in an integrated file environment because simpler data semantics are easier to enforce within application programs. Normalizing a collection of entity specifications for database design improves their data integrity with respect to update anomalies and can also decrease data redundancy. In this case simpler entity specifications facilitate the enforcement of data semantics by the DBMS software. It is important to note that normalization is a design process that seeks to minimize update anomalies and redundancy, not necessarily to eliminate them entirely.

Recall from Section 8.3 that update anomalies are undesirable side effects that occur when performing insertion, modification, or deletion transactions on an integrated set of files or a database. We can minimize these side effects by carefully designing the associations (shared attributes) among entities. Update anomalies are undesirable because they violate the semantics of the information represented by data items within a file or database. Clearly, semantic constraints (or interpretation rules) must be enforced so that stored data is consistent and valid. Once data semantics are violated, it becomes difficult to distinguish valid data values from erroneous data values.

In this chapter we start by describing various associations among attributes. Next we consider the process of normalization. Finally, we present an example of a normalized, integrated set of entity specifications.

9.1 Associations among Entity Attributes

Associations among attributes are the semantic constraints of, or facts about, the information being stored as data. There are three possible kinds of associations between two attributes: a 1:1, a 1:N, or an M:N association. That is, one attribute can select or determine one or many values of the other attribute. Assume for the moment that attribute A determines attribute B. This means that if two instances of an entity have the same value for A they must have the same value for B. One could say about a 1:1 association between attributes A and B that attribute A determines a value of attribute B. The primary key of a record is a **determinant** for the remaining attributes. Thus a 1:1 association is an example of a **single-valued dependency**. In contrast, 1:N and M:N associations are examples of **multivalued dependencies**. If there is a 1:N multivalued dependency between attributes A and B, a value of A can determine many values of B (from within a set of possible B values). With an M:N association a value of attribute A can determine a finite set of B values, and a value of attribute B can determine another finite set of A values.

	Attributes		Dependencies
1.	Key	$\longrightarrow$ Nonkey	Functional
2.	Part of key	$\longrightarrow$ Nonkey	Partial
3.	Nonkey	$\longrightarrow$ Nonkey	Transitive
4.	Nonkey	$\longrightarrow$ Part of key	Boyce-Codd

Where determinant value $\longrightarrow$ attribute value

FIGURE 9.1 Functional dependencies

In this discussion we implicitly assume the direction of the associations. For example, in a 1:1 association between attributes A and B, either attribute can be considered the determinant. A 1:N association can be viewed as either 1:N (where A determines several B values) or as N separate 1:1 associations (where each of N values of B determines the same A value). We have assumed a left-to-right association in presenting examples of 1:1 and 1:N dependencies in this book. We do not discuss associations where B determines A; they are assumed. An M:N association, however, is two 1:N associations. In the section on M:N multivalued dependencies we examine these associations in both directions. First, however, we consider single-valued dependencies.

Single-Valued Dependencies

If an attribute (or set of attributes) determines every other attribute in the entity specification, the determinant is a candidate key for the entity. The primary key is selected from the candidate keys. The choice of one candidate key as the primary key should be based on the usefulness of the various candidate keys for a particular application. An entity can have many candidate keys but, by definition, only one primary key. We assume here that nonkey attributes include candidate keys because a primary key has already been selected.

There are four kinds of single-valued dependencies among the attributes of an entity. They are listed in Fig. 9.1. The first, where a primary key determines a nonkey, is the desired single-valued dependency, because the determinant is a primary key attribute. Thus the dependency is known and can be declared, in both the file and DBMS environments. The remaining three kinds of dependencies represent associations whose semantics must be maintained by application programs. A DBMS, for example, cannot easily enforce semantics based on the last three forms because the determinant is not a primary key. The single-valued dependency is not declarable and is thus unknown to the DBMS. As an example, consider the entity specifications and instances of Fig. 9.2.

PROF (PID, OFFICE, PNAME, DEPT)
composite key is (pid, office)

20	413	Barnes	CS
21	414	Smith	CS
25	404	Gumb	CS
34	304	Wong	EE
55	402	Katz	EE
57	402	Schwartz	EE
27	414	Schwartz	CS

MEMBER (OFFICE, DEPT)
key is office

414	CS
413	CS
404	CS
304	EE
402	EE

Dependencies:

1. PID $\longrightarrow$ PNAME, OFFICE, DEPT
2. OFFICE $\longrightarrow$ DEPT

Dependency graph:

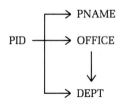

FIGURE 9.2 Example professor entities

The two specifications define entities containing data about faculty in a school. Professors have unique identification numbers (PID) and share their offices with a colleague in the same department. The example in Fig. 9.2 is not the best possible specification for the given functional dependencies. In fact, there are problems with the example that illustrate the four representations of single-valued dependencies in an entity specification. We now consider these problems.

In the example, PID is the candidate key for the PROF entity and OFFICE is the primary key (only candidate) of the MEMBER entity. Let us assume that PID and OFFICE together are chosen to be the composite key for PROF (both attribute values are required to form the key) and that OFFICE is the key for MEMBER. If PID is a candidate key for PROF, then by augmentation PID and OFFICE also uniquely select record instances of PROF. In fact, many composite candidate keys containing PID could be generated and considered for the role of primary key. (Bear in mind that we are using this example for illustrative purposes, and it is not intended to be the best specification of entities to store this data.) The composite key in this example is inefficient because it contains extraneous attributes. Such inefficient key usage can easily occur in a file system that becomes integrated over time by various application programs. For example, key usage of this sort could arise from the precedents set using paper files before office automation.

The entity PROF, with the composite key (PID, OFFICE), is an example of how nonkey attributes can be determined by part of a composite key (item 2 in Fig. 9.1). This is because the semantics of the information in PROF is that PID alone determines values of PNAME and DEPT. This could be represented in a simpler manner by making PID alone the key of PROF. In this way we are selecting a minimal but sufficient primary key.

Observe that, given dependency 2 in Fig. 9.2, OFFICE selects DEPT in entity specifications MEMBER and PROF. In PROF this dependency is an example of a nonkey attribute determining another nonkey attribute. As we stated at the beginning of this chapter, the goal of normalization is to design entity specifications such that an application program or DBMS can efficiently enforce rules about how attributes are associated. To this end we aim to develop entity specifications in which key attributes determine nonkey attributes. One way to accomplish this goal is to have many entity specifications that represent simple associations. An example here would be to replace the entity specifications of Fig. 9.2 by those shown in Fig. 9.3. Notice that the two entities are also less redundant with respect to their data items. Figure 9.2 contains 38 data items whereas Fig. 9.3 contains 31. Furthermore, all single-valued dependencies are determined by keys.

The various possible dependencies among attributes have formal names and definitions. We present these now to facilitate later discussions.

Dependencies. The term "dependencies" refers to the association among entities. An attribute (or set of attributes) B is functionally dependent on attribute (or set of attributes) A if, for each value of A, there is one value of B associated with it. Thus if two instances of an entity have the same value for A, they must also have the same value

PROF.1 (PID, PNAME, OFFICE)
key is pid

20	Barnes	413
21	Smith	414
25	Gumb	404
34	Wong	304
55	Katz	402
57	Schwartz	402
27	Schwartz	414

MEMBER (OFFICE, DEPT)
key is office

413	CS
414	CS
404	CS
304	EE
402	EE

Dependencies:

PID $\longrightarrow$ PNAME, OFFICE
OFFICE $\longrightarrow$ DEPT

Dependency graph:

PID $\longrightarrow$ OFFICE $\longrightarrow$ DEPT
$\longrightarrow$ PNAME

FIGURE 9.3 Revised professor entities

for B. Ideally, every nonkey attribute is functionally dependent on the entity's key. As illustrated in Fig. 9.1, the four general types of single-valued dependencies are **functional dependencies, partial dependencies, transitive dependencies**, and **Boyce-Codd dependencies**. Note that dependencies are defined in terms of a collection of entity specifications and are not limited to the range of one specific entity specification. That is, if a particular dependency exists between attributes in one entity specification the same dependency exists in other entity specifications that contain the attributes in question.

Functional dependencies. A dependency is functional if an attribute B of an entity specification is determined by the entire set of attributes A and not on any proper subset of A. Consider, for example,

Entities:

E1 (A1, A2, A3, B, C)   composite key is (a1, a2, a3)
E2 (A1, A3, C)   composite key is (a1, a3)
E3 (F, G, H, I)   key is f
E4 (H, I)   key is h
E5 (M, N, O, P)   composite key is (m, n)

Dependencies:

A1, A2, A3 ⟶ B, C
A1, A3 ⟶ C
F ⟶ G, H, I
H ⟶ I
M, N ⟶ O, P
P ⟶ M

Dependency graph:

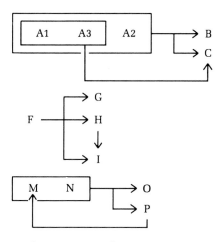

FIGURE 9.4 Example entity specifications

entity specification E1 in Fig. 9.4, which has as a composite primary key the set of attributes (A1, A2, A3). Attribute B is functionally dependent on the primary key because values of A1, A2, and A3 are needed to select a value of B.

Partial dependencies. A dependency is partial rather than functional when a nonkey attribute B of an entity specification is dependent on a subset of the composite primary key attribute A. In the example of Fig. 9.4, attribute C is partially dependent on the primary key (A1, A2, A3) because only values of A1 and A3 are needed to select a value of C. This partial dependency is illustrated by the two paths originating from all or part of the composite key (A1, A2, A3) and terminating at attribute C in the dependency graph in Fig. 9.4. Given the functional dependencies in E2, E1 has both a functional and a partial dependency.[1]

Transitive dependencies. A transitive dependency exists within an entity specification when the nonkey attributes contain functional dependencies among themselves. For example, consider the specifications of E3 and E4 in Fig. 9.4. In the specification for E4 the primary key H determines the attribute I. In the specification for E3 the primary key F determines the attributes G, H, and I. Within E3 there is therefore a transitive dependency, since F can select I through the functional dependency declared in E4. In other words, there are two paths to selecting I in E3. One can access an instance of I based on a value of F either directly or indirectly (transitively) from F to H and then from H to I. Note the two paths from F terminating at attribute I in the dependency graph in Fig. 9.4.

Boyce-Codd dependencies. A Boyce-Codd dependency exists within an entity specification when a nonkey attribute determines part of a composite primary key attribute set. An example is the specification for E5 in Fig 9.4. There is a Boyce-Codd dependency between P and M because M is part of a composite primary key and P is a nonkey. If P were a candidate key, however, there would not be a Boyce-Codd dependency.

Multivalued Dependencies

A multivalued dependency exists when an attribute can determine more than one value (from a finite set of values) for another attribute. In this case there is not a one-to-one association between the determinant and the set of determined attributes. Diagrammatically a multivalued dependency is shown as a double-headed arrow: $G \twoheadrightarrow M$. As an example of multivalued dependencies, consider the entity specification TEXTS in Fig. 9.5.

This specification contains two independent multivalued dependencies. In TEXTS, information about courses and textbooks is stored according to book identification number (BID), course number (COURSE), and course section number (SECTION). A book may be used in many courses and a course may use many books; hence the

---

1. The functional dependencies described above are often called **fully functional dependencies**. We use "functional dependencies" for brevity.

TEXTS (BID,   COURSE,   SECTION)
composite key is (bid, section)

20	CS132	456
20	CS132	457
20	CS182	458
30	CS182	458
20	CS182	459
30	CS182	459
38	CS242	461
42	CS242	461
38	CS242	463
42	CS242	463
42	CS440	540

Dependencies:

BID ⟶ COURSE
COURSE ⟶ BID
COURSE ⟶ SECTION

Dependency graph:

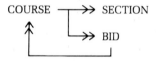

FIGURE 9.5 Example of multivalued dependencies

dependency between COURSE and BID is M:N. Because a course can
have multiple sections, the dependency between COURSE and SEC-
TION is 1:N. We will assume that all sections of the same course use
the same textbooks. Because of these semantics and multivalued dependencies, many redundant data items are needed to represent all
of the instances of TEXTS in Fig. 9.5. There are 11 instances of TEXTS,
requiring a total of 33 individual data values for attributes. Of the 33
data values there are only 15 unique values. The remainder represent
data redundancy. The redundant values are the result of generating
the cross product of the independent multivalued dependencies. The
cross product contains all combinations of the record instances. The
two multivalued dependencies (COURSE ⟶ BID, BID ⟶ COURSE)
and (COURSE ⟶ SECTION) are independent because there is no
direct dependency between SECTION and BID. The course name, not
the section number, determines a textbook. (Textbooks could possibly
be assigned to courses before section numbers are allocated.)

As mentioned earlier, an interesting observation is to look at multivalued dependencies in both directions. That is, the 1:N association is an example of a multivalued dependency from left to right (for each COURSE there can be several SECTIONS) and a single-valued dependency from right to left (for each SECTION there is only one COURSE). The M:N association, on the other hand, represents a multivalued dependency in both directions (1:M and 1:N respectively). We will discuss the implications of this observation in Chapter 11.

Now let us insert a new record of type TEXTS to see what can go wrong. If we insert a record with the values

    07, CS242, 461

one section of course CS242 has one more required text than the other sections. This is a violation of the semantics of the entity specification. As will be shown later, given the semantic constraints, we can declare more appropriate and simpler entity types. Such types will make this particular semantic violation impossible. In the next section we examine techniques for designing entity specifications that are relatively robust with respect to update anomalies and that also minimize data redundancy.

9.2 Normalization: Entity Design through Decomposition

Normalization is a design process that takes a set of entity specifications (or dependencies) and generates another set of entity specifications that (1) preserves the original semantics, (2) eliminates partial, transitive, and Boyce-Codd dependencies, and (3) minimizes data redundancy. After normalization the resulting associations are more easily implemented and will evidence fewer update anomalies. The normalization process can be defined by seven categories of associations that are called **normal forms**. Normal forms, as we will see, are assertions about allowable attribute associations.

Domain Key Normal Form

The goal of normalization is a form called domain key normal form (DKNF). DKNF is the most restrictive normal form and incorporates all the properties of the less restrictive forms. When a collection of attributes conforms to the requirements of DKNF, the dependencies in the data are represented by keys determining nonkeys [80]. This is an area of active research; there is currently no deterministic algorithm for transforming any set of dependencies into

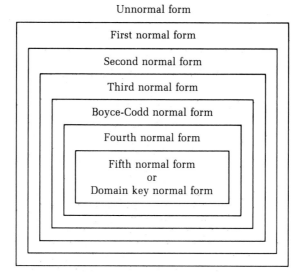

FIGURE 9.6 Nesting of normal forms

DKNF. DKNF is a goal for the integrated file and DBMS database designer.

The other normal forms are more easily achieved and defined with respect to each other. We describe them from the least restrictive form to the most restrictive. The relationships among the normal forms are depicted in Fig. 9.6.

Unnormal Form

An entity specification is in unnormal form (UNF) if any of its attributes is not an atomic data item. Examples of nonatomic data items are multifield records and lists. Consider the entity specifications

    Q (R, S, T, U)   key is R
    T (W, X)   key is W

Note that T is a component of Q, so that in entity Q, attribute T is a structured value. That is, there is more than one data value contained in T. T is, in fact, another entity specification. Another way of writing Q is

    Q (R, S, (W, X), U)

Entity Q could be represented alternatively as

Q.1 (R, S, W, U)

since W is the primary key for entity T (and hence can determine a value for X). A set of entities like Q.1 is often called a **flat file**. Flat files are common in file environments, since a flat file is a file of nonvariant logical records.

First Normal Form

An entity specification is in first normal form (1NF) if it is not in UNF. That is, all its attributes are atomic, not structures. All flat files are at least 1NF.

Second Normal Form

An entity specification is in second normal form (2NF) if it is in first normal form and every nonkey attribute is functionally dependent on the primary key. There is no partial dependency between a nonkey attribute and the key. Note that the primary key of an entity specification can be a composite of attribute values. If the primary key is a single attribute, there can be no partial dependency and hence the specification must be in at least 2NF. For example, consider the entity specifications for E1 and E2 in Fig. 9.4. There is a partial dependency in E1; attribute C is dependent on only part of the primary key. This partial dependency violates 2NF. E1 can be changed to have properties of 2NF entities by eliminating attribute C (see E1.1 in Fig. 9.7).

Insertion and deletion anomalies can exist for 2NF entity specifications. For example, consider the entity BOOKSTORES in Fig. 9.8. There are two violations of 2NF. Try to identify them. For example, the deletion of the record with the value 20 for BID and the value Waldens for STORE will cause a loss of information about the address of Waldens. The intent was to delete a book from a store; not to delete a store! There are problems with insertions too: information concerning only STORE could not be added without a value for BID. Yet we could know about a bookstore without knowing about any particular book it stocks. It would be convenient to be able to represent just a STORE and the corresponding address. Second normal form anomalies can be eliminated by splitting one entity specification into two entity specifications. In Fig. 9.9 we show the results of doing this to remove both violations of 2NF from the BOOKSTORES entity specification. As we will see there can still be update anomalies.

Consider for a moment the candidate key (F, G, H) of E3.1 in Fig. 9.7. Clearly the entire set of attributes determines the individual attributes. Yet this candidate key has many extraneous attributes. In normalization to 2NF we seek to identify a minimal key containing the necessary attributes to determine an entity.

Entities:

E1.1 (A1, A2, A3, B)	composite key is (a1, a2, a3)
E2 (A1, A3, C)	composite key is (a1, a3)
E3.1 (F, G, H)	key is f
E4 (H, I)	key is h
E5.1 (M, N, O)	composite key is (m, n)
E5.2 (N, P)	composite key is (n, p)
E5.3 (P, M)	key is p

Dependencies:

(A1, A2, A3) $\longrightarrow$ B
(A1, A3) $\longrightarrow$ C
F $\longrightarrow$ G, H
H $\longrightarrow$ I
(M, N) $\longrightarrow$ O
(N, P) $\longrightarrow$ N, P
P $\longrightarrow$ M

Dependency graph:

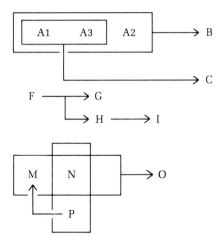

FIGURE 9.7 Revised entity specifications

Third Normal Form

An entity specification is in third normal form (3NF) if it is in second normal form and there are no transitive dependencies among the nonkey attributes. Entity E3 in Fig. 9.4 violates 3NF because H can determine I and neither is the key. This 3NF violation can be corrected by removing attribute I from E3, as shown in entity E3.1 in Fig. 9.7.

BOOKSTORES (BID, TITLE, STORE, QUANTITY, ADDRESS)
composite key is (bid, store)

20	Pascal	Union	16	School
20	Pascal	Tams	5	Reseda
20	Pascal	Waldens	10	Mall
30	Data S	Union	25	School
30	Data S	Tams	10	Reseda
38	Files	Union	33	School

Dependencies:

(BID, STORE) $\longrightarrow$ QUANTITY, ADDRESS, TITLE
BID $\longrightarrow$ TITLE
STORE $\longrightarrow$ ADDRESS

Dependency graph:

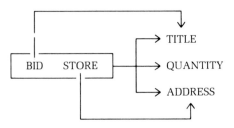

FIGURE 9.8 Violation of 2NF

Consider entity specifications STUDENTS.2 and ADVISERS in Fig. 9.10, which represent information about student advising. Because departments have different curricula requirements, a student should be advised by a faculty member in the department of his or her major. There is a transitive dependency in STUDENTS.2. SID determines values for DEPT transitively via PID. The transitive dependency in STUDENTS.2 exists because of one of the functional dependencies in ADVISERS. Clearly there is redundant data that can cause problems with updates. For example, if the record selected in ADVISERS by PID = 115 is modified so that DEPT = CE, there would be inconsistent data across the two files of records. The adviser of student 200 would be from a department (CE) different from that of the student (EE). With the given semantics, the above change to ADVISERS would either produce different and inconsistent data values in the STUDENTS.2 and ADVISERS files or require an update of all redundant dependencies. In a file processing environment, an application program would have to know all possibly redundant files to update. Depending

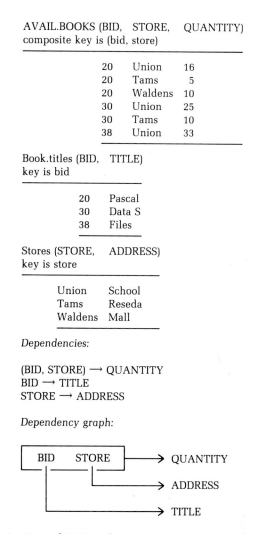

AVAIL.BOOKS (BID, STORE, QUANTITY)
composite key is (bid, store)

20	Union	16
20	Tams	5
20	Waldens	10
30	Union	25
30	Tams	10
38	Union	33

Book.titles (BID, TITLE)
key is bid

20	Pascal
30	Data S
38	Files

Stores (STORE, ADDRESS)
key is store

Union	School
Tams	Reseda
Waldens	Mall

Dependencies:

(BID, STORE) $\rightarrow$ QUANTITY
BID $\rightarrow$ TITLE
STORE $\rightarrow$ ADDRESS

Dependency graph:

FIGURE 9.9 Elimination of 2NF violations

on the DBMS, redundant data can be updated by the DBMS software (preferred) or by application programs.

Removal of the extraneous storage of attribute DEPT in STU-DENTS.2 would eliminate the transitive dependencies. Examine the 3NF version of relations STUDENTS.3 and ADVISERS in Fig. 9.11. Note that all the information is retained with reduced storage. Given the entities in Fig. 9.11 the previous update would enforce the constraint that adviser and student are in the same department. Now it

STUDENTS.2 (SID,   SNAME,   DEPT,   PID)
key is sid

100	Johnson	EE	107
150	Slominski	CS	208
200	Johnson	EE	115
250	Bruno	EE	107
300	Wang	CS	210

ADVISERS (PID,   PNAME,   DEPT)
key is pid

107	Roberts	EE
208	Solomon	CS
115	El Naga	EE
210	Horgan	CS

Dependencies:

SID $\longrightarrow$ DEPT, SNAME, PID
PID $\longrightarrow$ DEPT, PNAME

Dependency graph:

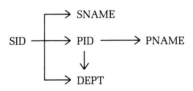

FIGURE 9.10 Violation of 3NF

is obvious that a change of El Naga's department from EE to CE would necessitate a change of adviser for Johnson (SID = 200) if the student is to remain in the EE department.

Boyce-Codd Normal Form

An entity specification is in Boyce-Codd normal form (BCNF) if it is in 3NF and it does not contain any Boyce-Codd dependencies. That is, all determinants are candidate keys. Recall that a candidate key is a potential primary key. Stated differently, every functional dependency is the consequence of a key rather than a nonkey. In Fig. 9.4, E5 violates BCNF although it is valid 3NF. E5 violates BCNF because the nonkey P determines M, part of the composite key (M, N).

STUDENTS.3 (SID,   SNAME,   PID)
key is sid

100	Johnson	107
150	Slominski	208
200	Johnson	115
250	Bruno	107
300	Wang	210

ADVISERS (PID,   PNAME,   DEPT)
key is pid

107	Roberts	EE
208	Solomon	CS
115	El Naga	EE
210	Horgan	CS

Dependencies:

SID $\rightarrow$ SNAME, PID
PID $\rightarrow$ PNAME, DEPT

Dependency graph:

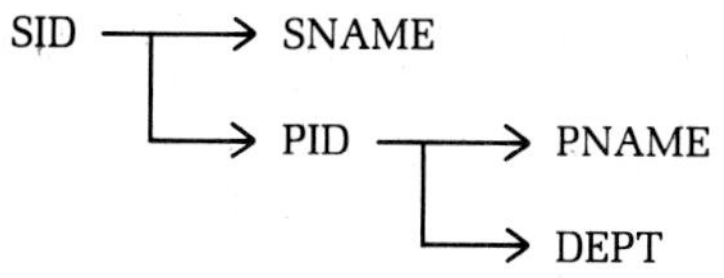

FIGURE 9.11 Elimination of 3NF violations

One normalization of entity specification E.5 creates three entity specifications: E5.1, E5.2, and E5.3 (see Fig. 9.7). In entity specification E5.1 the composite key (M, N) determines attribute O. In entity specification E5.2 the composite key (N, P) determines a unique combination of attributes N and P. In other words, the composite key determines itself: it is an identity association. This is called a **trivial dependency**. For simplicity we have not shown trivial dependencies except when they are necessary for normalization. Finally, in entity specification E5.3 the key P determines the attribute M. Trivial dependencies are not shown in this and later dependency graphs.

Consider, as an example, the association that might exist among teaching assistants (TA), students (SID), courses (CNAME), and rooms (ROOM). Let us assume that students enroll in courses before teaching assistants are assigned. In such a situation the entity specification

CLASSROOM as shown in Fig. 9.12(a) might exist after students are enrolled and teaching assistants are assigned to classrooms. For this example assume that a teaching assistant is assigned to a single course and a student in a course has only one teaching assistant.

CLASSROOM.1 in Fig. 9.12(b) shows the result of inserting TA into entity CLASSROOM. There is a Boyce-Codd dependency because CNAME (part of a key) is dependent on TA (a nonkey). Boyce-Codd normal form can be achieved by creating entity specifications in which each entity represents a single dependency. In this case the initial classroom entity specification is retained and two new specifications are established to represent the associations between TA and CNAME and between TA and SID. Example entities for these specifications are listed in Fig. 9.13.

Fourth Normal Form

An entity specification is in fourth normal form (4NF) if it is in BCNF and there is at most one independent multivalued dependency within the entity. Entity specifications that violate 4NF should be avoided because of the high data redundancy required to represent all cases of the 1:N associations and because of update problems. Figure 9.5 illustrated the redundancy in the entity TEXTS. Recall that TEXTS had an M:N multivalued dependency between course name and book identification (COURSE $\twoheadrightarrow$ BID and BID $\twoheadrightarrow$ COURSE) and a 1:N multivalued dependency between course name and course section (COURSE $\twoheadrightarrow$ SECTION and SECTION $\twoheadrightarrow$ COURSE). The two multivalued dependencies are independent since book identification and course section are unrelated. Fortunately, TEXTS can be normalized so as not to violate 4NF. This is done by creating separate entity specifications for each multivalued dependency. Figure 9.14 depicts a solution in 4NF with entities CLASS.TEXTS and CLASS.SECTIONS. Note that while the number of different entity specifications has increased (from 1 to 2), the number of data values stored has decreased (from 33 to 26).

At the end of Section 9.1 we presented an example of an insertion anomaly with the TEXTS entity specification. Let us examine the effects of inserting the record

07, CS242

into CLASS.TEXTS. There is no anomaly because the semantic constraint in CLASS.TEXTS is that all sections of the same course have the same reading requirements.

Fifth Normal Form

An entity specification is in fifth normal form (5NF) if it is in 4NF and the dependencies cannot be decomposed into simpler entity specifications without loss of information. Normalization to fifth normal

CLASSROOM (SID,   CNAME,   ROOM)
composite key is (sid, cname)

351	CS132	E107
352	CS132	E107
353	CS132	E136
351	CS122	E139
356	CS122	E136

Dependencies (dependency graph):

(a) Entity CLASSROOM before TA

CLASSROOM.1 (SID,   CNAME,   ROOM,   TA)
composite key is (sid, cname)

351	CS132	E107	Sun
352	CS132	E107	Sun
353	CS132	E136	Zavala
351	CS122	E139	Carter
356	CS122	E136	Carter

Dependencies:

(SID, CNAME) $\rightarrow$ ROOM, TA
TA $\rightarrow$ CNAME

Dependency graph:

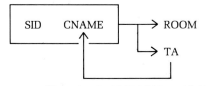

(b) Entity CLASSROOM.1 with TA

FIGURE 9.12 Entity CLASSROOM before and after adding TA

CLASSROOM (SID,   CNAME,   ROOM)
composite key is (sid, cname)

351	CS132	E107
352	CS132	E107
353	CS132	E136
351	CS122	E139
356	CS122	E136

COURSE-ASSISTANT (TA,   CNAME)
key is ta

Sun	CS132
Zavala	CS132
Carter	CS122

STUDENT-ASSISTANT (SID,   TA)
composite key is (sid, ta)

351	Sun
352	Sun
353	Zavala
351	Carter
356	Carter

Dependencies:

(SID, CNAME) $\rightarrow$ ROOM
TA $\rightarrow$ CNAME
(SID, TA) $\rightarrow$ SID, TA

Dependency graph:

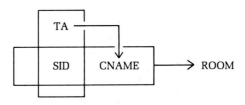

FIGURE 9.13 Boyce-Codd normal form example entities

CLASS.TEXTS (BID,   COURSE)
composite key is (bid, course)

20	CS132
20	CS182
30	CS182
38	CS242
42	CS242
42	CS440

CLASS.SECTIONS (COURSE,   SECTION)
key is section

CS132	456
CS132	457
CS182	458
CS182	459
CS242	460
CS242	461
CS440	540

Dependencies:

COURSE ⟶ BID
COURSE ⟶ SECTION
SECTION ⟶ COURSE

Dependency graph:

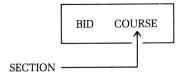

FIGURE 9.14 Elimination of 4NF violations

form reduces data redundancy due to multivalued dependencies. If an entity specification can be rewritten as two or more entity specifications, each having fewer attributes and without losing any dependencies, it is not in 5NF. Naturally we must exclude cases where the new specifications have the same key as the old one and differ only in nonkey entities. These cases are excluded because the determinants are the same and so the decomposition is trivial. For example, consider the decomposition of entity specification D (A, B, C, E), where A is the key into D.1 (A, B) and D.2 (A, C, E). Nothing has been gained!

ASSIGNMENTS (PNAME, DEPT, COURSE)
composite key is (pname, dept, course)

Jones	Math	Fortran
Jones	CS	Fortran
Brown	EE	Num. Methods
Brown	Math	Num. Methods
Brown	CS	Logic
Abbott	CS	Num. Methods
Abbott	Math	Fortran
Cowan	EE	Dig. Circuits
Cowan	CS	Fortran

FIGURE 9.15 Entities in 5NF

Consider the entity specification ASSIGNMENTS in Fig. 9.15. Assume that departments offer courses in many topic areas and that professors, being highly versatile, can teach many types of courses for many departments. With no semantic constraints on the attributes, we need all three fields in one entity. The primary key is the combination of all three fields. The entity specification cannot be decomposed further: it is in 5NF.

Now consider the effect of adding a semantic constraint that says that if a professor teaches a certain course and he teaches for a department that offers that course, then he must teach the course for that department. Under these conditions, we can represent the ASSIGNMENTS entity specification by three smaller entity specifications with less redundancy. First note that the entities of Fig. 9.15 violate the new constraints; Fig. 9.16 shows a revised set. The entities marked * have been added to meet the new constraints. For example, in Fig. 9.15 Brown teaches for the EE, Math, and CS departments and teaches Num. Methods and Logic. The CS department offers a course in Num. Methods, so Brown is assigned to teach it.

The entity specification of Fig. 9.16 is not in 5NF because we can represent the same information by the three two-field entity specifications of Fig. 9.17. Note that we need all three two-field entity specifications. Check this by eliminating in turn each of the three specifications of Fig. 9.17. See what three-field entities you derive from the remaining two specifications. You should find that in each case you get illegal entities, that is, entities not in Fig. 9.16. For example, if we eliminate the OFFERINGS entity specification we might deduce erroneously from EXPERTISE and AFFILIATIONS that Cowan teaches Fortran for the EE department.

If a 4NF entity specification cannot be constructed from smaller entity specifications, then the 4NF entity specification is also a 5NF

ASSIGNMENTS (PNAME, DEPT, COURSE)
composite key is (pname, dept, course)

	PNAME	DEPT	COURSE
	Jones	Math	Fortran
	Jones	CS	Fortran
	Brown	EE	Num. Methods
	Brown	Math	Num. Methods
	Brown	CS	Logic
*	Brown	CS	Num. Methods
*	Abbott	CS	Fortran
	Abbott	CS	Num. Methods
	Abbott	Math	Fortran
*	Abbott	Math	Num. Methods
	Cowan	EE	Dig. Circuits
	Cowan	CS	Fortran

FIGURE 9.16 Violation of 5NF

entity specification. We will discuss the notion of reconstructing entities without loss of information in Chapter 12.

Research on normalization is a current and active process. The material we have just discussed is the product of the efforts of many individuals. Codd [81, 82] defined the first three normal forms and the Boyce-Codd normal form. Fagin [80, 83, 84] introduced 4NF, 5NF, and DKNF. The following sources present more sophisticated and formal treatments of normalization than we present in this text: Stout and Woodworth [85], Beeri, Fagin, and Howard [86], Bernstein [87], Fagin [88], and Sagiv [89]. In addition, several database and database management textbooks other than our own have descriptions and examples of the normalization process.

Normalization and Efficiency

In the preceding discussion we considered the benefits of normalization. Normalization reduces update anomalies and data redundancy by eliminating from an entity specification dependencies where the determinant is not the key. Entity specifications are often more complex; they contain many dependencies. In such cases normalization will create a larger set of simpler entity specifications. This results in more files in an integrated file environment. This is also true in a database environment where all entities with the same specification are stored in a file.

For some data processing tasks, efficiency is the price paid for normalization. This price is paid when transactions must access many rather than few files. For example, consider the entities in Fig. 9.16.

AFFILIATIONS (PNAME,   DEPT)
composite key is (pname, dept)

Jones	Math
Jones	CS
Brown	EE
Brown	Math
Abbott	CS
Abbott	Math
Cowan	EE
Cowan	CS

EXPERTISE (PNAME,   COURSE)
composite key is (pname, course)

Jones	Fortran
Brown	Num. Methods
Brown	Logic
Abbott	Fortran
Abbott	Num. Methods
Cowan	Fortran
Cowan	Dig. Circuits

OFFERINGS (DEPT,   COURSE)
composite key is (dept, course)

Math	Fortran
Math	Num. Methods
CS	Fortran
CS	Logic
CS	Num. Methods
EE	Num. Methods
EE	Dig. Circuits

FIGURE 9.17 Elimination of 5NF violations

These data values could be used to generate a report listing classes being taught. Using the normalized entities in Fig. 9.17 would make this report generation less efficient (more file accesses and more complexity) than using the less normalized entities in Fig. 9.16. In addition, modification of key values can often require more file accesses given a normalized set of entity specifications. In general, however, the modification of nonkey attributes is more efficient in a normalized environment. Normalization, on the whole, is desirable and results in a better data processing environment. However, certain data processing tasks are hindered by highly normalized entity specifications.

Thus, in each application, the designer must balance the gains in data management against the possible loss in efficiency when determining the level of normalization required. In some cases it is sufficient to normalize only the single-valued dependencies and maintain multivalued semantics with application programs.

9.3 SECS Example Database Record Design

The example in this section concerns current and past courses offered by a School of Engineering and Computer Science (SECS), and we will also use this example in the succeeding chapters on databases. A database with these entities could be used to facilitate student advising, to check on prerequisites, to determine the students and the instructor for a course section, and to register students in sections of courses. (There is some overlap between the entities specified here and the SECS example for integrated files that we presented in Chapter 8.) For this database design we will need information about professors, students, and courses. Because a complete solution to this design would be too long for our purposes in this textbook, we make some simplifying restrictions about the information required and the associations allowed. However, we encourage you to generalize this restricted example to a school you are currently attending or have attended in the past. Before we present the dependencies among the attribute set, we briefly present the semantics concerning professors, students, and courses.

We need information about professors (PROFS) to establish advising associations between professors and students, and to specify which professor teaches a specific course section. The attributes we consider for professors are name (PNAME), a unique identification number (PID), office number (OFFICE#), and major department (DEPT). Here we assume that the earlier semantics regarding the dependencies among offices and departments do not exist.

For students, it is important to represent current information and information about past semesters. Current student (STUDENT) information should specify name (SNAME), a unique identification number (SID), major (MAJOR), grade point average (GPA), units of course work completed (SUNITS), and MAJOR prerequisite course completed (SPREREQ). In addition, we must maintain information about students' past performance in courses completed. This information should specify the course name, semester, year, and grade a student received (CNAME, SEMESTER, YEAR, and GRADE).

Course (COURSE) information shall include a unique name (CNAME), prerequisites for the class (PREREQ), and units (UNITS).

$$PID \longrightarrow PNAME, OFFICE\#, DEPT$$
$$PID \longrightarrow\!\!\!\rightarrow SID, SNUM$$
$$CNAME \longrightarrow SPREREQ, UNITS$$
$$CNAME \longrightarrow\!\!\!\rightarrow SNUM$$
$$SNUM \longrightarrow CNAME, PID, ROOM, BEGIN, END$$
$$SNUM \longrightarrow\!\!\!\rightarrow SID$$
$$SID \longrightarrow PID, SNAME, SPREREQ, MAJOR, GPA, SUNITS$$
$$SID \longrightarrow\!\!\!\rightarrow PID, SNUM$$
$$(SID, SEMESTER, YEAR, CNAME) \longrightarrow GRADE$$

FIGURE 9.18 Dependencies among SECS example attributes

Because schools often offer the same course at different times, we postulate the existence of course sections (SECTION). Each section will have a unique identification number (SNUM), a reference to course (CNAME), a room (ROOM), and a time interval (BEGIN and END). For course and student prerequisites we will assume that each course has a single prerequisite course that represents the most restrictive such course. For example, the prerequisite course for an introduction to files and databases might be an introductory course on data structures.

Before examining the associations among entities, we should make sure that all the entity specifications described so far are in at least first normal form. A possible violation of first normal form could exist in a student entity where information about past performance is represented as a list of course names and grades. To remove this violation we postulate a new entity called STUD.REC that will contain student records. Each instance of a STUD.REC will represent the grade obtained in one class by one student. Thus, STUD.REC should contain SID, SEMESTER, YEAR, CNAME, and GRADE.

Next we must specify the associations among the entities. Figure 9.18 lists the dependencies that exist among the example attributes. These dependencies represent the associations that exist between professors and students, courses and sections, professors and sections, students and past class grades, and students and sections. In Fig. 9.19 we introduce **Bachman diagrams** to represent the associations among these entities. A Bachman diagram [90] depicts entity names inside boxes and an association between two entities as a line with arrows at each end. If each end has a single arrow, the association is 1:1. If one end has a single arrow and the other a double arrow, the association is 1:N. An M:N association is represented by a line with a double arrow at each end.

There are two multivalued dependencies between professors and students. A professor can advise many students, while in our example,

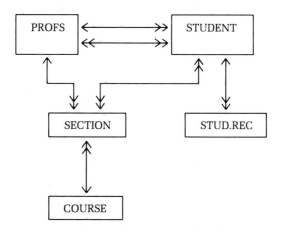

FIGURE 9.19 Initial associations among SECS example entities

a student has a single adviser. The adviser association is 1:*N*. In addition, a student may have many professors as instructors and a professor can be the instructor of many students (*M:N* association). Both professors and students have associations with course sections. A professor teaches several course sections and each section has a single instructor (1:*N* association). A student enrolls in several course sections, and a section has several students (*M:N* association). Each course has several class sections, but a class section is an instance of a single course (1:*N* association). Clearly, the associations among professors, students, and course sections require normalization to provide a robust design. The associations among professors, students, student records, courses, and sections are illustrated in the Bachman diagram in Fig. 9.19.

The associations between students and student records and between course sections and courses are straightforward. We will examine these associations first and then address the more complicated design issues (professors, students, and courses). First, consider students and the record of their past performance. The STUD.REC entity was specified earlier to eliminate embedded lists within the STUDENT entity specification. Since there is a single instance of a "SID, SEMESTER, YEAR, CNAME, GRADE" record for each grade a student has obtained, the association between STUDENT and STUD.REC is 1:*N*. The composite key for a STUD.REC entity is (SID, SEMESTER, YEAR, CNAME). Second, the association between COURSE and course SECTION is 1:*N* and the key of COURSE is CNAME. We show examples of the STUD.REC, SECTION, and COURSE entities in Fig.

STUD.REC (SID, SEMESTER, YEAR, CNAME, GRADE)
composite key is (sid, semester, year, cname)

261	Spring	80	CS132	C
261	Spring	80	M150A	C
261	Fall	80	CS122	B
261	Spring	81	CS182	C
118	Spring	79	M150B	A
118	Fall	80	CS182	B

SECTION (SNUM, CNAME, ROOM, BEGIN, END)
key is snum

550	CS332	E417	MWF1000	1050
551	CS480	E419	TTH0930	1050
461	CS242	E107	MWF1300	1350
463	CS242	E216	TTH1300	1420
464	CS232	E107	MWF0900	0950

COURSE (CNAME, PREREQ, UNITS)
key is cname

M150A	M150B	5
CS242	CS182	3
CS332	CS232	3
CS480	CS380	4

FIGURE 9.20 Examples of STUD.REC, SECTION, and COURSE entities

9.20. Given the dependencies in Fig. 9.18, the STUD.REC, SECTION, and COURSE entities in Fig. 9.19 are normalized.

The design of professor, student, and section associations is not as obvious as above. We start this design process by examining a worst case. Consider the entity specification PROFS-STUDENT-SECTION presented in Fig. 9.21. This entity contains all combinations of the associations among the entities PROFS, STUDENT, and SECTION. For completeness, example instances of entities PROFS and STUDENT are also shown. The attributes PIDI and PIDA are used here to represent professors that are instructors and advisers respectively. Examine the entity PROFS-STUDENT-SECTION and list the problems normalization should resolve. Determine your normalized solution before continuing.

There are two major problems with the dependencies in the entity specification PROFS-STUDENT-SECTION. First, since SID determines PIDA and SNUM determines PIDI, there are partial dependencies within the composite key (SID, SNUM). Second, the advising and

PROFS-STUDENT-SECTION (PIDI, SID, PIDA, SNUM)
composite key is (sid, snum)

20	261	20	461
21	118	21	463
20	115	21	550
20	118	21	464
21	115	20	463

PROFS (PID, PNAME, OFFICE#, DEPT)
key is pid

20	Barnes	413	CS
11	Mishra	413	EE
21	Smith	414	CS

STUDENT (SID, SNAME, MAJOR, SPREREQ, GPA, SUNITS)
key is sid

261	Brown	Math	CS182	2.8	39
118	Gomez	CS	CS182	3.2	51
115	Fisher	CS	CS232	2.5	63

FIGURE 9.21 Examples of professor, student, section associations

instructing associations between professors and students are independent and multivalued. This violates fourth normal form and produces data redundancy. For example, there is no need to specify more than once that Smith is Gomez's adviser. Both of these problems can be resolved by decomposition. We will consider the instructing association between students and professor before examining the advising association.

The M:N dependencies between professors (PIDI) and students can be extracted from the PROFS-STUDENT-SECTION entity into an entity specification we name SECT.STUD (see Fig. 9.22). This entity specification contains attributes SNUM and SID and has the composite key (SNUM, SID). Each entity represents the fact that student SID is enrolled in course section SNUM. The 1:N association between professor and section can be represented by placing the appropriate PID (PIDI) in the SECTION entity to reference the instructor (see SECTION.1 in Fig. 9.22).

A similar solution could be applied to generate an entity representing the advising association between professors (PIDA) and students. This entity (ADVISER) would contain the attributes PID and

SECT.STUD (SNUM,   SID)
composite key is (snum, sid)

461	261
463	118
550	115
464	118
463	115

SECTION.1 (SNUM,   CNAME,   PID,   ROOM,   BEGIN,   END)
key is snum

SNUM	CNAME	PID	ROOM	BEGIN	END
550	CS332	20	E417	MWF1000	1050
551	CS480	21	E419	TTH0930	1050
461	CS242	20	E107	MWF1300	1350
463	CS242	21	E216	TTH1300	1420
464	CS232	20	E107	MWF0900	0950

STUDENT.1 (SID,   SNAME,   MAJOR,   PID,   SPREREQ,   GPA,   SUNITS)
key is sid

SID	SNAME	MAJOR	PID	SPREREQ	GPA	SUNITS
261	Brown	Math	20	CS182	2.8	39
118	Gomez	CS	21	CS182	3.2	51
115	Fisher	CS	21	CS232	2.5	63

FIGURE 9.22 Normalized instruction and advising associations

SID. We do not adopt this solution here because it would result in redundant data. Since the advising association is 1:N, we can insert the appropriate PID (PIDA) value into the existing STUDENT entity (see STUDENT.1 in Fig. 9.22). In this solution we have eliminated an additional entity specification and redundant copies of attribute SID. As an exercise, generate the corresponding instances for the adviser entity specification and compare them with the solution presented in Fig. 9.22. Be sure to count all data items in entities STUDENT, AD-VISER, and PROFS.

The resulting normalized entity specifications and dependencies are depicted in Fig. 9.23. Note that we are adopting simpler names for the normalized STUDENT.1 (STUDENT) and SECTION.1 (SEC-TION) entity specifications because we will continue these examples in Chapters 11 and 12. If each entity specification were stored as a separate file, one could develop application programs to determine, among other things, the students a professor advises, the past grade for a student in a class, the instructor of a class section, and the students enrolled in a section. These are left as exercises for the

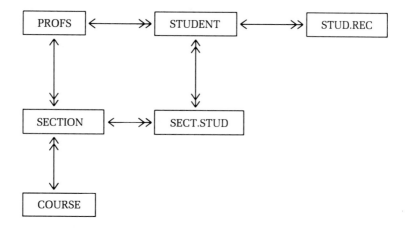

Entity specifications:

1. PROFS (PID, PNAME, OFFICE#, DEPT)
   key is pid
2. COURSE (CNAME, PREREQ, UNITS)
   key is cname
3. SECTION (SNUM, CNAME, PID, ROOM, BEGIN, END)
   key is snum
4. STUDENT (SID, SNAME, MAJOR, PID, SPREREQ, GPA, SUNITS)
   key is sid
5. STUD.REC (SID, SEMESTER, YEAR, CNAME, GRADE)
   composite key is (sid, semester, year, cname)
6. SECT.STUD (SNUM, SID)
   composite key is (snum, sid)

Dependencies:

PID $\rightarrow$ PNAME, OFFICE#, DEPT
CNAME $\rightarrow$ PREREQ, UNITS
SNUM $\rightarrow$ CNAME, PID, ROOM, BEGIN, END
SID $\rightarrow$ SNAME, SPREREQ, PID, MAJOR, GPA, SUNITS
(SID, SEMESTER, YEAR, CNAME) $\rightarrow$ GRADE

FIGURE 9.23 Entities and dependencies for SECS example

reader. Recalling the discussion of Chapter 8, you should consider the possible accessing techniques applicable for this set of integrated files.

In Chapters 11 and 12 we will present three common data models that are implemented in various database management systems: the hierarchical, network, and relational models. Chapter 11 describes the hierarchical and network data models, which are implemented as trees and graphs respectively. Chapter 12 describes the relational data model, which is implemented using flat files or tables.

Summary

In this chapter we have examined factors that designers should consider when developing specifications for interrelated entities. Entity specifications should be robust with respect to update anomalies. The process of developing robust specifications is called normalization. Normalization generates entity specifications such that all logical constraints are the function of keys determining nonkey attributes.

To clarify normalization we defined several normal forms (UNF, 1NF, 2NF, 3NF, BCNF, 4NF, 5NF, and DKNF) with examples. The normal forms describe the types of dependencies allowed between attributes within an entity specification. In a sense, normal forms are assertions about the entities. The first, second, third, and Boyce-Codd normal forms describe properties of entities with single-valued dependencies. The fourth and fifth normal forms describe the properties of entities with both multivalued and single-valued dependencies. Domain key normal form—the specification that all logical constraints (semantics) are represented as the consequence of keys determining nonkeys—is a type of normal form specification different from the others. DKNF differs from the other normal forms because there are no rules to apply that will always transform a set of entities from a lower form to DKNF. However, DKNF and 5NF are reasonably equivalent forms with respect to permissible assertions about the associations among attributes within and across a set of entities. The nomenclature and process of normalization is an active research area and will continue to affect database management systems.

In conclusion, the goal of normalization is to specify simple entities that clearly represent the semantics of the information being stored. That is, an entity should represent a single association or dependency of a key that determines nonkeys. In the next three chapters three general data models for DBMS will be discussed.

Exercises

1. For the following entity specifications and functional dependencies, determine the normal form of each entity, and normalize the set of entities.

Entities:

R1 (B, E, A, C, H)   composite key is (b, e)
R2 (S, U, R, F)   composite key is (s, u)
R3 (N, O, W)   key is n

Dependencies:

(B, E) → A, C, H
   C → H
   A → B
(S, U) → R, F
   U → F
   N → O, W
   W → O

2. The primary key and the dependencies are given for each of the following five entity specifications. For each specification (1) give the highest normal form that the specification is in (1NF, 2NF, 3NF, or BCNF), and (2) if the specification is not in BCNF, give equivalent specifications that are.

a) R1 (E, F, G, H)   primary key is e

   Dependencies: E → F, G, H   and   F → G

b) R2 (M, N, O)   primary key is m

   Dependencies: M → N, O

c) R3 (I, J, K, L)   composite primary key is (i, j, k)

   Dependencies: J → K   and   (I, J, K) → L

d) R4 (P, Q, R, S)   composite primary key is (p, q)

   Dependencies: (P, Q) → R, S   and   R → S

e) R5 (A, B, C, D)   composite primary key is (a, b)

   Dependencies: (A, B) → C   and   B → D

3. Consider the following entity specification and dependencies. First classify each of the dependencies and then normalize the entity specification.

(A, B, C, D, E)   composite primary key is (a, b)

Dependencies:

(A, B) → C, D
   A → E
   C → B, D

4. For the set of dependencies below, draw the dependency graph and derive a set of normalized entity specifications.

$(G, B) \rightarrow C, D$
$(C, D) \rightarrow B, E$
$C \rightarrow D, F$
$D \rightarrow E$
$H \rightarrow R$

5. Assume that you need to keep track of the majors and campus club memberships of students at a university. Each student has a student identification number. Also a student may have several majors and belong to several clubs. What entity specifications would you design and what are the semantics represented?

6. Choose an institution you know fairly well and define a set of normalized entity specifications. Be sure to specify your initial semantics (dependencies). Some example institutions are professional athletic leagues (baseball, football), citizens and their community service activities, or church membership and church service groups.

7. Normalize the following entity specification.

R (A, B, C, D, E, F)   key is a

Dependencies:

$A \rightarrow B, C, F$
$A \rightarrow D, E$
$B \rightarrow A$
$C \rightarrow F$

8. Adapt the SECS example entities to the school you are attending or have attended. First, specify the attributes you wish to represent and the dependencies that exist. Next, draw dependency graphs for your attribute set, and develop normalized entity specifications from the dependencies.

9. Assume that the normalized SECS entity specifications presented at the end of this chapter are separate direct-access files. Design application programs that would (1) determine a list of all students enrolled in a course section, (2) generate a list of all students a professor advises, and (3) list all the sections of a course. What access techniques would you use? Compare your solutions to the examples in Chapter 8.

10. Given the semantics provided below, determine the effects, if any, the choice of primary key (A or B) has on update modifications (insertion, deletion, or changing a nonkey value).

```
R  (A,  B,  C,  D)
   1   6  Z  Y
   2   7  Y  Z
   3   8  W  X
   4   9  X  W
   5  10  T  U
```

Dependencies:

A → B, C, D

B → A, C, D

11. Can normalization be automated? If so, what input would a normalization program require? What limitations might it have? (Hint: see the paper by Sagiv [89].)

12. Why does a Boyce-Codd dependency not exist when a nonkey attribute determines the key? Consider the entity specification and dependencies below. Compare the dependencies U → T and C → B.

R1 (A, B, C, D)   composite key is (a, b)
R2 (T, U, V, W)   key is t

Dependencies:

(A, B) → C, D

C → B

T → U, V, W

U → T

Suggestions for Further Reading

C. J. Date, *An Introduction to Database Systems,* 3rd ed. (Reading, Mass.: Addison-Wesley, 1981).

W. Kent, "A simple guide to five normal forms in relational database theory," *Communications of the ACM,* 26(2), pp. 120–125 (February 1983).

D. M. Kroenke, *Database Processing: Fundamentals, Design, Implementation,* 2nd ed. (Palo Alto, Calif.: Science Research Associates, 1983).

10

Database Management Systems

10.1 Presents the advantages and disadvantages of data processing in a DBMS environment.

10.2 Enumerates the major functions that a DBMS should provide.

10.3 Introduces the architectural components of multiuser DBMS's together with the software utilities that allow the definition and creation of a database.

10.4 Examines the life cycle of a database.

In this chapter, which begins the database portion of this text, we introduce and discuss common aspects of database management systems (DBMS's). Succeeding chapters will address specific database issues. Chapters 11 and 12 present example data models used to represent information logically in a database. In Chapter 11 the hierarchical and network database models are considered. Chapter 12 describes the relational database model and contrasts the three data models. Chapter 13 concerns data integrity, concurrent access, and security issues for DBMS's. Finally, Chapter 14 presents a brief overview of current and future research topics in DBMS's and discusses the optimization of query processing, database machines, and distributed database systems.

In Chapter 8 we examined problems that may be encountered when processing data in an integrated file environment. To a certain extent, a set of integrated files can be considered a physical database that is used without database management support. Here we use the term "database" to refer to data processing in a DBMS environment. In Chapter 9 we discussed issues for designing (normalizing) the logical records to be used either in a set of integrated files or in a database.

Normalization can minimize possible update anomalies with integrated files. Normalization does not, however, provide independence between application programs (the logical view of the data) and integrated files (the physical data). In this chapter we introduce data processing in a DBMS environment and show how a DBMS can provide insulation between logical and physical databases. We also introduce and discuss the major components of a DBMS.

In simple terms, a DBMS is a collection of software and hardware components that enables individuals to process large amounts of associated data. To do this a DBMS must be able to configure a computer system with secondary storage so that it can define, create, store, update, archive, and manage integrated data files. Furthermore, many application programs should be able to use the data at the same time. Although many DBMS's exist for single-user personal computers, more complex DBMS's—those that exist on multiuser, multitasking computers—are the focus of this and later chapters.

10.1 Data Processing with a DBMS

Assume for the moment that you have to set up a data processing environment containing many files of records that are highly related (perhaps partially redundant). Assume further that the data will be used concurrently by different applications. An example is the SECS environment defined at the end of Chapter 1. The following two different user groups and example applications are based on the SECS database. The first user group is students. One application gives them information about which professor is teaching a specific section of a class, the professor's office hours, and the professor's phone number. The second user group is professors. Various applications allow them to view information about the past performance of students in prerequisite classes and to update data about their current classes. With such applications many students and professors may request the same data records at the same time. A DBMS would enable you to set up such a data processing environment easily.

Advantages of Using a DBMS

There are six main advantages to using a DBMS rather than an integrated file environment. These advantages reflect greater flexibility in data processing capabilities. First, more information can be stored in the same amount of space in a database than in a file system. For example, the storage requirements of database pointers are usually less than the requirements for redundant data values or symbolic keys. Furthermore, information about the associations among data records is stored in the database. (The storage of associations among records in the database leads to the next two advantages, which also increase a database's information capacity.) Second, DBMS's have a greater degree of independence between program (logical view of data) and the data (physical database). Since intra- and interrecord associations are stored in the database, the application programs do not need to store associations among records as code. Third, databases have less data redundancy. Storing the associations (pointers) among data values can greatly reduce data redundancy. Fourth, DBMS's make it easier to generate answers to requests for one-of-a-kind reports using existing report generators and **query language** interfaces. Query languages and report generators can also reduce the number of applications that must be coded by programmers. Fifth, DBMS's allow more sophisticated programming. Complex applications may be performed more efficiently in a DBMS. Sixth, and finally, DBMS's manage data better because of minimized data redundancy and the existence of support personnel who maintain the database separately from application programs.

Disadvantages of Using a DBMS

There are four major disadvantages to using a DBMS rather than an integrated file processing environment. These disadvantages reflect increased costs and system vulnerability. First, DBMS's are more vulnerable than file-based systems because of the centralized nature of a large integrated database. Lately there has been a trend toward distributing databases to reduce the impact of system failure. (We will discuss this issue in more detail in Chapter 14.) Second, because many users may be accessing the database when a failure occurs, the recovery process is more complex. It is harder to determine what the state of the database was prior to failure. Although audit trails and incremental backups facilitate recovery, sometimes a failure results in lost transactions. Third, the sophisticated programming in a DBMS requires longer design and implementation time for new application programs. Modification of existing application programs also takes more effort. Thus all programming time is increased. Finally, hardware, software, and personnel costs are higher for DBMS's. Personnel costs are increased because of the experience and knowledge required to write applications against databases and to support databases.

10.2 Functions of a DBMS

A database exists so that concurrent users can extract information for various applications with high system reliability and at a reasonable cost. The functions of a DBMS are concerned with providing efficient flexible data processing capabilities without compromising data validity. Because efficiency is of no use if the data is not valid, we first examine the DBMS functions concerned with maintaining data validity. Next, we examine the DBMS functions that support efficient and flexible data processing. Finally, we examine the DBMS administration support functions that facilitate database design, utilization, and maintenance.

Maintaining Data Validity

The validity of the data in a database system represents the degree of certainty users have (1) that data values are correct, (2) that access to the data is restricted to approved applications, and (3) that concurrent access is properly synchronized. These issues reflect the DBMS functions of providing data integrity, security, and shared data.

Data integrity. The degree to which data values are correct is a measure of data integrity. Recall from Chapter 9 that all copies of the same data must have the same value. The integrity of the data has been lost if this is no longer true. Which value is to be considered correct and which incorrect in such a case? We will discuss data integrity further in Chapter 13.

Database security. A breach of database security is extremely serious. At the same time, restricting access to sensitive data is difficult. Within a community of database users there often exist subsets of individuals who require access to different portions of the database. Allowing all users to access all data would make the preservation of data validity more difficult. Clearly the ability to limit access to data on the basis of need reduces the possible sources of unauthorized access and so increases integrity. As we will see in Chapters 11, 12, and 13, access rights to a database can be controlled in the logical declaration of the database and in its physical implementation.

Shared data. Concurrent access is another factor that affects data validity. It is economically desirable to have concurrent access for both read and modify operations on a database because many applications can be productive simultaneously. However, the synchronization of concurrent access to the same data is extremely important for maintaining data validity. If many application programs are trying to update data in an interleaved manner, false data values may result. We will discuss this issue in more detail in Chapter 13. Here it suffices to state that DBMS's provide mechanisms that either explicitly or implicitly enable one application to "lock out" other concurrent applications while a data record is modified. In such a system the blocked applications typically wait in a queue for the shared resource to be released.

Efficient and Flexible Data Processing

In addition to maintaining data validity, a good DBMS should also facilitate efficient and flexible data processing. First, a DBMS should provide users with flexible access paths to shared data. Second, high-level data manipulation (programming) languages should be available to users.

Flexible access to data. After having studied the first part of this book, you should be aware of the access mechanisms that a DBMS can provide. A DBMS provides mechanisms by which the designer of the logical structure can either specify the access technique (and logical storage area) to be implemented for records or utilize system-provided defaults. Access techniques available usually include hashing, a B-tree variant index, and plex (graph) linkage. We discussed the appropriateness of various access mechanisms in Chapter 8. The designer can specify data access mechanisms when compiling the logical structure of the database. The logical database is compiled using a **data definition language** (or data description language, DDL).

In addition, flexible data access can be provided by using a logical translation, or filter, between the application program and the logical database. We examine this filter in more detail in Section 10.3 on DBMS architecture. Here it suffices to mention that different application programs perceive the data in a structure that is optimal for their requirements. Thus, several applications can be executed concurrently using shared records. Furthermore, the logical declarations of the records accessed can vary from application to application. A DBMS with the capability of perceiving data structured in an optimal manner should increase programmers' productivity in developing and maintaining software.

Data manipulation languages (DML). The second category of DBMS functions for flexible data processing includes query and application programming languages for data manipulation. A query language is typically a nonprocedural interface for users. "Nonprocedural" implies that programs cannot be written within the language. Rather, users ask questions (queries) about data values stored in the database, and the DBMS determines the operations needed to satisfy the requests. For example, given the SECS entity specifications described in Chapter 9, one could use a query language to display information about a particular professor:

```
SELECT PROFS WHERE PID = 11
```

This query would return (display or print) the contents of the professor record for Professor Mishra. In Chapter 12 we will see examples of queries that can be posed on a normalized relational database. Non-procedural query languages are suitable for data retrieval by both nontechnical and technical individuals. Nontechnical individuals, such as managers, accountants, and secretaries, can use the query system to ask questions easily and rapidly. Technical individuals, such as programmers and system support personnel, can use query languages to verify the results of application programs and to check the validity of the stored data.

A good DBMS should also support extended compilers for a wide range of application programming languages. (The compilers must be extended to allow programs to make access requests to the DBMS.) This enables programmers to choose the language that is best suited for the task or to choose the language in which they are most proficient. Furthermore, the ability to support a wide range of languages leads to portability, across DBMS's, of applications written in different languages. For example, a DBMS site that writes applications in PL/1 can install applications written in COBOL at other installations if the DBMS has a COBOL interface.

Database Administration

The third DBMS component concerned with efficient and flexible data processing is its administration. Database administration involves design, implementation, and maintenance. Although small databases with few applications and users have fairly simple administration requirements, they have some of the same requirements as large multiuser systems. Application programmers usually perform the administrative functions in a small database environment. Commonly, such a database is used by a single user at a time. In the case of a large DBMS supporting concurrent users, database administration is the concern of the database administrator (DBA).

Database administrator. The database administrator is responsible for designing, creating, loading, and maintaining the database. Often the DBA is a group of people rather than one person. The DBA is a centralized source for information about the current state of the database and the scheduling of changes to the database for the application programmers and users. The DBA arbitrates problems encountered when several applications share data but there is doubt about data ownership and responsibility. The DBA serves to maintain data integrity, enforce security precautions, and minimize redundant data by controlling the design and implementation of the database.

Database design and implementation. An essential function of a DBMS is to provide the tools to design both the logical and physical structure of a database. Both the logical and physical database declarations are compiled with DBMS tools available to the administrator. As we will see in Section 10.3, declarations for a database have two levels. The **logical database** is the common logical declaration for all entity specifications, and the **functional databases** are the entity specification developed for specific groups of applications. The functional databases are derived from the declarations in the logical database. DBMS's provide the administrator with data definition languages (DDLs) for logical and functional database compilation. Examples of declarations in a psuedo DDL for hierarchical, network, and relational database models are provided in the next two chapters.

The logical database must be mapped onto the actual data files. This mapping is described in the **physical data description module** by the DBA. The physical data description is compiled using a DBMS-provided language. (For example, this language is called the **device media control language**, or DMCL, in the network database model.)

Database maintenance. Database administration is also facilitated by tools that allow the database to be backed up, or archived, and that allow data to be recovered from the archives. These functions are similar to operating system utilities that provide backup and recovery functions for files. In addition, however, a DBA requires utilities that can repair the associations between data records stored in the database. Such repair is different from backing up to a known version of the data base because it attempts to reconstruct lost logical associations (pointers) between records.

10.3 Architecture of a DBMS

Our discussion on the architecture of a DBMS includes two main topics. The first is an introduction to the software and hardware components of a DBMS, some of which we briefly discussed in the presentation of DBMS functions. The second topic concerns the way in which the architecture of a DBMS implements logical and physical data independence. Without such data independence, the goals of a DBMS would be difficult to achieve.

Components of a DBMS

There are numerous configurations for DBMS's, and it would take a lengthy discourse to present them here. Instead, our goal is to describe an abstract, or general, architecture with features in common with most DBMS's. The architecture we describe is based both on the

ANSI/SPARC [91] and the CODASYL DBTG [92] reports. Where appropriate, we will introduce the terminology used in these reports. Figure 10.1 depicts a diagram of a DBMS architecture.

Figure 10.1 shows that the architecture is composed of hardware (the direct-access storage devices [DASD's] used to store the physical database) and software (all other components). This architecture is a layered structured architecture. That is, both procedural applications (such as inventory) and nonprocedural query systems interface to a functional database. The functional database is called an **external view** in the ANSI/SPARC model and a **subschema** in the CODASYL model. The functional database is the application program's (or user's) view of the database. It represents the database as the application knows it. Several applications can use the same functional database, and there can be many functional databases.

When an application requests a record, the request is expressed in terms of the functional database. The functional database, however, can vary greatly from the actual logical structure of the database. Thus, the data request is translated from the declarations of the application (the functional database) to the declarative structure of the logical database. There is only one logical database. In the ANSI/SPARC model the logical database is called the **conceptual view**. In the CODASYL model it is known as the **schema**.

The logical database receives the translated data request from the functional database and again translates the request so that the logical/physical database mapping module can determine the actual storage location of the data to be accessed from a DASD. The logical/physical mapping module typically contains routines to access data by hashing, ordered primary indexes (for example, B-trees and B$^+$-trees), and secondary indexes.

Data Independence

Data independence is desirable because it reduces costs and increases the flexibility of data processing. Logical data independence is achieved by buffering the applications from the logical database. Physical data independence is achieved by buffering the logical database from the physical database (DASD).

Logical data independence, which means that changes in the logical database structure have a minimal effect on application programs, is highly desirable because of the costs involved in software maintenance. Without logical data independence certain application programs would have to be modified and recompiled every time the logical database was reorganized. The functional database serves as a translation buffer and is the module by which logical data independence is achieved. By translating the application's view of the

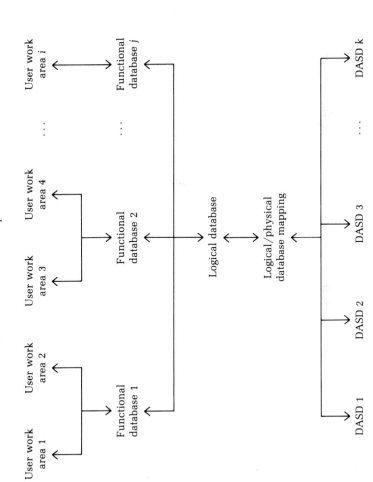

Database components

- Run unit
- Application program
- Query interface

Synonyms

- Subschemas
- External view
- External schema

- Schema
- Conceptual view
- Conceptual schema

- Data structure description

- Internal view
- Internal schema

| User work area 1 | User work area 2 | User work area 3 | User work area 4 | ... | User work area i |

| Functional database 1 | Functional database 2 | ... | Functional database j |

Logical database

Logical/physical database mapping

| DASD 1 | DASD 2 | DASD 3 | ... | DASD k |

FIGURE 10.1 Generalized DBMS architecture

database into the logical database, the functional database module can accommodate changes in the logical database while minimizing modifications to the applications. When the logical database is recompiled, the functional databases must also be recompiled (with a functional database DDL) so that the old application requests will be translated into the structure of the new logical database. Logical databases are reorganized for many reasons, including the need to store additional fields in specific records, reorganization of the institution using the database, and the need to improve database efficiency.

Physical data independence means that changes in the physical storage of the database have minimal effect on the logical database. A DBA might change a physical database to accommodate new storage hardware or restructure it to increase efficiency. It would be time-consuming to recompile the logical database and possibly the functional databases every time the physical storage is changed. Recompilation of the logical/physical mapping module reduces the likelihood that reorganization of the physical storage will necessitate reorganization of the logical database.

10.4 Database Life Cycle

Here we present the database life cycle for the network database model that we will discuss in Chapter 11. We chose this model because it is the most complex type of database to establish. The general database life cycle is the same for the hierarchical and relational databases, but the design stage is usually simpler. The three phases of the database life cycle are modeling, implementation, and maintenance. In the following sections we examine these phases in more detail. To facilitate this presentation, Table 10.1 shows the personnel (users), database components (compiled modules), and languages available in this DBMS environment.

Database Modeling

Conceptually there are two possible starting points in the life cycle of a database. First, a database might be created in an environment where there is either manual data processing or where all data processing is carried out using files and application programs. Second, an existing database might be restructured into a logically new database. In both cases the database designer should use a model of how data is (or will be) processed to determine entity specifications, associations among entities, functionally different applications (user groups), and access, security, and privacy rights.

TABLE 10.1 Components, users, and languages in a DBMS environment

Components	Users	Languages
User work area	Application programmers	Programming languages with DML statements
	Query users	Query language
	DBA	
Functional database	Application programmers	DML statements in application programs
	DBA	Query language
		DDL
Logical database	DBA	DDL
Logical/ physical mapping	DBA	DMCL
	System programmers	System programming languages
DASD		

An explicit model of how data is processed is available to the designer who is to restructure an existing database. Also, a good model for how the database is to be reconfigured is usually available. It is when there is no existing database that data processing is usually not well defined. In this situation the designer must spend much time studying how data is manually processed or how various file-based applications are interconnected. Interviewing the personnel involved in data processing is the dominant technique for developing such models. We recommend that the designer use diagrammatic techniques such as **data flow diagrams** and Bachman diagrams in such interviews to facilitate understanding and clarify the model.

After developing an initial representation of the way in which data is processed, the designer can develop entity specification and data semantics, normalize the entity specifications (develop a prototype logical database), and develop prototype functional databases. These prototypes can then be discussed with the user community to ensure that they will satisfy the necessary applications. The process of developing the database prototypes may take several iterations. (For a more elaborate description of this process, see Kroenke [93].)

Database Implementation

Database implementation involves designing and compiling the necessary database components, loading the database, and compiling application programs to run against the database.

Logical and functional database definition. After the DBA staff has a collection of normalized entity specifications and users' perspectives, they can begin to compile the logical and functional databases. Three stages are involved. First, the logical database is written and compiled using a schema DDL. The resulting schema object module represents all record type (data) and set type declarations (semantics). Second, the logical/physical mapping module is written and compiled in a DMCL. The resulting physical data description object module defines the physical structure of files used (blocking characteristics, buffers, etc.). Whenever the DBMS makes calls to the host operating system to open files, the information in the logical/physical module is used. Third, the functional databases are written and compiled using a subschema DDL. A subschema object module contains the necessary routines to derive the functional database record and set types from the logical database.

After the database components have been created, a physical database exists that contains information about the data to be stored within the database. At this point there is no actual data in the database—it must be loaded with its actual data values.

Loading the database. There are two ways to load a database. The first is to input data interactively. This is usually a menu-driven procedure and is more appropriate for relational databases. The second method is to load the database from existing data files. This technique is commonly used in the network and hierarchical models. Clearly, loading a database from a collection of files requires utility programs designed to read data files and write to the database schema.

Database application programs. Application programs accessing a database typically contain embedded database DML commands. Such programs are usually compiled by means of a **preprocessor**. A DML preprocessor extracts the DML statements from the source program before compilation and replaces them with statements that permit access to the database. When the preprocessor is finished, the resulting source program is then compiled into an application object program. To operate successfully, the preprocessor must be given information in the application program specifying the functional database and declaring the logical records accessed. The preprocessor uses the translation routines in the functional database module to generate correct data access statements for the logical database. Figure 10.2 shows the compilation steps for application programs.

Database Maintenance

Once created, a database enters the maintenance phase of its life cycle. The database stays in this phase until it is restructured. After

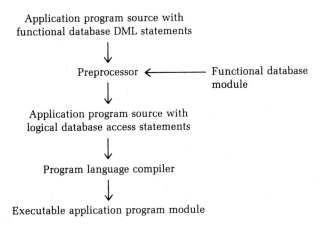

FIGURE 10.2 Compilation of application source program with DML

a database is restructured, the new database enters its maintenance phase. Thus maintenance, which is the responsibility of the DBA office, is the predominant phase of a database's life cycle. Database maintenance consists of two classes of events: (1) monitoring a working DBMS and (2) recovering from a DBMS failure. We briefly describe these classes of events here. (We will address DBMS recovery strategies in more depth in Chapter 13.)

Monitoring a working DBMS. It is the responsibility of the DBA staff to oversee the performance of a viable DBMS. This includes serving as a conduit for communication between the user community and the operations staff and monitoring the performance of the DBMS across applications. The DBA staff represents the users by investigating user reports of system failures or anomalies in application program performance. In addition, the DBA staff makes available information about the current configuration of the database, documentation standards, and acceptable user actions. By conveying this information to the user community, the DBA represents the operations staff.

Database performance is monitored with DBMS utilities that provide diverse statistics on storage utilization, access time, and general system throughput. When database access performance degrades to an unacceptable level, the DBA staff typically reorganizes the physical database and installs a new logical/physical mapping module. When the logical structure of the database is changed the database modeling and implementation phases are performed.

Recovering from DBMS failure. When a DBMS fails—there are numerous causes of failure—it must be recovered. A difficult problem in database recovery is determining the cause of the failure. Recovery diagnostics are hard to generate when concurrent transactions are being applied to the database. This is a major disadvantage of all DBMS's. There are two major strategies for database recovery: archiving and rollback. Both strategies require that the DBMS keep a **transaction log** of all actions performed on the database. It is advisable to log a transaction before it is performed. When a failure occurs there is then a record of the active transactions.

Archiving is the simplest but the least preferred recovery technique. In this method the database is copied (archived) periodically. After a failure the database is restored from the most recently archived copy. Once the database is restored, the appropriate part of the transaction log can be applied to the recovered database. Of course, the cause of the original failure must not be repeated. The disadvantage of this approach is the time it takes to repeat the entire transaction log from the time the database was last archived.

Rollback, the second approach, begins with the database in its failed state and attempts to undo all transactions that did not complete normally before failure. A transaction is undone by aborting the task that issued it and restoring the affected records to their state before the transaction was initiated. If this can be done, then the resulting database should be in a valid state. With a recovered database, the aborted transactions can be modified and resumed. This approach is faster than archiving because it works backward from the failure point.

Summary

In this chapter we discussed database data processing and presented the functions a general DBMS should provide, the architectural components of a DBMS, and the life cycle of a database. A DBMS is a combination of hardware and software that enables users to apply many applications concurrently to the same data. Such systems greatly improve data processing flexibility by providing logical and physical data independence, data integrity, security, and centralized system administration. The disadvantages of a DBMS are its hardware, software, and personnel costs and its vulnerability to system failure. In addition, recovery is a complex process for DBMS's. The advantages, however, are greater than the disadvantages for large data processing environments where information is a valued resource. In Chapters 11 and 12 we will discuss three different data models used in commercial DBMS's. In Chapter 13 we will consider database concurrency, integrity, and security issues in greater depth, and in Chapter 14 we will present future trends in database architecture and performance.

Exercises

1. Determine the DBMS's available at your institution. In manuals for these systems read about the major topics covered in this chapter: their architectural components, implementation steps, transaction logging, and recovery techniques.

2. Many schools have databases in the library for literature searches and in the career planning and placement offices for career counseling. Determine if your school has such facilities. If so, use the facilities to gain some experience interacting with a DBMS.

3. From the SECS entity specifications and applications presented in Chapter 9, determine groups of applications. Categorize applications by data usage and develop functional entity specifications for each group.

11

The Hierarchical and Network Data Models

11.1 Describes the properties of the hierarchical data model and presents an example hierarchical description of the SECS database derived from the entity specifications in Chapter 9.

11.2 Presents the syntax for a hierarchical pseudo data definition language (DDL) with an example for the SECS database.

11.3 Presents and describes the syntax for hierarchical pseudo data definition language (DML) commands.

11.4 Analyzes the hierarchical data model.

11.5 Describes the network data model and presents an example network description of the SECS database derived from the entity specifications in Chapter 9.

11.6 Discusses the syntax for a network pseudo DDL and an example and describes the declaration of functional databases (subschemas) of the logical database.

11.7 Presents the syntax of a network pseudo DML.

11.8 Presents an analysis of the network data model.

In this chapter we present the properties of the hierarchical and network data models, analyze the models' ability to represent M:N dependencies, and give examples of their data manipulation commands. We describe the hierarchical data model primarily as an introduction to the network data model, because it has been shown that hierarchical databases are not competitive with network databases. In fact, we will see that the hierarchical model can be regarded as a subset of the network data model.

11.1 Properties of the Hierarchical Data Model

The hierarchical data model organizes data according to associations that are represented as trees. Such a tree is called a **hierarchical definition tree**. A **hierarchical database** is a collection of records (nodes) connected in a forest of disjoint trees. Each database tree includes a root record and its descendant records. In a hierarchical data model:

1. There is a collection of record types (R1, R2, R3, . . . , Rn).

2. There is a collection of associations connecting all the records in one data structure. These associations are the links between the nodes in the database trees.

3. There is only one association between any two distinct record types. Thus there is no need to label the links. Furthermore, there can be no self-referencing link. Each record except the root has only one parent.

Advantages and Disadvantages of the Hierarchical Model

The hierarchical data model has three advantages. First, the tree structure is easy to conceptualize; thus a schema for a database can be easily understood. Second, the restriction of having only an ancestor-descendant association between different record types results in a small set of DML commands sufficient for record processing. Third, the restricted linkage allowed among record types facilitates implementation of hierarchical database management systems.

Unfortunately, the restricted linkage that gives the hierarchical model its advantages is also the cause of its major disadvantage. The model cannot adequately represent the true semantics among entities that have M:N associations. Furthermore, few sets of naturally occurring objects are associated in a hierarchical fashion. Thus the hierarchical model forces the database designer to use multiple, redundant database trees to represent nonhierarchical associations. We present examples in the next section.

Redundancy caused by multivalued dependencies can be minimized through the use of **logical links**. A logical link [94] associates a virtual record in one database tree with an actual record in another database tree. The virtual record replaces a redundant copy of the actual record with a reference to the actual record. This approach reduces data storage and, more important, eliminates possible integrity problems. If there is only one copy of the actual data, there cannot be any inconsistent yet semantically redundant instances of a record across database trees.

SECS Hierarchical Data Definition Trees

Figure 11.1 illustrates three hierarchical definition trees for our example SECS database. This example is derived from the SECS entity specifications of Chapter 9. The three distinct trees are necessary to represent associations when a record has a 1:1 or 1:N association with more than one parent record or is part of an M:N association. For example, consider the records SECTION and SECT.STUD in the professor and course definition trees. In this example the SECTION record has two different parents across the two trees. Furthermore, the records SECT.STUD and SECTION are part of an M:N multivalued association (we will elaborate on this shortly).

M:N associations and multiple parents are resolved through the use of logical links. There are logical links (not shown) between all records of the same type (same name) in Fig. 11.1. In addition, there are logical links between all occurrences of SECT.STUD (student in section) and STUDENT. Thus there is an M:N association between SECTION and STUDENT (SECT.STUD) that is not explicit in Fig. 11.1. Once the logical links are known we must determine which instance of a record is the actual record and which are instances of the virtual records. Such determination is part of the data definition process of each hierarchical database tree. Thus, the database administrator (DBA) would have to determine which parent of the SECTION record is to be a logical parent and which is to be an actual parent when designing the professor and course definition trees.

11.2 Hierarchical Data Definition

A hierarchical definition tree represents the semantics of the record types to be declared and instantiated in a hierarchical database. The designer declares the hierarchical database by compiling record descriptions written in a DDL for a particular database management system. Since our intent in this book is to describe general concepts and not specific systems, our examples and coverage of issues relating to the declaration of the logical structure of a database will be abstract. In keeping with our language-free (system-free) orientation we present an example hierarchical data definition in a pseudolanguage. Our pseudo DDL is, however, abstracted from existing systems. Actual (runnable) examples are not provided; they would require the reader to be familiar with a specific DBMS DDL in more detail than is necessary to illustrate a database data model. However, after reading this section you should be able to transfer this information to an actual DBMS DDL.

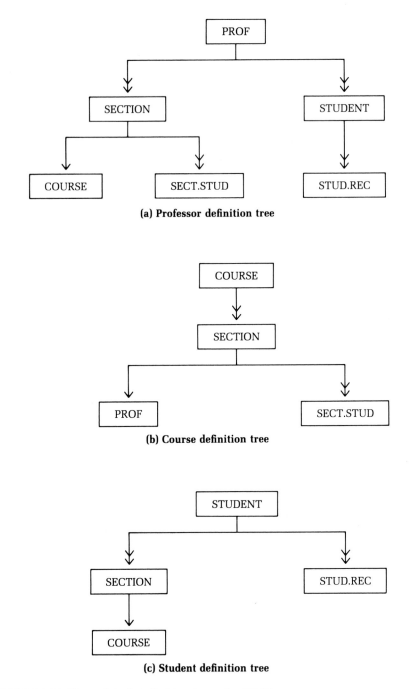

(a) Professor definition tree

(b) Course definition tree

(c) Student definition tree

FIGURE 11.1 Hierarchical definition trees for SECS

A Hierarchical Pseudo DDL

Data definition is a process by which the designer declares various record types that can exist in a database and the linkages (pointers) maintained among them. A hierarchical database can consist of numerous database trees with intra- and intertree logical linkages. Each database tree, record, record field, and link must be named and its type must be specified. The database tree declaration provides a name, an access technique, a data set name, and a storage device that holds the database tree [94, 95]. Furthermore, each record declaration within a database must specify the record's type and length (bytes for storage), and estimate its frequency of occurrence. Each record declaration must also specify its parent record within the current database tree and its logical parents from other database trees. Record field declarations must often also provide type, length, and position (byte offset within record) information. A syntax for a hierarchical pseudo DDL is presented in Fig. 11.2. We use square brackets ([ ]) to indicate optional statements in Fig. 11.2 and braces ({ }) to indicate a set of alternatives. The declaration of logical links to virtual records and parents are examples of optional statements.

SECS Hierarchical Data Definition Example

An example data definition is provided for the COURSE database tree in Fig. 11.3. In this example the root record COURSE is an actual record that declares logical links to virtual course records in the PROF and STUDENT database trees. The PROF record is an example of a virtual record. Thus its definition declares links to a logical parent (the actual PROF record) in the PROF database.

11.3 Properties of a Hierarchical DML

The following DML examples are loosely based on IMS [94]. IMS uses the data manipulation language DL/1. Within DL/1 traversal of database trees is based on a preorder algorithm. Within a database tree there exists a **currency pointer** to enable record-by-record processing. The currency pointer references the record in the tree currently accessible by an application program. The preorder traversal can be written as:

PREORDER TRAVERSAL

If record not visited
    then visit record
    else if no descendants or all descendants visited
        then return to parent
        else traverse to leftmost descendant not visited

(* Declare database tree name, access technique, file name, and device. *)

DEFINE DB NAME = database name, ACCESS = an access technique
DATASET NAME = file name, DEVICE = device identifier

(* Declare root record name field, its virtual duplicate records
in other database trees, and remaining fields. *)

```
RECORD NAME      = record name,
                   LENGTH = byte count for record,
                   TYPE = {integer, real, character, . . .},
                   FREQ = expected occurrence count
[LOGICAL NAME    = (virtual record name, database tree name)]
FIELD NAME       = field name [specify if (UNIQUE KEY) or not],
                   LENGTH = i,
                   TYPE = . . . ,
                   POSITION = j

                      .
                      .
                      .

                   repeat for all record field declarations

                      .
                      .
                      .
```

(* Declare remaining nonroot records of database tree. For each
record declare the name field, parent record within database
tree, virtual parents from other database trees, virtual
duplicate records in other database trees, and remaining fields. *)

```
RECORD NAME      = record name
                   PARENT = name of parent within current tree
                             [LOGICAL,
                              name of logical parent,
                              name of database for logical parent]
                   length, type, and frequency specification
                   [POINTER = pointer to logical parent]
[LOGICAL NAME    = (virtual record name, database name)]
FIELD NAME       = field name [specify if (UNIQUE KEY) or not],
                   length, type and position specification

                      .
                      .
                      .

                   repeat for all necessary field declarations

                      .
                      .
                      .
```

FIGURE 11.2 Hierarchical pseudo data definition example

(* Declare Course database, its access technique, filename, and device. *)

DEFINE DB NAME = COURSE-DB, ACCESS = an access technique
DATASET NAME = COURSE-FILE, DEVICE = device identifier

(* Declare Course as root record with virtual duplicates in the
Prof. and Student database trees. *)

RECORD NAME   = COURSE,
                  length, type, and frequency specification
LOGICAL NAME   = (COURSE, PROF-DB)
LOGICAL NAME   = (COURSE, STUDENT-DB)
FIELD NAME   = CNAME (UNIQUE KEY),
                  length, type, and position specification
FIELD NAME   = field declarations for remaining attributes:
                  PREREQ, UNITS

RECORD NAME   = SECTION,
                  PARENT = COURSE
                  length, type, and frequency specification
LOGICAL NAME   = (SECTION, PROF-DB)
LOGICAL NAME   = (SECTION, STUDENT-DB)
FIELD NAME   = SNUM (UNIQUE KEY),
                  length, type, and position specification
FIELD NAME   = field declarations for remaining attributes:
                  CNAME, PID, ROOM, BEGIN, END

(* Declare the Prof. record. The Prof. record in this database
is a virtual record. Thus, its logical parent record and
database must be specified in addition to its parent record
within the current database. *)

RECORD NAME   = PROF,
                  PARENT = SECTION,
                          LOGICAL, PROF, PROF-DB,
                  length, type, and frequency specification
                  POINTER = LOGICAL PARENT
FIELD NAME   = PID (UNIQUE KEY),
                  length, type, and position specification
FIELD NAME   = field declarations for remaining attributes:
                  PNAME, OFFICE#

RECORD NAME   = SECT.STUD,
                  PARENT = SECTION
                          LOGICAL, STUDENT, STUDENT-DB,
                  length, type, and frequency specification
                  POINTER = LOGICAL PARENT
FIELD NAME   = SID (UNIQUE KEY), . . .

FIGURE 11.3 Course database data definition example

In any hierarchical DML there are two operations of importance: retrieval and modification. All modification requests must be carried out after the currency pointer has been positioned by the traversal. In the next section we present the general form of statements in our pseudo DML for performing record retrievals and modifications.

Hierarchical Retrieval

There are three general retrieval modes:

GET UNIQUE record-id WHERE qualification

> This command retrieves the leftmost record that satisfies the constraints of the qualification. Traversal begins at the root.

GET NEXT [record-id WHERE qualification]

> This command retrieves the next (preorder) record from the current location that satisfies the qualifications. Recall that the brackets are used to represent an optional clause. Thus, GET NEXT would retrieve the next sequential record from the current position.

GET NEXT WITHIN PARENT [record-id WHERE qualification]

> This command obtains records within the family of the parent record. The parent is selected by a previous GET command. Whereas GET NEXT will continue traversal to the end of the database, GET NEXT WITHIN stops searching at the rightmost immediate descendant of the parent.

Hierarchical Record Modification

There are three modification commands and one concurrency control command.

HOLD

> This command is used to lock out any other concurrent users from accessing the current record while modifications are in progress. The subsequent modification commands will release the hold.

INSERT record

> Stores new record and connects to parent record. Parent must be selected by previous GET command.

REPLACE record

> This command updates the current record with the new record. The current record must have been set with a GET and HOLD.

DELETE record

> This command performs a physical deletion of the current record and all of its descendants. Note that one can logically delete a record by REPLACING the record with null information fields while retaining all the pointer linkages.

SECS Hierarchical DML Examples

Returning to our SECS example, let us suppose, for example, that we wish to retrieve information about a specific student. Furthermore, assume that our currency pointer is set to the root of the STUDENT database tree as defined in Fig. 11.1. To retrieve information about a student the student's identification number (SID) would have to be known since it is the unique key for the STUDENT record type. The retrieval DML command would be:

```
GET UNIQUE STUDENT WHERE SID = SID number
```

As another example, consider changing the office of the professor teaching a particular section of a course. Clearly, one would first have to retrieve the professor record and then modify the value for the office field. Let us assume that the professor's PID (a unique identifier) is unknown. In this case retrieval can be accomplished from the COURSE database tree by:

```
GET UNIQUE COURSE WHERE CNAME = course title
GET NEXT WITHIN PARENT SECTION WHERE SNUM = section number
GET NEXT WITHIN PARENT PROF
```

After the professor's record has been located, the office number could be changed by:

```
HOLD
LET PROF.OFFICE# = new office number
REPLACE
```

I I.4 Analysis of the Hierarchical Data Model

The advantages of the hierarchical model are that the data model is simple to comprehend because of the parent-offspring and logical link associations. This enables the use of a concise and easy-to-use

DML. In addition, the constrained set of associations facilitates implementation.

There are two disadvantages of the hierarchical model. First and foremost, the limited set of associations and strict hierarchical nature require an indirect implementation of M:N mappings (via multiple interconnected database trees). Second, the strict hierarchy can make insertions and deletions complex at times. If one is careless when deleting, vital data can be lost due to the **triggered deletion** of descendants. A triggered deletion occurs when the parent of a record is physically deleted from the database tree. As a side effect, the descendant records are also deleted, which may be unintentional. The use of logical deletions (replacing valid data with values representing a deleted record) eliminates triggered deletions. However, to restore storage utilization, one may have to reorganize the tree after many logical deletions.

11.5 Properties of the Network Data Model

The network database model represents the associations among record types in a graph (plex) structure. Thus a record type may have numerous associations with other record types. Clearly, the network structure is less restricted than the hierarchical data model. In a network data model:

1. There is a collection of record types (R1, R2, R3, . . . , Rn).

2. There is a collection of named links (associations) connecting different record types. The links define sets that consist of owner records and member records. Links can represent 1:1 and 1:N associations.

3. There can be no self-referencing link. That is, a record type cannot be both the owner and a member of the same set type.

4. An instance of a record type cannot exist in more than one instance of a specific set type. A record can, however, exist in more than one different set type at a time.

5. M:N associations are not directly implementable because of the fourth property. However, a many-to-many association can be represented in a network by interposing an intermediate record type between the two record types having an M:N association.

M:N Associations in a Network

Clearly the network model is more powerful than the hierarchical model in terms of expressing the associations that may exist among different entities. Unfortunately, it still cannot implement M:N associations directly. Let us look at how M:N associations can be represented indirectly. Suppose that we wish to represent the fact that a course could require many books and that a specific book may be required for many courses. This is clearly an M:N association.

Because associations are presented as sets in a network model, we must state our example in terms of sets. Let the set REQUIRED BOOKS have as an owner a CLASS record and have as members BOOK records. Consider the problem posed when one class (CS132) requires two books (Pascal and CS132 Notes) and another class (CS182) requires three books (Data Structures, Pascal, and CS182 Notes). The Pascal book is required by both courses. This situation violates the fourth property of network databases: the same book is a member of two instances of the same set type. Figure 11.4(a) illustrates the set violation, set instance, and set specification.

In a network database we have to create an intermediate record type and two set types to represent the M:N association between CLASS and BOOK. The new record type could be named CLASS TEXT and the new set TEXT BOOK. The owner of the set TEXT BOOK is a BOOK record and the members are CLASS TEXT entities. The second set REQUIRED BOOKS would have the same owner record as before, but the new members would be CLASS TEXT entities. Figure 11.4(b) represents the new network. Notice that no instance of a record type is a member of more than one instance of the same set type. With this example, the books required for a particular class can be determined through a two-step process: first, find the CLASS TEXT record that is a member of the REQUIRED BOOKS for the class; and second, find the BOOK record that is the owner of the CLASS TEXT record obtained in the first step.

SECS Network Data Diagram

Figure 11.5 contains an example network database diagram for the SECS database. This database is derived from the SECS entity specifications in Chapter 9. As you can see, the diagram is similar to the representation of the SECS entity specifications in Fig. 9.23. The salient difference in Fig. 11.5 is the explicit labeling of set name, owner record, and member record.

11.6 Network Data Definition

The logical definition of a network database is called its schema. Each schema description has four components: the schema entry, area (or realm) entry, record entry, and set entry [96]. We discuss the schema entry and area entry together. Figure 11.6 illustrates, in a pseudo DDL, the mandatory portions of each component as it might be expressed in a network schema DDL. Again, note that this is an introductory

Bachman diagram:

Set instance:

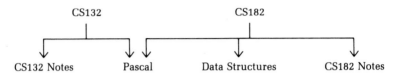

Set specification:

Set name	Owner record	Member record
REQUIRED BOOKS	CLASS	BOOK

(a) Violation of set membership

Bachman diagram:

Set instance:

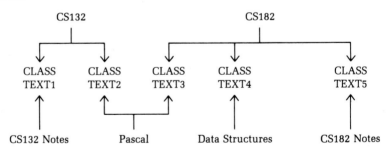

Set specification:

Set name	Owner record	Member record
REQUIRED BOOKS	CLASS	CLASS TEXT
TEXT BOOK	BOOK	CLASS TEXT

(b) Valid *M:N* set membership implementation

FIGURE 11.4 Set memberships

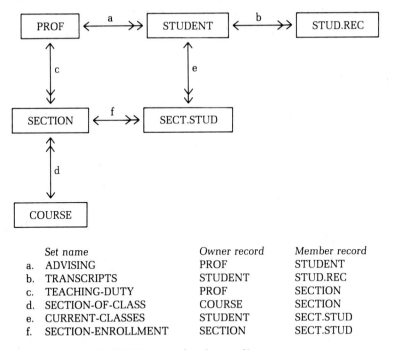

Set name	Owner record	Member record
a. ADVISING	PROF	STUDENT
b. TRANSCRIPTS	STUDENT	STUD.REC
c. TEACHING-DUTY	PROF	SECTION
d. SECTION-OF-CLASS	COURSE	SECTION
e. CURRENT-CLASSES	STUDENT	SECT.STUD
f. SECTION-ENROLLMENT	SECTION	SECT.STUD

FIGURE 11.5 Example SECS network schema diagram

example only. Many nuances to schema declaration and options are omitted here for brevity. The example schema syntax is loosely derived from the IDMS network database [97] and the CODASYL DDL report [98].

The schema description entry declares the schema name and can optionally specify the author, date, and installation, as well as remarks. The file entry associates logical file names with actual direct-access files used to store the physical database. The area (realm) entry is used to specify the logical name of a subdivision of addressable space in the database used to store records. A file may contain many complete areas or portions of areas. Similarly, an area can reside on more than one file.

Optional specifications for schema and subschema declaration can restrict and enforce which applications can perform certain operations. Such optional specifications are made in the area, record, and set entries to declare various privacy and error handling options. Privacy options enable the database designer to restrict the DML statements usable within an entry. A **privacy lock** is typically defined as a literal (password) and is specified in the subschema declarations.

SCHEMA DESCRIPTION

SCHEMA NAME IS schema name
FILE NAME IS file name ASSIGN TO actual operating system file names
AREA NAME IS area name

RECORD DESCRIPTION

RECORD NAME IS record name
      RECORD ID integer id
      LOCATION MODE IS {DIRECT   given a db.key
                        CALC   given an attribute and a
                                   hash function
                    VIA   given a set name
                    SYSTEM system provides access mode}
      WITHIN {area or owner area}
      DATA NAME data item name and standard COBOL data description
               for each attribute of the record

SET DESCRIPTION

SET NAME IS set name
      ORDER IS {FIRST, LAST,
              PRIOR, NEXT,
              SORTED, DEFAULT}
      MODE IS CHAINED
      OWNER IS {record name with db.key position specification
              SYSTEM}
      MEMBER IS record name
          LINKED TO OWNER db.key position specification
          {MANDATORY, OPTIONAL}
          {AUTOMATIC, MANUAL}

FIGURE 11.6 Network pseudo data description (schema) syntax

Error-handling options specify database procedures to be invoked on detection of an error state for specific DML commands. The use of error trapping can facilitate error recovery. More generally, database procedures can be specified to be invoked both before and after specific DML commands. Error-handling features can also be declared in the schema and subschema.

The record description entry is used to declare records that can exist in the schema. Each record entry has two components, a record subentry and a data subentry. The record subentries specify the name of the record, how it can be accessed (location mode), and where it may reside. The three location modes available are:

1. DIRECT db.key.
   Record is assigned db.key that determines placement within a defined area. A db.key is a physical record address plus a logical record offset.

2. CALC [procedure name] USING attribute list
   DUPLICATES ARE [NOT] ALLOWED.
   db.key formed from attributes in list and hashed on system or user-supplied procedure.

3. VIA set-name SET.
   Record is stored on basis of set membership.

The data subentry declares the record's attribute fields. An optional clause for the data subentry can be used to specify data storage.

The set description entry declares the associations among the various record types. It specifies the name, owner, and members of each set. Because a record can be a member of many set types and also be an owner of many other set types, the number of pointer linkages (database key or DB.KEY positions) between records varies with record type. Different record types require different numbers of owner, next member, and prior member links. The assignment of pointer values to these links creates instances of sets. Set membership is dynamic, and records of the same type may or may not belong to a set instance. Thus the number of valid set pointers varies with time.

The network implementation restriction that an instance of a record type cannot exist in more than one instance of a particular set type is necessary to ensure a fixed number of pointer linkages for any record type. In addition, a consistent rule for assigning set linkages into a record's set pointer (DB.KEY) positions is necessary. Given such a rule, when a record instance is created, space is allocated for all required pointers and the set linkages are assigned as needed. For example, if a record can belong to three sets with owner, prior, and next pointers it requires nine DB.KEY positions (assuming it is not the owner of any other sets). The DB.KEY positions specified in the set declarations for this example could be cardinals ranging from 1 to 9.

We must also specify the insertion mode for set members. Four possible membership categories result from the combinations of (1) two ways to do member insertion at member creation and (2) whether or not the member must always belong to a set:

1. MANUAL membership. The application program must insert members into sets.

2. AUTOMATIC membership. At record creation the record is inserted as a member of relevant sets by the DBMS.

3. OPTIONAL membership. The record can be inserted into, or removed from, a set by an application program. The record does not have to belong to an instance of a set type.

4. MANDATORY membership. The record must belong to an instance of a set type. The record can be removed only by deletion from the database.

Thus membership is specified by optional-manual (member does not have to be in the set and must be manually inserted into the set), optional-automatic (member can exist outside the set and is initially inserted into the current instance of the set), mandatory-manual (member must be in the set and is inserted by the application program), or mandatory-automatic (member must be in the set and is initially inserted by the DBMS). Various network DBMS's offer additional set membership options. Optional features of the set description entry include duplicate membership and storage order specification.

SECS Network Schema Example

Figure 11.7 contains an example schema declaration for the portion of the SECS network diagram of Fig. 11.5 containing the two sets CURRENT-CLASSES and SECTION-ENROLLMENT. This example illustrates the representation of an M:N association in the network model. Note that the record declaration for SECT.STUD does not require any data item declarations. This is because this record only contains pointer linkages to represent the M:N association of STUDENTS and SECTIONS.

Network Subschema Definition

In addition to defining a network schema, the database designer can also define numerous subschemas (functional databases). Subschemas provide additional logical independence between the application programs and the schema. Simply stated, a subschema maps the schema into a logical description more suitable for an application program (or related set of application programs). Usually the perspective the subschema provides to the application program is a subset of the schema. This enables applications to process the database without having to know the entire schema. Subschemas can rename records or create new record types from data items in records declared within the schema or derived from values known to the schema. Furthermore, when the schema is reorganized (recompiled), new subschemas can be compiled to map the new schema into the old subschemas, allowing application programs to execute with a minimum of modification.

The subschema declarations are syntactically similar to the schema declaration. The designer must name all subschemas and specify

SCHEMA DESCRIPTION

SCHEMA NAME IS SECS-SCHEMA-EXAMPLE
FILE NAME IS SECS ASSIGN TO SECS.DAT
AREA NAMES IS SECS-REGION

RECORD DESCRIPTION

RECORD NAME IS STUDENT
      RECORD ID IS 100
      LOCATION MODE IS CALC USING SID DUPLICATES NOT ALLOWED
      WITHIN SECS-REGION
      DATA NAME . . . declarations follow for:
          SID, SNAME, SPREREQ, MAJOR, GPA, SUNITS

RECORD NAME IS SECT.STUD
      RECORD ID IS 102
      LOCATION MODE IS VIA SECTION-ENROLLMENT
      WITHIN SECS-REGION

RECORD NAME IS SECTION
      RECORD ID IS 103
      LOCATION MODE IS CALC USING SNUM DUPLICATES NOT ALLOWED
      WITHIN SECS-REGION
      DATA NAME . . . declarations follow for:
          SNUM, CNAME, PID, ROOM, BEGIN, END

SET DESCRIPTION

SET NAME IS CURRENT-CLASSES
      ORDER IS SORTED
      MODE IS CHAINED
      OWNER IS STUDENT   NEXT DB.KEY POSITION IS cardinal
                                 PRIOR DB.KEY POSITION IS cardinal
      MEMBER IS SECT.STUD   NEXT DB.KEY POSITION IS cardinal
          LINKED TO OWNER   OWNER DB.KEY POSITION IS cardinal
                                 PRIOR DB.KEY POSITION IS cardinal

          OPTIONAL MANUAL

SET NAME IS SECTION-ENROLLMENT
      ORDER IS FIRST
      MODE IS CHAINED
      OWNER IS SECTION   NEXT DB.KEY POSITION IS cardinal
      MEMBER IS SECT.STUD   NEXT DB.KEY POSITION IS cardinal
          LINKED TO OWNER   OWNER DB.KEY POSITION IS cardinal
          MANDATORY AUTOMATIC

FIGURE 11.7 SECS network schema example

their areas. In addition, the designer must declare all record descriptions and sets. The subschemas must be compiled after schema compilation. Subschema compilation enforces type correspondence among declarations of the same record items. It is for this reason that some network database implementations (for example, IDMS [97]) require that the same names be used in the subschema and schema. Subschemas can set privacy locks that are different for different users. Further, they can restrict the record and set-processing DML commands a subschema user can issue.

Consider, as an example, sets CURRENT-CLASSES and SECTION-ENROLLMENT in Fig. 11.5. Both are concerned with students and their enrollments in sections of classes. One could imagine several subschemas developed for this data in a university environment. We would expect a subschema devised to allow students to access information about courses to have different declarations and capabilities than a subschema developed for professors to access course information. The professor subschema could allow full access to information about students (that is, SID, GPA, SPREREQS, SUNITS, MAJOR). The student subschema should, considering privacy rights, enable students to know only the names of students enrolled in a particular class section. In this manner queries made through the professor subschema would operate on a logically different database than queries about course enrollment made through the student subschema.

11.7 Properties of Network DML Commands

As with the hierarchical data model, currency pointers are necessary for navigation through the network model. A collection of currency pointers is maintained for each executing application (**run unit**). This collection contains values referencing the last record processed by the application, the last record processed for each record type, and the last record processed for each declared set type. Thus the processing of records in a network database consists of setting a currency pointer, obtaining the referenced record, and then processing the record.

Recall that records can be stored in the network on the basis of either database keys or membership in a set. Thus there are two categories of DML commands, those that process records by database keys and those that process records on the basis of set membership. Processing by database keys can utilize computational and primary index techniques; processing on the basis of sets requires traversing set linkages. We present example network DML commands for retrieval, modification, and set maintenance and then present examples drawn from the SECS database.

Retrieval in a Network

There are two general data selection facilities in the network model. The first is based on database keys and the second utilizes sets:

1. Retrieval DML commands using database keys:

FIND record name USING db.key

> The db.key must first be set:
> MOVE CURRENCY STATUS FOR record name RECORD TO db.key.

FIND [NEXT DUPLICATE WITHIN] record name RECORD

> Selects first or next occurrence of record whose calc keys match those specified by application program. Calc key must first be set by:
>
> MOVE 'value' TO calc key for record.

2. Retrieval DML commands using set membership:

FIND [OWNER IN set name OF] CURRENT OF
  {record name RECORD
  set name SET
  area name AREA
  RUN UNIT}

> Locates current record.

FIND {NEXT
      PRIOR
      FIRST
      LAST
      Nth} [record name] RECORD OF {SET
                                       AREA}

FIND OWNER RECORD OF set name SET

FIND record name VIA [CURRENT OF] set name [USING attribute list]

> Where set is qualified by,
> MOVE 'value' TO attribute list.

GET record name

> Once the current record of the run unit is determined by the above FIND statements, the GET statement obtains and holds the record for processing.

Record Modification in a Network

There are three general network data modification DML commands. These commands are concerned with writing, modifying, and deleting records.

STORE record name

> Assigns db.key to implement set linkages. If set membership is mandatory-automatic then the record is arbitrarily linked to the current occurrence of each set type of which it is a member.

MODIFY record name

> Updates record value after record has been found and attribute values changed in user's local copy.

DELETE record name [{ONLY
                       SELECTIVE
                       ALL }]

> If no option, record deleted if and only if all sets it owns are empty. The ONLY option deletes record and all mandatory members. The SELECTIVE option deletes record and mandatory and optional members if they do not belong to other sets. The ALL option deletes all members regardless of membership status.

Network Set Maintenance

In addition to retrieval and modification commands there are also several DML commands for set maintenance. Set maintenance involves the assignment and modification of linkages between the owner record and member records when records are inserted into and deleted from the database. Before using these commands one must establish the current record.

CONNECT record name INTO {ALL
                            set name list}

> Set membership must be manual.

DISCONNECT record name FROM {ALL
                              set name list}

> Set membership must be optional.

SECS Network DML Examples

We now show how some of the DML commands presented above might be used in our SECS example. Assume that a professor wishes to retrieve information about students enrolled in a section of his class. We shall examine two cases: one where a unique key value is known, and one where set membership is known.

In the first example let the unique identification number (SID) of the student in whom we are interested be 817456. Student information could be obtained by the following commands:

```
MOVE 817456 TO SID IN STUDENT
FIND STUDENT USING SID
GET STUDENT
```

In this example the FIND command sets the currency pointers for the run unit, student record, and all sets containing students to the student record with SID = 817456.

In the second example, let us suppose that the professor wishes to obtain a student's record but knows only the student's major (ART) and the section (SNUM = 55104) in which the student is enrolled. The record can be obtained by the following commands:

```
MOVE 55104 TO SNUM
FIND SECTION USING SNUM
FIND FIRST SECT.STUD RECORD OF SECTION-ENROLLMENT
FIND OWNER RECORD OF CURRENT-CLASSES
GET STUDENT
REPEAT UNTIL STUDENT IS FOUND
    WHILE CURRENT STUDENT'S MAJOR IS NOT ART
        FIND NEXT SECT.STUD RECORD OF SECTION-ENROLLMENT
        FIND OWNER RECORD OF CURRENT-CLASSES
        GET STUDENT
    DISPLAY STUDENT
    QUERY USER IF STUDENT IS FOUND
```

The first statement sets the value for SNUM so that the FIND SECTION command can determine the necessary current SECTION record. Setting the SECTION record determines the current instance of the SECTION-ENROLLMENT set. This enables us to obtain the first SECT.STUD member record and as a by-product set the currency pointer for the CURRENT-CLASSES set. The owner of CURRENT-CLASSES is a student enrolled in section SNUM. The value of the MAJOR field of the student's record can be examined. If the student is not an ART major, then we examine the next student in the section.

This student's record is obtained by retrieving the owner of the CURRENT-CLASSES set of which the next SECT.STUD record is a member. This loop would continue until the current student's major is ART. The outer repeat loop handles the case where there is more than one ART major in a course section.

Notice how complex the set-based retrieval example is. To manipulate the data in a network database the application programmer must know all the set definitions and the existing currency pointers. This programming is both detailed and difficult. In addition, some updates require that the application programmer explicitly maintain the set linkages. This can occur during record insertion when set membership is manual, and also when set membership is optional and a record is being removed from a set.

11.8 Analysis of the Network Data Model

In summary, the network model is more flexible than the hierarchical data model. Using sets, the network model can represent diverse types of associations among record types. Although the network model cannot directly implement M:N associations (because of its restrictions on set membership), it can represent such mappings with an indirect set. Another advantage of the network model compared with the hierarchical model is the absence of triggered deletions.

The major disadvantage of the network data model is its complexity and structure. To write application programs that process data stored in the network, the programmer must know the logical structure of the database. This places a heavy burden on the programmer. **Navigation** or searches through the network database is not simple, and application programs written for a network DBMS tend to be complex and not easily modified.

Summary

In this chapter we briefly examined the hierarchical and network data models. The properties of each data model were presented along with a pseudo DDL and DML syntax. Examples were provided from the SECS database. Both data models have been used extensively to implement commercial DBMS's. Of the two, the network model is more powerful because of its greater design flexibility and extended DML capabilities. Unfortunately, neither data model can directly represent M:N associations.

Both data models are sufficient to perform the database functions specified in Chapter 10. They both provide mechanisms for data integrity, security, concurrent data processing, minimal data redundancy, relative flexibility in data access techniques, and DML. Furthermore, the architectures of both models provide for logical and physical data independence. DBMS's based on the hierarchical or network data model are typically used for data processing activities on very large databases. Typical applications are payroll, sales orders, and inventory.

Exercises

1. Exercise 5 in Chapter 9 required that you design a system to keep track of students at a university with respect to their major and their membership in campus clubs. Each student had a student identification number, could have several majors, and could belong to several clubs. Take your entity specifications and semantics from that problem and develop both a hierarchical and a network data diagram.

2. Given your hierarchical and network data diagrams from Exercise 1, write pseudo DML commands to list the majors of all students belonging to a specific club.

3. Choose an institution with which you are familiar and define a network schema or data diagram. Some example institutions are professional athletic leagues (baseball, football), citizens and their community service activities, or church membership and church service groups. List the records and their data fields and specify set owners and members.

4. Given the schema developed in Exercise 3, develop a few subschemas for different applications. For example, a baseball team schema might support three subschemas for application programs used by players, management, and coaches.

5. If you have a hierarchical or network database management system available, compile the schemas and subschemas for Exercises 1 through 4 above.

6. Write the pseudo schema DDL statements for the four sets listed in Fig. 11.5 not specified in Fig. 11.7.

Suggestions for Further Reading

C. J. Date, *An Introduction to Database Systems*, 3rd ed. (Reading, Mass.: Addison-Wesley, 1981).

D. M. Kroenke, *Database Processing: Fundamentals, Design, Implementation*, 2nd ed. (Palo Alto, Calif.: Science Research Associates, 1983).

D. C. Tsichritzis and F. H. Lochovsky, *Data Models* (Englewood Cliffs, N.J.: Prentice-Hall, 1982).

12

The Relational Data Model

12.1 Describes the basic conceptual model with examples of relations.

12.2 Considers how a relational database could be defined.

12.3 Examines the three levels of relational DML.

12.4 Presents examples of the relational DML using the SECS database.

12.5 Compares the advantages and disadvantages of the hierarchical, network, and relational data models and briefly presents the concept of a multimodel DBMS.

In this chapter we outline the features of the relational database model. We then compare the relational model with the hierarchical and network models. In addition, we briefly discuss the advantages and disadvantages of multimodel DBMS's.

The relational data model has a certain elegance and simplicity compared with the network and hierarchical models. For this reason it is becoming widely used. However, doubts have been cast on the efficiency with which certain relational operations can be performed. To circumvent these difficulties, large data processing environments may use two loosely linked DBMS's: a network DBMS for extensive record-by-record processing and a relational DBMS for query transactions and reports. Future DBMS's may provide both a relational and network database interface to users. However, the debate between the merits of the two models may become moot with the advent of database machines. We will consider possible future database systems in Chapter 14.

12.1 Properties of the Relational Model

Use of the relational model was proposed by Codd [81].[1] A **relation** is a subset of the cross product of sets of attribute values. More pre-

---

1. Chamberlin [99] provides an introduction to the relational model and traces

SCHEDULE (INSTRUCTOR, COURSE, ROOM)

Abbott	100	12
Fisher	105	2
Fisher	105	10
Baker	101	12
Carter	100	8
Carter	101	12

FIGURE 12.1 Tabular representation of a relation

cisely, given a collection of sets $D_1, D_2, \ldots, D_N$ (not necessarily distinct), R is a relation on the N sets if it is a set of ordered N-tuples $(d_1, d_2, \ldots, d_N)$ such that d_i belongs to D_i. Sets $D_1, \ldots, D_N$ are the **domains** of R, and N is the **degree** of R.

Consider, for example, a university department with 5 instructors, 6 courses, and 18 rooms in which to hold classes. In any particular semester, the schedule of classes is likely to contain only a small subset of the 540 possible combinations (5 $\times$ 6 $\times$ 18). This and all relations can conveniently be represented by a table. Figure 12.1 shows a possible relation on the instructor, course, and room sets. Each row in the table represents a **tuple**. The relation's degree is the number of attributes in each of its tuples.

From the definition of a relation, certain properties of the tabular representation follow. These are:

1. All tuple entries are atomic (scalar).
2. All entries in a particular column are drawn from the same set.
3. Each column has a name unique within the table.
4. All rows are distinct.
5. Neither row order nor column order is important.

Another viewpoint, which is often useful, is to think of each N-tuple in the relation as a point in the space defined by the attribute sets. In the case of the example above, the 3-tuple (Carter, 100, 8) is one point in a three-dimensional space.

Note the comparative simplicity of the relational model. Tables are simple in structure, and there are no pointers from one record to

---

its development. Codd [100] reviews the motivation behind the development of the model.

another. Relational DBMS's began to appear comparatively quickly after Codd's model was introduced, although many were of a limited nature. Kim [101] surveyed some early systems. In the next sections we look at data definition and manipulation in the relational model.

12.2 Relational Data Definition

In Chapter 9 we discussed normalizing a set of entities. The same techniques apply to relations. In fact, all the example entity specifications in Chapter 9 that were at least of first normal form (1NF) were valid relation specifications. A major advantage of the relational model is that it can directly represent M:N associations. Figure 9.14 in Chapter 9 contains the relations CLASS.TEXTS and CLASS.SECTIONS. Both relations are examples of multivalued dependencies.

Specifying and creating a relational database is usually simpler than creating a hierarchical or network database because relations have a simpler structure. There are no explicit links between relations. One can distinguish between actual relations and **views.** Views are virtual relations defined in terms of actual relations and/or other views. "View" is the relational term for what we have called a functional database.

Relation Specification: Logical Database

In some systems it may be necessary to specify only the name of the relation and the amount of storage to reserve for each of the fields. The statement below shows how an employee relation might be declared using the INGRES query language QUEL [71]. We do not use a pseudo DDL here because the relational DDL is sufficiently abstract.

```
CREATE EMPLOYEE (NUMBER = I2, NAME = C20, = I2, MANAGER = I2,
                 ADDRESS = C20, DEPT = I2)
```

In QUEL, "I" fields reserve space for one-, two-, or four-byte integers. The "C" fields reserve space for character strings.

We may wish to go further and, for example, specify a key field and nondefault values for some domains. A similar employee relation might be declared using the Troll interface language [102] for the PLAIN Data Base Handler [103] as follows:

```
RELATION EMPLOYEE [KEY NUMBER] OF
    NUMBER, MANAGER : INTEGER;
    NAME, ADDRESS   : STRING;
    SALARY          : SALARY;
    DEPT            : INTEGER (100..999);
    END;
```

The QUEL commands to establish the relations for the SECS database example are as follows:

```
CREATE PROFS (PID = I1, PNAME = C15, OFFICE = I2, DEPT = C2)
CREATE COURSE (CNAME = C15, PREREQ = C15, UNITS = I1)
CREATE SECTION (SNUM = I4, CNAME = C15, PID = I1, ROOM = C6,
               BEGIN = C4, END = C4)
CREATE STUDENT (SID = C8, SNAME = C15, SPREREQ = C15, MAJOR = C5,
               GPA = F4, SUNITS = I2)
CREATE STUD-REC (SID = C8, SEMESTER = C5, YEAR = I2, CNAME = C15,
               GRADE = C1)
CREATE SECT-STUD (SNUM = I4, SID = C8)
```

As with the previous DBMS models, the logical database declarations in the relational model establish domains and field sizes; no actual data values exist yet.

Relational Views: Functional Databases

In setting up views we are in effect defining functional databases (subschemas). When a query involving a view is processed, it is modified to operate on the appropriate real elements. For example, suppose that to convey messages to students a certain application needs information about when, where, and from whom students take classes. We could define a virtual relation based on the relations given above. In QUEL, the definition would be:

```
DEFINE VIEW STUDENT (SECT-STUD.SID,
                     SECTION.ROOM,
                     DURATION = SECTION.END — SECTION.BEGIN,
                     PROFS.PNAME)
        WHERE SECT-STUD.SNUM = SECTION.SNUM
        AND PROFS.PID = SECTION.PID
```

There is no problem with retrieving from views, but there may be problems in updating views. The difficulty in updating a view is common to all functional databases. Some attributes in a derived view may be computed from the logical database relation. For instance, in the definition above the attribute "duration" is computed from two attributes in the logical database. If the computed value is changed, there is no corresponding value in the logical database to update. If we update the duration field, what part of the section tuple would we expect to be modified? One can think of computed view attributes as similar to a procedure parameter passed by value.

12.3 Three Levels of Relational DML

Having established that data can be held in relations, what operations are available to extract useful information? There are three levels of DML commands: **relational calculus, relational algebra,** and **tuple-by-tuple processing.** Relational calculus, devised by Codd [104], is a non-procedural query DML. It is nonprocedural in the sense that the user specifies the properties of the information to be operated on rather than the detailed steps by which the operation is to be carried out. The DBMS analyzes the request and performs the necessary operations. Relational algebra is a procedural language in which the user specifies operations. However, the specifications contain no references to access paths. In other words, the specification is independent of how the relations are actually stored. The lowest of the three levels is a tuple-by-tuple language in which individual tuples from relations can be accessed. Here there is need to know the access paths.

In our discussion below we briefly mention tuple-by-tuple processing and compare relational calculus commands with equivalent relational algebra commands. Our examination of relational DML focuses on relational algebra and calculus.

Tuple-by-Tuple DML

The tuple-by-tuple command level requires data processing strategies similar to the DML shown for the hierarchical and network data models. Using a tuple-by-tuple language one can process the rows in a relation one by one. In this manner one could process all the rows in a relational database if one so desired. We do not examine the tuple-by-tuple command level further for two reasons. First, it is similar to previously discussed DML. Second, because the strength of the relational model, from the user's perspective, is in the relational algebra and calculus we concentrate on those commands.

Relational Algebra

Relational algebra was devised by Codd [105]. If two sets of N-tuples are relations on the same collection of domains, then conventional set operations, for example, union, intersection, and difference, can be applied to them. The operators we discuss here can be applied to two dissimilar relations. We consider four operators: two monadic

SANDWICHES (LOCATION,   BREAD,   FILLING,   HEAT,   PRICE)

Union	Rye	Cheese	Cold	2.35
Roof	Wheat	Cheese	Hot	1.80
Union	Whole	Turkey	Hot	2.60
Pub	Wheat	Spam	Cold	1.75
Pub	Rye	Beef	Hot	2.30
Union	Rye	Beef	Cold	2.50
Roof	Wheat	Beef	Hot	2.00
Pub	Whole	Ham	Cold	1.95
Roof	Rye	Ham	Hot	2.10
Union	Rye	Turkey	Hot	2.60
Union	Wheat	Spam	Cold	1.75
Pub	Rye	Turkey	Hot	2.60
Pub	Whole	Cheese	Cold	2.40
Pub	Wheat	Spam	Cold	1.70

FIGURE 12.2 Sandwich for lunch relation

or unary (selection and projection) and two dyadic or binary (join and division).[2] We give examples of their use in the text and provide exercises at the end of the chapter for further practice. Relational algebra (and calculus) is a "functional" language in that each operation returns as its result a relation. In contrast, the network model DML is a "procedural" language. The relation in Fig. 12.2 will be used in the examples.

Selection. Selection is the simplest of the four relational algebra operators. It can be thought of as picking out one or more rows from a relation. In the notation we adopt, the general form is:

relation2 ← SELECT relation1
             WHERE condition

The resulting relation (Relation2) is a subset of the original (Relation1). The result contains those tuples for which the specified condition is true. In our example relation, we could use selection to find hot sandwiches that sell for less than 2.40. Figure 12.3(a) shows the appropriate selection command and Fig. 12.3(b) shows the resulting relation. Note that the result of a selection operation has the same domains as the relation from which the selection was made.

---

2. Only three are needed to be complete: selection, projection, and join. Other operators can be defined in terms of these three.

HOTNCHEAP ← SELECT SANDWICHES
WHERE (HEAT = "Hot" and PRICE < 2.40)

(a) Selection command

HOTNCHEAP (LOCATION, BREAD, FILLING, HEAT, PRICE)

Roof	Wheat	Cheese	Hot	1.80
Pub	Rye	Beef	Hot	2.30
Roof	Wheat	Beef	Hot	2.00
Roof	Rye	Ham	Hot	2.10

(b) Resulting HOTNCHEAP relation

FIGURE 12.3 HOTNCHEAP sandwich selection

Projection. Projection is the second monadic operation. Whereas selection processes a relation by rows, projection can be thought of as processing the relation by columns (though see below). In our notation the general form is:

relation2 ← PROJECT relation1
ON [attribute, attribute, . . .]

The resulting relation (Relation2) is almost the result of selecting the specified columns from the relation. It is not quite a column selection because there will be no duplication of rows in the result. Thinking in terms of the N-dimensional space mentioned earlier will show how the projection is actually obtained.

Suppose we wish to find out the bread/filling combinations of sandwiches available. We can use the command in Fig. 12.4(a) to generate the BREADFILL relation listed in Fig. 12.4(b). Note that there are only 10 tuples in Fig. 12.4 compared with the 14 tuples in Fig. 12.2. The difference is the number of duplicate rows eliminated during the projection.

Because of their "functional" nature, operators in relational algebra can be nested. Suppose, for example, we wish to find all the places serving ham sandwiches. We could first find the entries for ham sandwiches and then project the result on location. The command and result are shown in Fig. 12.5.

Join. The join operator is dyadic and comes in a number of forms. We denote the most general of them as follows.

relation3 ← JOIN relation1, relation2
WHEN condition

BREADFILL ← PROJECT SANDWICHES
ON [BREAD, FILLING]

(a) Projection command

BREADFILL (BREAD,   FILLING)

Rye	Cheese
Wheat	Cheese
Whole	Turkey
Wheat	Spam
Rye	Beef
Wheat	Beef
Whole	Ham
Rye	Ham
Rye	Turkey
Whole	Cheese

(b) BREADFILL relation

FIGURE 12.4 Sandwich bread and fillings projection

Every tuple in the resulting relation is a concatenation of a tuple from relation1 with a tuple from relation2. Two tuples are concatenated if the specified condition holds. To illustrate the dyadic operators we need a second example relation, which we show in Fig. 12.6. It indicates the sandwich preferences of a small group of people.

We could use the join operation to find those places where the people in TASTES might go to lunch. Let us assume that they are willing to compromise on the heat of the sandwich filling and that they are not willing to spend more than 2.20. The operation we perform is shown in Fig. 12.7(a). The effect is to join a tuple from the

FIGURE 12.5 Places to eat ham sandwiches

HAMPLACES ← PROJECT (SELECT SANDWICHES
WHERE FILLING = "Ham"
)
ON [LOCATION] .

(a) Nested relational commands

HAMPLACES (LOCATION)

Pub
Roof

(b) Resulting HAMPLACES relation

TASTES (NAME, FILLING, HEAT)

Brown	Turkey	Hot
Brown	Beef	Hot
Brown	Ham	Hot
Jones	Cheese	Cold
Green	Beef	Hot
Green	Turkey	Cold
Green	Cheese	Cold

FIGURE 12.6 TASTES: a sandwich preference relation

SANDWICH relation with one from the TASTE relation if and only if the FILLING attributes of the two tuples are the same and the PRICE attribute in the SANDWICH tuple is not more than 2.20. Figure 12.7(b) shows the result.

Note that we have used subscripts in Fig. 12.7 to have unique column headings in the result. It is worth noting that a series of projections of a relation R cannot, in general, be "joined" back together to reconstitute R. R can be recreated if each of the projections includes the primary key or, in general, the same candidate key.

Equijoin. The equijoin operation is a special case of the join operation. We denote it as follows:

relation3 ← EQUIJOIN relation1, relation2

Two tuples are concatenated if they have equal values of common attributes. Consider the result of

FIGURE 12.7 Join of TASTES and SANDWICHES

WHEREAT ← JOIN TASTES, SANDWICHES
    WHEN TASTES.FILLING = SANDWICHES.FILLING
      AND SANDWICHES.PRICE ≤ 2.20

(a) Join command

WHEREAT (NAME, $FILLING_1$, $HEAT_1$, LOCATION, BREAD, $FILLING_2$, $HEAT_2$, PRICE)

Brown	Beef	Hot	Roof	Wheat	Beef	Hot	2.00
Brown	Ham	Hot	Pub	Whole	Ham	Cold	1.95
Brown	Ham	Hot	Roof	Rye	Ham	Hot	2.10
Jones	Cheese	Cold	Roof	Wheat	Cheese	Hot	1.80
Green	Beef	Hot	Roof	Wheat	Beef	Hot	2.00
Green	Cheese	Cold	Roof	Wheat	Cheese	Hot	1.80

(b) Resulting WHEREAT relation

CANDIDATES (NAME, $FILLING_1$, $HEAT_1$, LOCATION, BREAD, $FILLING_2$, $HEAT_2$, PRICE)

Brown	Turkey	Hot	Union	Whole	Turkey	Hot	2.60
Brown	Turkey	Hot	Union	Rye	Turkey	Hot	2.60
Brown	Turkey	Hot	Pub	Rye	Turkey	Hot	2.60
Brown	Beef	Hot	Pub	Rye	Beef	Hot	2.30
Brown	Beef	Hot	Roof	Wheat	Beef	Hot	2.00
Brown	Ham	Hot	Roof	Rye	Ham	Hot	2.10
Jones	Cheese	Cold	Union	Rye	Cheese	Cold	2.35
Jones	Cheese	Cold	Pub	Whole	Cheese	Cold	2.40
Green	Beef	Hot	Pub	Rye	Beef	Hot	2.30
Green	Beef	Hot	Roof	Wheat	Beef	Hot	2.00
Green	Cheese	Cold	Union	Rye	Cheese	Cold	2.35
Green	Cheese	Cold	Pub	Whole	Cheese	Cold	2.40

FIGURE 12.8 Equijoin of TASTES and SANDWICHES

CANDIDATES ← EQUIJOIN TASTES, SANDWICHES

Two tuples are joined if they have the same value of FILLING and HEAT. The result of this equijoin is shown in Fig. 12.8.

Natural join. The equijoin operator inevitably produces column duplication in the result. It is therefore convenient to define a variant that, in some ways, is the most useful form of the join operation. This **natural join** also joins two tuples if common attributes are equal but discards duplicate occurrences of identical columns in the result. From now on, we will call this operation the join operation. The natural join operation with TASTES and SANDWICHES is shown in Fig. 12.9(a), and its result is shown in Fig. 12.9(b). We can find candidate places to eat by projecting the result of the natural join operation on name and location. Figure 12.10(a) shows the operation and Fig. 12.10(b) the result.

Implementation of the join operator. The simplest implementation of the join operator would take each tuple in relation1 in turn and examine its relationship with each tuple in relation2. If there are N_1 tuples in relation1 and N_2 tuples in relation2, then there would be $N_1 \times N_2$ tuple-tuple evaluations. However, this would usually be unacceptably inefficient. Ways have been proposed for implementing a join more efficiently (see, for example, Todd [106]). We can imagine that the number of comparisons could be reduced if it were possible to access tuples in sequence by an attribute used in the join. In the case of an equijoin we would be interested in determining as quickly as possible whether or not a tuple in relation1 matched any in relation2.

TASTY ← JOIN TASTES, SANDWICHES

(a) Natural join command

TASTY (NAME,   FILLING,   HEAT,   LOCATION,   BREAD,   PRICE)

Brown	Turkey	Hot	Union	Whole	2.60
Brown	Turkey	Hot	Union	Rye	2.60
Brown	Turkey	Hot	Pub	Rye	2.60
Brown	Beef	Hot	Pub	Rye	2.30
Brown	Beef	Hot	Roof	Wheat	2.00
Brown	Ham	Hot	Roof	Rye	2.10
Jones	Cheese	Cold	Union	Rye	2.35
Jones	Cheese	Cold	Pub	Whole	2.40
Green	Beef	Hot	Pub	Rye	2.30
Green	Beef	Hot	Roof	Wheat	2.00
Green	Cheese	Cold	Union	Rye	2.35
Green	Cheese	Cold	Pub	Whole	2.40

(b) Resulting TASTY relation

FIGURE 12.9 Natural join of TASTES and SANDWICHES

We leave further consideration of possible techniques as exercises for the reader (see Exercises 3 and 4).

Division. Division is the second dyadic operator we consider. We denote it as follows:

relation3 ← DIVIDE-BY relation1, relation2

FIGURE 12.10 Natural join and projection

CANEAT ← PROJECT (JOIN TASTES, SANDWICHES)
ON [NAME, LOCATION]

(a) Projection on a join operation

CANEAT (NAME,   LOCATION)

Brown	Union
Brown	Pub
Brown	Roof
Jones	Union
Jones	Pub
Green	Pub
Green	Roof
Green	Union

(b) Resulting CANEAT relation

PEOPLE ← PROJECT TASTES
ON [NAME]

(a) Projection command

PEOPLE (NAME)

_____

Brown
Jones
Green

_____

(b) Resulting PEOPLE relation

FIGURE 12.11 People to find food for relation

If relation1 is of degree $M + N$ and relation2 is of degree N, the result is of degree M. An example of the divide operator may serve as the best introduction.

Assume that we are interested in finding places where everyone in our example may eat together and find something to his or her taste. The relation CANEAT in Fig. 12.10(b) gives us candidate places for each person. We project TASTES on NAME to find the people in our set; this is shown in Fig. 12.11.

We can now use division to find places where everyone can eat together. Figure 12.12(a) shows the operation and Fig. 12.12(b) the result.

Having seen an example, let us now define the divide operation. Using our prototype call above, treat each tuple in relation1 as if it consisted of two parts. The first part (the Y component) comprises the set of attributes that relation1 has in common with relation2. The second part (the X component) consists of the remaining attributes. The result of the division is a subset of the X components. For a tuple to appear in the resulting relation, it must appear in relation1 concatenated with each of the tuples in relation2. Consider the example

FIGURE 12.12 Result of division

ALLEAT ← DIVIDE-BY CANEAT, PEOPLE

(a) Division command

ALLEAT (LOCATION)

_____

Union
Pub

_____

(b) Resulting ALLEAT relation

ORDER (FILLING, HEAT)

Cheese	Cold
Turkey	Hot
Beef	Hot

(a) Food order

WHEREALL ← DIVIDE-BY (PROJECT SANDWICHES
ON [lOCATION, FILLING, HEAT]
), ORDER

(b) Division on the results of a projection command

WHEREALL (LOCATION)

Pub

(c) Resulting WHEREALL relation

FIGURE 12.13 Second example of division

of Fig. 12.12. The only locations where all three of the people can eat are the union and the pub.

Consider a second example. Figure 12.13(a) contains a relation with information about a lunch order. We can use division to find out which food outlet can satisfy the complete order, that is, can serve all the items on it. The appropriate operation is shown in Fig. 12.13(b) and the result in Fig. 12.13(c). Note that we do not divide SANDWICHES directly by ORDER. If we did, the result would be a relation with attributes LOCATION, BREAD, and PRICE. There would be a tuple in the result only if all the tuples in ORDER were in SANDWICHES with the same location, bread, and price.

Relational Calculus

Query languages based on relational calculus are found in most commercial relational DBMS's. We give examples in notation based on those languages rather than on the calculus itself. To illustrate the difference between relational calculus and relational algebra, we will show how some of the examples given in the section on relational algebra would be expressed.

Figure 12.14 shows the relational calculus equivalents of the examples of Figs. 12.3, 12.4, and 12.5. Figure 12.14(a) shows the equivalent of a simple selection, Fig. 12.14(b) the equivalent of a simple projection, and Fig. 12.14(c) a projection of a selection.

Figure 12.15 shows relational calculus equivalents of the examples of Figs. 12.7, 12.8, and 12.9, which were concerned with various

RETRIEVE INTO HOTNCHEAP (SANDWICHES.ALL)
        WHERE (SANDWICHES.HEAT = "Hot" and SANDWICHES.PRICE < 2.40)

(a)

RETRIEVE INTO BREADFILL (SANDWICHES.BREAD, SANDWICHES.FILLING)

(b)

RETRIEVE INTO HAMPLACES (SANDWICHES.LOCATION)
        WHERE SANDWICHES.FILLING = "Ham"

(c)

FIGURE 12.14 Relational calculus selections and projections

forms of the join operation. Figure 12.15(a) shows a general join. Figure 12.15(b) shows the equivalent of our equijoin example (note that we have to make the condition explicit here). Figure 12.15(c) shows the equivalent of our natural join example. In addition to making the condition explicit, we have to eliminate the redundant columns in the result because the operation does not perform this function.

In relational calculus it is sometimes necessary to introduce **relational variables.** A typical example is where a relation is being joined with itself (in the corresponding algebra the relation appears in both operands of a join). Consider the relation of Fig. 12.16. Suppose we wish to find the names of employees managed by someone earning more than 50,000. Let us also retrieve the manager's name. Figure 12.17(a) shows how the query might be posed in relational algebra.

FIGURE 12.15 Relational calculus joins

RETRIEVE INTO WHEREAT (TASTES.ALL, SANDWICHES.ALL)
        WHERE (TASTES.FILLING = SANDWICHES.FILLING
                AND SANDWICHES.PRICE < 2.20)

(a)

RETRIEVE INTO CANDIDATES (TASTES.ALL, SANDWICHES.ALL)
        WHERE (TASTES.FILLING = SANDWICHES.FILLING
                AND TASTES.HEAT = SANDWICHES.HEAT)

(b)

RETRIEVE INTO TASTY (TASTES.ALL, SANDWICHES.LOCATION,
                SANDWICHES.BREAD, SANDWICHES.PRICE)
        WHERE (TASTES.FILLING = SANDWICHES.FILLING
                AND TASTES.HEAT = SANDWICHES.HEAT)

(c)

EMPLOYEES (NAME, NUMBER, MANAGER, SALARY)

Able	1	5	30000
Baker	2	3	60000
Charles	3	0	85000
Dunn	4	3	52000
Elliot	5	0	40000
Foxx	6	5	30000
Grant	7	4	35000

FIGURE 12.16 Employee relation

We use our earlier subscripting conventions for differentiating columns in RESULT. Figure 12.17(b) shows the result of the join. The left half of a tuple represents employee information; the right half represents the same information for the employee's manager. Figure 12.17(c) shows the result of the projection. An equivalent relational calculus query is as follows:

```
RANGE OF A, B IS EMPLOYEES
RETRIEVE INTO RESULT (A.NAME, B.NAME)
        WHERE (A.MANAGER = B.NUMBER AND B.SALARY > 50000)
```

FIGURE 12.17 Managerial enquiries: algebraic solution

```
RESULT ← PROJECT (JOIN EMPLOYEES, EMPLOYEES
                WHEN (MANAGER₁ = NUMBER₂ AND SALARY₂ > 50000)
              )
        ON [NAME₁, NAME₂]
```

(a)

$NAME_1$, $NUMBER_1$, $MANAGER_1$, $SALARY_1$, $NAME_2$, $NUMBER_2$, $MANAGER_2$, $SALARY_2$

Baker	2	3	60000	Charles	3	0	85000
Dunn	4	3	52000	Charles	3	0	85000
Grant	7	4	55000	Dunn	4	3	52000

(b)

RESULT ($NAME_1$, $NAME_2$)

Baker	Charles
Dunn	Charles
Grant	Dunn

(c)

Think of A and B as pointers ranging over the EMPLOYEES relation. We want the NAME fields of the two tuples they point to when the specified condition is satisfied.

Relational algebra and calculus have been shown to be equivalent (see, for example, Klug [107]), but relational calculus is a more natural query interface. Therefore most relational query systems are based on the calculus. There are, however, limits on the power of relational calculus. A common example of this concerns a managerial hierarchy. Suppose we have an employee relation such as that of Fig. 12.16 in which each employee tuple contains the employee name and the name of the employee's immediate supervisor. Although it may be trivial to find those supervised directly by employee X, it is beyond the power of relational calculus to find those supervised by X either directly or indirectly.[3]

In Chapter 11 we showed how both hierarchical and network databases could be established for the SECS data processing example of Chapter 1. In each case we showed how three example transactions could be performed. In the next section we show how similar transactions might be formulated using a relational DML.

12.4 SECS Relational DML Examples

On page 308 we gave example relation declarations for the SECS database. Because a relational database is conceptually simpler than either of the other two models, the DML commands are correspondingly simpler.

The first transaction is to retrieve a student record given the student identification number. In the relational model this requires selecting a tuple from the appropriate relation. A suitable DML statement is

```
RETRIEVE (STUDENT.ALL)
      WHERE STUDENT.SID = 817456
```

The second transaction is to change the office number of a professor. For example, suppose we want to move Professor Jones to room 419. Again, a single relation is involved. An appropriate statement is

```
REPLACE PROFS (OFFICE = 419)
      WHERE PROFS.PNAME = 'Jones'
```

---

3. If X supervises Y and Y supervises Z, then X supervises Z indirectly. Of course this could go on for an arbitrary number of levels.

For our final transaction, we will retrieve all art majors in section number 55104. Two relations are involved in this case. A suitable DML statement is

```
RETRIEVE (STUDENT.ALL)
        WHERE STUDENT.MAJOR = 'Art'
        AND STUDENT.SID = SECT-STUD.SID
        AND SECT-STUD.SNUM = 55104
```

12.5 Comparison of Database Data Models

In Chapter 11 and in this chapter we described the hierarchical, network, and relational data models. We now compare their major advantages and disadvantages. Michaels, Mittman, and Carlson [108] present a good comparison of the relational and network approaches. Our comparison is based on each model's understandability, representational power, space and time efficiency, and ease of use. We also take a look at the architecture and properties of multimodel DBMS's.

Comparison of the Three DBMS Data Models

A data model is understandable if users can easily comprehend the associations represented by the model. A data model's understandability is primarily affected by the explicitness of the connections between associated record types and by the simplicity of the associations. Thus the hierarchical data model is easy to understand because the only association allowed between different record types is that of parent-descendant. The network data model, on the other hand, is less understandable due to the numerous set associations allowed. The relational data model is the least understandable because the associations among relations are not explicitly represented; rather, they exist through shared attributes.

A model's understandability is also related to its representational power. Representational power is the ability of a data model to establish 1:1, 1:N, and M:N associations between record types. All three data models can easily represent 1:1 and 1:N associations. Their ability to represent M:N associations, however, differs greatly. The hierarchical model has the worst representational power. A hierarchical model must represent M:N associations indirectly as two 1:N associations in different database trees. This reduces its understandability for M:N associations. The network data model has better representational power, but cannot directly represent M:N associations. It must establish an intermediate record type and two set declarations. This obscures the underlying M:N dependency. The relational model has the best representational power because it can directly represent M:N associations. Although the M:N association is directly representable, it is not easily understood in the relational model because the associations are not explicitly stated.

The hierarchical and network models are roughly equivalent in their space efficiency. Their storage space is well utilized because they implement associations by pointers rather than data values. In addition, application programs can exploit the pointer linkages and currency pointers to minimize time for transactions. The relational model is not as efficient in time and space. This is because associations are stored by redundant attribute values, not pointers. Transactions can take a long time in the relational model because associations must be derived dynamically.

The application programmer's ease of use of the DML for the three models also varies. (We do not consider query language interfaces here because the user's prerequisite knowledge of the logical database is theoretically equivalent across all data models.) Again, the hierarchical and network data models are roughly equivalent. Both are more difficult to use than the relational model. The DML for the hierarchical and network DBMS are procedural. Application programmers must know both how the functional database is declared and how it is stored in order to develop efficient applications. Furthermore, navigation through the network with its many currency pointers can be difficult to comprehend. With the "functional" relational DML, application programmers request information in terms of information content, not associational linkage.

In summary, the hierarchical and network data models (1) are more understandable, (2) have less representational power, (3) are more space and time efficient, and (4) are more difficult to use than the relational model. We believe that the hierarchical data model has historical significance only and will not be the basis of many future DBMS's. Network DBMS supporters claim three advantages over the relational model: a more "natural" structure for modeling associations, a more efficient DML, and minimal data redundancy. Relational DBMS advocates claim that the relational data model is simpler and more uniform. Furthermore, they claim that the relational model provides greater data independence and that its DML is easier to use.

Next we briefly present the multimodel DBMS concept and contrast it to single data model DBMS's.

Multimodel DBMS's

As we have seen, DBMS's provide flexible data processing compared with an integrated file processing environment. There are, however, three problems associated with a DBMS based on a single data model. First, the data model may not be well suited for specific applications. As an example, a relational model is well suited for ad-hoc report generation, while a network model is not. Second, conversion of applications from one DBMS data model to a different DBMS data model is a difficult task. Third, it is hard to transmit data between DBMS's based on different data models.

A **multimodel DBMS** can reduce these difficulties. A multimodel DBMS must be able to support equivalent, multiple, logical databases and DML's for different data models. Two databases based on different data models are equivalent when three conditions are met. First, they must represent the same collection of data items and associations. Second, they must be able to translate the DML commands for one model into equivalent commands in another model. Third, the same changes to the database must be made by equivalent DML commands. To simplify our discussion we assume here that a multimodel DBMS supports both a network and relational representation of the same database. Such a DBMS enables users to perceive a network or relational functional database and can support network and relational DML commands. For a good introduction to multimodel DBMS concepts, see Larson [109].

How would a multimodel DBMS address the three problems associated with a single-model DBMS mentioned above? First, with a multimodel DBMS, application programmers can choose the data model to suit the application or their expertise. For example, one might choose a relational perspective to develop a user interface for queries and a network perspective for a large batch job for updating numerous records. Second, conversion of applications from different data models is unnecessary in a multimodel DBMS because both data models are available. Third, communication problems between different DBMS data models are minimized by having common data models.

There are two design approaches for implementing a multimodel DBMS: mapping and composite. We show both approaches in Fig. 12.18. The mapping approach translates one data model into another. For example, a relational data model might be mapped onto an actual network database. This approach is somewhat analogous to functional and logical database mappings as described in Chapter 10. The mapping approach, for our example, requires the generation of a relational model of the database from an actual network database. In addition, relational DML commands would have to be translatable to network commands.

The composite approach requires the development of a common logical database that embeds both relational and network representations of all dependencies into a common record/relation declaration. Both DML command sets would have to maintain the composite

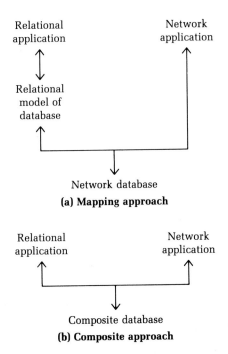

(a) Mapping approach

(b) Composite approach

FIGURE 12.18 Mapping and composite multimodel DBMS's

record declarations and set memberships. The interested reader is encouraged to read the examples of the mapping and composite approaches to multimodel DBMS's provided by Larson [109].

There are foreseeable disadvantages to multimodel DBMS's. A multimodel DBMS is less understandable, is slower in carrying out transactions, and requires more storage than a single-model DBMS. Declaring a multimodel DBMS would require more complex DDL, probably with different syntax for the network DDL and the relational DDL. With the composite approach, the logical database would not be as understandable. Translation of DML commands across data models would slow the transaction speed. Finally, more storage would be used because either all associations would be redundantly stored (composite approach) or a secondary logical database would have to be maintained (mapping approach). Nevertheless, we believe that multimodel DBMS's will become more available in the near future and that they will combine the capabilities of the network and relational models.

Summary

The relational database model has many advantages. First, relations can be conveniently implemented as tables. Second, the relational model can directly represent M:N associations among relations and is easy to define. Third, the relational model provides three levels of DML commands to support varied data processing activities. Typical commercial relational DBMS's provide a language similar to relational calculus. A disadvantage of the relational model is performance on query processing. Often query resolution can produce large intermediate relations and require extensive searching of the database. This is because a join, in essence, dynamically builds the associative links that exist within a network database. Query optimization is an important research effort in relational database systems. In Chapter 14 we will discuss future database technology important to relational systems such as query optimization and database machines.

We compared the three DBMS data models according to their understandability, representational power, efficiency, and usability. The hierarchical and network models represent dependencies in a more understandable manner than the relational model. The relational model has the greatest representational power because it can directly implement M:N dependencies. The network model is the most efficient because applications can exploit the existence of various currency pointers. Finally, the DML for the relational model is the easiest to use. The concept of a multimodel DBMS was discussed and compared with the traditional single-model approach.

Exercises

1. Assume that a database contains the following relations:

   CLASSES (TICKET-#, DEPARTMENT, INSTRUCTOR)
   ENROLLMENTS (ID-#, MAJOR, TICKET-#)

   Students from a number of different majors take computer science courses. Give a relational algebraic expression that produces the answer to the following query:

   "Find those majors such that, in each computer science class, there is at least one student with the major."

2. Using the relations of Exercise 1, give an expression that yields a list of the instructors who have at least one computer science major in their class.

3. Describe how each of the following might be used to increase the efficiency of a join operation:

a) sorting

b) indexes

c) recording maxima and minima of attributes in a relation

4. Consider the equijoin and natural join operations. How might hashing be used to reduce the number of tuple-tuple evaluations?

5. Is the join operator associative? That is, is the following expression true?

JOIN A, (JOIN B, C) ≡ JOIN (JOIN A, B), C

6. Implement a means of storing relations and allow users to issue queries and to perform select and project operations (including nested operations).

7. Extend your answer to Exercise 6 so that natural join and division operations can be performed.

8. Extend your answer to Exercise 7 so that users can store the result of a query as a new relation. Test your system on the examples in this chapter.

9. Show that each of the four relational algebra operators (select, project, join, and division) can be expressed in relational calculus.

13

Issues in Database Implementation

13.1 Considers ways in which the integrity of data may be maintained.

13.2 Examines the problems caused by allowing concurrent access to a database.

13.3 Discusses measures that might be implemented to preserve the security of data in a database.

As microcomputers have grown in power, it has become feasible to run database management systems on them. A number of systems are currently available. However, in general, the designers of such systems have fewer problems to solve than designers of DBMS's for minicomputer and mainframe systems. A typical microcomputer operates in a single-user nonmultitasking environment. Minicomputers and mainframes, on the other hand, tend to support multiple concurrent users with multitasking. In this chapter we briefly consider three issues that must be addressed by the designers of DBMS's for multiuser and multitasking environments: data integrity, concurrent access, and data security. These are active research areas; in this chapter we give only a brief introduction to some of the problems. We encourage you to read the referenced papers.

In this chapter we use the INGRES relational database [71] to illustrate some of the capabilities found in DBMS's, and we use a pseudo DDL based on SQL and QUEL.

13.1 *Integrity of Databases*

The problem of preserving the integrity of data in a database can be viewed at a number of levels. At a low level it concerns ensuring that the data is not corrupted by hardware or software errors. We looked at some aspects of this problem in Section 2.5, and we consider it further in this chapter. At a higher level, the problem of preserving database integrity concerns maintaining an accurate representation of the real world. Assuming that we can start with a completely empty database, the integrity problem becomes one of checking updates to ensure that they do not violate some set of user-supplied constraints. We therefore need a mechanism to specify what constraints data must satisfy and an enforcement mechanism.

Specification of Constraints

A DBMS should include a mechanism by which integrity rules can be specified in a high-level language. A rule would typically have three components:

1. the conditions under which it should be applied, for example, before deleting an instructor record
2. the condition that is to be tested, for example, that there are no class records for the instructor
3. the action to take if condition 2 is found to be false, for example, abort the deletion and write a warning to the error log

Constraints in INGRES. The INGRES system allows users to specify integrities on a relation. The following statement is an example:

```
DEFINE INTEGRITY ON EMPLOYEE IS EMPLOYEE.SALARY < 100000          (1)
```

This statement specifies that values of the salary attribute in the employee relation must be less than 100,000. When an integrity constraint is issued, the current values of relevant data are checked to ensure that the integrity holds initially. (There is a simple way for users to see which integrities are currently in force on a particular relation.) In terms of the general form above:

1. The constraint will be checked when a change is made to the salary field.
2. The condition to be tested is that the new salary is less than 100,000.
3. In the version of INGRES we use,[1] the designers decided that violations would not be flagged. Instead bad updates are simply not performed.

---

1. Berkeley INGRES rather than Relational Technology INGRES.

It would be useful if the system could distinguish between insertions of new records and modifications of existing ones. The action taken in the case of an error condition may be different in the two cases. For example, a faulty new record might be inserted but offending fields left blank. An invalid modification, on the other hand, would leave the existing record unchanged.

Integrity Enforcement

It is better for enforcement of integrity rules to be handled centrally by the DBMS rather than by individual application programs. In this way enforcement will be consistent and difficult to circumvent. We can conceive of a subsystem in the DBMS concerned with integrity that screens transactions and rejects those that violate current integrity rules. Alternatively, integrity rules could be compiled into application programs automatically.

INGRES enforcement. INGRES handles integrities by modifying those transactions that can change data (replace and append) [110]. Statement (2) shows a QUEL statement as entered by a user. Its purpose is to give employees a 10% pay raise.

```
REPLACE EMPLOYEE(SALARY = EMPLOYEE.SALARY * 1.1)                    (2)
```

Statement (3) shows the query after the system has modified it in the light of the constraint of Statement (1). The query modification is transparent to the user.

```
REPLACE EMPLOYEE(SALARY = EMPLOYEE.SALARY * 1.1)
WHERE EMPLOYEE.SALARY * 1.1 < 100000                               (3)
```

Types of Constraints

Constraints can be classified broadly according to whether they apply to single fields in isolation or involve a set of fields or records. The example in Statement (1) is a single field constraint. Only the new value of that field must be checked. No other records are involved. An example of a constraint involving a set of records would be one that checks primary keys for uniqueness. For example, in a file holding a schedule of classes, no two records should have the same section number. When inserting a new record, a check should be triggered that examines existing primary keys. A similar kind of constraint would be one that ensures that in a file of employee records a manager earns more than any employee he/she manages. This might be specified in a pseudo DDL as follows:

```
RANGE OF E, M IS EMPLOYEE
INTEGRITY ON EMPLOYEE IS: M.SALARY > E.SALARY
                 OR E.MANAGER ≠ M.NUMBER
```

An integrity constraint can involve more than one file. For example, we may wish to specify that the instructor field in a new class record must be the primary key of an existing record in the file of instructors.

With either type of constraint the condition may be specified in absolute terms, as in Statement (1), or in terms of the previous state of the database. For example, in updating student records we may wish to have a constraint that checks to make sure that the number of classes taken never decreases. In the case of employee records, we may wish to ensure that the number of hours worked, or years in the pension plan, never decreases.

The mechanisms described above can be regarded as protecting data against logical damage, that is, cases where hardware and software operate correctly but the new state of the database is invalid. Next we consider what might be done when data becomes corrupt due to hardware or software errors.

Database Recovery

Data corruption can be classified as either **localized corruption** or **nonlocalized corruption.** Localized corruption is the result of some failure, for example a system crash, at some specific time t. Typically, a DBMS includes utilities that can be run to clean up the effects of transactions in progress at the time. For example, consider a system that writes updates to a temporary file rather than applying them to a database immediately. If there is a failure during the creation of the temporary file, that file can be discarded and the application program rerun. If there is a failure during the subsequent processing of the temporary file, then a recovery utility can pick up from the last transaction performed and run to completion.

Nonlocalized corruption is a more serious problem. Typically a periodic integrity check reveals that data has become corrupt between time t_i and the present. A solution here is to restore the database to its state at time t_i and to reperform the transactions that were carried out since t_i. For this to be possible, copies of a database must be taken from time to time (this might happen as part of general filestore backups), and the DBMS must keep a log of transactions carried out.

Hinxman [111] describes a low-overhead update/recovery scheme that is applicable to many small databases with comparatively low transaction rates and no DBA or special recovery software. In this scheme updates are not applied to the database immediately but are written to a serial file. At the end of the user's interaction with the database, a batch program is generated. When run, the batch program updates the database from the serial file. The batch job updates a file by copying it to a temporary file, updating the contents of the temporary file, and finally replacing the original file by the updated copy.

A suitable mechanism for rerunning batch jobs in the event of system failure minimizes the probability of localized failures. If the serial file is kept rather than deleted after a batch run, there is no need for special software for recovery from nonlocalized failures. The set of serial files constitutes the system log. The appropriate set of batch jobs can be run again following the restoration of an old version of the database.

Another way in which data might become corrupt in a multiprocessing system is through the unwanted interactions of two transactions running at the same time. We look at this problem next.

13.2 Concurrency in DBMS's

It is important that two or more processes operating at the same time on a particular part of the database do not interfere with each other in unintended ways. If the processes are only retrieving data, such interactions will not occur. Difficulties arise if one or more of the processes is updating data. In a typical multiprocessing system, active processes are given small bursts of CPU time in turn. In this manner a single process often executes in a series of noncontiguous time intervals. A particular process cannot be considered indivisible, and the execution of many independent processes may overlap. Consider some of the effects of this in the following two examples. Let P1 and P2 represent independent processes.

Example 1: P1 outputs X. P2 adds 1 to X.

Example 2: P1 subtracts 1 from X. P2 subtracts 1 from X.

We assume that to update a value in a database the value has to be read into main memory, modified, and then written back. Problems occur because the sequence is interruptible. While we are holding in main memory what we think is the most current version of a variable, it may be updated on secondary storage by another process. In example 1 the value output by P1 will only be the final value of X if P2 completes before P1 starts. Similarly, in the second example X will be reduced by 2 only if the two processes run consecutively. We want the parallel execution of processes to be equivalent to their serial execution in some order. We consider two broad classes of solution to the concurrent access problem: **locking** and **timestamping.**

Data Locking

In general, a process may request a lock on a data item from some arbitrator. An S-lock (shared lock) allows other processes to read but not write to the item. This is appropriate if the process will read but not change the item. An X-lock (exclusive lock) prevents other processes from reading or writing the item. This is appropriate if the process may change the data item. To permit as much parallelism as possible, we would like the lockable unit to be as small as possible. Thus, rather than locking out an entire database, we would prefer to have the DBMS lock, for example, a particular file being updated or perhaps just a single record. In some cases, this locking mechanism is explicit in the DML of a DBMS (see pseudo DML examples in Chapter 11). The locks are released when the process terminates.

This solution sounds simple, but care is needed to avoid **deadlock.** Consider a situation where P1 has locked file A and needs a lock on file B, while at the same time process P2 has locked file B and now needs a lock on file A. Deadlock occurs because neither process can proceed. A solution is for no process to be allowed to start until it has locked all the resources it needs. This is essentially the strategy adopted by INGRES [71, 4.2]. (To avoid further complications, the request for locks should not be interruptible by any other request for locks.) One difficulty of this approach, however, is that a process may not know what it is going to need until it has started running.

An alternative strategy, therefore, is to have a mechanism for detecting deadlock when it occurs. We could have a dependency graph indicating which processes are waiting until which others are completed. A cycle in the graph indicates deadlock. Alternatively, if two or more processes are stalled for a certain period of time, then we could conclude that deadlock has occurred. A way out of the deadlock is to "roll back" one or more processes. That is, any transactions the process has performed are undone and any resources it has locked are freed. The process is placed on a queue to be restarted later.

Process Timestamping

Consider example 2 above and the read-modify-write sequence of operations performed by P1 and P2. Assume that the order in which they occur is as shown in Fig. 13.1. Note that the effect of P1 is nullified by the write operation of P2, the net effect being that X is decreased by only 1 instead of 2. How can P2 detect, when it performs the write operation, that it has been using what is now an outdated version of X? One solution is for the system to maintain access and update times for data objects, such as X, and assign a **timestamp** to each process. In the case of a simple single-processor system, the

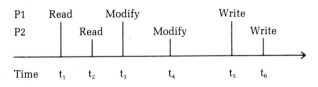

FIGURE 13.1 Transaction overlap

timestamp could be the time at which each process is started. If the clock used is sufficiently fine-grained, timestamps will be unique. We will assume that timestamps are issued in ascending order.

A read operation can now be rejected if the timestamp for the process issuing the read request is lower than the last update time for the data. It is rejected because the data has been updated since the process started. Similarly, a write operation will be rejected if the data about to be overwritten has been read or written since the start of the process issuing the write request. If the data has been written, then the write operation about to be issued may be based on out-of-date information. If it has been read since the process started, then some other process may be using data that will soon be out of date.

If a read or write operation is rejected, the process issuing it is rolled back (as described earlier) and restarted (with a higher timestamp). Although this method will avoid deadlocks, restarting a process is probably more expensive than waiting until it can proceed.

We have been concerned up to now with keeping data free from the effects of logical and physical errors and eliminating transaction errors due to the side effects of concurrently running processes. Even if these sources of error are eliminated, data may still be vulnerable to unauthorized modification unless security measures are implemented. We briefly consider the security problem next.

13.3 DBMS Security

Most users require that their data be protected against unauthorized access and update. It can be argued that the extent to which security measures are implemented should depend on the costs that would be incurred if data is destroyed or disclosed against the wishes of the owner. If the data is of little importance, it may not be worth implementing elaborate security. However, we must assume that all data is valuable in a general-purpose database system and that consequently the DBMS must provide users with protection mechanisms. In this section we briefly outline some aspects of the problem. Note that a DBMS running under an operating system may be able to use the underlying file protection mechanisms (see pp. 40–41 in Chapter 2) and utilities such as encryption programs.

Security Granularity

Security measures in database systems can be classified according to their granularity. What is the smallest unit that can be given individual protection? Typically a data owner can control access to individual record fields. For example, a user Y may be given permission to read either the name field or the salary field of an employee record (but not both together). Thus Y could obtain either a list of salaries or a list of names and thus could not correlate the two lists. It is useful to be able to have value-dependent controls. For example, a user X has permission to access names and salaries of all employees but is allowed to modify only the salaries of those managed by X. Finally, sophisticated systems may have temporal or spatial controls. For example, only the personnel office may be allowed to change a name or address, and only the packing department may reduce the recorded quantity on hand of a part.

Security Specification

In some DBMS's the DDL used to compile functional databases on the logical database provides high-level language mechanisms for defining user access. In such cases the DBA staff authorizes, designs, and compiles the access features for a group of application programmers. In other systems, users are able to grant and revoke permissions in a more dynamic manner. Fig. 13.2 shows how we could do this using pseudo DDL.

Figure 13.2(a) shows how we can allow users of an employee file to access names or salaries (but not both at the same time). An attempt to access both fields at the same time would be trapped. Figure 13.2(b) shows how we allow X to read both the name and the salary of employees reporting to X. X can read both fields at the same time. In addition, X has permission to change the salary of a subordinate.[2] Finally, Fig. 13.2(c) shows how temporal and spatial constraints can be specified. Only user "dispatch" can update the quantity-on-hand

---

2. Rather than have to enter a permission for each possible manager it would be more convenient to be able to enter something like

```
PERMIT READ OF EMPLOYEE (NAME,SALARY) TO ALL
        WHERE EMPLOYEE.MANAGER = LOGINNAME
```

and have the system make the appropriate substitution when a transaction is executed.

PERMIT READ OF EMPLOYEE (NAME) TO ALL
PERMIT READ OF EMPLOYEE (SALARY) TO ALL

(a) Fields permission

PERMIT READ OF EMPLOYEE (NAME,SALARY) TO X
      WHERE EMPLOYEE.MANAGER = "X"
PERMIT REPLACE OF EMPLOYEE (SALARY) TO X
      WHERE EMPLOYEE.MANAGER = "X"

(b) Value-dependent permission

PERMIT REPLACE OF PARTS (QOH) TO DISPATCH
      AT TERMINAL05
      FROM 0730-1730
      ON MON TO SAT

(c) Spatial and temporal permission

FIGURE 13.2 Permission specifications

(QOH) field of parts records. Moreover, this user can make changes only if logged in at a particular terminal (terminal05) and only during normal working hours. In INGRES the owner of a relation can add, modify, and delete permissions that are themselves protected just as any other data objects.

Security Enforcement

A possible method of enforcement is to have an arbitrator section of the DBMS check each transaction and determine whether or not security would be breached if it were executed. INGRES enforces security in a manner similar to its enforcement of integrities (see Statement 2); QUEL (DML) statements are modified before execution. For more details, see Stonebraker and Wong [112]. Although some breaches of security may be accidental, others may be part of a concerted scheme to bypass controls. For this reason the DBMS should log transactions that are rejected for security reasons.

Security and Statistical Databases

A particular kind of security problem is posed by **statistical databases.** A statistical database provides only summary data (for example totals, averages, and counts) about the records it contains. Individual records in the file may contain sensitive information. Examples of statistical databases are collections of medical reports and tax returns. Users are normally prohibited from accessing individual records directly. However, a security problem is caused by the fact that information contained in a particular record may be deduced by an appropriate series of legitimate commands.

Assume, for example, that there is a tax return database containing social security number, sex, city, age, profession, salary, taxes, dependents, and charitable contributions for each of a large sample of people. Assume further that available operations are:

COUNT predicate
TOTAL field WHERE predicate

The COUNT operation returns the number of records satisfying the predicate, and the TOTAL operation returns the total of the values in the specified field for records satisfying the predicate. The primary key (social security number) is not permitted in a predicate. Legitimate enquiries of this database might include finding the average salary paid to college professors, the number of chiropractors, and the average number of dependents claimed by female residents of San Jose.

The general form of attack on the database is to use the COUNT operation to find a means of identifying a unique record. A similar sequence of operations using the TOTAL operation then allows one to determine values of individual fields in the record. Consider the following example.

Suppose we know that a friend is included in the sample. Being curious, we would like to know how much he gave to charity last year. By making appropriate general enquiries we may be able to extract this information, even though a direct query (using the primary key of his record) is not allowed. Suppose our friend is a driving instructor. We can find out how many driving instructors are in the database as follows:

```
COUNT PROFESSION = 'Driving instructor'
```

The result is likely to be greater than 1; a large database will probably contain many driving instructors. Consequently, we add an additional condition, our friend's city of residence.

```
COUNT PROFESSION = 'Driving instructor'
      AND CITY = 'Northridge'
```

This time we are lucky. There is only one Northridge driving instructor in the database, so the count returned is one. We now have a predicate that holds for exactly one record in the database, and we can use it to discover otherwise protected information. Thus we can easily find out how much our friend gave to charity by means of the following enquiry:

```
TOTAL CHARITABLE CONTRIBUTIONS
     WHERE PROFESSION = 'Driving instructor'
     AND CITY = 'Northridge'
```

Although statistical queries can reveal supposedly protected data, possible countermeasures are available. Denning and Schlorer [113] classify countermeasures broadly as **restrictions** and **perturbations.** Restrictions prohibit certain queries. Perturbations add "noise" to the results of queries.

Query restrictions. Restriction techniques can be subdivided according to whether or not the queries previously posed are taken into account in deciding whether to allow the current one. Consider some approaches that take into account only the current query.

One restriction technique is to limit the number of attributes that can be specified in a query. If this limit were one in our example system, then the second COUNT query above would not be allowed. This technique, however, does not guarantee that a COUNT query always gives a result greater than one. A better solution, therefore, is for the DBMS to refuse to answer queries where the size of the set of records satisfying the predicate is either too small or too close to the size of the database. For example, if N is the number of records in the database, COUNT operations yielding results less than K or greater than $N - K$ (for some threshold K) would not be allowed.

Although this countermeasure stops us using some predicate P that uniquely identifies a record, it does not stop attacks based on set differences. Thus it can be circumvented fairly easily. In our example the query

```
COUNT PROFESSION = 'Driving instructor'
     AND CITY = 'Northridge'
```

would be inadmissible, but we could issue the following query:

```
COUNT PROFESSION = 'Driving instructor'
```

We assumed earlier that the number of driving instructors is reasonably large. If it is above the threshold, we make the following query:

```
COUNT PROFESSION = 'Driving instructor'
     AND CITY ≠ 'Northridge'
```

The result is one less than the result of the previous query, showing again that our friend is the only Northridge driving instructor in the database. His charitable contributions can be discovered using a similar pair of TOTAL queries.

Here the predicate

```
PROFESSION = 'Driving instructor' AND CITY ≠ 'Northridge'
```

is an **individual tracker** for our friend. It is an admissible predicate that allows us, in conjunction with a more general predicate, to track down information in a particular record. Similarly,

```
CITY = 'Northridge' AND PROFESSION ≠ 'Driving instructor'
```

is also an individual tracker for this particular record. In general, if the predicate "C1 AND C2" is inadmissible because too few (or too many) records satisfy it, then we can try C1 followed by "C1 AND NOT C2." (Alternatively, we could follow C2 by "C2 AND NOT C1.")

Note that an individual tracker is based on a particular inadmissible predicate. We can generalize the idea. Denning, Denning, and Schwartz [114] showed that there is usually a **general tracker** for a particular database. A general tracker is a predicate that we can use to find the answer to any inadmissible query. What we need is a predicate T that is true for between $2K$ and $N - 2K$ records, where K is the system threshold introduced earlier. Now, given an inadmissible predicate P, we find the size of the set of records for which P is true (assume that this size is less than K) as follows:

1. Find the size of the set satisfying P OR T. (Because T satisfies at most $N - 2K$ records and P satisfies $< K$ records, this query is admissible.)

2. Find the size of the set satisfying P OR NOT T. (If the size of the set satisfying T is between $2K$ and $N - 2K$, then so is the size of the set satisfying NOT T. Thus this query is also admissible.)

3. Add the results of queries 1 and 2 and subtract the size of the database (found by adding results of COUNT T and COUNT NOT T). This gives us the size of set P.

As can be seen from Fig. 13.3, the size of set P is the amount by which the sum of the sizes of sets "P OR T" and "P OR NOT T" exceeds the total number of records.

Consider our example again. The predicate "SEX = Male" would appear to be a good candidate for a general tracker. We could first find the total number of records in the database by combining the results of

```
COUNT SEX = 'Male'
```

and

```
COUNT SEX ≠ 'Male'
```

Next we combine the results produced by

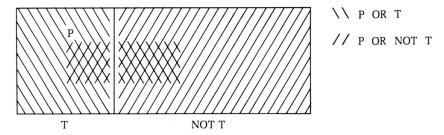

\\ P OR T

// P OR NOT T

T   NOT T

FIGURE 13.3 Security compromise using general tracker

```
COUNT SEX = 'Male' OR (PROFESSION = 'Driving instructor'
                       AND CITY = 'Northridge')
```

and

```
COUNT SEX ≠ 'Male' OR (PROFESSION = 'Driving instructor'
                       AND CITY = 'Northridge')
```

In our example, the second total will be one greater than the first, showing that there is one Northridge driving instructor. See Denning [115] for more discussion of trackers. Next we look at an alternative form of defense.

Data perturbation. A perturbation technique deliberately distorts the results of a query. For example, a random quantity could be added to the result of a TOTAL operation. However, the quantities should not be completely random. It is important that the perturbations be consistent. A particular query posed on a particular database should always give the same result. In addition, if the same information can be derived from more than one query, then those queries should return the same answer. For example, the query

```
COUNT PROFESSION = 'Secretary'
```

should return the same number as the sum of the results of the queries

```
COUNT PROFESSION = 'Secretary' AND SEX = 'Male'
COUNT PROFESSION = 'Secretary' AND SEX ≠ 'Male'
```

One perturbation solution to this problem is to round numeric data to the nearest value of some multiple M.

A general perturbation method (devised by Denning [116]) is to devise some function (F) that takes as parameter a predicate (P) and a record (R) satisfying P. The function determines whether or not R should be ignored in the operation (see Fig. 13.4). A possible function could treat predicate and record as bit strings and produce its result

Predicate: SEX = "Male" AND CITY = "Pasadena"

Candidate Records

Sex	City	Age	Profession ...	F(P, R)
M	Pasadena	21	Programmer	1
M	Pasadena	39	Taxi Driver	0
M	Pasadena	27	Photographer	0
M	Pasadena	54	Actor	1

FIGURE 13.4 General perturbation function

by bit operations. A disadvantage of this method is that if it were implemented generally, significant overhead may be incurred. However, compromise is no longer possible using the general tracker approach.

Summary

In this chapter we have briefly considered implementation aspects of a DBMS concerned with the reliable and secure processing of transactions in a multiuser, multiprocessing environment.

Integrity concerns the maintenance of correct information in a data collection. If we start with an empty database, it may be sufficient to enforce integrity constraints when records are inserted or changed. The DBMS should provide a mechanism for users to specify conditions that must hold on the data.

In a multiaccess environment more than one user may wish to access a particular database at a particular time. Without any controls, transactions may interact in unexpected and unwanted ways. One way of preventing this is to require a process to request all the resources it needs when it first executes. A process must not start until it has locked all its resources. Alternatively, read and write operations can be monitored to check whether data has been accessed or modified since the process started.

Data is a valuable resource and must be protected. Enforcement of security measures in a DBMS should be centralized to avoid compromise. In a conventional database, a typical mechanism is to allow data owners to issue and withdraw permissions. The DBMS checks current permissions at transaction time. Protecting data in a statistical database, however, is a difficult problem. Currently there appears to be no general solution. Techniques that add security may result in loss of information to enquirers or lead to inefficiencies.

Exercises

1. Devise a fast test that a DBMS might use to reduce the work needed to check the uniqueness of the primary key of a new record.

2. Assume that concurrency in the example of Fig. 13.1 is controlled by timestamps. At what time will a read or a write operation be rejected? Draw a diagram showing how both processes will eventually be completed.

3. Access to multiuser systems is often controlled by means of passwords. Could access to parts of a database be similarly controlled? How would this work if the data were to be accessible from a batch program? Where would passwords be stored?

4. In the restriction data security technique described in the section "Security and Statistical Databases," why is it necessary to have both a high and a low cutoff value? Suppose only a lower bound had been implemented. Devise a way of showing that there is only one Northridge driving instructor that takes advantage of the missing upper bound.

5. Implement a simple statistical database. Allow users to perform COUNT and TOTAL operations. Implement one of the security measures discussed in this chapter.

Suggestions for Further Reading

C. J. Date, *An Introduction to Database Systems*, vol. 2 (Reading, Mass.: Addison-Wesley, 1983).

E. B. Fernandez, R. C. Summers, and C. Wood, *Database Security and Integrity* (Reading, Mass.: Addison-Wesley, 1981).

14

Advanced Database Topics

14.1 Discusses query languages and the query optimization problem.

14.2 Examines database machines and, in general, attempts to distribute the processing of database transactions at a single site.

14.3 Looks at distributed database systems, that is, systems where data is spread over different sites.

In this final chapter we briefly present some advanced database topics. These are active research areas and we encourage you to read the referenced papers and books. Our principal aim here is to describe some of the problems rather than to present solutions.

14.1 Query Languages and Optimization

We interpret the term "query language" broadly to cover the means by which users may describe transactions to be performed on a database. In this section we examine both some forms the interface may take and also the problem of performing transactions efficiently.

Query Languages: User Interface

We can classify user interfaces to databases in many ways. For example, we can classify according to the medium (e.g., graphics versus text) or according to the command language (e.g., procedural versus nonprocedural). We give examples of some representative systems in the following discussions.

Graphics versus text. There is a trend toward providing graphic (for example, forms-based) interfaces to database systems. In such systems users can issue queries and perform updates without having to learn a command language. This is a natural interface, particularly

SID	SNAME	SPREREQ	MAJOR	GPA	SUNITS
	P.X		Comp Sci	P.Y	>100

FIGURE 14.1 Query by Example

in commercial environments where many transactions are based on forms.

Query by Example [117] is an early system with a graphic interface. The underlying database is relational. When operating on a particular relation, a user sees a template for a tuple on the terminal. Suppose, for example, that we wish to retrieve, from the STUDENT relation of the SECS database, the names and grade point averages of computer science majors who have completed more than 100 units. We would select the STUDENT relation, a template for a tuple would be displayed, and we would make appropriate entries in fields (see Fig. 14.1). The user enters the condition that must be true in a selected tuple and indicates the fields to be displayed by preceding identifiers with P. X and Y here are arbitrarily chosen place holders. They can be considered domain variables that range over the domain on which the corresponding attribute was defined. Query by Example can also process queries involving more than one relation.

A number of "visual programming" (forms-based) tools can front-end INGRES. An umbrella program Application-by-Forms allows users to select utilities to create forms and report formats. INGRES/Query is similar to Query by Example. Users can perform queries and updates. In updating a tuple, for example, values on the screen can be overtyped. The user has the option of updating the actual database data.

Natural language interface. Query by Example provides a nonprocedural interface. That is, a user specifies the effect of a transaction rather than the means by which it is to be performed. Therefore users do not need to know how data is organized. However, the interface is artificial, as are most query languages. Is it possible for users to communicate with a DBMS in a natural language?

Limited-domain information retrieval systems with natural language interfaces have been in existence for many years. The BASE-BALL system [118], for example, could answer queries such as "What teams won eight games in July?" or "Who beat the Red Sox on August 23?" More recently, natural language query systems for real databases have been developed. Examples are RENDEZVOUS [119], PLANES [120], and LADDER [121]. Note that all three are designed to process queries rather than general transactions. Some of the problems with natural language systems are generality, vocabulary, parsing, and ambiguities. We examine these problems individually.

Generality. The LADDER system uses the general LIFER parser [122]. A **parser** is a program that can determine whether or not an arbitrary string of symbols is in a given language. Typically the language must be defined by a grammar. A parser should be both powerful and easily portable to different databases. The LIFER parser is powerful, but a lot of work is needed to implement it on a new database system.

Vocabulary. Most systems require a dictionary containing syntactic and/or semantic information about the words a user may enter. RENDEZVOUS is atypical in that words that are not found in its dictionary do not cause problems. It assumes that the type can be determined from context or that the user can be asked to supply further information.

Parsing. It is desirable to have the parser, in addition to checking the validity of a query, construct a representation of its syntactic structure. Approaches to parsing differ. RENDEZVOUS uses a bottom-up method; it applies a series of rewrite rules to the query. On the other hand, the LIFER parser tries to match user queries with stored templates. Some systems use grammars based on the syntax of symbols; others use grammars based on the meanings (semantics).

Ambiguities. Natural language may be ambiguous. Consider the number of ways in which it is possible to interpret metaphorical phrases like "Time flies like an arrow." (Time is shot from a bow, time flies favor arrows, and so on.) PLANES, after analyzing a query, generates a paraphrase of it. If the user indicates that the paraphrase is equivalent to the query, then the system executes it. RENDEZVOUS can enter into a number of different forms of dialog with the user to resolve uncertainties.

Menus. A promising recent development is the use of menus to circumvent some of the problems of parsing a string of characters. In a typical system (Texas Instruments NLMenu—see, for example, Tennant [123]) users can build up a query by selecting query elements from menus. In some contexts, menus contain current values for particular attributes in a database. Selection of menus and selection from menus is constrained to avoid error. Apart from implementation advantages, menu systems are portable and easy to use. Much of the interface can be generated from the database itself.

ENROLLMENTS (STUDENT-ID, TICKET#)
CLASSES (TICKET#, INSTRUCTOR, DEPT)
DEMOGRAPHICS (STUDENT-ID, NAME, CITY, MAJOR)

(a)

RETRIEVE DEMOGRAPHICS.NAME
        WHERE DEMOGRAPHICS.CITY = "LA"
        AND DEMOGRAPHICS.STUDENT-ID = ENROLLMENTS.STUDENT-ID
        AND ENROLLMENTS.TICKET# = CLASSES.TICKET#
        AND CLASSES.DEPT = "Math"

(b)

FIGURE 14.2 Relation domains and example query

Query Optimization

In this section we consider techniques designed to improve the efficiency with which a query can be answered, or in general, with which a transaction can be performed. Optimization is concerned with minimizing some cost function. ("Amelioration" would actually be a better term than "optimization" because, in general, there is no guarantee that the solution will be the least expensive one.) The cost function is likely to have a number of components, for instance, communication cost, CPU time, number of I/O transfers, response time for the user, and amount of scratch space required. The weight given to these components will vary from installation to installation.

As an example of the ways in which a query can be answered, consider the relations of Fig. 14.2(a) and the problem of finding the names of the students from Los Angeles (LA) taking at least one math class. The query as posed by a user might be as shown in Fig. 14.2(b). One way to proceed is first to join all three relations and from the result select those tuples having DEPT = "Math" and CITY = "LA." Finally, NAME is projected. In relational algebra this strategy could be denoted as:

```
PROJECT (SELECT (JOIN CLASSES,
                        (JOIN ENROLLMENTS, DEMOGRAPHICS)
                )
            WHERE CITY = 'LA' AND DEPT = 'Math'
        )
ON [NAME]
```

This solution is likely to lead to a large intermediate result. Consider the degree of the result of the join operations and the number of tuples it contains. Intuitively we might decide that it is better to use the attribute values given in the query to eliminate as many tuples as possible at an early stage. This strategy could be expressed:

```
PROJECT (JOIN CLASSES WHERE DEPT  =  'Math',
                (JOIN ENROLLMENTS,
                        DEMOGRAPHICS WHERE CITY  =  'LA'
                )
        )
ON [NAME]
```

There is, however, at least one better strategy that reduces the size of the intermediate results still further (see Exercise 1).

The current trend is for top-down optimization (Jarke and Koch [124]). Four steps are involved. First, the query is transformed into an internal representation that has the same expressive power as the original language. Second, the internal form is standardized, simplified, and ameliorated. For example, it may be rearranged to reduce cost. (See Talbot [125] for a number of techniques that can be applied here.) Third, the modified internal form is mapped to alternative sequences of primitive operations. Finally, the least expensive sequence is selected.

In practice, the third and fourth steps could be combined. Mapping into a sequence would be abandoned if it becomes clear that the sequence will be more expensive than the best sequence found so far. Of course we are assuming that we can estimate the cost of a strategy before it is executed. For this to be feasible, information in addition to the schema must be available. For example, we need to know if indexes (primary or secondary) are available. A sophisticated system might also record the frequencies of various attribute values in relations.

A query optimizer is a software solution to the problem of reducing the cost of a transaction or increasing the throughput of a DBMS. However, even an optimal strategy will sometimes take an unacceptably long time to run on conventional hardware. An alternative way to improve performance is through the use of special-purpose hardware and/or unconventional configurations. We look at some aspects of this solution next.

14.2 Database Machines

The Von Neumann architecture was not designed with database processing in mind. Von Neumann machines execute one instruction at a time on a single processor that therefore becomes a bottleneck in the system. Relational operations in particular may require many CPU cycles. There are precedents for delegating special operations to special-purpose processors. For example, floating point arithmetic processors are common, and graphic display processors are becoming increasingly common. In this section, we interpret the term **database machine** broadly to include all attempts to utilize special hardware to improve the performance of database operations. We consider a configuration with a database machine to be one in which some of the processing of database transactions is performed somewhere other than on the processor running the application programs. This covers a wide spectrum of possibilities, ranging from intelligent storage devices to special-purpose processors.

Database machines have been developed comparatively slowly, for two main reasons. First, the development of clever query optimizers, as discussed in Section 14.1, reduced some of the incentive for developing database machines. Second, the concept of sharing transaction processing has been generalized beyond a simple specialized processor into distributed database systems, which we discuss in Section 14.3. However, database machines are beginning to fulfill some of their early promise [126]. We consider two broad classes of configuration that have been proposed and some example database machine products.

Figure 14.3(a) shows a conventional configuration. We see that the computer running the application programs (AP) is the same as that running the DBMS. Both run under an operating system (OS) that controls input/output (I/O). A first step might be to move input/output processing to an intelligent device controller with memory and processing capability. This is depicted in Fig. 14.3(b). The controller could be given commands to find all records with particular attributes in a particular file. To the main computer this **back-end processor** acts as an **associative memory**. A second step is to move the DBMS out of the main machine (see Fig. 14.3c). The back-end machine now is typically a computer in its own right. Text retrieval systems have special requirements for which conventional DBMS's are not the best solution, but they can also benefit from special hardware. We will discuss associative memories, back-end processors, and a hardware solution to a text retrieval problem (even though it is not, strictly speaking, a database machine).

Associative Memories

In a read operation, a conventional memory device is given an address and returns the contents of that address. An associative memory, on the other hand, is given a key value or set of key values and returns the addresses of the data elements where the key field matches the search values. Even more usefully, it might return nonkey fields

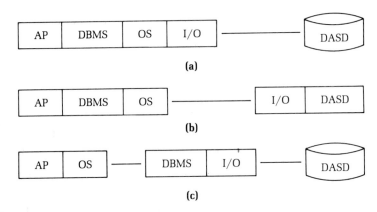

FIGURE 14.3 Alternative configurations for database processing

from those locations. An associative main memory can readily be constructed, although it may be expensive. In such a memory, multiple identical circuitry compares the search pattern with each cell simultaneously and indicates whether or not there is a hit. It is not feasible to do precisely the same with a secondary storage device such as a disc. We can come close, though. We could have a read/write head for each track and thus scan the whole disc in the time it takes for it to rotate once. It may be more practical, however, to have a read/write head for each surface. Although this would be much slower, it would still scan the disc in a few seconds.

What could we do with the parallel streams of bits as they come off the disc? We need processing capability to perform search operations. In addition, the processor for each stream would need buffers to hold sections of the bit stream and to hold values from the CPU for comparisons. There would have to be circuitry for performing simple arithmetic and logical operations. The processing units could be independent of each other or could have some means of interacting. Information about record formats would be stored on the disc or downloaded from the CPU.

The interface with the associative disc may be high level or low level. CAFS (see page 34) has a low-level interface. It basically does record/field selection according to criteria down-loaded from the CPU. Addis [16] demonstrates how to construct an interpreter that processes high-level relation-based queries and then uses CAFS capabilities.

Back-end Database Processing

One of the earliest back-end configurations was the XDMS system described by Canaday et al. [127]. XDMS comprised two conventional machines. The host was a Univac 1108 and the back end was a Digital Scientific META-4. Maryanski [128] surveys a number of other prototypes. More recently, a number of special-purpose database machines have reached the market.

Britton-Lee's IDM 500 series are back-end machines that can be shared by up to 64 different hosts. They perform many functions in addition to transaction processing, including audits, backups, and recovery. An optional accelerator unit (a high-speed processor) scans disc pages as they are brought into memory. The data manipulation language is IDL (Intelligent Database Language), which is similar to INGRES QUEL. Parsing is done on the host and the parse trees are passed to IDM. B*-trees are used for indexing. Although benchmarking of DBMS's and back-end machines is in its infancy, Britton-Lee [129] claims that use of IDM will reduce host CPU usage by up to 90%. In addition, Britton-Lee reports that database management functions will be accomplished in a third of the time needed on a conventional host-resident DBMS.

Teradata Corporation's DBC/1012 uses multiple microprocessors connected in a patented network to achieve high performance. In its full configuration the system can store a terabyte (10^{12} bytes) of data. It too can be shared by multiple hosts. A database is distributed as evenly as possible over the storage units to maximize potential parallelism.

At times the throughput of a two-processor system might be limited by one or other of the processors. It is possible that such bottlenecks could be detected and that the level at which the processors communicate could be altered dynamically. For example, if the DBMS machine were overloaded, the application machine might do more of the checking and optimization of the transactions. Similarly, if the application machine were being heavily used, transaction parsing could be delegated to the back-end machine.

A beneficial side effect of a back-end configuration is increased security. On a conventional machine, databases are typically stored as part of the general file system. As such they might be accessible to normal file operations and thus bypass DBMS security. They might even be vulnerable to direct disc addressing. However, if the data is on a machine that accepts only validated database transactions, compromise is likely to be more difficult.

Full-Text Information Retrieval

In Section 7.4 we considered the STAIRS information retrieval system. We saw how it can satisfy a variety of simple queries by means of an extensive, space-consuming index. Considerable time is required to process the inverted lists for a very large text database. This may be unacceptable if queries are frequent.

Processing of a typical full-text collection differs from conventional database processing. Usually the size is much larger, operations are read only and queries are very simple (typically finding documents containing a pattern of words or characters). Hollaar *et al.* [130] introduce a design for a hardware-enhanced information retrieval system and describe an application (the Patent Office) where such a high-performance system is required. Like CAFS, their machine can scan data as it streams off discs. Logic for various classes of pattern matching is implemented in VLSI. Indexes are used to reduce the area of the discs that has to be searched. Given the text-searching hardware, the indexes do not need to be as precise as the STAIRS indexes. A coarser index might indicate, for example, simply that word "X" appears in a particular context (such as the title or abstract) of a particular document. Clearly there are trade-offs in determining index coarseness. A coarser index results in larger scan areas.

Various papers in Hsiao [131] give more detailed information about some back-end designs. Shemer and Neches [132] describe the origins of the Teradata DBC/1012 system. In a sense, the database machines we have described are a simple form of distributed computing. Processing is partitioned between the main CPU and another element of the system. In the next section we consider characteristics of more general distributed systems.

14.3 Distributed Database Systems

The model we use to illustrate distributed database systems is that of a network of machines each running a DBMS. Parts of the database (possibly overlapping) are located at each node of the network. However, a user of the database is largely unaware of its distributed nature. In addition to the rationale behind database distribution we look briefly at some aspects of the design of and transaction processing with distributed DBMS's.

Rationale for Data Distribution

Why distribute a database? We considered this question briefly in Chapter 1. Data distribution can reduce communications costs when a database must be accessed from a number of scattered sites. Distribution of its data may match the distributed nature of an organization. In addition, data distribution may have integrity benefits. If data is replicated, the effect of data loss at a particular node (either temporary or permanent) might not be catastrophic. Note, however, that replication decreases security; the more copies there are of an item, the higher the probability of unauthorized access. In addition, the opportunity for inconsistent data is increased and updating is more expensive.

Design of a Distributed Database

The design of a conventional database typically consists of two major steps: design of the overall logical view (schema) and physical implementation. The design of a distributed database has an intermediate step: to decide on the allocation of data to nodes in the network.

Data allocation. We consider the data allocation problem in the context of distributing a new database (rather than combining existing ones). For simplicity, we use the relational model and follow Ceri, Pernici, and Weiderhold [133] in breaking the problem down into three subproblems: horizontal fragmentation, vertical fragmentation, and allocation of fragments to nodes. (Not all these steps are found in all systems. For example, distributed INGRES [134] supports horizontal but not vertical fragmentation.)

Horizontal fragmentation. What subsets of tuples of a particular relation should be considered fragments that can possibly be stored at different nodes? A predicate would be stored with each fragment indicating the condition satisfied by all tuples in the fragment.

Vertical fragmentation. How can the set of domains of a relation be partitioned? (Note that in order to avoid loss of information, tuples in each vertical fragment must include a candidate key.)

Allocation of fragments to nodes. This can be broken down further into nonredundant allocation (where a fragment is only at one node) and redundant allocation (where a fragment is at two or more nodes).

SECS example. Consider the SECS example database from page 308 and assume that the departments in the school are on different university sites. Assume further that communication costs are significant (perhaps public phone lines must be used). The fragmentation and data allocation depend on the application programs that are expected to be run at each node. We might tackle the three subproblems outlined above as follows.

When considering horizontal fragmentation we look for application programs that use particular subsets of the tuples in a relation. A possible horizontal fragmentation of the STUDENT relation is to partition according to major. A department in the school is likely to have many occasions on which it processes only its own majors. A second (overlapping) fragmentation might partition according to grade point average. Those students with a grade point average of less than 2.0 might be of interest in particular application programs.

When partitioning vertically we consider the fields of a tuple that are used together. For instance, during class registration, the SID and SPREREQ fields of a STUDENT record are used to verify prerequisites. In assigning advisers, the SNAME and MAJOR fields are of interest. Note that in the latter case the key field (SID) would have to be included in the fragment to avoid loss of information.

For the problem of allocating fragments to nodes, assume that each department is a node on the network. It would seem sensible to allocate a STUDENT record to the corresponding major department. Similarly, we would allocate a SECT-STUD record to the department offering the class. This allocation is nonredundant. In addition, however, it would be useful for a STUDENT record to be allocated to all departments from which the student is taking a course. Similarly a SECTION record could be allocated to all departments having students in the class.

Allocation algorithms. Solutions to various combinations of the three data allocation subproblems have been developed (see [133]), but because of its complexity, there is as yet no general design for the whole problem. Consider a database as small as the SECS example and the large number of possible fragmentations and allocations. Ceri, Pernici, and Weiderhold envisage an interactive design environment with a human expert helping to reject infeasible partial solutions.

Transaction Processing with Distributed Databases

The fact that data is distributed has implications for transaction processing. How do we find the data we need? How do we lock it? How can we find an efficient transaction execution strategy?

Catalogs. Assume that **catalogs** at each node indicate the location of fragments, that is, allocation of data to nodes. The catalogs become a distributed system in their own right. Is there a complete catalog at each node? One option is to replicate completely information necessary to identify the site of data and to store purely local information locally. Local information would include performance statistics and available access methods.

Concurrent processing. Although timestamping has been investigated, **two-phase locking** seems to be the technique most widely used for concurrency control in distributed systems. In this technique, a transaction has two phases. In the first, new locks are acquired; in the second, locks are only released (no new locks are acquired). It is desirable to go further than this and require that a transaction not release its X-locks (exclusive locks) until ready to commit its actions. At commit, the DBMS guarantees that the results will take effect. Deadlock detection is more prevalent than deadlock avoidance in distributed systems. In most systems deadlock is detected by a time-out mechanism: a transaction that exceeds its waiting time is aborted. It will be rolled back and restarted later.

Data replication. Replication occurs when a logical object is represented by more than one physical object. There is, of course, the integrity problem of keeping the copies consistent. The overhead necessary in preserving integrity should be transparent to the user. In a distributed system there are particular problems if part of the network holding a copy of a data item is temporarily inaccessible. Various solutions have been proposed. One is for a node to go through a start-up ᴗequence before it goes on the air to the rest of the network. This sequence would include reading a list of changes that should be applied to its data.

Replication has consequences for data locking. How should the values of locks on copies of a logical data item be related? There are a number of strategies. For instance, if an item is read-locked, then only the lock on the particular copy need be set. On the other hand, if an item is write-locked then all copies should also be write-locked. However, a consequence of this strategy is that if a node holding one of the copies of an item to be write-locked is inaccessible, then the write process cannot proceed because not all locks can be set. Observe that it is sufficient to adopt a strategy whereby a write-lock is set in a majority rather than all of the nodes holding a copy of the item.

We have outlined some of the ways in which data could be kept consistent. However, it is not difficult to conceive of applications where it is permissible for integrity to slide a little. It may not be essential for all copies of a data item to be identical all the time. Transmission costs can thus be reduced by not broadcasting changes every time one copy of a data item is modified. In an inventory, for example, provided that the quantity on hand does not fall below some limit, it may be sufficient to bring copies into line perhaps once a day. Local logs would keep the necessary information.

Transaction optimization. Optimization is concerned with finding the least expensive transaction execution strategy. It is particularly important in a distributed database because bad strategies can be very expensive. In a distributed system the optimizer has to take into account the cost of moving data from node to node. Different authorities give this component different weight relative to local processing costs.

Its importance is likely to depend on the bandwidth of communication lines. As an example of some aspects of optimization we consider some actions taken for one class of query.

There have been a number of investigations into the processing of relational algebra operations involving unary operations and joins. The unary operations tend to be straightforward; they can be performed at the node(s) holding the appropriate fragment(s). More difficult, however, is deciding how best to perform joins where operands are at different nodes. A number of techniques make use of the **semi-join** operation[1] (see, for example, Bernstein and Chiu [135]). This is because

```
JOIN X, Y          ≡ JOIN   (SEMI-JOIN X, Y
WHEN condition              WHEN condition
                           ),Y
                     WHEN condition
```

We are getting from the semi-join only those tuples which can possibly be in the result of the join. Consider the following example.

Example. At site A we have the STUDENT relation

STUDENT (SID, SNAME, SPREREQ, MAJOR, GPA, SUNITS)

and at site B we have the SECT-STUD relation

SECT-STUD (SNUM, SID)

At site A we want information about students enrolled in classes.

---

1. We denote the semi-join operation

    relation3 ← SEMI-JOIN relation1, relation2
              WHEN condition

It can be defined in terms of other relational algebra operators as follows.

    SEMI-JOIN R1, R2 ≡ PROJECT (JOIN R1, R2
    WHEN condition   WHEN condition
)
                    ON [attributes of R1]

That is, the result of the semi-join is a subset of the tuples of R1: those contributing to the join of R1 and R2. Semi-joins can thus be used to perform efficient joins of relations at two sites.

Suppose we need the result of

    JOIN R1, R2
    WHEN R1.P = R2.Q

where R1 is at site 1 and R2 is at site 2. A sequence of operations to produce the join is

More precisely, if a student with grade point average of less than 2.0 is enrolled in one or more classes, we want the student record and list of those classes. One strategy for getting this information is to transmit the whole of the SECT-STUD relation from B to A and do the processing at A. However, if we suppose that few students have grade point average of less than 2.0 and, of these, few are enrolled in classes, we will be sending much unnecessary information. An alternative strategy is:

1. At site A, select students with a grade point average of less than 2.0.

2. At site A, project SIDS.

3. Send list of SIDS to site B.

4. At site B, perform a semi-join and get tuples from SECT-STUD with SIDS in the list.

5. Send the subset of SECT-STUD to site A.

6. At site A, join the subset from B with the students selected in step 1.

In general, if data required for a transaction is at different sites, we need some scheme for devising a least-cost strategy. Can the processing of the data be performed at more than one site? To what site is it best to send partial results? If transmission costs dominate the cost function for a distributed query, then query optimization may become a problem of finding the best sequence of semi-joins.

Summary

In this chapter we have examined advanced database topics, including query languages and optimization, database machines, and distributed database systems.

---

a) send from site 2 to site 1 the result of
   PROJECT R2 ON [Q]

b) compute at site 1
   R1' ← SEMI-JOIN R1, R2
        WHEN R1.P = R2.Q

c) send R1' (subset of R1) to site 2

d) compute at site 2
   JOIN R1', R2
   WHEN R1'.P = R2.Q

The trend in query languages seems to be toward providing graphic-based nonprocedural interfaces. Graphic interfaces are usually easier for casual users to learn. Although there have been many experimental systems with natural language interfaces, there are considerable problems in processing unconstrained input. Providing menus of phrases and attribute values may solve some of these problems, however.

There are often many ways in which a particular transaction can be carried out. Criteria for deciding which is the best vary from installation to installation. In some cases CPU usage is most important; in others the amount of temporary working space required may be critical. Typically, an optimizer generates a number of strategies from the transaction, computes costs, and selects the least expensive procedure. It is possible that examination of intermediate results may result in a change of strategy.

Apart from transaction optimization, another way of increasing throughput is to distribute some of the processing of a transaction. There are a number of alternatives to running the application programs and DBMS on the same processor. One option is to add processing power to a disc so that it can scan for records satisfying certain conditions. A second option is to add a back-end processor dedicated to running the DBMS. Full-text information retrieval has particular requirements that may be satisfied by a combination of intelligent discs and conventional indexing techniques.

If a database must be accessed from a number of locations, then distributing it is one way of reducing communication costs. However, there is currently no complete algorithm for determining the optimal distribution of data fragments. If data is replicated in this distribution, database reliability will be increased although security may be diminished. Distribution complicates some aspects of database operation. Transaction processing is complicated by the necessity to locate the data and apply concurrency controls to more than one site. Finding the optimal way of processing a transaction has additional dimensions: the processing may be carried out at a number of sites.

Exercises

1. Find a better solution to the problem of finding math students from Los Angeles discussed on pages 346–347.

2. Consider the semi-join example on pages 355–356. Could the semi-join operation have been performed at site A rather than site B? What would be the sequence of operations? What would be an appropriate sequence if the final result were required at B rather than A?

Suggestions for Further Reading

C. J. Date, *An Introduction to Database Systems*, vol. 2 (Reading, Mass.: Addison-Wesley, 1983).

Special issue of *IEEE Computing* (on database machines) (March 1979).

S. Ceri and G. Pelagatti, *Distributed Databases: Principles and Systems* (New York: McGraw-Hill, 1984).

Glossary

Address space. Set of valid addresses.

Adjacent siblings. In a multiway tree, two nodes that have the same parent node and are referenced by adjacent pointers in the parent.

Archiving. The act of copying parts or all of a database (or file system) onto off-line storage (for example, magnetic tape). Archives can be used to restore a failed set of files.

Associative memory. Memory that can be accessed by specifying content rather than addresses.

Bachman diagram. A diagrammatic design technique used to represent the single-valued and multivalued dependencies that exist among logical record types.

Back-end processor. A processor to which part of the processing of a transaction (at least the file I/O) can be delegated.

Batch updating. A file updating process in which transactions are collected and an update program is run periodically. This contrasts with processing the transactions immediately.

Bit map/vector. A one-dimensional array of bits used to indicate whether each of a set of objects has a particular property. Useful for inverted indexes where an attribute has a limited set of values.

Block. Usually synonymous with physical record, that is, the unit of transfer between a secondary storage device and main memory.

Blocking factor. The number of logical records packed into a physical record (block).

Boyce-Codd dependency. The dependency of part of a key attribute on a nonkey attribute.

bpi (bits per inch). A measure of recording density. Typically it refers to the number of bits in an inch of a track (tape or disc).

Bucket. In the context of a hash file, the unit of a file having a particular address.

Buddy bucket. Two buckets are buddies if they are pointed to by external nodes with the same parent.

Candidate key. A field or combination of fields that will uniquely identify a record in a file. A candidate key is a potential primary key.

Catalog. A data structure that holds information about the location and representation of data items.

Category. A subdivision of software based on logical and physical data dependencies.

Check bytes. Information computed from and stored with data values. Used to detect read/write errors.

Closed addressing. The collection of hash overflow resolution methods in which overflow records are found by following pointers rather than calculating addresses.

Clustering. A defect of the linear probe overflow technique for hashing in which records tend to bunch together in full buckets.

Collision. Occurs in hashing when two logical records hash to the same address.

Composite key. A candidate key comprising more than one attribute.

Concatenation. Joining together. Concatenation of adjacent sibling nodes is used in B-trees as a solution to node underflow.

Conceptual view. The logical database description in the ANSI/SPARC DBMS architecture. See also Logical database; Schema.

Currency pointer. In the hierarchical and network database models, a pointer required by the DML commands that allows record-by-record processing. In the hierarchical model there is one currency pointer that references a logical record for each database tree. In the network model there can be a currency pointer for each record type, set type, and area.

Cylinder. A set of tracks (one on each surface) having the same radius on a multisurface disc pack. All tracks in a cylinder can be referenced without movement of the read/write heads.

Data definition language (DDL). A DBMS language used to describe the logical properties of records and the associations among records. Also called a data description language.

Data description language. See Data definition language.

Data flow diagram. A diagrammatic design technique that can represent a data processing application as a graph where the processes acting on data are nodes and the transmission of data between processes are edges. Data flow diagrams are useful in modeling an existing database or manual data processing actions prior to designing a new database.

Data manipulation language (DML). An extended application programming language with DBMS commands for data access.

Database. A collection of integrated files designed to serve multiple applications.

Database administrator. A person or group of people responsible for the design and supervision of a database.

Database machine. Hardware designed to increase the throughput of a DBMS.

Database management system (DBMS). A collection of programs that allows the creation and maintenance of a database. A DBMS should insulate user programs from the physical database. A DBMS handles mapping from program perspectives to actual storage.

Deadlock. Occurs when none of a set of processes can proceed because each is waiting for a resource held by another.

Degree. The number of domains over which a relation is defined. It is the number of columns in the tabular representation of the relation.

Deletion anomaly. Occurs when a deletion operation removes more information than was intended.

Determinant. Attribute(s) on which some other attribute is functionally dependent. See Functional dependency.

Device controller. Hardware responsible for the low-level operation of a device such as a disc (or set of discs).

Device media control language. A DBMS language used to describe the physical storage of data.

Direct-access file. File in which all records are equally accessible at any time.

Direct-access storage device (DASD). The media, typically a disc pack, used to hold data so that all parts are equally accessible.

Directory. In a filestore, a file holding information about a set of files. In the extendible hashing file organization, a directory points to leaves (buckets) holding records.

Distributed database. A database located at more than one site. Typically, its distributed nature is not apparent to users.

Domain. In a relation, a set of values from which tuple values are drawn.

Double hashing. A hashing technique to reduce clustering. In double hashing the linear probe step size is the result of a second function applied to the key.

Dummy partition. A partition assumed to be in a file so that the total number of partitions matches a target distribution required by the polyphase merge algorithm.

Dynamic index. An index that may change shape as the indexed file is modified.

Encrypted text. Text after it has passed through an encryption process that typically makes it incomprehensible without the use of a corresponding decryption process.

Entity. Any distinguishable object about which information is stored. A logical collection of attribute values.

Entity specification. The declaration, or naming, of the attributes of an entity.

Extensible file. A file that can change size dynamically (shrinking as well as growing). Sometimes called a dynamic file.

External memory. See Secondary memory.

External sorting. Sorting in which, at any time, some (usually most) of the data being sorted is in secondary (external) memory rather than primary memory.

External view. In the ANSI/SPARC model, the user program's perspective on a database. See also Functional database; Subschema.

File. A named collection of data almost always held on a secondary storage device.

File pointer. Part of a high-level language interface to a file. It references the current accessible logical record.

File-use ratio. The proportion of records in a file used in a run of an application program.

File variable. A variable in a program that can be associated with a file. Typically the association is used in the transfer of data to and from the file.

Filestore. Collection of files maintained for users by an operating system.

Fixed head. An unmoving read/write head on a data storage device. Because each track has a separate read/write head, the heads do not need to move.

Flat file. A file in which the fields of records are simple atomic values. Relational databases require flat files.

Formatting information. Data written to a secondary storage medium so that it can subsequently hold retrievable data.

Full backup. An archiving process in which all of a set of files is copied (as opposed to copying only those that have been modified since a particular time).

Fully functional dependency. Attribute Y is fully functionally dependent on a set of attributes X if it is functionally dependent on the whole of the set X and not on any proper subset of X.

Functional database. Our term for the user program's view of a database. The functional database is a compiled module written in a database description language or DDL. See also External view; Subschema.

Functional dependency. A record attribute Y is functionally dependent on attribute X if when two records have the same value of X they also have the same value of Y. See also Fully functional dependency.

General tracker. A predicate that can be used to bypass certain security measures in a statistical database and find the answer to any inadmissible query.

Generation. In the context of a file that is updated periodically, a particular version of the data. For example, generation 67 is updated to form generation 68. In the context of computer systems, a generation is a categorization of the hardware and software components.

Grid. An orthogonal partitioning of a space resulting from partitions on each dimension.

Grid array. Part of the grid directory that holds pointers to buckets.

Grid block. A subdivision of a space partitioned by a grid.

Grid directory. In a grid file organization, a k-dimensional structure that keeps track of the assignment of buckets to grid blocks.

Hard-sectored disc. A disc in which sectoring is established by physical means, for instance, holes in the disc.

Hash function. A function that maps a set of keys onto a set of addresses.

Hashing. A storage and retrieval technique that uses a hash function to map records onto store addresses.

Header block. Data at the beginning of a file or storage device that indicates the size, format, creation date, and miscellaneous information about the following data.

Hierarchical database. A database in which the associations among records are constrained to be tree-structured. A record can be the child of one parent and the parent of several descendants.

Hierarchical definition tree. A structure that defines the record associations in a hierarchical database.

Hit ratio. The proportion of read/write requests that can be satisfied from a cache memory.

Home buckets. In a hash file, the buckets with addresses that can be produced by the hash function.

Hopscotch. A technique for placing records on a disc to minimize rotational latency.

Incremental backup. A copying process in which the only files copied to an archive are those that have been modified since a particular time.

Index. Typically a data structure of (key, address) pairs used to decrease file access times.

Indexing. A technique for reducing storage and retrieval times by using an index to point to data areas.

Individual tracker. A predicate that can be used to retrieve information from a particular record in a statistical database.

Insertion anomaly. Occurs when partial information (usually incomplete records with no key) cannot be stored because of the record types available.

Interblock gap. The space between data blocks on a magnetic tape.

Internal memory. See Primary memory.

Inverted file. An index from which the records in the main file with a particular attribute value can be determined.

Key. A field or set of fields by which a record may be accessed. See also Composite key.

Key space. The set of values for a key.

Latency. In general, waiting time. Often used to mean the delay in a disc transfer while the appropriate sector rotates to a read/write position.

Linear probe. A method of searching for free space (to resolve overflow in hashing) by examining file/table entries at fixed intervals. A type of open addressing.

Linear scales. Part of the grid directory in the grid file organization. A linear scale holds the partition points of a domain.

Linked storage. A data structure in which elements contain pointers to other elements.

Localized corruption. Data corruption occurring at a known time from a known cause.

Locking. A technique for preventing conflicting concurrent operations on a data item.

Logical data independence. The insulation of user programs from changes in the logical database. Logical data independence is achieved by using functional databases.

Logical database. Our term for the compiled module that contains the logical description of a database. The logical database is written in a data description language. See also Conceptual view; Schema.

Soft-sectored disc. A disc on which sector size is established by writing formatting information.

Sort-merge. A sorting technique that partitions data to be sorted, sorts the partitions, and then merges the sorted partitions.

Splitting. Dividing a node. A solution to node overflow in a B-tree.

Start/stop mode. A mode of operation of a tape drive in which the tape stops after reading or writing each block.

Static index. An index that does not change shape as the indexed file is modified.

Statistical database. A database from which a user is allowed to extract only summary information.

Status bits. Bits typically found at the beginning of a disc track indicating the state of the track.

Streaming mode. A way of driving tape in which the tape does not stop after processing a block if there are more blocks to be processed.

String. See Partition.

Structure clash. In Jackson's design method [33], occurs when there is a mismatch between the structures of an input and an output file.

Subschema. The network database model's term for the functional database or the user program's perspective on the database. See also External view; Functional database.

Synchronization bits. Bits written to a disc during formatting to help reliable reading.

Synonyms. Two keys that hash to the same value.

Thread. In the context of secondary indexing, a pointer chain that links records having a particular attribute value.

Timestamp. A unique data item (typically a time-related integer) assigned to a process.

Timestamping. A technique for detecting potential conflicting operations on data items.

Track. The projection onto a recording surface of a position of a read/write head. The positions where data can be stored on a disc or tape.

Track identification bits. Bits written during disc formatting to identify tracks.

Transaction. An operation performed on a set of data. Queries, insertions, deletions, and modifications are typical transactions.

Transaction log. A collection of all updates made on the database. Useful when trying to recover from a database failure because it specifies the user programs active when the database failed.

Transitive dependencies. If Y is dependent on X and Z is dependent on Y, then Z is transitively dependent on X.

Triggered deletion. Occurs in a hierarchical database when the physical deletion of a record triggers the deletion of its descendants.

Trivial dependency. The dependency of an attribute on itself.

Tuple. A row in the tabular representation of a relation.

Tuple-by-tuple processing. Use of a low-level DML for relational processing requiring knowledge of relational storage.

Two-phase locking. A locking scheme with two distinct phases. During the first it may set locks; during the second it is allowed only to release locks.

Underflow. In the context of B-trees, occurs when the number of records in a node falls below a minimum.

Update anomaly. An undesirable side effect caused by an insertion, deletion, or modification.

Vertical parity. In a tape block, the check applied across the tape, typically to the bits of a byte.

View. A term used to describe a perspective on a database. There are external, conceptual, and internal views of databases.

Write permit ring. A ring that can be placed in the back of a tape reel. When such a ring is present the tape can be written to. Removal of the ring makes the tape read-only.

Write-through policy. A policy that may be adopted in the maintenance of a cache memory so that when a cache item is written to, the same change is made to the appropriate item in the slower memory.

References

1. S. Ceri and G. Pelagatti, *Distributed Databases: Principles and Systems*, McGraw-Hill, New York, 1984.
2. E. Onuegbe, S. Rahimi, and A. R. Hevner, "Local query translation and optimization in a distributed system," *Proceedings of the NCC*, vol. 52, pp. 229–239, AFIPS Press, May 1983.
3. R. Epstein and M. R. Stonebraker, "Analysis of distributed data base processing strategies," *Proceedings of the Sixth International Conference on Very Large Data Bases*, pp. 92–101, Montreal, Canada, October 1–3, 1980.
4. J. P. Fry and E. H. Sibley, "Evolution of data-base management systems," *ACM Computing Surveys*, vol. 8, no. 1, pp. 7–41, March 1976.
5. R. W. Hamming, "Error detecting and correcting codes," *Bell System Technical Journal*, vol. 29, pp. 147–160, April 1950.
6. M. Hofri, "Should the two-headed disk be greedy?," Technical report #250, Computer Science Department, Technion—Israel Institute of Technology, Haifa, Israel, August 1982.
7. K. Townsend, "Winchesters and floppies keep pace with user needs," *Computing*, pp. 6–7, November 14, 1983. COMPEC '83 Supplement.
8. R. Bernhard, "Bubbles take on disks," *IEEE Spectrum*, vol. 17, no. 5, pp. 30–33, May 1980.
9. D. Gifford and A. Spector, "The TWA reservation system," *Communications of the ACM*, vol. 27, no. 7, pp. 650–665, July 1984.
10. S. H. Kaisler, "Fifth IEEE Symposium on Mass Storage Systems," *IEEE Computer Architecture Technical Committee Newsletter*, pp. 1-i–1-58, June 1984.
11. C. Johnson, "IBM 3850—Mass storage system," *Proceedings of the NCC*, vol. 44, pp. 509–514, AFIPS Press, May 1975.
12. Masstor Systems Corporation, *M860 Mass Storage System: Equipment Description*, Masstor Systems Corporation, Santa Clara, Calif., 1984.

13. Masstor Systems Corporation, *M860 Mass Storage System: System Description*, Masstor Systems Corporation, Santa Clara, Calif., 1984.

14. R. W. Mitchell, "Content addressable file store," *Proceedings of the Online Database Technology Conference*, London, England, April 1976.

15. R. Sharpe, "A potential winner in need of support," *Computing: The Magazine*, pp. 20–21, February 21, 1985.

16. T. R. Addis, "A relation-based language interpreter for a content addressable file store," *ACM Transactions on Database Systems*, vol. 7, no. 2, pp. 125–163, June 1982.

17. D. G. Howe and A. B. Marchant, "Digital optical recording in infrared-sensitive organic polymers," *Proceedings of the Society of Photo-Optical Instrumentation Engineers Conference on Optical Data Storage*, pp. 103–115, Incline Village, Nev., January 1983.

18. L. Fujitani, "Laser optical disk: The coming revolution in online storage," *Communications of the ACM*, vol. 27, no. 6, pp. 546–554, June 1984.

19. Storage Technology Corporation, *7440 Optical Media Unit Specifications*, Storage Technology Corporation, Louisville, Colo., 1984.

20. J. S. Vitter, "An efficient I/O interface for optical discs," *ACM Transactions on Database Systems*, vol. 10, no. 2, pp. 129–162, June 1985.

21. A. J. Smith, "Cache memories," *ACM Computing Surveys*, vol. 14, no. 3, pp. 473–530, September 1982.

22. P. J. Denning, "On modeling program behavior," *Proceedings of the NCC*, vol. 40, pp. 937–944, AFIPS Press, May 1972.

23. D. W. Barron, *Computer Operating Systems*, Chapman and Hall, London, 1971.

24. A. N. C. Kang, R. C. T. Lee, C. L. Chang, and S. K. Chang, "Storage reduction through minimal spanning trees and spanning forests," *IEEE Transactions on Computers*, vol. C-26, no. 5, pp. 425–434, May 1977.

25. J. Martin, *Computer Data-Base Organization*, Prentice-Hall, Englewood Cliffs, N.J., 1977. 2nd ed.

26. F. Rubin, "Experiments in text file compression," *Communications of the ACM*, vol. 19, no. 11, pp. 617–623, November 1976.

27. D. A. Huffman, "A method for the construction of minimum-redundancy codes," *Proceedings I.R.E*, vol. 40, pp. 1098–1101, September 1952.

28. M. Pechura, "File archival techniques using data compression," *Communications of the ACM*, vol. 25, no. 9, pp. 605–609, September 1982.

29. G. V. Cormack, "Data compression on a database system," *Communications of the ACM*, vol. 28, no. 12, pp. 1336–1342, December 1985.

30. R. G. Gallagher, "Variations on a theme by Huffman," *IEEE Transactions on Information Theory*, vol. IT-24, no. 6, pp. 668–674, November 1973.

31. T. A. Welch. "A technique for high-performance data compression," *Computer*, vol. 17, no. 6, pp. 8–19, June 1984.

32. K. Jensen and N. Wirth, *Pascal: User Manual and Report*, Springer-Verlag, Berlin, 1974.

33. M. A. Jackson, *Principles of Program Design*, Academic Press, London, 1975.

34. J. C. Molluzzo, "Jackson design techniques for elementary data processing," *ACM SIGCSE Bulletin*, vol. 13, no. 4, pp. 16–20, December 1981.

35. M. Stubbs, "Resolution of structure clashes by structure inversion," *Computer Bulletin*, vol. 2, no. 39, pp. 8–11, March 1984.

36. M. Stubbs, "An examination of the resolution of structure clashes by structure inversion," *Computer Journal*, vol. 27, no. 4, pp. 354–361, November 1984.

37. B. Dwyer, "One more time—how to update a master file," *Communications of the ACM*, vol. 24, no. 1, pp. 3–8, January 1981.

38. J. Inglis, "Updating a master file—yet one more time," *Communications of the ACM*, vol. 24, no. 5, p. 299, May 1981.

39. B. Dwyer, *Communications of the ACM*, vol. 24, no. 8, pp. 538–539, August 1981. Author's response to technical correspondence.

40. D. E. Knuth, *The Art of Computer Programming, Vol. 3: Sorting and Searching*, Addison-Wesley, Reading, Mass., 1973.

41. G. M. Barnes and P. D. Smith, "Experiments with file accessing techniques," *ACM SIGCSE Bulletin*, vol. 15, no. 4, pp. 3–7, December 1983.

42. N. H. Macdonald, L. T. Frase, P. S. Gingrich, and S. A. Keenan, "The Writer's Workbench: Computer aids for text analysis," *IEEE Transactions on Communications*, vol. COM-30, no. 1, pp. 105–110, January 1982.

43. L. L. Cherry and W. Vesterman, "Writing tools—the STYLE and DICTION programs," Computer Science Technical Report No. 91, Bell Laboratories, Murray Hill, N.J., 1981.

44. G. Miranker, L. Tang, and C. K. Wong. "A 'zero-time' VLSI sorter," *IBM Journal of Research and Development*, vol. 27, no. 2, pp. 140–148, March 1983.

45. C. A. R. Hoare, "Partition: Algorithm 63, Quicksort: Algorithm 64, and Find: Algorithm 65," *Communications of the ACM*, vol. 4, no. 7, pp. 321–322, July 1961.

46. H. W. Six and L. Wegner, "Sorting a random access file in situ," *Computer Journal*, vol. 27, no. 2, pp. 270–275, August 1984.

47. J. Bradley, *File and Data Base Techniques*, Holt, Rinehart and Winston, New York, 1982.

48. W. D. Frazer and C. K. Wong, "Sorting by natural selection," *Communications of the ACM*, vol. 15, no. 10, pp. 910–913, October 1972.

49. T. G. Lewis and M. Z. Smith, *Applying Data Structures*, Houghton Mifflin, Boston, 1982. 2nd ed.

50. R. L. Gilstad, "Polyphase merge sorting—an advanced technique," *Proceedings of the AFIPS Eastern Joint Computer Conference*, vol. 18, pp. 143–148, 1960.

51. S. P. Ghosh and V. Y. Lum, "An analysis of collisions when hashing by division," *Information Systems*, vol. 1, no. 1-B, pp. 15–22, 1975.

52. W. Buchholz, "File organization and addressing," *IBM Systems Journal*, vol. 2, pp. 86–111, June 1963.

53. V. Y. Lum, P. S. T. Yuen, and M. Dodd, "Key-to-address transform techniques: A fundamental performance study on large existing formatted files," *Communications of the ACM*, vol. 14, no. 4, pp. 228–239, 1971.

54. W. W. Peterson, "Addressing for random-access storage," *IBM Journal of Research and Development*, vol. 1, no. 2, pp. 130–146, 1957.

55. P.-A. Larson and A. Kajla, "File organization: Implementation of a method guaranteeing retrieval in one access," *Communications of the ACM*, vol. 27, no. 7, pp. 670–677, July 1984.

56. W. Litwin, "Virtual hashing: a dynamically changing hashing," *Proceedings of the Fourth International Conference on Very Large Data Bases*, pp. 517–523, West Berlin, September 13–15, 1978.

57. P.-A. Larson, "Dynamic hashing," *BIT*, vol. 18, pp. 184–201, 1978.

58. R. Fagin, J. Nievergelt, N. Pippenger, and H. R. Strong, "Extendible hashing—a fast access method for dynamic files," *ACM Transactions on Database Systems*, vol. 4, no. 3, pp. 315–344, September 1979.

59. R. A. Frost, "Algorithm 112—Dumping the index of a dynamic hash table," *Computer Journal*, vol. 24, no. 4, pp. 383–384, 1981.

60. M. Scholl, "New file organizations based on dynamic hashing," *ACM Transactions on Database Systems*, vol. 6, no. 1, pp. 194–211, March 1981.

61. M. Tamminen, "Order preserving extendible hashing and bucket tries," *BIT*, vol. 21, no. 4, pp. 419–435, 1981.

62. D. R. McGregor and J. R. Malone, "Design for a robust, simple

and highly reliable filestore," *Software Practice and Experience*, vol. 11, no. 9, pp. 943–947, September 1981.

63. IBM Corporation, "OS ISAM logic," Order form GY28-6618, IBM Corporation, White Plains, N.Y., 1966.

64. D. G. Keehn and J. O. Lacy, "VSAM data set design parameters," *IBM Systems Journal*, vol. 13, no. 3, pp. 186–212, 1974.

65. W. A. Martin and D. N. Ness, "Optimizing binary trees grown with a sorting algorithm," *Communications of the ACM*, vol. 15, no. 2, pp. 88–93, February 1972.

66. G. M. Adel'son-Vel'skii and E. M. Landis, "An algorithm for the organization of information," *Doklady Academiia Nauk SSSR*, vol. 146, no. 2, pp. 263–266, 1962. English translation in *Soviet Mathematics*, vol. 3, no. 5, pp. 1259–1263, 1962.

67. R. Bayer and E. McCreight, "Organization and maintenance of large ordered indexes," *Acta Informatica*, vol. 1, no. 3, pp. 173–189, 1972.

68. D. Comer, "The ubiquitous B-tree," *ACM Computing Surveys*, vol. 11, no. 2, pp. 121–137, June 1979.

69. G. D. Held and M. R. Stonebraker, "B-trees re-examined," *Communications of the ACM*, vol. 21, no. 2, pp. 139–143, February 1978.

70. P. L. Lehman and S. B. Yao, "Efficient locking for concurrent operations on B-trees," *ACM Transactions on Database Systems*, vol. 6, no. 4, pp. 650–670, December 1981.

71. M. R. Stonebraker, E. Wong, P. Kreps, and G. D. Held, "The design and implementation of INGRES," *ACM Transactions on Database Systems*, vol. 1, no. 3, pp. 189–222, September 1976.

72. G. Salton and M. J. McGill, *Introduction to Modern Information Retrieval*, McGraw-Hill, New York, 1983.

73. D. Fife, K. Rankin, E. Feng, J. Walder, and B. Marron, *A Technical Index of Interactive Information Systems*, Systems and Software Division, Institute for Computer Science and Technology, National Bureau of Standards, Washington, D.C., March 1974.

74. National Library of Medicine, *MEDLARS, The Computerized Literature Retrieval Service of the National Library of Medicine*, Department of Health, Education and Welfare, Washington, D.C., January 1979. Publication NIH 79-1286.

75. IBM World Trade Corporation, *STAIRS, Storage and Information Retrieval System*, IBM World Trade Corporation, Stuttgart, Germany, 1973. General Information Manual No. GH 12.5107.

76. D. C. Blair and M. E. Maron, "An evaluation of retrieval effectiveness for a full-text document-retrieval system," *Communications of the ACM*, vol. 28, no. 3, pp. 289–299, March 1985.

77. J. Nievergelt, H. Hinterberger, and K. C. Sevcik, "The grid file:

An adaptable, symmetric multikey file structure," *ACM Transactions on Database Systems*, vol. 9, no. 1, pp. 38–71, March 1984.

78. R. H. Davis and P. Coumpas, "A dynamic file organization model," *Computer Journal*, vol. 27, no. 2, pp. 143–150, May 1984.

79. R. H. Davis, "A note on dynamic file organization models," *Computer Journal*, vol. 27, no. 3, p. 284, August 1984.

80. R. Fagin, "A normal form for relational databases that is based on domains and keys," *ACM Transactions on Database Systems*, vol. 6, no. 3, pp. 387–415, September 1981.

81. E. F. Codd, "A relational model of data for large shared data banks," *Communications of the ACM*, vol. 13, no. 6, pp. 377–387, June 1970.

82. E. F. Codd, "Further normalization of the data base relational model," in *Courant Computer Science Symposia No. 6: Data Base Systems*, ed. R. Rustin, Prentice-Hall, Englewood Cliffs, N.J., 1972.

83. R. Fagin, "Multivalued dependencies and a new normal form for relational databases," *ACM Transactions on Database Systems*, vol. 2, no. 3, pp. 262–279, September 1977.

84. R. Fagin, "Normal forms and relational database operators," *Proceedings of the ACM SIGMOD International Conference on the Management of Data*, pp. 153–160, Boston, Mass., May/June 1979.

85. Q. F. Stout and P. A. Woodworth, "Relational databases," *American Mathematical Monthly*, vol. 90, no. 2, pp. 101–118, February 1983.

86. C. Beeri, R. Fagin, and J. H. Howard, "A complete axiomatization for functional and multivalued dependencies," *Proceedings of the ACM SIGMOD International Conference on the Management of Data*, pp. 47–61, Toronto, Canada, August 1977.

87. P. A. Bernstein, "Synthesizing third normal form relations from functional dependencies," *ACM Transactions on Database Systems*, vol. 1, no. 4, pp. 277–298, December 1976.

88. R. Fagin, "The decomposition versus synthetic approach to relational database design," *Proceedings of the Third International Conference on Very Large Data Bases*, pp. 441–446, Tokyo, Japan, October 1977.

89. Y. Sagiv, "An algorithm for inferring multivalued dependencies with an application to propositional logic," *Journal of the ACM*, vol. 27, no. 2, pp. 250–262, April 1980.

90. C. W. Bachman, "Data structure diagrams," *Data Base*, vol. 1, no. 2, pp. 4–10, Summer 1969. (Journal of ACM SIGBDP.)

91. D. C. Tsichritzis and A. Klug, eds., "The ANSI/X3/SPARC DBMS framework: Report of the study group on data base management systems," *Information Systems*, vol. 3, pp. 173–191, 1978.

92. CODASYL DBTG, "CODASYL data base task group report," *ACM Conference on Data System Languages*, New York, 1971.

93. D. M. Kroenke, *Database Processing: Fundamentals, Design, Implementation*, Science Research Associates, Palo Alto, Calif., 1983. 2nd ed.

94. IBM Corporation, "Information Management System (IMS/VS)," IBM Corporation, White Plains, N.Y., 1975. General Information Manual No. GH 20-1260.

95. D. Kapp and J. F. Leben, *IMS Programming Techniques*, Van Nostrand Reinhold, New York, 1978.

96. T. W. Olle, *The CODASYL Approach to Data Base Management*, Wiley, New York, 1978.

97. Cullinane Corporation, *Integrated Database Management System (IDMS) Data Definition Languages*, Cullinane Corporation, Boston, 1975.

98. CODASYL Data Description Language Committee, "Data Description Language Journal of Development," U.S. Government Printing Office, Washington, D.C., 1973. Document C13.6/2:113.

99. D. D. Chamberlin, "Relational data-base management systems," *ACM Computing Surveys*, vol. 8, no. 1, pp. 121–137, March 1976.

100. E. F. Codd, "Relational database: A practical foundation for productivity," *Communications of the ACM*, vol. 23, no. 2, pp. 109–117, February 1982.

101. W. Kim, "Relational database systems," *ACM Computing Surveys*, vol. 11, no. 3, pp. 185–211, September 1979.

102. M. L. Kersten, A. I. Wasserman, and R. P. van der Riet, *Troll Reference Manual*, Medical Information Science, University of California, San Francisco, December 1982.

103. M. L. Kersten and A. I. Wasserman, "The architecture of the PLAIN data base handler," *Software Practice and Experience*, vol. 11, no. 2, pp. 175–186, February 1981.

104. E. F. Codd, "A database sublanguage founded on the relational calculus," *Proceedings of the ACM-SIGFIDET Workshop, Data Description, Access and Control*, pp. 35–68, San Diego, November 11–12, 1971.

105. E. F. Codd, "Relational completeness of data base sublanguages," in *Courant Computer Science Symposia No. 6: Data Base Systems*, ed. R. Rustin, pp. 67–101, Prentice-Hall, Englewood Cliffs, N.J., 1972.

106. S. Todd, "Implementing the join operator in relational databases," IBM Scientific Center Technical Note 15, IBM Scientific Center, Peterlee, England, 1974.

107. A. Klug, "Equivalence of relational algebra and relational calculus query languages having aggregate functions," *Journal of the ACM*, vol. 29, no. 3, pp. 699–717, July 1982.

108. A. S. Michaels, B. Mittman, and C. R. Carlson, "A comparison

of the relational and CODASYL approaches to data-base management," *ACM Computing Surveys*, vol. 8, no. 1, pp. 125–151, March 1976.

109. J. A. Larson, "Bridging the gap between network and relational database management systems," *Computer*, vol. 16, no. 9, pp. 82–92, September 1983.

110. M. Stonebraker, "Implementation of integrity constraints and views by query modification," *Proceedings of the ACM SIGMOD International Conference on the Management of Data*, pp. 65–78, San Jose, Calif., May 1975.

111. A. I. Hinxman, "Updating a database in an unsafe environment," *Communications of the ACM*, vol. 27, no. 6, pp. 564–566, June 1984.

112. M. Stonebraker and E. Wong, "Access control in a relational database management system by query modification," *Proceedings of the ACM Annual Conference*, pp. 180–186, San Diego, November 1974.

113. D. E. Denning and J. Schlorer, "Inference controls for statistical databases," *Computer*, vol. 16, no. 7, pp. 69–82, July 1983.

114. D. E. Denning, P. J. Denning, and M. D. Schwartz, "The tracker: A threat to statistical database security," *ACM Transactions on Database Systems*, vol. 4, no. 1, pp. 76–79, March 1979.

115. D. E. Denning, "Are statistical data bases secure?," *Proceedings of the NCC*, vol. 47, pp. 525–530, AFIPS Press, June 1978.

116. D. E. Denning, "Secure statistical databases with random sample queries," *ACM Transactions on Database Systems*, vol. 5, no. 3, pp. 291–315, September 1980.

117. M. M. Zloof, "Query by Example," *Proceedings of the NCC*, vol. 44, pp. 431–437, AFIPS Press, May 1975.

118. B. F. Green, A. K. Wolf, C. Chomsky, and K. Laughery, "Baseball: an automatic question answerer," in *Computers and Thought*, ed. E. A. Feigenbaum and J. Feldman, pp. 207–216, McGraw-Hill, New York, 1963.

119. E. F. Codd, "How about recently? (English dialog with relational data bases using RENDEZVOUS version 1)," in *Databases: Improving Usability and Responsiveness*, ed. B. Shneiderman, Academic Press, New York, 1978.

120. D. L. Waltz and B. A. Goodman, "Writing a natural language data base system," *Proceedings of the Fifth International Joint Conference on Artificial Intelligence*, pp. 144–150, Cambridge, Mass., August 22-25, 1977.

121. G. G. Hendrix, E. D. Sacerdoti, D. Sagalowicz, and J. Slocum, "Developing a natural language interface to complex data," *ACM*

Transactions on Database Systems, vol. 3, no. 2, pp. 105–147, June 1978.

122. G. G. Hendrix, "Human engineering for applied natural language processing," *Proceedings of the Fifth International Joint Conference on Artificial Intelligence*, pp. 183–191, Cambridge, Mass., August 22–25, 1977.

123. H. R. Tennant, "Menu-based natural language understanding," *Proceedings of the NCC*, vol. 53, pp. 629–635, AFIPS Press, July 1984.

124. M. Jarke and J. Koch, "Query optimization in database systems," *ACM Computing Surveys*, vol. 16, no. 2, pp. 111–152, June 1984.

125. S. Talbot, "An investigation into logical optimization of relational query languages," *Computer Journal*, vol. 27, no. 4, pp. 301–309, November 1984.

126. D. K. Hsiao, "Data base machines are coming, data base machines are coming!," *IEEE Computer*, vol. 12, no. 3, pp. 7–9, March 1979.

127. R. E. Canaday, R. D. Harrison, E. L. Ivie, J. L. Ryder, and L. A. Wehr, "A back-end computer for database management," *Communications of the ACM*, vol. 17, no. 10, pp. 575–582, October 1974.

128. F. J. Maryanski, "Backend database systems," *ACM Computing Surveys*, vol. 12, no. 1, pp. 3–25, March 1980.

129. Britton-Lee, Inc., *IDM 500 Series: The Logical Approach to Efficient Database Management*, Britton-Lee, Inc., Los Gatos, Calif., 1984.

130. L. A. Hollaar, K. F. Smith, W. H. Chow, P. A. Emrath, and R. L. Haskin, "Architecture and operation of a large, full-text information-retrieval system," in *Advanced Database Machine Architecture*, ed. D. K. Hsiao, pp. 256–299, Prentice-Hall, Englewood Cliffs, N.J., 1983.

131. D. K. Hsiao, ed., *Advanced Database Machine Architecture*, Prentice-Hall, Englewood Cliffs, N.J., 1983.

132. "The genesis of a database computer," *IEEE Computer*, vol. 17, no. 11, pp. 42–56, November 1984. Interview with Jack Shemer and Phil Neches of Teradata Corporation.

133. S. Ceri, B. Pernici, and G. Wiederhold, "An overview of research in the design of distributed systems," *IEEE Database Engineering Bulletin*, vol. 7, no. 4, pp. 46–51, December 1984.

134. M. R. Stonebraker and E. Neuhold, "A distributed database version of INGRES," *Proceedings of the Second Berkeley Workshop on Distributed Data Management and Computer Networks*, Berkeley, Calif., May 25–27, 1977.

135. P. A. Bernstein and D. M. Chiu, "Using semi-joins to solve relational queries," *Journal of the ACM*, vol. 28, no. 1, pp. 25–40, January 1981.

Index